Ani Maamin

Biblical Criticism, Historical Truth, and the Thirteen Principles of Faith

MAGGID

Joshua Berman

ANI MAAMIN

*Biblical Criticism, Historical Truth,
and the Thirteen Principles of Faith*

Maggid Books

Ani Maamin
Biblical Criticism, Historical Truth, and the Thirteen Principles of Faith

First Edition, 2020

Maggid Books
An imprint of Koren Publishers Jerusalem Ltd.

POB 8531, New Milford, CT 06776-8531, USA
& POB 4044, Jerusalem 9104001, Israel
www.maggidbooks.com

Cover Photo: Carvings of slaves at Abu Simbel, www.shutterstock.com

The publication of this book was made possible
through the generous support of *The Jewish Book Trust*.

ISBN 978-1-59264-538-1, *hardcover*

A CIP catalogue record for this title is
available from the British Library

Printed and bound in the United States

עַל בָּנֵינוּ וְעַל דּוֹרוֹתֵינוּ, וְעַל כָּל דּוֹרוֹת

… for our children, for our generations, and for all generations…

Explore the world and explore Torah.
And when approaching Torah,
"Turn it over, and turn it over, for all is therein…
become gray and old therein…
do not move away from it,
for you have no better portion than it."
(Pirkei Avot 5:22)

Annette and Mitch Eichen

ୡୠ

Dedicated to

Mr & Mrs Michael and Hilda Aaronson

whose love and dedication to their children
are an inspiration and a signal of transcendence.

Author's Dedication

In dedication to
Rabbi Yakov Bieler
my first rebbe

Contents

Acknowledgments

The Mishna in Avot (1:6) tells us, "Make for yourself a teacher, and acquire for yourself a friend." Teachers we look up to for guidance and wisdom; friends we look out to for camaraderie and companionship. Over the years, I have made many friends and colleagues – as a student at Princeton, while learning at Yeshivat Har Etzion, as a professor at Bar-Ilan University, and in my hometown of Beit Shemesh. During the composition of this book, many of these friends became my teachers. Researching and writing outside of my field of biblical studies mandated that I seek out their wisdom and learning for various chapters of this book, especially those that address the Thirteen Principles of Faith. There is a special *nachas* that one feels when the reciprocal and bilateral nature of friendship gives way to a sense of hierarchy, and you become the beneficiary of a friend's specialized wisdom. It is the *nachas* of your friend becoming, for a moment, your *rebbe*, your teacher. For their willingness to read and critique my work, I would like to thank Yitzchak Blau, Michael Broyde, Eli Clark, Adam Ferziger, Yoel Finkelman, Yehuda Galinsky, David Henshke, Aton Holzer, Eric Lawee, Marc Shapiro, Moshe Shoshan, Gil Student, Chaim Waxman, and Jeffrey Woolf. The generosity of their time, however, should not be construed as approval or agreement with all that I have written here, and I alone am responsible for the arguments contained in this book.

There is a special group of people I wish to thank, who have no idea how much they have given me through their personal example and through hours and hours of heartfelt conversation. Without them, simply, I could not have written this book. These are individuals who have shown me what it is to be a person of deep faith and deep scholarly integrity. These are people who are unafraid of speaking truth to power and who are my comrades in arms in combating some of the erroneous paradigms that prevail in the field of biblical studies. My thanks to Richard Averbeck, John Bergsma, Daniel Block, Jens Bruun Kofoed, Georg Fischer SJ, Jim Hoffmeier, Benjamin Kilchör, Michael LeFebvre, Sandra Richter, Jean-Pierre Sonnet SJ, John Welch, Nicolai Winther-Nielsen, and Markus Zehnder. Following Numbers 10:31, I say to you all, "You have shown me how to camp in the wilderness, and you have served as eyes for me."[1]

Sections of this book have appeared in slightly altered form elsewhere, and I would like to acknowledge the original forums in which these materials appeared. Chapters 1 and 4 and the first part of chapter 6 originally appeared within an eight-part series that I published on Orthodoxy and biblical criticism on the website of Gil Student, torahmusings.com. Chapter 3 appeared originally as "Was There an Exodus?" in *Mosaic* magazine.[2] The latter part of chapter 6 is taken from my essay, "What Is This Thing Called Law?" which appeared in *Mosaic* magazine.[3] Chapter 7 appeared originally as "How the Torah Revolutionized Political Thought" on Aish HaTorah's website, aish.com.[4] Chapter 11, with slight modification, appeared as "Orthodox Rabbinic Exceptions to the Thirteen Principles of Faith: The Dynamics of Boundary Permeability" in *Modern Judaism*.[5]

---

1. All translations of biblical passages are my own in consultation with existing translations.
2. March 2, 2015, available at https://mosaicmagazine.com/essay/history-ideas/2015/03/was-there-an-exodus/.
3. December 1, 2013, available at https://mosaicmagazine.com/essay/uncategorized/2013/12/what-is-this-thing-called-law/.
4. December 29, 2012, available at https://www.aish.com/sp/ph/How-the-Torah-Revolutionized-Political-Thought.html.
5. Joshua Berman, "Orthodox Rabbinic Exception to the Thirteen Principles of Faith: The Dynamics of Boundary Permeability," *Modern Judaism* 39, no. 2 (2019): 161–83.

My thanks to Matthew Miller and Reuven Ziegler of Koren Publishers for their enthusiastic support of this project and for enabling this dream to come true for me. My thanks also to Deena Glickman for her scrupulous editing of my manuscript, as well as to managing editor Ita Olesker, proofreader Tali Simon, and indexer Reuben Meghnagi. Special thanks to Mitch and Annette Eichen and to Edward Aaronson for sharing my vision for this project and for offering their generous support.

At the age of fourteen, I began studies at the Ramaz Upper School in New York and was placed in Rabbi Yakov Bieler's Gemara class. The chemistry with the class was special and we had the good fortune of having Rabbi Bieler as our *rebbe* for the full four years of high school. We learned Gemara, but even more than that, we learned what it was to be an *eved Hashem*, as much through who he was as through what he said and taught. At a time when it was becoming fashionable for teachers to project chumminess, Rabbi Bieler radiated dignity and gravity. Where other teachers wanted to instill a love of Torah, Rabbi Bieler sought to instill within us a reverence for Torah. Where other teachers did what they could to make the Torah accessible, Rabbi Bieler preached the value of *amelut baTorah*, toiling in Torah. Our work, he promised, would be difficult but rewarding. And it is my prayer that readers of this book will share that experience as well. In Rabbi Bieler's class, challenging topics were never avoided and complexity was embraced. Forty years on, it is a privilege to dedicate this work to him.

Introduction

As Pinhas bared his soul to me, I could see he was a man of courage. Visiting with his wife and family from the United States, he had walked for more than an hour from the other side of Beit Shemesh on a blistering Shabbat afternoon to speak with me in our home. But his journey had begun long before that. Pinhas had received a typical Orthodox upbringing, attending twelve years of yeshiva day school followed by yeshiva study in Israel. He had rebelled at one point, but it meant that when he returned to *yiddishkeit*, he did so out of choice. He had given deep thought to what it all meant, and that made his commitment to Torah and mitzvot all the more profound. Now in his mid-thirties, Pinhas was an ordained *musmakh* and a passionately committed educator.

For Pinhas, the desire to know and understand was part and parcel of his *avodat Hashem*. An eclectic reader, Pinhas stumbled onto academic approaches to the Tanakh. Scholars, he saw, raised interesting and valid questions about the Torah, questions he had never heard raised by his teachers and *rebbeim*. Though he searched, he could not find answers within classical rabbinic sources that he felt were satisfactory. Pinhas found himself in an unfamiliar place: deeply committed to his *yiddishkeit*, but troubled by gnawing questions that would not disappear. "I lose sleep over these questions," he confided.

"Even worse, I feel dishonest. Outwardly I affirm all sorts of things in my *davening* and when I'm standing before kids teaching. Inwardly, though, I struggle."

Over the past several years it has been my highest calling to oblige people like Pinhas, people driven by an intense desire for religious and spiritual integrity, who have sought my counsel, sometimes in my living room, sometimes in the local branch of Aroma Espresso Bar, sometimes as a "guest" in their home via Skype. I receive a steady stream of emails from individuals, young and old, Orthodox and non-Orthodox, Jewish and even non-Jewish, seeking guidance on how to understand the relationship between what they were taught in piety and the troubling questions they face from their encounter with academic biblical studies. In this volume, I share my own strivings for such integrity as a scholar and as an *eved Hashem*.

The subject is threatening to some. Many rabbis and educators would not dare broach this topic for themselves, and certainly not with their students and congregants. This is indeed sensitive and at times complex material. And we have a long-standing tradition that difficult issues in halakha and religious worldview are often best handled discreetly, on an individual basis, each according to his or her need and understanding, and not in published form. But there are times in the life of the community when we come to what I would term a "tipping point." This is the point at which a sensitive issue has begun to gain traction. What once vexed only scattered individuals now troubles a small but growing part of the community. The cost of not publicly addressing the issue begins to outweigh the cost of confronting the issue in the open. In this situation, the smart money says that bold leaders will emerge winners by taking the lead on the issue, and "owning it," as it were, controlling the communal agenda and helping to offer guidance.

Educators often fear that raising anything associated with academic biblical studies in the classroom will cause more harm than good. My experience and that of many other educators suggests otherwise. I smile when a student in a gap year program says to me, "Oh, I'm not bothered by biblical criticism; my *rebbe* talked to us about that in high school." Did her teacher raise – let alone solve – the entire gamut of challenges that academic biblical studies raises? I doubt it. But young men and women who express this sentiment remind us of something very important: when a young mind is first introduced to anything relating to academic biblical studies by a beloved and trusted educator, it sends the message that we need not be afraid. Ninety percent of the battle is already won, and the chances that that student will experience a crisis of faith later on are diminished. We sabotage our best educational efforts when we pretend critical approaches to the Bible do not exist, and therefore need not even be acknowledged. When our more thoughtful students discover these alternative approaches – often after they have left Orthodox educational environments – they arrive at a reasonable conclusion: if my teachers never acknowledged any of this, it must be because the tradition has nothing to say in its defense. Worse, they feel hoodwinked, wondering why the wool was pulled over their eyes. With courage and resources, educators can make a huge difference by demonstrating even slight familiarity with some of the methods and claims of the academy. The motto of the New York State Lottery circa 1980 is equally apt here: you gotta be in it to win it.

The Orthodox engagement with the challenges of biblical criticism today is more robust than any since prewar Germany. To my mind, however, the current state of the discussion is deficient in four respects.

First, I am troubled by the blind and obsequious manner in which some in the Orthodox world view the authority of the academy as the repository of ultimate truth. We find individuals who identify as Orthodox and proclaim acceptance of "the findings of biblical criticism," with no attendant caveat of what they *do not* accept. Let me be clear: I am not speaking about a failure to establish theological red lines. What I mean is that in some quarters there is no critical eye turned on the criticism itself. Everything is accepted in the name of truth, but nothing is rejected in the name of truth. "The findings of biblical criticism" are embraced whole hog, as it were. Go to the major academic conferences in biblical studies and you will see that there is hardly a conclusion anymore that is accepted consensus. The field is more fractured concerning its most basic methodologies and conclusions than ever before. Ironically, there is far more criticism of "the findings of biblical criticism" among the critics themselves than there is in certain corners of the halakhically observant community.

Now, one could say in their defense that lay individuals are not trained biblicists; they are not privy to the latest debates in the top journals of the field. It is unfair to expect non-specialists to articulate learned positions about such things. But this apology veils a deeper spiritual and cognitive malady. Today some are prepared to pledge their unflinching allegiance to any position of the academy, because by doing so they demonstrate their autonomy from tradition, and ostensibly their commitment to the pursuit of truth. As a teacher at a Jewish day school once put it to me: "Often, I find that students might not be so well informed about the meaning of a scientific or archaeological claim. It's enough that many academics holding respected titles have advanced a certain way of understanding something." When individuals assume that every utterance of a rabbinic figure on any subject – even beyond issues of Jewish learning – is authoritative by virtue of his Torah learning, we arrive at the problem called *Daas Torah*. When other individuals are prepared to accept "the findings of biblical criticism," but cannot state the academic positions they find suspect, when they fawn over academics because of the titles they bear, without checking whether cultural presuppositions and ideological biases have colored their interpretations, we arrive at a similar problem – *Daas Mada*.[1]

Second, the state of Orthodoxy's encounter with biblical criticism is deficient because it is engaged begrudgingly, solely through a defensive posture as a fulfillment of R. Elazar's dictum, *Da mah lehashiv la'epikoros*, "Know what to retort to the heretic" (Mishna Avot 2:14).[2] Instead, Orthodoxy should celebrate the insights afforded by understanding the Torah in its ancient Near Eastern context. The light this context sheds is not on a small detail here or there. Rather, a wide array of dazzling insights emerges – insights that can be harmonized with traditional teachings, as I hope this book will demonstrate. If there are indeed seventy *panim*, or "faces," to the Torah, its ancient Near Eastern context is one of them. If

---

1. Elsewhere I have expanded upon the corrupting role of culture and intellectual currents in influencing the field of biblical studies. See my essay, "The Corruption of Biblical Studies," *Mosaic*, July 10, 2017, available at https://mosaicmagazine.com/essay/2017/07/the-corruption-of-biblical-studies/.
2. All translations of mishnaic and talmudic literature in this volume are my own in consultation with existing translations.

we see scant sign of this in our classical sources, it is only because these ancient texts were largely hidden from our Sages – indeed as they were from critical scholarship – until the late nineteenth century. We should view the merit to develop and appreciate these insights as an opportunity granted to our generation.

Third, the state of the discussion concerning Orthodoxy and its relationship with biblical criticism is deficient because published contributions on the topic are universally brief – either in essay or blog form. This book is the first effort by a single author to address these issues in a full-length monograph. The comprehensive analysis afforded by a lengthy treatment is crucial, because so many of the issues in this inquiry are interconnected. Consider the question of the historical accuracy of the Torah's account of the Exodus. One can indeed pen a single essay that summarizes the evidence for and against. But that will hardly do the issue justice, because to understand how the Torah reports the event of the Exodus, we need to understand how the cultures of the ancient world reported historical events generally. This in turn begs the question of whether it is appropriate to view the Torah – ostensibly a timeless document – in ancient context. And so a discussion of the Exodus account's historical accuracy really requires three interrelated discussions. Only a full-length volume allows treatment of the issues and their interdependence with a consistent and coherent voice.

Fourth and finally, the state of Orthodox engagement with biblical criticism is deficient because it has run roughshod over a subtle, rarely discussed, but crucial factor: the factor of *locale*, *where* the discussions are held. Over years of discussing these issues I have discovered that looking at the same sources and the same evidence, Orthodox Jews in America speaking English and Israeli Orthodox Jews speaking Hebrew carry on different sorts of conversations about these issues. Consider the American term "Centrist Orthodoxy." The term reflects the reality that this expression of Orthodoxy, now more than a century old, has always had competition. From the left, alternative expressions of Judaism have long posed theological competition, and these liberal movements have jockeyed with Centrist Orthodoxy for adherents. Meanwhile, Centrist Orthodoxy has also had to look over its right shoulder, no less. For a generation now, more right-wing expressions of Orthodoxy have also provided Centrist Orthodoxy with theological competition and a contest for adherents. The result is that public discussion of hot-button issues within Centrist Orthodox circles is often stifled and limited. Thinkers and writers rightfully feel compelled to establish clear and strong boundaries between themselves and the movements to the left. There are many Orthodox Jews who believe that even addressing the issue of Orthodoxy and biblical criticism implicitly serves liberal agendas. The fear is not without basis. Find a website that discusses Orthodoxy and also eagerly embraces biblical criticism and you are likely to find elsewhere on that website entries that challenge rabbinic authority and call for a liberalization of halakhic practice. Helpful and creative positions that might be supported by a new reading of the sources are rejected, or never even stated, because they seem to play into the agenda of the competition to the left.

Meanwhile, looking to their right, Centrist Orthodox thinkers and writers will fear – again, legitimately – being pegged by the right as being too left-wing. The claim, "I believe *x*, but if I say so publicly, I'll create *shiddukh* (matchmaking) problems for my daughter" is but one symptom of this dynamic. Centrist Orthodoxy is where Orthodoxy's most fruitful thinking could come from, on a range of sensitive issues. But precisely by virtue of its being in the center, it is boxed in by socio-religious forces that stifle broad and open conversation.

Contrast this with the situation in Israel. Indeed, there is much in common between the attitudes and theological proclivities of Centrist Orthodox authorities in the United States and Religious Zionist thinkers and leaders in Israel. Religious Zionism, however, has never termed itself "Centrist" Orthodoxy. Indeed, within the Israeli socio-religious landscape it occupies no "center" in the way that Centrist Orthodoxy does in North America. Religious Zionist thinkers and leaders have no need to consider ideological threats from movements just to the right or just to the left. In Israel, there is practically no competition for adherents that equals the challenges facing Centrist Orthodoxy in North America. The result is that on a range of hot-button issues, Religious Zionist leaders and thinkers often entertain ideas and positions that would be nonstarters in the English-speaking world.

Some conclude that when Centrist Orthodox figures consider the threats from the right and from the left as they formulate halakha, or as they articulate points of theology, they are wrongly engaging in "politics." They say that we should simply read the sources, and let the chips fall where they may. I reject this approach. I take it as axiomatic that the needs of the community are part and parcel of both the halakhic and the theological rabbinic tradition. From time immemorial, different authorities at different times have come to different halakhic and theological conclusions on the basis of the very same rabbinic sources, because of the needs of their respective times and places. Therefore, in our own time as well we need to be open to the possibility that on a range of issues – halakhic and theological – decisions taken by authorities and communities in one locale might not be appropriate for those in another.

While some will agree that it is high time for Orthodoxy to address the claims of academic biblical studies, they may well ask: How can the material in this volume be trusted? After all, I am an Orthodox rabbi; surely my viewpoint is biased. The question is an important and legitimate one, and begs a discussion about motivation and bias in academic research more generally. Feminist scholars write from a feminist perspective; disabled scholars write from the perspective of disability studies; scholars produce work so that it will find favor in the eyes of their thesis advisors or defend claims they made in earlier publications. There is no end to the possible motivations that drive scholars to produce their work. Ultimately, motivation and agendas are entirely irrelevant when determining the quality of academic work; articles undergo blind peer review, and with very good reason. Academic arguments must rise or fall solely upon the rational and critical merits of the claims based on the evidence. The scholarly positions I stake out in this book have all been previously published in the most distinguished forums within the field of biblical studies. Does this mean that most scholars in the field have read my work and adopted my positions? It does not. But it does mean that a wide range of scholars who do not share my affiliation and orientation have vetted these arguments and have found them worthy of scholarly attention and discussion. Looking in from the outside, laypeople may conjure an image of biblicists as a guild with a strong set of conclusions that are accepted truths. The fact of the matter is that today there is robust debate within biblical studies about nearly every major issue – even ones that were long thought to have been settled.

In this book I make no effort to be comprehensive in the range of issues I raise, nor exhaustive about the evidence I adduce. To do so would require many volumes. Instead, I address the issues that I sense are of greatest concern to the types of people that over the years have turned to me for guidance. I present academic arguments in ways that will allow the layman to follow without getting bogged down in detail, with a premium on covering ground. I do not think of my work here as *the* definitive Orthodox standpoint. Rather, I hope readers will view these sources and arguments as resources as they arrive at their own conclusions to the issues. For those wishing to see fuller presentations of the evidence, or alternative views within the scholarship, I provide references to my academic publications where these can be found.

As I mentioned earlier, our engagement with texts and concepts from the ancient Near East opens up new vistas for us, shedding great light on previously hidden aspects of the Torah. But there is one aspect of this type of study that I find absolutely exhilarating both as a scholar and as a Jew, and it is something that we will see again and again throughout this book. Here is an illustration of the type of inquiry I have in mind, from an example outside of biblical studies.

Consider this: When did Jews who endured the Holocaust first become survivors? The question borders on the absurd. What answer could one give to such a question? At the moment they were liberated? From the moment the war ended? From the moment they arrived in a new land? But more than anything else, the question seems absurd, because it is just obvious: Jews who endured the Holocaust are survivors. They just are.

But it turns out that Jews who endured the Holocaust really did not become survivors until the late 1970s. By that I mean that until then, it was actually unusual for such Jews to be called *survivors*. When Jews first reached the shores of the United States from the horrors of wartime Europe, they were referred to with any number of designations: *refugees, displaced persons, liberated prisoners, immigrants, greenhorns*, or the Yiddish version, *greene*. The refugees kept a low profile, focusing on building new lives and fitting in. Those around them did not want to hear their stories, and encouraged them to Americanize. Rarely were they called *survivors*.

The watershed moment came in 1978, when the television mini-series *Holocaust* was broadly viewed by millions of Americans. Interest grew in the historical plight of an oppressed group of people.[3] The various labels referred to earlier all bore connotations of passivity and victimhood. Now able to share their collective story in prime time, Jews could highlight and share their trauma. The process allowed Jews to take back their power and strength, and the new way of thinking about such Jews was not as immigrants, but as *survivors*, a term that connotes resilience, perseverance, and even ingenuity. With so few survivors remaining today, we are filled with an ever-greater sense of reverence for them and their heroism. Their stories are for us sacrosanct. It seems so natural to us to view them this way that it is difficult to imagine that it was ever any other way. But it truly was. And only by appreciating the gulf between our perceptions and those of earlier generations can we grasp just how limited our perspective is.

I cite this example because it powerfully illustrates what we will see again and again throughout this book. Ideas and terms that we take for granted as obvious, universal, and timeless turn out, upon inspection, to be contingent, a function of time and place. We suddenly realize that what seemed obvious to us was only so because we see things through the limited fishbowl of our own lives and our own world. We suddenly realize that once upon a time, people thought about things in a very different way.

Indeed, our forefathers in the time of the Tanakh thought and wrote in ways that differ greatly from the ways that we do. Consider the following words and concepts: *belief, law, history, author, fact, fiction, story, religion,* and *politics.* When did the concept of an "author" begin? Since when have humans engaged in recording "history"? We would surely say that these concepts must be nearly as old as civilized man himself. But, as we shall see, that assumption is mistaken. We routinely assume that the Tanakh is a book of *beliefs, history,* and *law;* that it understands clearly the difference between *fact* and *fiction;* that it is dedicated to imparting lessons about both *religion* and *politics.* In

---

3. Diane L. Wolf, "What's in a Name? The Genealogy of Holocaust Identities," *Genealogy* 1, no. 4 (2017), available at https://www.mdpi.com/2313-5778/1/4/19/pdf.

fact, as we shall see, the Tanakh has no knowledge of even any one of them. We will see that there is no word in either biblical or talmudic Hebrew that corresponds to *any* of these terms. This is the surest sign that a conceptual gulf exists between us and our forefathers. Only once we understand what separates our world from theirs can we begin to address many of the challenges to Orthodoxy raised in its encounter with the decidedly modern field of biblical criticism. We will see that a wide range of concepts we take as simple and universal are in fact anachronistic and modern, and that these modern presuppositions – rarely recognized, but ever present – are the source of a great deal of misunderstanding about the Tanakh.

This book contains two parts. Part I is devoted to an appreciation of the Tanakh in historical context. Chapter 1, "The Rabbinic Mandate to Understand the Torah in Ancient Near Eastern Context," sets the table for the entire section. Many of the challenges raised by critics concerning the historical accuracy and coherence of the text of the Torah emerge precisely because scholars have for too long ignored the ways and the degree to which the Torah is a literary creation of the ancient world. The questions often raised are founded on the anachronistic assumption that ancient readers and writers must have written and thought in the same ways as we do today. This chapter demonstrates that some of our greatest sages believed that aspects of the Torah could only be appreciated by understanding its ancient context, and did not see this as compromising the eternal validity of its import and message.

Chapter 2, "But Is It History? The Historical Accuracy of the Tanakh," focuses on *how* the Tanakh relates to us the events that befell our forefathers, the rules the Tanakh employs for what it will tell us about those events. Here we will see an instance in which we become aware of the fact that ideas and concepts that we take for granted as being obvious and eternally true turn out to be a construct of our own time and place. When we are speaking of *history, fact,* and *fiction,* we must realize that we are utilizing modern categories of thought – categories that the modern mind has constructed. We think that history simply means a discussion of past events with factual accuracy. We assume that this history has existed for, well, all of history. But it has not. The concept *history* itself has a history and we need to understand how it came to be.

Only by doing so can we understand how our sacred sources – biblical and rabbinic – relate to us the events that befell our forefathers.

Chapter 3, "*Avadim Hayinu*: Exodus, Evidence, and Scholarship" well illustrates the lessons learned in chapter 2 about how the Tanakh relates historical events. Perhaps no issue addressed in this book has garnered as much interest – and as much angst – as the question of the historicity of the Torah's account of the Exodus. Here I examine claims and counterclaims for the Exodus, and provide insights and comparisons with Egyptian texts that are to my mind the strongest evidence for the historicity of the Exodus.

A major point of contention for Orthodoxy is the critical claim that the Torah is riddled with inconsistencies which can only be explained as the product of irreconcilable viewpoints. Nowhere is the question of inconsistency more pressing and widespread than in the relationship between the book of Deuteronomy – *Sefer Devarim* – and the earlier books of the Torah. In serial and wholesale fashion we find that the stories and laws related in this book seem to stand at odds with earlier versions of the same stories and same laws found elsewhere in the Torah. Yet here, too, viewing the Torah in its ancient Near Eastern setting sets the entire issue in a different light. In chapter 4, "Narrative Inconsistencies: The Book of Deuteronomy and the Rest of the Torah," I present the standard critical position concerning these seeming inconsistencies and lay bare the *academic* difficulties of that approach. From there, I introduce a particular genre of writing that is crucial for understanding the narrative discrepancies between Deuteronomy and earlier accounts in the Torah: the ancient Near Eastern treaties between sovereign and vassal kings. I demonstrate that in this literature, the vassal would routinely receive from the sovereign king differing and conflicting accounts of the history of their relationship. I explain why this was so and how it sheds light on the relationship between the narratives of Israel's behavior in Deuteronomy and those contained in the earlier books.

Narrative inconsistencies in the Torah are not limited to the discrepancies we find between the accounts of the book of Deuteronomy and the earlier books of the Torah. Indeed, they may be found throughout the Torah, and scholars often take these inconsistencies to be signs of editing as they seek to recreate the history of the text's development.

This approach is broadly known as *source criticism*. Many find source criticism satisfying because it strives to make sense out of passages that are difficult to understand. But how reliable is this type of inquiry? Increasingly, scholars are calling into question whether it is really possible to work back from a received text, such as the Tanakh, and recreate its prior stages of development. In chapter 5, "Critiquing Source Criticism: The Story of the Flood," I take the parade example of source criticism – the Flood story of Genesis 6–9 – and highlight eight methodological flaws endemic to this approach.

In chapter 6, "Legal Inconsistencies: The Book of Deuteronomy and the Rest of the Torah," I turn to the vexing question of the seeming discrepancies between laws in the Torah. My focus here will be on the book of Deuteronomy, where many mitzvot given earlier in the Torah are repeated – sometimes, as we shall see, in ways that seem incommensurate with the earlier versions of the mitzva elsewhere in the Torah. First, I will survey the approaches within rabbinic sources to the questions of legal discrepancies between the book of Deuteronomy and the other books and why many people do not find them satisfying. I will then present the source-critical approach to the issue, and note the problems inherent in that approach from within its own frames of reference – from an *academic* perspective. In the second part of the discussion, I will claim that we today use the word "law" and think of legal texts in ways that are distinctly modern and anachronistic, and I will examine legal writings from the ancient Near East to recapture how people of the time understood how law works. From there, I will move to law in the Tanakh generally and demonstrate that the lessons learned from ancient legal writings help us understand why law seems to change so often and so easily in the Tanakh. Moreover, we will see that the way in which the legal texts were read and interpreted in the time of the Tanakh is quite different from the way in which we read and interpret halakhic texts today. The chapter closes by demonstrating that the conclusions reached here are in concert with provocative comments by the Netziv (Rabbi Naftali Tzvi Yehuda Berlin, 1816–1893) and Rabbi Tzadok HaKohen Rabinowitz of Lublin (1823–1900) about the fluid and changing nature of halakha. Fluidity and change in halakha are very threatening propositions today, and for good reason. But it is important to understand how and why the halakha evolved from a more fluid system to one that is more resistive of change, and the concepts developed in this chapter help us understand this evolution in how halakha works.

But if, indeed, the Torah must be viewed in ancient Near Eastern context – written according to the human conventions of that period – what confidence can we have that it bears a divine imprint? In chapter 7, "But Is It Divine? How the Torah Broke with Ancient Political Thought," I reveal how understanding the Torah in ancient context also demonstrates how utterly removed it is from the norms of its time, expressing political thought that was millennia ahead of its age. In ways that were astonishingly new and counterintuitive, in ways that served the purposes of no known interest group, the political philosophy of the Torah rises like a phoenix out of the intellectual landscape of the ancient Near East. Throughout the ancient world the truth was self-evident: all men were *not* created equal. It is in the five books of the Torah that we find the birthplace of egalitarian thought. When seen against the backdrop of ancient norms, the social blueprint espoused by the Torah represents a series of quantum leaps in a sophisticated and interconnected matrix of theology, politics, and economics.

The question of the origins of the Torah goes to the very heart of Orthodox belief and practice and is the subject of Part II, "Appreciating Principles of Faith and the Principle of Torah from Heaven." The question of what a Jew must believe about the origins of the Torah is inextricably bound with the question of the status and acceptance of the Thirteen Principles of Faith. As with all matters of rabbinic tradition, these subjects have a long history. And as with all matters of rabbinic tradition, what recent authorities have ruled and taught carries the greatest weight for contemporary thought and practice. To appreciate the distinctive qualities and authority of the Thirteen Principles in general and how the sages of Israel have related to the question of the Torah's origins in particular, we must trace these issues from the beginning. Chapter 8, "From the Mishna to the Rambam's Thirteen Principles of Faith," explores how our earliest authorities related to the origins of the Torah and the question of principles of faith, from the Mishna until the composition of the Rambam's Thirteen Principles. Here we probe several crucial questions: When and where did the notion of "fundamental principles" of Judaism arise? Just what did it mean that a proposition was "a fundamental principle"? What are the various opinions within talmudic sources concerning the origins of the Torah? Were these various opinions considered by their expositors to be "fundamental principles" of the Jewish faith? If not, why not? The Rambam was not the first major rabbinic figure to compose a list of principles of faith. How did his principles differ from those proposed by his predecessors, and why?

Beliefs matter and they matter halakhically. *Posekim* since the *Shulḥan Arukh* have unanimously adopted the halakhic definition of heretic as that defined in the Rambam's *Mishneh Torah*, in the third chapter of *Hilkhot Teshuva*, halakhot 6–8. They do so without referencing the Rambam's formulation of the Principles of Faith in his introduction to the tenth chapter of Sanhedrin, in his Commentary on the Mishna. In chapter 9, "The Rambam's Principle of Torah from Heaven: From His Introduction to *Perek Ḥelek* to the *Mishneh Torah*," I probe the question: How does the Rambam's delineation of the principle of "Torah from heaven" in the *Mishneh Torah* differ from his treatment of this issue in the eighth of his Thirteen Principles in the Introduction to *Perek Ḥelek*?

Today we take it as axiomatic that the Rambam's Thirteen Principles are *the* fundamental principles of the faith. But that status was a long time in coming. In chapter 10, "The Thirteen Principles from The Rambam until the Dawn of Emancipation," I trace how this acceptance grew from the time of the Rambam in the twelfth century until the dawn of Emancipation at the end of the eighteenth century. But just what did "acceptance" of the principles mean at that time? And what version of the principles was it that gained acceptance?

The beginning of the Emancipation movement at the end of the eighteenth century engendered far-reaching consequences for the socio-religious condition of Jews across Europe. For the first time, the prospect of legal and social equality caused large numbers of Jews to abandon the beliefs and practices of the tradition. Rabbinic leaders faced unprecedented challenges in meeting these new realities. Within this new and threatening situation, the role and prominence of the Thirteen Principles took on new dimensions. Contemporary Orthodoxy has accepted both a commitment to the halakha and to the Thirteen Principles as binding. But they have been accepted in different ways, and the acceptance of each is governed by different rules. Understanding that difference is the subject of chapter 11, "The Thirteen Principles as Boundary Marker: The Nineteenth and Twentieth Centuries."

The search for spiritual and intellectual integrity inevitably brings one to junctures where there are questions but no apparent answers. In the afterword to this volume, "When We Are Left with Questions," I probe how our sages responded to potentially damning evidence concerning the Torah and its transmission, and adopt their approach as a guiding light for our own encounter with similar questions.

What blessing should a person say upon the publication of a book of Torah insights? Rabbi Jacob Emden (Altona, Hamburg, 1697–1776) was of the opinion that one should recite the blessing of *Sheheheyanu*.[4] Our sources, he reasoned, speak of reciting this blessing on the acquisition of new items that are of a material nature, such as articles of clothing. Certainly, then, one should recite the blessing when a person publishes a book of insights about the Torah, which is of infinitely greater worth. Moreover, he wrote, such a book would bring pleasure and merit not only to its author, but to all those who learn from it as well. If that is the case, then surely I should recite *Sheheheyanu* on the publication of this book, which I pray will bring reaffirmation of our tradition for readers long tormented by challenging questions.

But not all of our authorities agreed with this ruling, among them the Klausenberger Rebbe, Rabbi Yekutiel Yehuda Halberstam (1905–1994). He ruled that far from reciting *Sheheheyanu*, one who publishes a book of Torah insights should actually recite the blessing *Dayan HaEmet* – the blessing we recite upon news of a death![5] He reasoned that in an entire volume devoted to Torah elucidation it was inevitable that an author would err at some point, leading, Heaven forfend, to the misguidance of all who read it. And if that is the case, then surely I should recite *Dayan HaEmet*, as this book touches upon a range of complex and unexplored issues and the nuances and implications of nothing less than the principles of our faith.

---

4. *Mor UKetzia* (Altona, Hamburg: Beit HaMehaber, 1760/1), sec. 223.
5. *Shut Divrei Yatziv* (Union City, NJ: Hitahdut HaTalmidim, 1980), *Orah Hayim* 92.

And so in joy for the opportunity to share my reflections with others, and in the trembling hope that I have done so in a responsible manner, I conclude with a dual blessing: *Barukh sheheḥeyanu vekiyemanu vehigiyanu lazman hazeh, uvarukh Dayan HaEmet.*

Part I
The Tanakh in Historical Context

Chapter 1

The Rabbinic Mandate to Understand the Torah in Ancient Near Eastern Context

To fully understand the Torah and its way of conveying ideas and messages, we must seek to understand the Torah in its ancient Near Eastern context. As we will see in the coming chapters, many of the challenges raised by critics concerning the Torah's historical accuracy and the coherence of the text emerge precisely because scholars have for too long ignored the ways and the degree to which the Torah is a literary creation of the ancient world. The questions often raised are founded on anachronistic assumptions – that ancient readers and writers must have written and thought in the same ways as we do today.

But is it religiously legitimate to say that the Torah reflects the way ancients thought and wrote? Is not the Torah eternally valid and above time? Do we not slight the Torah when we propose that it expresses itself in a manner that is culture-dependent or more relevant for one generation than another? These questions are crucial not only when we consider Orthodoxy's engagement with biblical criticism. They are critical whenever we wish to study the Torah on its literal – or *peshat* – level. And therefore, this book must begin by exploring these issues at the outset.

One can marshal a wide spectrum of opinions on this topic, indeed, as with so many issues in rabbinic thought. My aim in this chapter is to demonstrate both (1) that some of our greatest sages maintained that the Torah not only can be read, but *must* be read, in precisely this way, and (2) that reading the Torah in its ancient context is a sacred enterprise and does not denigrate the sanctity or "eternal" nature of the *kitvei hakodesh* – our sacred Scripture.

THE RAMBAM'S DOCTRINE OF GRADUAL DEVELOPMENT IN THE DIVINE PLAN

The Rambam (or Maimonides, 1135–1204) offers us a particularly rich and detailed meditation on the importance of reading the Torah in its ancient context. To probe his thinking, I would like to examine his well-known – but often misunderstood – explanation of animal sacrifice in the *Guide for the Perplexed*. As many know, the Rambam saw the institution of animal sacrifice in the Torah as concessive in nature. Israel knew no form of worship other than the worship of idols she had seen in Egypt. The Almighty chose, therefore, to establish norms of worship in a form the nation could recognize.[1] Over two lengthy chapters of the *Guide* (3:32 and 3:46), the Rambam identifies the specific heathen practices relating to the god Ares, Hindu practice, and the cultic norms of an ancient culture he knew as Sabean. He sees the minutiae of the *avoda* – sacrificial service – recorded in the Torah as a vehicle to reform those norms. He explains specific mitzvot, such as the prohibition against using honey or leavened bread in the sacrificial worship of the Temple, in light of these ancient practices.

The Rambam stresses that the mitzvot he explains through ancient context do not constitute an exhaustive list. He bemoans

---

1. Although this opinion is popularly associated with the Rambam, it actually is found earlier, in the Midrash (Leviticus Rabba 22:8).

the fact that he is removed in place and time from the ancient world and cannot fully appreciate the reforms inherent in each aspect of the *avoda*:

> Most of the "statutes" (*ḥukkim*), the reason of which is unknown to us, serve as a fence against idolatry. That I cannot explain some details of the above laws or show their use is owing to the fact that what we hear from others is not so dear as that which we see with our own eyes. Thus my knowledge of the Sabean doctrines, which I derived from books, is not as complete as the knowledge of those who have witnessed the public practice of those idolatrous customs, especially as they have been out of practice and entirely extinct since two thousand years. If we knew all the particulars of the Sabean worship, and were informed of all the details of those doctrines, we would clearly see the reason and wisdom of every detail in the sacrificial service, in the laws concerning things that are unclean, and in other laws, the object of which I am unable to state.[2]

In his Letter on Astrology, the Rambam writes of his efforts to learn about the ancient world:

> I also have read in all matters concerning all of idolatry, so that it seems to me that there does not remain in the world a composition on this subject, having been translated into Arabic from other languages, but that I have read it and have understood its subject matter and have plumbed the depth of its thought. From those books it became clear to me what the reason is for all the commandments that everyone comes to think of as having no reason at all, other than the decree of Scripture.[3]

---

2. *Guide for the Perplexed*, III:49. All translations of the *Guide for the Perplexed* in this volume are taken from the M. Friedländer translation (1903), available online on several sites.
3. Text found in Isadore Twersky, ed., *A Maimonides Reader* (New York: Behrman House, 1972), 465–66.

These passages demonstrate that the Rambam holds that many matters in the Torah can be understood only by gaining access to the cultures of the ancient world. Probing the Rambam further, however, we learn that familiarity with the ancient world is not only crucial for understanding the mitzvot. Such study for the Rambam has theological significance: it allows us to discern God's caring and fostering nature. But why and how does the study of Torah in ancient context help us understand God's caring and fostering nature?

To grasp this point, we need to appreciate where his discussion of sacrifice appears in the *Guide*, beginning in section III, chapter 32. As is well known, the Rambam ascribes rationales for the mitzvot in chapters 35–49. Chapter 32 is an introductory chapter to that effort. The chapter explores the divine hand evident in processes of *development*, by which the Rambam means development of all kinds: the physiological development of men and beasts, and the spiritual and psychological development of individuals and of nations. The chapter opens as follows:

> On considering the Divine acts or the processes of Nature we get an insight into the prudence and wisdom of God as displayed in the creation of animals, with the gradual development of the movements of their limbs and the relative positions of the latter, and we perceive also His wisdom and plan in the successive and gradual development of the whole condition of each individual.

For the Rambam, when we discern the wonders of physiological development, we more fully apprehend the Almighty's prudence, plan, and wisdom. The point here is not merely an appreciation of the Divine Clockmaker, as it were, a recognition of the wonders of physiology. The Rambam here draws our attention to how physiological mechanisms develop step by step. The Rambam then extends his recognition of the divinely guided processes of development from the realm of animal physiology to the realm of national flourishing:

> Many precepts in our Law are the result of a similar course adopted by the same Supreme Being. It is, namely, impossible to go suddenly from one extreme to the other; it is therefore

according to the nature of man impossible for him suddenly to discontinue everything to which he has been accustomed.... By this Divine plan it was effected that the traces of idolatry were blotted out, and the truly great principle of our faith, the Existence and Unity of God, was firmly established.... It was in accordance with the wisdom and plan of God, as displayed in the whole Creation, that He did not command us to give up and to discontinue all these manners of service.

The Rambam's discussion of animal sacrifice, therefore, is much more than an exploration of the rationale of a given mitzva. It is certainly much more than an apologetic for an institution that some might say was a source of embarrassment for the Rambam. Rather, it is an appreciation of the guiding path of slow, spiritual growth afforded Israel by the Almighty, which is part and parcel of His wisdom in guiding the step-by-step growth and development of all creatures in all ways. When we attain a greater understanding of the cultic practices of the ancient world, we can more fully appreciate how the Almighty accommodated Israel's spiritual mindset. The Rambam further notes the divine hand of developmental guidance at work concerning national character. He explains that when the Israelites left Egypt – as the Torah tells us – the Almighty did not want to lead the children of Israel to the Promised Land via the coast, or "via the Philistine route" (Ex. 13:17). He sees this as an expression of the same developmental guidance that the Almighty offers Israel through the medium of animal sacrifice:

> It was the result of God's wisdom that the Israelites were led about in the wilderness till they acquired courage. For it is a well-known fact that traveling in the wilderness, and privation of bodily enjoyments, such as bathing, produce courage, whilst the reverse is the source of faint-heartedness.... In the same way the portion of the Law under discussion is the result of divine wisdom, according to which people are allowed to continue the kind of worship to which they have been accustomed, in order that they might acquire the true faith.

The Rambam strives to understand as much as he can about ancient Near Eastern culture. Doing so enables him to discern the prudence and wisdom of the divine hand and the divine plan. The Rambam maintains that the Torah's cultic prescriptions are a broad mélange of continuities *and* discontinuities with ancient Near Eastern practice. A deep recognition of the interplay between the two enables us to apprehend how the Almighty nurtures Israel's spiritual development in incremental steps.[4] Our own study of the Torah in ancient Near Eastern context can be animated by the same impulse: to discern how the Torah orchestrates the play between continuity and discontinuity with ancient culture.

As is well known, the Rambam had detractors who strenuously disagreed with his accounting of the sacrifices, notably the Ramban (or Nahmanides, 1194–1270) in his comments on Leviticus 1:9. I note, however, the points staked out by the Ramban in his claim, and more significantly, the points he does not make. The Ramban expresses reservations on two accounts. First, he feels that it would simply be ineffective to try to wean Israel off of sacrifice by perpetuating that very institution. Second, he notes that the Torah at a number of points suggests loftier purposes for the sacrifices and nowhere portrays them merely as a stopgap measure or as concessive in nature. What is noticeably absent from the Ramban's exposition is the claim that it is insulting to the Torah to suggest it speaks with more immediacy to earlier generations than to later ones. In fact, the Ramban also suggests elsewhere that ancient context is necessary for understanding certain passages of the Torah. In his commentary on Exodus 6:25, for example, he questions why the Torah would point out that Elazar the *kohen* married someone from "the daughters of Putiel," with no indication of who this Putiel was or why he was deserving of distinction. One of the Ramban's suggestions is that Putiel was known to his generation. Moreover, the Ramban approvingly cites the Rambam's accounting of the prohibition of *orla*, which disallows

---

4. Fascinating in this regard is the well-known talmudic statement (Shabbat 88b–89a) that the Torah was composed 974 generations prior to Creation, which would seem to negate a view that it was written with a given generation in mind. Yet the context of that passage reveals precisely the opposite; the angels question why the Torah was given to Moses and the Almighty essentially responds that the Torah was written specifically for the generation of the Exodus.

deriving benefit from the produce of a tree in its first three years, as a response to ancient Near Eastern practices (commentary on Lev. 19:23). Put differently, the Ramban allows that the Torah may have spoken with more immediacy to its own generation than to later ones. Similarly, the Ramban writes (commentary on Ex. 28:2) that the some of the priestly garments were patterned after royal attire of the time.

RALBAG'S BELIEF THAT THE TORAH COMMUNICATES THROUGH THE LITERARY CONVENTIONS OF ITS AGE

Figures like the Rambam and the Ramban tell us that understanding ancient Near Eastern realities can help us appreciate the specific details of isolated passages of the Torah. But another prominent medieval figure, Ralbag (or Gersonides, 1288–1344), stresses the importance of grasping the Torah within its ancient context, because this context will better help us understand the very way in which the Torah conveys its ideas. For Ralbag, such context contributes to our understanding of the Torah's poetics, the literary devices and conventions that it employs to convey the divine message. The final two weekly *parashot* of the book of Exodus raise a well-known question: The *parashot* of *Teruma* and *Tetzaveh* lay out in great detail the component parts of the Tabernacle that Bezalel is to construct. Why does the Torah repeat all of these details, nearly verbatim, in its narration of the construction of the Tabernacle in *Parashat Vayak'hel* and *Parashat Pekudei*? Ralbag raises this question at the conclusion to his commentary on the book of Exodus and his answer is fascinating on a number of levels:

> We ought to attend to a most puzzling issue here in this account, and in many of the Torah's accounts, and that is, that owing to its perfection, the Torah should not contain anything repetitious or extraneous. Yet we see here [in these last two *parashot* of the book of Exodus] repetitiousness without purpose. It would have been sufficient for the Torah to state, "And Bezalel the son of Uri the son of Hur made the Tabernacle, as commanded by the Lord." Moreover, we encounter such repetitiousness at many junctures in the Torah, and to this day, we have not found a compelling explanation for this. Perhaps we may say that it was the

convention at the time of the giving of the Torah to fashion literature in this way and that the prophet expresses himself through
the conventions of the times.[5]

Ralbag displays a remarkable degree of cultural humility. He realizes that
aesthetics are not universal. He understands that the mark of literary
perfection for one age may not be held in the same regard by another.
No less striking is his realization that even the Torah could not express
itself in some form of "divine Esperanto," whereby the divine word
would communicate with equal clarity to all human listeners. Ralbag
recognizes that it is the limitation of man that precludes this. He does
not expect that the Torah would communicate according to the conventions of fourteenth-century Provence, nor should we expect the Torah
to communicate according to the canons of modern Western literature,
whose roots are in the thought of Aristotle. Ralbag expects the Torah
to communicate according to the conventions of the ancient Near East.
What is most remarkable about Ralbag's remarks is that without any
exposure to the compositions of the ancient Near East, his conjecture is
precisely on the mark. One of the hallmarks of composition – of many
types of genres – in the ancient Near East is a predilection for what
appears to contemporary tastes as unaesthetic repetition.[6] No doubt,
Ralbag would have rejoiced to know this as a fact.

Even as the Rambam and Ralbag engage ancient Near Eastern
texts to help us understand the Torah, for many, there is a certain hesita-
tion to do so that stems from the realm of religious psychology. When
you sit to learn, there is a certain aura of *Kedusha* that you feel as you
open a textured, cranberry-colored *sefer* from left to right. Somehow,
Pritchard's *Ancient Near Eastern Texts* just doesn't do it. There is almost
a feeling that such materials, even if not forbidden, are surely from the
world of *ḥullin*, the wider, general world, and somehow encroach upon
the holiness of the endeavor of Talmud Torah. In our world, where an
atmosphere of holiness – *Kedusha* – is such a fragile thing, the feeling is

---

5. The translation is my own.
6. Jerrold S. Cooper, "Symmetry and Repetition in Akkadian Narrative," *Journal of the American Oriental Society* 97 (1977): 508–12.

understandable. However, figures like the Rambam, Ralbag, and Abarbanel (1437–1508) freely and seamlessly integrated non-Torah materials into their study of the Torah. Their model of how to integrate these materials into a proper understanding of Torah should offer us the religious security blanket to do the same. Rabbi Abraham Isaac HaKohen Kook (1865–1935) also wrote that we should expect the Torah to incorporate preexisting laws from the ancient Near East, when these laws possess a moral foundation. He writes:

> Many things that are found in the Torah, be they commandments or narrative accounts, are surely also to be found in similar form in the writings of earlier great and righteous figures of the gentile world. The great divine light that extends to the prophecy of our master Moses clarified and purified these elements, separating out those traces of impurity and error. All that has merit from these practices and accounts are gathered by the divine desire and retained to be performed and recounted. Israel has no need to take the credit of having created the first moral laws of the world, nor even for having introduced monotheism to the world.... The discovery in our time of the epigraphic archives of the civilizations of the ancient Near East and the parallels found between them and various aspects of the Torah should add light and rejoicing to all who truly seek out God.[7]

THE TORAH: CULTURE-DEPENDENT *AND* ETERNAL?

We have seen, then, at least two prominent sages who underscore the importance of grasping the Torah's ancient Near Eastern context. But if

---

7. See Rabbi Abraham Isaac HaKohen Kook, *LiNevukhei HaDor* (Tel Aviv: Yediot Aharonot, 2014), 167 and 174. See also Rabbi Abraham Isaac HaKohen Kook, *Eder HaYakar VeIkvei HaTzon* (Jerusalem: Mossad HaRav Kook, 1985), 42. See further the essay by Rabbi Chaim Navon on this subject, "Torah and Ancient Near-Eastern Law," http://etzion.org.il/en/torah-and-ancient-near-eastern-law. We can also add Ibn Ezra and Ibn Caspi to the list of those who utilized ancient Near Eastern customs to explain biblical passages; see Basil Herring, *Joseph Ibn Kaspi's Gevia' Kesef: A Study in Jewish Medieval Philosophic Bible Commentary* (New York: Ktav, 1982), 61–63 for specific instances.

there are aspects of the Torah that are indeed best understood in ancient context, in what sense is the Torah "eternal"?

The supposition of the Torah's "eternity," while correct, needs to be defined. Do we mean that its meaning is fixed, singular, and eternal? Such a position contravenes fundamental tenets of rabbinic Judaism. If this is the sense in which the Torah is eternal, then there is no room for Hillel HaZaken to introduce the seven principles through which he interpreted the Torah, nor is there room for R. Yishmael to introduce his thirteen additional principles of interpretation. Indeed, there would have been no room for any interpretation at all. All ages would need to understand the Torah in exactly the same manner. The "eternal" nature of the Written Torah, its multifaceted richness, is found only through the medium of the interpretative process of the *Torah Shebe'al Peh*. The Sages teach that there are seventy "faces" to the Torah. The simplest meaning, the *peshat*, is sometimes time-dependent, addressed to the generation that received the Torah. But its other meanings radiate throughout the millennia, allowing new perspectives and interpretations to thrive.

With this perspective, we can now address some of the most vexing questions posed by the field of academic biblical studies. In the remaining chapters of this section, we will see that the question of the historical accuracy of the Tanakh and the question of inconsistency and contradiction in the Torah take on a new light when these questions are examined in ancient Near Eastern context.

Chapter 2

But Is It "History"? The Historical Accuracy of the Tanakh

F
ew issues are as sensitive as the question of the historical accuracy of the Tanakh, and particularly of the Torah. For many people, what is at stake can be simply stated: If the events the Torah chronicles historically happened the way the Torah describes them, then the Torah is true. If the events in the Torah did not happen the way the Torah says they did, then the Torah is not telling us the truth – it is engaging in fiction masquerading as historical truth. Thus, many religious people feel compelled to affirm and demonstrate that the events of the Bible – all of them – are historically accurate. If even one event can be shown to have happened differently than the Bible's portrayal, the claim that our Tanakh is historically accurate and therefore "true" will be severely undermined. The stakes could hardly be higher.

In chapter 3, we will look at historical evidence for the Exodus, that is, we will look outside the Tanakh for confirmation of what is contained inside it, and weigh what we can from that evidence. Here, however, we will not discuss external evidence. Rather, in this chapter we focus on *how* the Tanakh relates to us the events that befell our forefathers, the rules that the Tanakh employs for what it will tell us about those events. In my introduction I noted that most of us probably assumed that Jews who endured the atrocities of the Holocaust were referred to as "survivors" and treated with heroic reverence from the moment of their liberation. Yet, we saw that the very term "survivor" and the attendant attitudes that accompany it were actually very late in developing; terming our brethren in such a way was actually a construct of a later age that developed and shaped how we looked upon the individuals who endured these experiences. What we will see here is very similar – an instance in which we become aware of the fact that ideas and concepts that we take for granted as being obvious and eternally true turn out to be a construct of our own time and place. And the key concept that we need to critically examine in this chapter is the concept of *history*, and the idea of an account of the past that is "historically" accurate.

Consider this: If you take all of biblical literature and all of rabbinic literature through the Middle Ages, you will not find anywhere a Hebrew term for "history." Of course, you can find innumerable discussions of the events of the past, but you will never find these referred to as "history"; you will never find that one who discusses the past is called "a historian." Or, consider this even more surprising observation: there is no Hebrew equivalent in biblical or rabbinic writings for the words *fact* or *fiction*. This is astonishing, because the rabbis were clearly attuned to the moral values of truth (*emet*) and falsehood (*sheker*). When a word in one culture has no precise translation in another culture, it is a sign that the two cultures exhibit not only a lexical gap, but a conceptual one as well. There is no word, and hence no clearly defined concept, in biblical and talmudic writings of a realm of statements or compositions that have the quality of representing "fact" as opposed to other statements or writings who receive the downgraded characteristic of "fiction."

The near-total absence of the conceptual categories of *history*, *fact*, and *fiction* from the biblical and rabbinic record speaks volumes about how far we as moderns stand from the world of our forefathers during those periods. It means that we are likely to find genres of writing here where these categories appear to us as blurred. When we speak of *history, fact,* and *fiction,* we must realize that we are utilizing modern categories of thought, that these are categories that the modern mind has constructed. We think that history simply means a discussion of past events with factual accuracy. We assume that this "history" has existed for, well, all of history. But it has not. The concept *history* itself has a history and we need to understand how it came to be. Only by doing that can we understand how our sacred sources – biblical and rabbinic – relate to us the events that befell our forefathers. Put differently, before we seek to understand the Tanakh, we must seek to understand ourselves.

In what follows, we will first lay bare the assumptions we make about the genre of writing that we term "history" and how those assumptions deviate from those that guided the way premodern authors and readers viewed authoritative accounts of the past. We will then illustrate this type of writing by looking at a few examples of biblical accounts of the past – the story of Rahab and the spies, passages that showcase the use of numbers in Tanakh – and what they signal to the reader about these events. From there we examine the concept of myth, and discuss why very few episodes in the Tanakh can be classified under that category. Our examination of modern constructs about historical writing, myth, metaphor, and meaning will lead us to conclusions about the ways in which the Tanakh relates to us the events of the past.

WHAT DO WE MEAN BY "HISTORY"?

Reading History: Basic Assumptions

Let us examine the unspoken assumptions we make when we engage a concrete piece of modern history writing. To help illustrate what I am getting at, here is a short excerpt from Michael Oren's account of the June 1967 war, *Six Days of War,* which was published by Oxford University Press in 2002 and was a *New York Times* bestseller. In this passage, Oren details the arrival of the paratroopers at the Western Wall:

> [General Mordecai] Gur received a delegation of Arab notables who proffered him the city's surrender, along with arms that had been stored in the mosques. To their surprise, the general

released them and allowed them to return to their homes. But neither he nor any of his staff knew how to get to the Western Wall, and were forced to ask an old Arab man for directions. He guided Gur through the Mughrabi Gate, exiting just south of the wall. A retaining structure of giant ashlars erected by King Herod, the wall was the only remnant of the Second Temple destroyed by the Romans in the year 70. Jews had not had access to the shrine, their holiest, for nineteen years.

As Gur descended, men from both the Jerusalem Brigade and the 71st paratroopers converged on the Wall, ecstatic and all but oblivious to the persistent sniper fire. [IDF Chief] Rabbi Goren broke free of the three soldiers Gur had designated to restrain him, and ran headlong to the wall. He said *Kaddish* – the mourner's prayer – blew his *shofar*, and proclaimed, "I, General Shlomo Goren, chief rabbi of the Israeli Defense Forces, have come to this place, never to leave it again." Crammed into the narrow space between the stones and the ramshackle dwellings of the Mughrabi Quarter, the soldiers broke into spontaneous songs and prayers. Above them, the Star of David was hoisted.[1]

When we as moderns read a passage of historical writing such as this, we do so with a set of presuppositions that we rarely think about or acknowledge. The presuppositions I draw attention to here will seem banal, perhaps even obvious. But they are important to identify because they are at odds with how people – including those living in the periods of the Tanakh and the Talmud – read accounts of the past before the modern age. Only by grasping that difference can we understand how the Tanakh relates to us the events of the past.

When you read a history book like Oren's *Six Days of War*, you do so with three sets of presuppositions. First, you harbor presuppositions about the nature of the *content* you will find in such a history book. Second, you have presuppositions about the *author*, the figure dubbed the "historian," even if his or her name is entirely unfamiliar to you.

---

1. Oren, *Six Days of War*, 245–46.

Finally, you maintain presuppositions about yourself as the *reader* of a modern history book. Let us unpack these presuppositions one at a time.

First, you harbor presuppositions about the *content* you will find in a history book. You know that Oren, like any writer, presents an interpretation of the material. No writer ever writes from a fully objective vantage point. But you assume that even while providing an interpretation of events, he provides you with factual information exclusively. If you give Oren the benefit of the doubt, you take as fact that the paratroopers really did reach the Western Wall via the Mughrabi Gate and that the flag of Israel really was hoisted above the wall. You assume that Oren has based his account on reliable sources. In fact, it is no coincidence that in the passage above, Oren chooses a direct quotation from Rabbi Goren. Rabbi Goren composed his account of the event, and that account represents a documentable, first-person source, written relatively close to the time of the event itself. Had Oren decades later interviewed a soldier who had been there, and that soldier had "quoted" what someone had said, that would not have been nearly as credible as a historical source written much closer to the event itself.

Further, you assume that Oren has done nothing to embellish the account in any way. By way of fact, the paratroopers arrived at the Western Wall in the late hours of the morning. Imagine Oren had written in his account, "and as the paratroopers reached the wall, the morning sun rose above the highest layer of its ancient stones." There would be great symbolism in that – indeed, the conquest of Jerusalem did open a new chapter in Israeli history – but a rhetorical flourish like this would be entirely out of place in what we consider to be a reliable work of history. Indeed, you correctly assume that were it to be discovered that he had embellished – fabricated would be a better word – even the slightest detail of the event, he would immediately be disbarred from the scholarly guild. That is because in your mind you categorize this as a work of *history*. You make a sharp divide between a work such as this, which must be fully factual, and other genres that use accounts of the past, such as historical novels like Leon Uris's *Exodus* about the founding of the State of Israel, or ballads such as Naomi Shemer's *Yerushalayim Shel Zahav*. You presume that Oren's book belongs to the genre of *fact*, not *fiction*. You live in a culture in which those terms are often value laden.

Things assigned to the category of *fact* are true and valuable. Things deemed to be merely fiction are false, even mendacious. You assume that Oren's presentations are his conclusions on the basis of careful scrutiny of original sources and the pertinent scholarship to those sources. You expect that he will advance his argument on the basis of evidence, citing those primary sources and the scholarly works that have shed light upon them. Put differently, you assume that there is a discipline called *history* that has well-established rules of inquiry that determine how this work was researched and written. In this case, that means that you trust that Oren knew how to access the various diplomatic and military archives in several countries, and that he knew how to compare and cross-validate the claims made by a wide array of actors. Because a historian like Oren must cite his sources, you know that he subjects himself to critique and examination: other scholars can review the evidence he marshals and either critique or confirm his findings.

You also assume that you will find no preaching or moralizing in his account. Oren is an ardent Zionist, but even if you share those same sentiments you would find it disconcerting to find in a work of history such as his a concluding remark: "and therefore all Jews should mark 28 Iyar each year as Yom Yerushalayim." That is not his mandate in a work of history and the work would be tainted in your mind had he done so. As a work of academic history, his presentation is expected to be an interpretation of facts. There is no room in such a work to preach explicit religious, moral, or civic lessons to you as a reader.

Second, when reading a book such as *Six Days of War*, you harbor implicit presuppositions about Michael Oren as the *author* of this book. You may know his name because he served as Israel's ambassador to the United States during the Obama presidency, but let us assume that his name meant nothing to you. You would still give him the benefit of the doubt as a reliable authority by dint of the degrees he holds; because of the standing he has in the academic community; because a panel of outside experts vetted his work; and because a prestigious publisher has chosen to commit its name to it. You assume that he has mastered the discipline of history and its critical methods. And those presumptions would be here justified. Prior to his political and diplomatic career, Michael Oren was a historian. He holds a doctorate in Near

Eastern Studies from Princeton University and his book was published by Oxford University Press. Yet, for all of his bona fides, his authority in our eyes is limited. In our milieu, these qualifications certify him solely to present before you the reader an interpretation of events past. They do not authorize him to ask anything of you, to command you, or even to recommend a course of action. Moreover, his background – his religious denomination, the community in which he was raised – are of ancillary interest at most, in terms of determining his qualifications to compose a work of history. Historians' personal backgrounds are so irrelevant that when they submit a study for publication in a scholarly journal, their name as author is kept from the experts who judge the work. Arguments in a work of historical scholarship, we presuppose, should be evidence-driven and independent of the author's identity.

Finally, you bring to your reading of a book such as Oren's presuppositions about yourself as a *reader*. Unwittingly, you see yourself as a consumer of this work. You read such a book volitionally, for the purpose of your edification. As this work is sold commercially, you or someone else paid the publisher for this opportunity. What you are doing is an exercise in inquiry and understanding; you wish to learn something about the history of modern Israel. But beyond coming to the book as a consumer, you also come to it as a judge. You know that many other competent scholars have written about this critical episode in Israel's history and you know that you can easily access their findings and opinions should you choose to. Implicitly, you will ask yourself, "Do I believe this is a compelling argument?" Most importantly, you reserve for yourself as reader the right to determine the ultimate meaning of what you are reading. Do Oren's findings mean that we should recite Hallel on Yom Yerushalayim? Do they substantiate the claims of those who believe that Israel illegally occupies East Jerusalem? You as reader reserve for yourself the right to incorporate his account within a larger web of meaning and significance, as you see fit. In our world, the historian or journalist provides the facts; the reader determines the meaning.

HISTORY VS. EXHORTATION: TWO DIFFERENT GENRES

If these presuppositions all seem quite obvious, they were not to premodern writers and readers, such as the Roman readers who read the so-called "historical" works of Cicero and Livy, or to the medieval readers who read the "historical" accounts of the monk, the Venerable Bede. History then and history now are alike in name only. In fact, to properly distinguish between accounts of the past that are read today, such as Oren's *Six Days of War*, and accounts of the past that were written and read in pre-modern times, we would do well to employ two different terms. In modern times we read works of *history*. This "history" employs all of the presumptions laid out above. In pre-modern times, however, it would be more correct to say that when people read accounts of the past, they were reading *exhortation*. That term captures many of the differences between accounts of the past written in the modern period and seemingly similar exercises from the pre-modern age. To understand what I mean by calling this genre of writing *exhortation*, let us return to the same three categories of assumptions that I laid out before: What was the nature of the *content* readers expected to find in these accounts of the deeds of the past? What did they assume about the *authors* of these works? What presuppositions did they make about their place as *readers* of these works? The answers to these questions are key to understanding how the Tanakh presents to us the events of the past.

First and foremost, pre-modern readers harbored expectations about the *content* they read or heard. Works such as Cicero's *De Republica* or Livy's *The History of Rome* or, in medieval times, the Venerable Bede's *A History of the English Church and People*, were works of *exhortation*. These writers never wrote with the disinterested aim of chronicling the past for its own sake. Rather, the deeds of the past were harnessed for rhetorical effect to persuade readers to take action in the present, to believe in the powers of a deity to deliver salvation, to exhibit bravery or other civic virtues.[2] For the historians of Rome, the deeds of the past were retold to instruct and to inspire. It was expected that writers would not only narrate the deeds of the past, but evaluate them as well, offering praise or blame. The lessons from the past were intimately connected to the public life of the state and had an educative

---

2. Gerald Press, "History and the Development of the Idea of History in Antiquity," *History and Theory* 16 (1977): 290.

purpose.[3] It was in this sense that Cicero remarked, *Historia magistra vitae*, "History is a teacher of life."[4]

The essential nature of these compositions as *exhortation* leaves us today trapped unaware by our modern binary categories of fiction and non-fiction.[5] As one modern scholar of these so-called "histories" has noted:

> We have no useful category for the realm inhabited by ancient historical texts: rather than being "literature," the works of ancient historians came far closer to the modern genres of non-fiction novel or popular, non-academic history, where a degree of embroidery and imagination is layered upon a basis of fact.[6]

While history and fiction were conceptually distinct in the Middle Ages, medieval accounts of the past are full of what we today would consider fictional elements: invented material (speeches, secret conversations, letters, and battle scenes), miracles, and type-scenes where the same ordered sets of activities seem to recur across works.[7] The Roman "historian" Cicero claimed that the facts as known to the writers were subject to rhetorical amplification and invention. This

---

3. John Marincola, "Ancient Audiences and Expectations," in *Cambridge Companion to the Roman Historians*, ed. Andrew Feldherr (Cambridge: Cambridge University Press, 2009), 19–22; Andrew Feldherr, introduction to *Cambridge Companion to the Roman Historians*, 4.

4. See similar sentiments for medieval history writing in Robert Bonfil, *History and Folklore in a Medieval Jewish Chronicle: The Family Chronicle of Aḥimaʿaz ben Paltiel* (Leiden, Netherlands: Brill, 2009), 28–29; John Burrow, *A History of Histories: Epics, Chronicles, Romances and Inquiries from Herodotus and Thucydides to the Twentieth Century* (New York: Knopf, 2008), 160.

5. J. E. Lendon, "Historians Without History: Against Roman Historiography," in *Cambridge Companion to the Roman Historians*, 57.

6. Ibid. See a similar appraisal of medieval materials in Suzanne Fleischman, "On the Representation of History and Fiction in the Middle Ages," *History and Theory* 22 (1983): 278–310.

7. Justin Lake, "Current Approaches to Medieval Historiography," *History Compass* 13:3 (2015): 90. For a full-length treatment of modes of embellishment in medieval historiography, see Ruth Morse, *Truth and Convention in the Middle Ages: Rhetoric, Representation, and Reality* (Cambridge: Cambridge University Press, 1991).

heritage of classical antiquity remained influential throughout the Middle Ages. Far from detracting from the veracity of a work, plausible fictional embellishments endowed an account with credibility. Often, these embellishments would give an account greater depth, enabling an author to probe the thoughts and motives of historical actors. They contributed to the value of the piece as *exhortation*. Such embellishments ensured that the piece would achieve what all assumed was its purpose: to inspire and instruct.[8] This is why many scholars of these materials question whether we can reconstruct fully accurate histories of these periods on the basis of these accounts.

One thing that readers did not expect to find in the historical accounts of Rome was a detail of the historian's sources. Roman "historians" are notoriously silent about the sources of their accounts.[9] This further underscores the fundamental truth that these records of the deeds of the past do not represent a sustained effort to arrive at fully factual truth. Rather, they are a harnessing of accepted historical details for the sake of exhortation. "History is written for telling, not proving," wrote the first-century Roman rhetorician, Quintilian (*Institutes of Oratory* 10.1.31).[10]

Pre-modern readers of these works of exhortation also harbored certain presumptions about the *authors* of these works that differ from those we harbor concerning modern writers of history. Such readers would never have assumed that these writers had special research training that qualified them to compose "historical" accounts. Livy was trained in rhetoric. Cicero famously described history as "a job for a public speaker" (*De Oratore* 2:62).[11] In Roman times there was no systematic study of history and no methodology for doing so.[12] Even in medieval times history was not a discipline that was taught; there was no option for a student to enroll himself in a course entitled "history" or to be examined in a field called "history."[13] Indeed, the first faculty in a field called "history" was

---

8. Lake, "Medieval Historiography," 91.
9. Marincola, "Ancient Audiences and Expectations," 19.
10. As translated in Lendon, "Historians Without History," 55.
11. Feldherr, introduction, 4.
12. Marincola, "Ancient Audiences and Expectations," 18.
13. Beryl Smalley, *Historians in the Middle Ages* (New York: Scribner, 1975), 11.

established in Berlin in 1810.[14] It is only with the rise of the academic discipline of history in the nineteenth century that the practice of annotation and citation of sources becomes de rigueur.[15] These pre-modern writers were authorities not on account of their mastery of sources or extensive training in the methodology of historiography. Instead, the authority of these writers stemmed from their standing in the community. The stature and status of the historian in classical Rome was gained by dint of the offices he held, or the armies he commanded. Practical experience was what made one worthy of writing of the deeds of the past, not the mastery of research methodology.[16] Their mandate was not to sift sources and to paint as accurate a picture of the past as possible, but rather to use what was known about the past to inspire and instruct.

Finally, pre-modern readers of historical accounts differed from their contemporary peers in the presumptions they had about themselves as *readers*. As I noted, contemporary readers are consumers, or even judges of the works they read. Modern historians give readers a way to verify information and to formulate different opinions by citing primary sources and referencing other scholarly works. The making of meaning for modern readers is a task left to the discretion of the reader. By contrast, ancient and medieval historians rarely present sources for cross-reference; the interpretation these writers offer and the lessons they exhort are stated in absolute terms.[17] The making of meaning concerning the events of the past was a task entrusted to the authors who composed these works. Few would have been the readers or listeners equipped to even begin to question the accuracy of the presentations they were reading or hearing. The works were held to be basically true. But their value was not measured in terms of how accurately their

---

14. Frederick Beiser, *The German Historicist Tradition* (Oxford: Oxford University Press, 2011), 22.

15. See discussion in Paul Veyne, *Did the Greeks Believe in Their Myths? An Essay on the Constitutive Imagination*, trans. Paula Wissing (Chicago: University of Chicago Press, 1988), 11.

16. Charles W. Fornora, *The Nature of History in Ancient Greece and Rome* (Berkeley: University of California Press, 1983), 54; cf. Marincola, "Ancient Audiences and Expectations," 18.

17. See discussion in Veyne, *Did the Greeks Believe*, 10.

depictions accorded with fact. Indeed, readers would have had no way of ascertaining those facts. Rather, the works were held in high esteem because of the standing and authority of the authors who had penned them. For the pre-modern reader of the deeds of the past, facts about the past were subsumed within a hortatory exhortation.

Here we come to the primary difference between modern compositions of history and pre-modern compositions of history. In our world, the primary encounter is between the reader and the facts he or she reads. In the pre-modern world, the primary encounter is between the reader and the authority of the exhorter. And when that exhorter or preacher is an esteemed man of letters, or an office holder in classical Rome, or a church father in the histories composed by the early Church, the reader no longer approaches these works as a consumer, or judge, the way a contemporary reader would. Such readers or listeners encounter accounts of the past from within a hierarchy in which the reader is subordinate to the exhorter, the preacher. The reader comes to learn not what factually transpired in times of yore. Rather, in a spirit of submission, the reader or listener engages these texts to learn the lessons those texts come to teach, via the lived example of individuals in the past.

THE TANAKH AS EXHORTATION

The books of the Tanakh were written and read along the lines of exhortation. These are works in which a degree of embroidery and rhetorical embellishment is layered upon a base of fact. The primary interest of all books of the Tanakh is to bring Israel to greater covenantal piety in its relationship with the Almighty. The Tanakh assumes that readers and listeners approach the biblical text in submission, with a desire to learn its lessons. The Tanakh assumes that readers leave it to the divinely inspired authors of the texts to determine the most effective way to cast the events of the past in order to transmit its lessons.

This can be very threatening for some on religious grounds, because it suggests that some aspects of the biblical accounts are not fully factual, but rather rhetorical. But this is threatening only if we allow ourselves to fall into the trap of buying into what our modern environment tells us. The environment we live in tells us that the more factual an account is, the truer it is, and hence the more valuable it is.

By contrast, the Tanakh – and indeed the entire rabbinic tradition – proceeds on different assumptions. The Tanakh is a valuable account of the past, not because all it records is fact. It is a valuable account of the past because of the divine authority behind it; it is valuable because it casts the events of the past in a way that ensures that we come away with the most important messages those events have to teach. Our modern environment tells us we should read the news or learn about past events and then process the facts for ourselves, determine their meaning on our own. Our sacred sources insist that we come to the sacred texts in submission with the belief and commitment that this alone is the best way to understand the meaning and lessons of the events that are portrayed. This is how God has authorized that we relate to these events.

For many this sounds new, and unintuitive. Why are there no rabbinic sources that lay this all out? Why are there no rabbinic sources that tell us how to determine what is fact and what is fiction? My answer is that for millennia our sages could not even have fathomed the underlying tenets of modern historiography that I laid out. They certainly believed that the events reported in the Tanakh had occurred. But they could not envision writing about the past in a way that aimed solely for factual representation and not exhortation and instruction. They had no notion of a writer trained in the methodology of sifting sources. They had no notion of a reader reading an authorized text and then judging its meaning for him- or herself. To foist these categories on these earlier generations of our Sages is to insist that they conceptualize in a way entirely foreign to them. Indeed, it would be akin to asking American Jews in the late 1940s why they referred to the recent immigrants from Europe as *greene* and refugees and not as "survivors." Our way of thinking about the writing of history came about through a conceptual revolution that postdated their time.

Let us move now from a broad and theoretical discussion to look at examples of passages in the Tanakh where it appears that the Tanakh simply details a factual account. Upon closer inspection, however, we will be able to discern that these passages cannot be fully factually accurate, that they employ a degree of rhetorical embellishment. These illustrations will allow us to appreciate what is gained when the Tanakh expresses these events of the past in the way that it does, rather than sticking to a realistic presentation of facts alone.

THE STORY OF RAHAB (JOSHUA 2)

Imagine you are asked to begin a dialogue with someone and instructed that while speaking to them, you must weave references to the first five of the Ten Commandments into your speech. Would you be able to do it? Would you be able to do so effortlessly? The chances are slim. And yet, this is what we find that Rahab does, as seen in her speech to the spies on the roof of her house, reported in Joshua 2:9–13. Let us see how she does this and what it tells us about the relationship between realism and embellishment in the way the Tanakh reports historical events.

In her soliloquy of verses 9–13, Rahab professes her belief in the potency of the God of Israel, seen through His salvation on Israel's behalf in Egypt and against kings Sihon and Og. She concludes that the townsfolk of Jericho are dispirited "because the Lord your God is God in the heaven above and on the land below" (Josh. 2:11). Her words echo language found twice in the Torah, in Deuteronomy 4:39 and 5:8. The former proclaims that God reigns "in the heavens above and on the earth below," while the same language is used in 5:8, proscribing the fashioning of graven images of anything "in the heavens above and on the earth below" (Ex. 20.4=Deut. 5.8). The story of Rahab reaches for this phrase in a call to the reader to engage one of those texts – the Ten Commandments. The immediate impression is that Rahab affirms God's sovereignty over the heavens and earth, just as Israel does through the instruction of the second commandment.

Other elements of terminology and motifs from the Ten Commandments are also tightly woven into her speech. Rahab affirms the first commandment (Ex. 20:2=Deut. 5:6): "I am the Lord your God who has taken you out of Egypt (אֲשֶׁר הוֹצֵאתִיךָ מֵאֶרֶץ מִצְרַיִם), the house of bondage." Rahab sees God's role in the Exodus in similar terms (Josh. 2:10): "For we have heard that the Lord dried up the waters of the Red Sea before you, as you came out of Egypt (בְּצֵאתְכֶם מִמִּצְרַיִם)."

Her request to the spies for shelter in verse 13 expressly mentions both her father and her mother (וְהַחֲיִתֶם אֶת אָבִי וְאֶת אִמִּי). No other figure in the Tanakh performs an action for the good of his or her parents, where the words "father" and "mother" both appear. This seems to invoke the language of Exodus 20:12 (=Deut. 5:16), "Honor your father and mother." Rahab is seen here performing what the Ten Commandments would consider a fulfillment of one's duties to father and mother. Indeed, the reward to one who honors one's father and mother, "so that you lengthen your days in the land" (Ex. 20:12=Deut. 5:16), is Rahab's reward (Josh. 6:25): "And Joshua delivered Rahab the harlot, her father's house, and all that was hers, and she dwelled in the midst of Israel to this very day."

Rahab's behavior also implicitly affirms the injunction of the third commandment against taking God's name in vain (Ex. 20:7=Deut. 5:11). She asks the spies to swear in the name of God that they will protect her and her family, putting all of her stock in the belief that the name of God is so sacrosanct that they would not dare take His name in vain and fail to abide by their oath (Josh. 2:12). The language of that commandment is echoed further on in the story. The Decalogue states that one who does not uphold his vow and takes God's name in vain shall not be "cleared" or "exonerated" (לֹא יְנַקֶּה; Ex. 20:6). The spies express their understanding that they will only be "clear" of the oath if they uphold it (Josh. 2:20): "And if you divulge our plan with you, we shall be clear of your oath (נְקִיִּם אֲנַחְנוּ מִשְּׁבֻעָתֵךְ)" (cf. Josh. 2:17).

Finally, Rahab demonstrates her fidelity to the spirit of the mitzva of Shabbat, the fourth commandment. To be sure, Rahab is not "Shabbat observant." Among the Ten Commandments, the commandment of Shabbat is the only one that offers a rationale for its observance, an explanation of its commemorative function. While Rahab may not refrain from work on Shabbat, she does display a keen appreciation of the events that the day is meant to commemorate. For the Decalogue in Exodus, the Shabbat is commanded, "because in six days the Lord your God created the heaven and the earth (אֶת הַשָּׁמַיִם וְאֶת הָאָרֶץ)" (Ex. 20:10). Rahab, as we already saw, affirms God's sovereignty over the heaven and earth in Joshua 2:11: "because the Lord your God is God in the heaven above and on the earth below" (הוּא אֱ-לֹהִים בַּשָּׁמַיִם מִמַּעַל וְעַל הָאָרֶץ מִתָּחַת).

In short, we have seen that the story of Rahab interweaves references to the first five of the Ten Commandments within the space of her five-verse soliloquy in verses 9–13. It seems unlikely that this is actually a verbatim transcript of what transpired. After all, Rahab – a Canaanite harlot – could hardly have known Hebrew, let alone the Ten Commandments. And even if she somehow was familiar with them as a text, it seems unlikely that under the pressure of the moment she could coincidentally weave all of these allusions into her address before the spies. Realistically speaking, it seems much more likely that Rahab and the spies spoke in a Northwest Semitic dialect intelligible to both sides, and that she spoke in the manner of simple folk and negotiated the terms of their rescue, and then hers. If we hear in the text references to the Ten Commandments, this is because the author of the story embellished the bare facts because he sought to inculcate a message that would be lost by merely recording a Hebrew transcription of their dialogue. What message and instruction are gained by casting this exchange in embellished fashion? Why weave dialogue with Decalogue?

According to the Torah (Deut. 20), all Canaanites were to be killed. However, Rahab saved the spies, and essentially, through them, the rest of Israel. But how could she be spared if the Torah had said she should be killed? The author of our story answers by showing that she is no ordinary Canaanite. By portraying her actions and her speech in ways that echo the first half of the Ten Commandments, the author demonstrates that she is not merely acting out of opportunism to save her own skin, but that she in fact believes deeply in the God of Israel. Through her "observance" or alignment with the Ten Commandments, she demonstrates that she is worthy of being spared and eventually taking up residence within the people of Israel (Josh. 6:25).

The book of Joshua could have presented a "historically accurate" version of the story. But the story would have been greatly impoverished. It would have told us exactly what happened and the manner in which things were precisely said. It would have failed to give us the primary message: that Rahab was a righteous woman, not only an opportunist, and thus fully worthy of being spared the fate of the other Canaanites. It is precisely the artifice of her monologue, the embroidery layered upon the base facts of the story, that gives us the truest presentation of the events: Rahab was worthy of being saved. Put differently, we see that the author of Joshua had two choices: He could present the truest version of the bare facts, at the risk of losing the true message of the story. Or he could ensure that we come away with the true lesson of her actions, at the expense of factual accuracy.

NUMBERS IN THE TANAKH

Throughout the writings of the ancient Near East we find that numbers are often unrealistically large, especially when reported in a military context, such as army size or the detail of booty taken from an enemy.[18] In the Tanakh as well, numbers may be used to reflect something other than what we would define as a quantitative reality. Below we see three examples in which numbers appear to function as markers of meaning.

1. The armies of Judah in the book of Chronicles

In the second book of Chronicles, we find troop figures for the armies of many of the kings of Judah. Concerning the first four of these kings, these figures are listed over six chapters. The army of Rehoboam, we are told, numbered 180,000 (II Chr. 11:1). The army of his son, Abijah, numbered 400,000 (II Chr. 13:3). The army of Asa was comprised of two units: one numbered 300,000 and the other numbered 280,000. Finally, the armies of Jehoshaphat, his son, consisted of five units. Those units numbered 300,000; 280,000; 200,000; 200,000; and 180,000 men (II Chr. 17: 14–18). These numbers are all quite large and cannot conform to any realistic picture of what we know about life in the Land of Israel at the time. In fact, the armies of Jehoshaphat total over one million soldiers! When we look at these numbers a little more closely, though, we see two trends. One is that some of the numbers are what we would term large round numbers – 200,000, 300,000, and 400,000. The other numbers we might term semi-rounded figures – 180,000 and 280,000, each of which appears twice. Put differently, the figures that are "semi-rounded," of which there are four, all end with eighty thousand. That seems a bit odd. After all, if the armies are presented as rounded to the nearest ten thousand, one would not expect that all four examples of armies that are not rounded to the nearest hundred thousand all happen to round to eighty thousand. For all of these reasons, it is difficult to read these figures as reflective of quantitative realities.

One perceptive scholar has recently discerned a clear pattern that points to the meaning inherent in these numbers. The sum of

---

18. See D. M. Fouts, "A Defence of the Hyperbolic Interpretation of Large Numbers in the Old Testament," *Journal of Evangelical Theological Studies* 40 (1997): 377–87.

Jehoshaphat's armies totals 1,160,000. This figure is exactly double the size of his father Asa's armies. The figure is also exactly equivalent to the sum of all the armies of the three kings of Judah who preceded him, recorded above.[19] The narrative of Second Chronicles casts Jehoshaphat as the most righteous of the kings of Judah – more so than any of his predecessors, or those that immediately followed him. The author of Chronicles uses troop numbers to convey that idea in keeping with an ancient convention of employing non-realistic numbers. As a reward for his righteousness, Jehoshaphat commanded not only the largest army but, rhetorically speaking, an army so large that it doubled the size of his father's armies and equaled the total of all those who preceded him. Put differently, the book of Chronicles depicts troop numbers not to convey reality but to convey meaning. There are many other numerical figures in the book of Chronicles that do not seem realistic and which we cannot as of yet explain in symbolic terms. However, the observation that Jehoshaphat's armies equaled the total of his predecessors surely cannot be coincidental. It represents a literary use of numbers in a way that is not intuitive for us today.

2. Seventy descendants of Jacob went down to Egypt

The Torah explicitly states that seventy descendants of Jacob went down to Egypt and lists the names of each (Gen. 46:8–27). The number of names listed and the final tally figure cross-validate each other and certainly give the impression that this is a full and quantitatively realistic census. However, a closer look at the name list and the summary figures it offers for each of the matriarchs reveals several problems. The greatest of these is that the census indeed includes seventy named individuals, but only two of these are women. It is inconceivable that the ratio of Jacob's male to female descendants was 34:1.[20] Had the census listed male members only, one might have concluded that the Torah was counting men alone. But by listing two women, it implies that women are also considered in this

---

19. Neriah Klein, "The Chronicler's Code: The Rise and Fall of Judah's Army in the Book of Chronicles," *Journal of Hebrew Scriptures* 17, no. 3 (2017): 1–20.
20. As noted in *Haamek Davar*, Gen. 46:7.

count. Moreover, the Torah emphasizes that Jacob went down to Egypt with all his daughters-in-law (Gen. 46:5, 15) and all his daughters and granddaughters (Gen. 46:7). Second, we see that the Torah states that the sons of Leah were thirty-three in number (Gen. 46:15), and yet there are only thirty-two names listed. Finally, a compound problem emerges when we contrast this census with that recorded in Numbers 26. When we compare the listing of the descendants of Benjamin here (Gen. 46:21) with the data recorded in the census of Numbers 26 (Num. 26:38–40) we discover discrepancies of every imaginable type: the number of descendants is different; the names differ; the birth positions differ; and some of the names listed in Genesis as sons of Benjamin appear in Numbers as grandsons. Other tribes exhibit similar discrepancies, but the greatest degree of discrepancy is found with regard to the genealogies for the tribe of Benjamin. If the census of Genesis 46 is taken as a realistic and factual account of how many souls descended to Egypt, it fails to provide names and numbers that are internally consistent; it fails to provide details that easily dovetail with other such lists, such as those in Numbers 26; and it fails to count those who actually descended according to one consistent rule, counting some women but not others. How may we account for all of these uneven details?

Anthropologists have long known that genealogies in pre-modern cultures are not merely records of birth order. They are dynamic records of status and hierarchy within the tribe. Thus, in one period the tribe will recall its forefathers as having been "born" in one order, while at a later period, some of the names will migrate within a given level of the genealogy, or even "move" up or down a generation, all depending on the merits and demerits of that individual's descendants.[21] If this sounds entirely foreign, it should not. This is, in fact, what we find with our own "memory" concerning the order and identity of the tribes of Israel. When Jacob's children were born, Joseph counted as one son. However, in time Joseph essentially assumed the position of firstborn, and received a double portion; Menashe and Ephraim assumed the status as "sons"

---

21. J. A. Barnes, *Models and Interpretations* (Cambridge: Cambridge University Press, 1990), 227–28.

of Jacob, equal to his other genealogical sons. The narrative of Genesis 48 and Jacob's blessing to Joseph's sons establishes this to be so. Thus, both the lists in Genesis 46 and in Numbers 26 reflect something other than mere genealogy by birth order.

Numbers in Genesis 46 are designed to reflect status, and this is seen most clearly with regard to the seeming "discrepancy" between the descendants of Leah; they are said to tally thirty-three, while the Torah lists only thirty-two names. Some might be tempted to write off the discrepancy as a scribal error. Yet all the ancient translations of the Bible, such as the Septuagint – which often seek to correct seeming "errors" in the text – maintain the version of the text preserved here in our Masoretic Text. When we look at the actual names listed in Genesis 46 – as opposed to the summary tally figures for each of the four matriarchs – a clear pattern emerges: the number of descendants of Rachel (fourteen; Gen. 46:20–21) is double the number of descendants of her handmaid, Bilhah (seven; 46:23–24). Similarly, the number of Leah's descendants (thirty-two; 46:9–14) is double that of her handmaid, Zilpah (sixteen; 46:16–17). This is achieved, though, only by applying different "rules" to the question of who is counted as a descendant of each of the wives. Rachel's descendants, for example, include grandsons – Menashe and Ephraim – whereas no other grandsons are included in this census, even though the Torah states that grandchildren were among those who descended to Egypt with Jacob (Gen. 46:7).

However, when we examine not the actual number of names listed for Jacob's descendants, but rather the summary tally totals, a different axis of significance emerges. The numbers form multiples of seven. There is a grand total of seventy descendants (Gen. 46:27). The descendants of Bilhah are seven (46:25). Those of Rachel total fourteen (46:22). Those of Leah (thirty-three; 46:15) and of Zilpah (sixteen; 46:18) total forty-nine. The message that emerges from an examination of these figures is that the "whole" of Israel represented a "significant" contingent – it "counts" seventy individuals.[22] Moreover, it is significant because its subdivisions are multiples of seven as well. Factually, there

---

22. See *Haamek Davar*, Gen. 46:7, who also sees symbolism in the figure of seventy descendants.

were far more than seventy members of Jacob's family who descended to Egypt, as claimed by the Netziv.[23] But the point of the list in the first place was never to offer a roll call. *We* call the list a census, but that label represents little more than our construction of what we think it is telling us. It is, in fact, an encoded way of demonstrating God's blessing to Jacob and his family as they descend to Egypt. There is no reason to doubt that there was a figure named Jacob, nor any reason to doubt that his extended clan descended to Egypt in a time of famine in the land of Canaan, an oft-occurring event, well-documented in Egyptian records of the second millennium BCE. But when we insist on viewing all of the details of an account as a record of facts, we are misleading ourselves, as we misread the text. Like the literature of all ages, the texts of the Torah and the Tanakh are composed with literary conventions in mind. Only by understanding how those literary conventions utilize figures and numbers to embellish a text and further bring out its teachings can we be assured of reading the text according to its intended *peshat* meaning.

3. Four hundred and eighty years in I Kings 6:1

Figures and numbers can serve as the bearers of meaning outside of census lists and troop counts as well. I Kings 6:1 reports that King Solomon began work on the Temple 480 years after the Exodus from Egypt. That number is problematic because it is difficult to reconcile this time span with the total number of years that seem to be chronicled in the book of Judges. It is also problematic because if it is assumed that Solomon reigned in the tenth century BCE, then the book of Kings places the Exodus in the fifteenth century BCE. However, there is abundant archaeological evidence from within the Land of Israel that Egypt retained control of Canaan until the thirteenth century BCE. It is not possible to reconcile a conquest of the land by Joshua on any scale before that.

The figure of 480 years indeed measures time, but in a non-literal way. In the third century BCE the Tanakh was translated into Greek in Alexandria, producing what is known as the Septuagint (often referred to as the LXX for short). The Septuagint is largely similar to our Tanakh, known as the Masoretic Text, but at many points we find differences

---

23. Ibid.

between the two. At the junctures where we find a discrepancy between the two versions, it is often difficult to know whether the Greek translators possessed a version of the passage that differed from the Masoretic Text, or whether those translators were working with a version highly similar to the Masoretic Text, but for various reasons elected to translate certain words or phrases differently. One way or another, we discover that in I Kings 6:1, the Septuagint states that King Solomon commenced work on the Temple 440 years after the Exodus from Egypt. How may we explain the difference between the Masoretic Text and the Septuagint? Why would a different version of the Tanakh read 440 years rather than 480? Alternatively, what might have driven a translator to make such a change?

Insight can be garnered when we look at the priestly genealogies in I Chr. 5:30–36:

> The sons of Aaron:
> Nadav, Avihu, Eleazar, and Itamar.
> Eleazar was the father of Phineas,
> Phineas the father of Avishua,
> Avishua the father of Bukki,
> Bukki the father of Uzzi,
> Uzzi the father of Zerahia,
> Zerahia the father of Meraioth,
> Meraioth the father of Amaria,
> Amaria the father of Ahituv,
> Ahituv the father of Zadok,
> Zadok the father of Ahimaaz,
> Ahimaaz the father of Azaria,
> Azaria the father of Yohanan,
> Yohanan the father of Azaria (it was he who served as *kohen* in the Temple Solomon built in Jerusalem).

Based on this list, how many generations elapsed between the Exodus and the building of the Temple? We know that Phineas was born in Egypt (Ex. 6:25). This means that Phineas's son, Avishua, was the first generation born after the Exodus. Counting the generations from there, on the basis of I Chronicles 5:30–36, it emerges that Azaria ben Yohanan, who served as the *kohen* in Solomon's Temple, was the twelfth generation following the Exodus. The figure of 480 years between the Exodus and the beginning of work on the Temple may be a way of stating that twelve generations had passed, where forty years stands as a trope for a generation. This would well explain an anomaly found in the book of Judges: while there are various tallies offered for the length of the rule of the different judges, a highly disproportionate number of them rule for either forty or eighty years. This could be the prophetic book's way of stating that they ruled for a generation. The Septuagint may have believed that although Azaria served as the *kohen gadol* when the Temple was completed, work on the Temple commenced during the lifetime of Azaria's father, Yohanan, which is to say eleven generations after the Exodus, which would be expressed as 440 years. Here, too, we may see how the Tanakh embellishes a text by using numbers in a non-literal fashion.

Looking at all the evidence provided in this section, some may ask: Why does the Tanakh not express its messages more clearly? Why not simply record Rahab's words more accurately and state that her belief was genuine? Why engage in the artifice of embellished dialogue? If the point of the census of Genesis 46 is to tell us something about the significance of the matriarchs Rachel and Leah over their handmaids – then just say it; why list quantitative figures that are inaccurate? Why not state in I Kings 6, simply, that Solomon built the Temple twelve generations after the Exodus?

It is indeed true that these modes of expression are not intuitive for us. But we would do well to adopt the intellectual and religious humility we saw exhibited in the commentary of Ralbag, cited in chapter 1. Recall, there, that Ralbag was troubled that the Torah exhibited unnecessary repetition in the Exodus chapters depicting the Tabernacle. These repetitions, he noted, violated his sense of literary perfection, and hence stood to undermine the standing of the Torah. Ralbag concluded that literary aesthetics and conventions are culturally dependent. The time and place in which the Torah was given employed a different literary aesthetic than the one that was intuitive for him. We can know little about the future with certainty. But we can know this: our children and grandchildren will look back at us in wonder at how we could not see things that to them are so clear and obvious; their children and grandchildren will express the same wonder about them. It is only by letting the text speak to us on its terms rather than ours that we can properly engage the meaning expressed to us by our holy texts.

HOW MUCH OF THE TANAKH IS FACTUAL?

Is the Tanakh Just Myth?

If the Tanakh deliberately portrays events in a way that is not always fully factual, how can we know that the Tanakh intends any of its depictions to be taken as factual in any way? Put differently, perhaps everything in the Bible is written to be myth – that is, a fictional metaphor composed entirely to inculcate ideas, but without reference to actual historical persons and events.

This understanding of how the Tanakh communicates should be rejected. To be clear: I say this notion should be rejected not because there is historical evidence for many of the Tanakh's claims, even though that may be so. Similarly, my rejection of this notion is not a religious one – even though overwhelmingly our classical rabbinic sources relate to the events depicted in the Tanakh as having actually occurred. Rather, we should reject the notion that the Tanakh was composed as an extended metaphor or fable on *academic* grounds. A few notes are in order here concerning what we know about myth in the ancient world and the ways in which the Tanakh presents us with a genre of writing that is distinct in style and content. These observations, in turn, lead us to the conclusion that the Tanakh intends for its accounts to be taken as having actually occurred.

What are the hallmarks of myth in the ancient world?[24]

1. Myths depict events as occurring outside of historical time (in our terms, the types of stories that begin, "Once upon a time, long, long ago..."), and have no reference to known figures and events that can be plotted on a timeline. Oftentimes, they are depicted as having transpired in the earliest days of mankind.

---

24. See Mary Magoulick, "What Is Myth?," available at https://faculty.gcsu.edu/custom-website/mary-magoulick/defmyth.htm.

2. Myths depict events as having transpired in a locale that might be named, but does not correspond to a locale that the reader/ listener can readily locate.

3. Myths typically mediate inherent, troubling dualities, reconcile us to the realities of human existence, or establish the patterns for life as we know it. They focus on basic human attributes: lust, greed, valor, relations with the gods, and so on.

4. Myths typically relate an isolated episode or a set of closely related episodes and tell of the actions of a small number of personalities and figures. Myths do not encompass many actors over many generations.

5. Myths typically employ supernatural events and figures, and present humans and gods as in direct communication with one another.

These characteristics are all closely related to one another. Because myth in the ancient world seeks to tell us some fundamental and unchanging truth about ourselves and the world we live in, it is placed outside of recognizable time and place. Because it wishes to highlight certain very clear messages, it limits its scope to a small number of key individuals over a relatively limited time frame.

Most of the Tanakh, however, does not conform to these parameters. The majority of the events in the Tanakh take place entirely in the human realm. They take place within known geographic settings. They are set in a timeline of one event in relation to another. Put differently, although myth was the normal way in the ancient world to convey ideas about man and his relationship to the gods, the Tanakh strove to create a new and different genre. This is no accident. The Tanakh is nothing if not a record of how God responds to Israel's actions across the history of their relationship in covenant. Biblical history traces the evolution of this relationship, and looks forward to future developments. The surrounding cultures of the ancient Near East believed that there was no force that unilaterally controlled world events; the gods were in tension with one another, and this tension played out in the chaotic turns of world events. By contrast, the Tanakh posits that the world is controlled by a God who purposefully directs human – that is to say historical – affairs according to His will. Moreover, we see that throughout the Tanakh the deeds and interactions of one generation of the people of Israel have implications for later generations as well. Things said to Abraham and actions taken by him have direct consequences for Isaac, and indeed for the rest of the people of Israel; the actions of one generation in the desert have consequences for the next. If, indeed, the Tanakh was written to be read as myth, why does it go out of its way to break from ancient convention and cast its stories within a historical continuum? Why does it emphasize over and over the interconnectedness of all generations of the people of Israel? Writing in this new convention makes sense only if the Tanakh assumes that it is telling us about individuals that really lived and events that really happened.

Whereas myth focuses on unchanging realities, in the Tanakh, God's interaction with Israel changes over the course of her history. Early in the arc of biblical history, God is still relatively sparing in His punishment. Thus, during the period of the Judges, Israel is wayward. But notice the limits of God's threats: there can be partial foreign conquest, but the specter of exile is nowhere seen. Later, as Israel continues to sin, in the book of Kings, God's patience has run its course, and this ends in exile. Or consider another example: Earlier in the Bible, God performs many miracles; later in the Bible, far fewer. God's interaction with Israel changes as her history progresses. But telling us that God's interactions with Israel change across history – as witnessed in the frequency of miracles and the severity of national punishment – only has coherence if, in fact, Israel really does have a history and it really does unfold along the lines of how the Tanakh reports it.

But let us assume that the narratives of the Tanakh – and all of the prophetic censures of Isaiah, Jeremiah, Ezekiel, and the rest of the prophets of Israel – do not refer to actual events, but were written to be read as mere metaphor. To what would this metaphor point? What would be the lessons of all these fables? Presumably, the lessons would be that God rewards Israel for proper behavior, and punishes her for improper behavior. Put differently, we would be asked to believe that the Tanakh teaches that God will guide Israel through history in the future, even though the proof text for this – the Tanakh itself – was never founded on Israel's actual history in the past.

Moreover, the claim that the Tanakh was composed as myth, and therefore does not address historical reality, is actually predicated on an anachronistic misunderstanding of how ancients related to their myths. Today we associate the word "myth" with fiction and fable. But for the ancients, myth was not symbolic knowledge.[25] Myths were not understood as metaphor where various elements of the constructed story correspond to something in the real world of human events. The ancients understood their myths as accounts of *real* events that either transpired in the past, or transpire continually in the struggles between the gods and in the ongoing relationships between the gods and humans. Those that claim that the events of the Tanakh do not depict reality because they were composed as "myth" engage in a fundamental category error. The term "myth" in its meaning as metaphor and symbolic knowledge is entirely a modern notion. We have no compositions from the ancient Near East in which individuals wrote narratives about the interaction between the human and divine realms that were intended as symbolic knowledge.[26] To refer to these compositions and to the texts of the Bible as "myth" in its modern sense of metaphor or fable is to take modern categories of thinking and writing and superimpose them upon the cultures of the past.

HOW MUCH FACT? HOW MUCH EMBELLISHMENT?
A BRIEF OVERVIEW OF RABBINIC SOURCES

As a whole, rabbinic sources presume that the accounts of the Tanakh tell of real events. Not surprisingly, it is in the rationalist tradition of rabbinic exegesis that we find authorities with an interest in parsing the facts of a story from its rhetorical embellishments. This tradition includes, first and foremost, the Rambam, but also later medieval exegetes such as Ralbag, Abarbanel, and Sforno. Many twentieth-century figures also share this orientation by virtue of living in an age in which Enlightenment, empiricism, and rationalism are so thoroughly entrenched. Within this tradition we find opinions that understand the account of the Garden of Eden and the story of Job as metaphor. The Garden of Eden takes place at the beginning

---

25. See James Barr, "The Meaning of Mythology in Relation to the Old Testament," *Vetus Testamentum* 7, no. 1 (1959): 1–10.
26. See Johan Degenaar, "Discourses on Myth," *Myth & Symbol* 4, no. 1 (2007): 1–14.

of time in a place that is difficult to identify geographically. It focuses on such basic issues as obedience to God, relationships between the sexes, and temptation. It features a small number of characters, including a talking serpent and a God who "walks" in the Garden. It is no wonder that figures such as the Rambam and Rabbi Abraham Isaac HaKohen Kook ascribed enormous importance to this account, but read it as metaphor and not as history, seeking out its instruction on that basis.[27] Likewise, we can well understand the opinion in Bava Batra 15a that Job never lived, and that his story is a *mashal*, which is to say an instructional tale. In this story, as well, we have a limited number of characters worked into a story across a limited time frame, devoted to a single issue – theodicy – in which God and humans speak to each other directly, and in which we find heavenly figures such as Satan. Other expositors, such as Abarbanel, Ralbag, and Sforno, maintained that the account of the Garden of Eden was a historical event, but sought to limit its supernatural elements, and in various ways referred to those as allegorical in nature. Rabbi David Zvi Hoffmann, the greatest halakhic decisor of early twentieth-century German Jewry, maintained that the story of the Flood recorded an actual event, but that the floodwaters covered only the plains of Mesopotamia, not the entire face of the earth.[28] The Rambam maintained that several of the Torah's accounts of encounters between humans and angels were not historical events, but visions to which the biblical figures were privy. He included in this category the account of the visits of the three angels (Genesis 18), the struggle between Jacob and the angel at the Jabbok River (Genesis 32), and the story of Balaam and his donkey (Numbers 22).[29] In his posthumously published work, *The Emergence of Ethical Man*, Rabbi Joseph B. Soloveitchik writes an intriguing section about miracles generally and the plagues of Egypt specifically.[30] Many have understood that Rabbi Soloveitchik maintained that the plagues were natural events whose timing caused historical metamorphosis. Implicit

27. Rambam, *Guide for the Perplexed*, I:2; II:30; Rabbi Abraham Isaac HaKohen Kook, *Igrot HaRaaya* (Jerusalem: Aguda LeHotzaat Sifrei HaRaaya Kook, 1943), 1:134.
28. Rabbi David Zvi Hoffmann, *Sefer Bereshit* (Benei Berak: Netzah, 1969), 140–41.
29. Rambam, *Guide for the Perplexed*, II:42, 47.
30. See Joseph B. Soloveitchik, *The Emergence of Ethical Man* (Jersey City, NJ: Ktav, 2005), 187–88, and the discussion by Lawrence Kaplan, "R. Joseph

in this understanding is that the simple reading of the plagues as super-natural is a literary embellishment.

The notion that rhetorical embellishment is an integral part of how the Tanakh relates to us the events of the past is explicitly adopted by the Midrash in its characterization of the information conveyed in the book of Chronicles. Chronicles (I Chr. 4:18) identifies Moses's mother as a descendant of the tribe of Judah, while according to the Torah (Ex. 2:1), she was from the House of Levi. The Midrash proposes the following resolution:

> "His wife the Judean woman" (I Chr. 4:18) .... The book of Chron-icles was given solely for the purpose of deriving exhortation (*lidaresh*). "His wife the Judean woman" refers to Yokheved. But was she indeed from the tribe of Judah (*Yehuda*)? Was she not from the tribe of Levi? Rather, she is thus named for she raised many Jews (*Yehudim*) in the world.[31]

With regard to other discrepancies found between the book of Chron-icles and other books of the Tanakh, several other midrashim likewise claim that "the book of Chronicles was given solely for the purpose of deriving exhortation."[32] There is here an explicit recognition that even a text that "looks" like history is actually primarily hortatory. Earlier we saw that a variety of biblical texts could employ rhetorical embellish-ment that departs from a fully realistic depiction of the events as they happened. These midrashim give us permission, particularly with the book of Chronicles, to seek out this license even more.

B. Soloveitchik on Miracles and Nature," July 9, 2006, http://hirhurim.blogspot.com/2006/07/r-joseph-b-soloveitchik-on-miracles_09.html. See similarly the understanding of the splitting of the Red Sea offered by Rabbi Jonathan Sacks, "Beshal-lach – Miracles," January 30, 2010, http://rabbisacks.org/covenant-conversation-5770-beshalach-miracles/. For a rationalist defense of miracles in the Bible, see the classic work by C. S. Lewis, *Miracles* (New York: HarperCollins, 2015).

31. *Yalkut Shimoni* I: Chr. 4.

32. Leviticus Rabba, 1:3; Ruth Rabba, 2:1; *Pesikta Zutra Shemot* 2:5; *Sekhel Tov* (Buber ed.) 2:10.

To conclude, when we approach our sacred texts, we do not do so in a vain search for the real facts behind the narrative so that we may then determine their meaning. We take it as axiomatic that the reporting of an event stripped down solely to its factual components will not accurately convey the message that we need to take from the event. Instead, we approach our texts seeking how the Almighty has authorized that these events be told. We welcome whatever embellishment may be added upon the basic factual dimension of the event, for we take it as religiously axiomatic that this is the only way to grasp how the Almighty wished for the event to be remembered and meditated upon by the ages. Viewing the Torah in ancient context allows us to appreciate the fine line between "history" and the recording of a real event adapted for the purpose of hortatory writing. We proceed now to see how these concepts can help us best understand the Torah's report of a single, seminal event: the Exodus from Egypt.

Chapter 3

Avadim Hayinu: Exodus, Evidence, and Scholarship

Perhaps no issue raised in this book has garnered as much interest – and generated as much angst – as the question of the historicity of the Torah's account of the Exodus. Excising the Exodus from Judaism would seem to undercut Judaism itself. After all, the biblical rationale for Israel's obligation to God is premised not on His identity as Creator, or on His supreme moral authority, but on the fact that the Israelite slaves in Egypt cried out to Him from their bondage and He saved them. This is the sole driving force behind the opening line of the Ten Commandments: "I am the Lord your God *who took you out of Egypt, the house of bondage*" (Ex. 20:2).

Were there no Exodus, it would seem, nearly all of Judaism's sacred texts over the centuries would have perpetuated a great lie. In response to the question posed by the child at the Seder meal, "How is this night different from all other nights?" a father would be obliged to reply, "Really, my child, there's no difference." And indeed, at many a contemporary Seder table where questions about the historicity of the Exodus arise, a new figure has emerged: next to the son who knows not how to ask sits the father who knows not how to answer.

In what follows, I offer that father three helpings of scholarship to assist him in formulating his answer.

WAS THERE AN EXODUS? A REVIEW OF THE ARGUMENTS

The case against the historicity of the Exodus is straightforward, and its essence can be stated in five words: a sustained lack of evidence. Nowhere in the written record of ancient Egypt is there any explicit mention of Hebrew or Israelite slaves, let alone a figure named Moses. There is no mention of the Nile waters turning into blood, or of any series of plagues matching those in the Bible, or of the defeat of any pharaoh on the scale suggested by the Torah's narrative of the mass drowning of Egyptian forces at the sea. Furthermore, the Torah states that 600,000 men between the ages of twenty and sixty left Egypt. Adding women, children, and the elderly, we arrive at a population in the vicinity of two million souls. There is no archaeological or other evidence of an ancient encampment that size anywhere in the Sinai Desert. Nor is there any evidence of so great a subsequent influx into the Land of Israel, at any time.

No competent scholar or archaeologist will deny these facts. Case closed, then? For those who would defend the plausibility of a historical exodus, what possible response can there be?

A GLARING LACK OF DOCUMENTARY AND ARCHAEOLOGICAL EVIDENCE?

Let us begin with the missing evidence of the Hebrews' existence in Egyptian records. It is true enough that these records do not contain clear and unambiguous reference to "Hebrews" or "Israelites." But that is hardly surprising. The Egyptians referred to all of their West-Semitic slaves simply as "Asiatics," with no distinction among groups – just as slaveholders in the New World never identified their black slaves by their specific provenance in Africa.

More generally, there is a limit to what we can expect from the written record of ancient Egypt. Ninety-nine percent of the papyri produced there during the period in question have been lost, and none whatsoever has survived from the eastern Nile Delta, the region where the Torah claims the children of Israel resided. Instead, we have to rely on monumental inscriptions, which, being mainly reports to the gods about royal achievements, are far from complete or reliable as historical records. They are more akin to modern-day résumés, and just as conspicuous for their failure to note setbacks of any kind.

We will have reason to revisit such inscriptions later on. But now let us consider the absence of specifically archaeological evidence of the Exodus. In fact, *many major events reported* in various ancient writings are archaeologically invisible. The migrations of Celts in Asia Minor, Slavs into Greece, Arameans across the Levant – all described in written sources – have left no archaeological trace. And this, too, is hardly surprising: archaeology focuses upon habitation and building; migrants are by definition nomadic.

There is similar silence in the archaeological record with regard to many conquests whose historicity is generally accepted, and even of many large and significant battles, including those of relatively recent vintage. The Anglo-Saxon conquest of Britain in the fifth century, the Arab conquest of Palestine in the seventh century, even the Norman invasion of England in 1066 – all have left scant, if any, archaeological remains. Is this because conquest is usually accompanied by destruction? Not really. The biblical books of Joshua and Judges, for instance, tell of a gradual infiltration into the Land of Israel, with only a small handful of cities said to have been destroyed. And what is true of antiquity holds true for many periods in military history in which conquest has in no sense entailed automatic destruction.

HOW MANY LEFT EGYPT? LOOKING AT
ALL OF THE TORAH'S EVIDENCE

The Torah's statement that some 600,000 men of fighting age left Egypt looms large in the case against the historicity of the Exodus. In fact, however, it is something of a red herring, and warrants a deeper discussion of its own. As we already saw in the previous chapter, census figures, troop totals, and other seemingly quantitative representations are, in fact, part of the hortatory embellishment of the true stories they depict, and we shall see that such is the case here as well. Despite the Torah's apparent declaration that Israelite men numbered 600,000 when they left Egypt, a wealth of material *from within the*

Torah itself points to a number dramatically and perhaps even exponentially lower. My discussion here proceeds in two parts. In the first, I examine the so-called census numbers in the Torah and determine that trends within the figures should lead us to conclude that the Torah itself does not consider these figures to be factual head counts. In the second part of the discussion, I examine evidence from elsewhere in the Torah that suggests that the number of Israelites that came out of Egypt was much smaller than what the figure of 600,000 men of fighting age would suggest.

THE CENSUS AND ISRAEL'S POPULATION

Let us begin with a closer look at the numbers. For one thing, the book of Numbers (3:43) records the number of firstborn Israelite males of all ages as 22,273. To have so few firstborn males in a population totaling in excess of two million would have required a fertility rate of many dozens of children per woman – a phenomenon unmentioned by the Torah and not evidenced in any family lineages from that period in other biblical or ancient Near Eastern sources.

Next we may turn to the census lists themselves in Numbers 1 and Numbers 26. There are several anomalies in these figures. On the one hand, the Torah presents us with a grand total in each chapter, and the breakdown of that figure by tribe. To our eyes, this certainly seems to be an attempt to communicate precisely the number of fighting-age men each tribe had to contribute. Yet, if these are indeed precise figures, how is it that they all look like they have been rounded off? Further, the totals of 601,730 and 603,550 in Numbers 1 and 26 respectively are the totals of precisely the tribal figures listed. But if the tribal figures themselves are each rounded off, then the summary figures are no longer accurate representations of the actual number of fighting-age males. Had the Torah not offered tally totals in each chapter, we could simply surmise that the tribal figures had been rounded off. It is the disparity between the seemingly rounded tribal figures and the precision of the tally totals that are a point of tension here.

---

1. Cf. Num. 26:7–10.

Census of Men of Military Age (20–60 Years)		
Tribe	Numbers 1	Numbers 26
Reuven	46,500	43,730 $(+250)^1$
Shimon	59,300	22,200
Gad	45,650	40,500
Yehuda	74,600	76,500
Yissakhar	54,400	64,300
Zevulun	57,400	60,500
Menashe	32,200	52,700
Ephraim	40,500	32,500
Binyamin	35,400	45,600
Dan	62,700	64,400
Asher	41,500	53,400
Naftali	53,400	45,400
Total	603,550	601,730
Census of Males One Month and Older		
Levi	22,000	23,000

Moreover, there is an unexplained discrepancy between the two lists. We can well imagine natural birth rates resulting in a marginal rise or drop for each tribe between the second year (as reported in Numbers 1) and the fortieth (as reported in Numbers 26). But note the massive increase witnessed in the tribe of Menashe – from 32,200 to 52,700. Even greater, note the drop witnessed in the tribe of Shimon, from 59,300 to 22,200. Nowhere does the Torah explain how or why these two tribes experienced such dramatic demographic shifts relative to the modest shifts in size witnessed in the other tribes. Were these factual figures, they would beg explanation.

Finally, witness an unusual pattern in the rounding off of these figures. None of the twenty-four tribes considered in the tallies of some 600,000 fighting men present figures that are rounded off to the nearest thousand. They seem rounded, in most cases, to the nearest hundred. Yet consider the bar graph below that charts the remainder in hundreds of each tribe:

Remainders in Hundreds Out of
Twenty-Four Tribal Military Census Figures

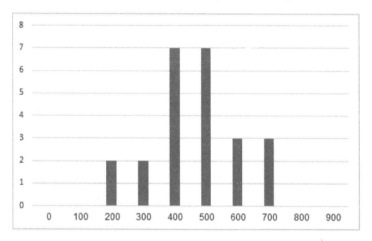

We can see here clear clustering toward the middle: most of the tribes have a "remainder" of either four hundred or five hundred. Some have two hundred or three hundred, and some have six hundred or seven hundred. But none are an even thousand or remainder of one hundred. And on the other side of the scale, none have a remainder of eight hundred or nine hundred. If the tribal figures represented factual birth figures, we would expect the remainders to be entirely random. This clustering suggests that the figures may come to suggest something other than precise census figures.

When we look farther afield in the Torah, we actually see ample evidence that Israel was a tiny populace. For one thing, the book of Exodus (23:29–30) claims that the children of Israel were so *few* in number as to be incapable of populating the land they were destined to enter. Similarly, in referring to them as the smallest nation on the face of the earth, the book of Deuteronomy (7:7) says they were badly outnumbered by the inhabitants of the land. Moreover, when Israel conquers parts of the land in the book of Joshua, there is no indication that the city-states there had populations of enormous size.[2]

Additionally, an encampment of two million – equivalent to the population of Houston, Texas – would have taken days to traverse. Yet the Torah (Ex. 33:6–11) does not remark upon that, either, instead describing Israelites routinely exiting and returning to the camp with ease. Nor does it register the bedlam and gridlock that would have been created by the system of centralized sacrifices mandated in the book of Leviticus. Consider, as well, the question of the staffing of the Tabernacle. How many *kohanim* were available during the trek in the desert to officiate in the offering of all these sacrifices? Aaron had four sons: Nadav, Avihu, Eleazar, and Itamar, two of whom, Nadav and Avihu, perished during the first year of the trek. At the very most, the number of adult male descendants of Aaron could not have exceeded a few dozen – hardly enough to minister to the sacrificial needs of two million people. Finally, in Exodus 15:27, the children of Israel are reported to be camping at a particular desert oasis that boasted seventy date palms – which, for a population of two million, would have to have fed and sheltered 30,000 people per tree!

Why is the figure of 600,000 fighting-age males so wildly out of sync with so many other elements in the Torah's desert account? In the previous chapter we already encountered census and military figures that were clearly symbolic in intent. We saw how the armies of Jehoshaphat equaled the size of all the armies of his predecessors in the Kingdom of Judah; we saw how Jacob's "seventy" descendants were really many more and that the figures included in Genesis 46 could be seen as markers of the significance of the wives of Jacob, Leah, and Rachel, over their handmaids, Bilhah and Zilpah. It should not surprise us in the least, therefore, to see that the figures listed in the desert census raise a host of problems when interpreted as factual representations of actual census figures, and also do not accord with a wide array of other passages in

---

2. It also goes without saying that there is no archaeological evidence that the Land of Israel contained tens of millions of inhabitants at this time (or, indeed ever), as would be necessitated by a literal reading of Deuteronomy 7:7 and the figure of 600,000 men of fighting age in the desert.

the Torah that suggest that the children of Israel at this time numbered dramatically fewer individuals.

THE SYMBOLISM OF CENSUS FIGURES

If these figures do not represent the actual number of fighting-age men, what do they represent? In biblical Hebrew, as in other Semitic languages, the word for thousand – *elef* – can also mean "clan," or "troop," and it is clear from individual occurrences of the word that such groups do not comprise anywhere near one thousand individuals. In the military context, the term may simply function as a hyperbolic figure of speech – as in, "Saul has killed his thousands, but David his tens of thousands" (I Sam. 18:8) – or serve some typological or symbolic purpose, as do the numerals seven, twelve, forty, and so on. In isolation, a census list total-ing some 600,000 men obviously refers to a certain sum of individuals; against the wealth of other data I have adduced here, it becomes difficult to say what that sum is.[3] Admittedly, though, viewing *elef* in these chap-ters as "troop" or "division" as opposed to a literal figure of one thousand men does not solve all of the difficulties raised by the text.

Yet we may take a cue from the "census" figures we saw in the previous chapter, and apply the same logic here. The sums indicated for each tribe are a reflection of status. It is not a coincidence that we have in the book of Numbers positive stories about the tribe of Menashe (such as the daughters of Tzlofhad [Numbers 21] and the exploits of Yair ben Menashe [Numbers 32]) and negative stories about the tribe of Shimon (Zimri, Numbers 25). Due to those events, it may be that Menashe receive a "raise" in numbers, and Shimon a "penalty." What is fascinating here is that the relative sizes of the tribes in the final census of chapter 26 neatly mirror the relative standing of each tribe within the blessings of Jacob to the brothers in Genesis 49. There, the two most celebrated tribes are Judah and Joseph. The least "blessed" tribes are

---

3. For an overview, see Moisés Silva, *New International Dictionary of Old Testament Theol-ogy and Exegesis*, vol. 1 (Grand Rapids, MI: Zondervan, 2014), 416–17, and Jerry Waite, "The Census of Israelite Men After Their Exodus from Egypt," *Vetus Testamentum* 60 (2010): 487–91. See also Neriah Klein, "The Chronicler's Code: The Rise and Fall of Judah's Army in the Book of Chronicles," *Journal of Hebrew Scriptures* 17, no. 3 (2017): 1–3, available at http://www.jhsonline.org/Articles/article_227.pdf.

Reuven, Shimon, and Levi, who are subject to censure from Jacob. The other tribes receive brief blessings. In Numbers 26, Judah and Joseph (i.e., Menashe and Ephraim) have much larger populations than any other tribe, both in excess of 75,000. At the bottom of the list are Shimon (22,200) and Levi (23,000), with all the other tribes tallying between 45,000 and 64,000. The clincher is this: Reuven (43,980, prior to the Korah rebellion) is nearly twice the size of the *smallest* tribe (Shimon). That is, Reuven, as a censured firstborn, receives the smallest possible double portion of blessing, at twice the size of the smallest tribe, Shimon. Seen through this prism, the "census" numbers are manipulated by the text of the Torah as a way of encoding status to the tribes in accordance with Jacob's blessings, just as the census of Genesis 46 was manipulated to ascribe status to the matriarchs Leah and Rachel.

Even if this approach is found wanting, my aim here is not to explain the meaning of the numbers in the census figures of Numbers 1 and Numbers 26. It may well be that we do not understand how to uncover the meaning of these numbers. My point, instead, is to show that when taken on its own terms, the Torah seems to suggest that the total figure to leave Egypt was not 600,000 men, but much fewer. The historicity of the Torah's account of the Exodus does not hinge on its seeming claim that millions left Egypt, because that claim fails to take into account the textual evidence raised here.[4]

---

4. Understanding the census numbers this way should pose no difficulty for normative belief or practice. The Kuzari refers to the mass-witness of the Revelation at Sinai by Israel. Naturally, like all before him, he assumes this to be a population of 600,000 men. Yet, the real gist of his argument is that a huge assembly bore witness to this event. His argument is no weaker if we assume that "only" enough people to fill a stadium were present. Additonally, although there is a common perception that the concept of a *reshut harabim* was defined by the size of the population of Israel present in the desert – *no authority holds this to be the case*. The Gemara does not even mention this figure and most *Rishonim* define a *reshut harabim* without reference to any number of people at all. *Tosafot* and other Ashkenazic *posekim* did – but their use of the numbers is itself instructive. *Tosafot* is the first to recognize (Eiruvin 6a, s.v. *Keitzad*) that there were not 600,000 *people* in the desert. There were 600,000 *men of fighting age.* In their own way, the *Tosafot* admit that we use the figure 600,000 to define a *reshut harabim* because that figure symbolically represents the people as a whole. To be sure, the *Tosafot* believed that there were indeed 600,000 men in the desert. But

A final note about this approach to the number of individuals who left Egypt – and it concerns a conspicuous but pervasive silence within our rabbinic sources: We believe, correctly, that the *baalei hamidrash* and the medieval commentators were careful readers of the biblical text. Above, I posed about a dozen questions that arise from the figures listed in the book of Numbers, as they related to one another, and as they relate to other passages in the Torah. These are all questions that are there on the surface of the text, and are obvious and perhaps even troubling once they are recognized. Remarkably, there is precious little treatment of any of them in the entire corpus of classical rabbinic literature. Why this "blind spot"?

I would suggest that the blindness is in our eyes and not theirs. We view the world through the prism of empiricism, logistical feasibility, and realities that are quantitatively and statistically analyzed. Seen through this prism, the figures of Numbers 1 and Numbers 26 are problematic. But this lens is a modern one, and one that was unfamiliar to our forefathers, the giants of the rabbinic exegetical tradition. It was so unfamiliar that it did not cross their minds that these were the types of questions that one would ask of the text.

In light of what we have seen so far, should the historicity of the Exodus still be denied by reason of absence of evidence? Or can we now invoke the familiar and all-too-true quip that absence of evidence is not evidence of absence?

THE EXODUS AND EGYPTIAN REALITY

Actually, there is more to be said than that. Many details of the Exodus story do strikingly appear to reflect the realities of late second-millennium Egypt, the period when the Exodus would most likely have taken place – and they are the sort of details that a scribe living centuries later and inventing the story afresh would have been unlikely to know:

---

their adoption of the figure toward symbolic ends suggests a way that pre-moderns related to numbers in literature, in a way greatly removed from our obsession with metrics, data, and statistics.

- There is rich evidence that West-Semitic populations lived in the eastern Nile Delta – what the Torah calls Goshen – for most of the second millennium. Some were slaves, some were raised in Pharaoh's court, and some, like Moses, bore Egyptian names.
- We know today that the great pharaoh Rameses II, who reigned from 1279 to 1213 BCE, built a huge administrative center out of mudbrick in an area where large Semitic populations had lived for centuries. It was called Pi-Rameses. Exodus (1:11) specifies that the Hebrew slaves built the cities of Pithom and Rameses, a possible reference to Pi-Rameses. The site was abandoned by the pharaohs two centuries later.
- In the Exodus account, pharaohs are simply called "Pharaoh," whereas in later biblical passages, Egyptian monarchs are referred to by their proper name, as in "Pharaoh Necho" (II Kings 23:29). This, too, echoes usage in Egypt itself, where, from the middle of the second millennium until the tenth century BCE, the title "pharaoh" was used alone.
- The names of various national entities mentioned in the Song at the Sea (Ex. 15:1–18) – Philistines, Moabites, Edomites, et al. – are all found in Egyptian sources shortly before 1200 BCE; about this, the book of Exodus is again correct for the period.
- The stories of the Exodus and the Israelites' subsequent wanderings in the wilderness reflect sound acquaintance with the geography and natural conditions of the eastern Nile delta, the Sinai Peninsula, the Negev, and Transjordan.
- The book of Exodus (13:17) notes that the Israelites chose not to traverse the Sinai Peninsula along the northern, coastal route toward modern-day Gaza because that would have entailed military engagement. The discovery of extensive Egyptian fortifications all along that route from the period in question confirms the accuracy of this observation.
- Archaeologists have documented hundreds of new settlements in the Land of Israel from the late thirteenth and twelfth centuries BCE, congruent with the biblically attested arrival there of the liberated slaves; strikingly, these settlements feature an absence of the pig bones normally found in such places. Major

destruction is found at Bethel, Yokneam, and Hatzor – cities taken by Israel according to the book of Joshua. At Hatzor, archaeologists found mutilated cultic statues, suggesting that they were repugnant to the invaders.

- The earliest written mention of an entity called "Israel" is found in the victory inscription of the pharaoh Merneptah from 1206 BCE. In it the pharaoh lists the nations defeated by him in the course of a campaign to the southern Levant; among them, "Israel is laid waste and his seed is no more." "Israel" is written in such a way as to connote a group of people, not an established city or region, the implication being that it was not yet a fully settled entity with contiguous control over an entire region. This jibes with the Bible's description in Joshua and Judges of a gradual conquest of the land.[5]

OUT-PHARAOHING THE PHARAOH

To sum up thus far: There is no explicit evidence that confirms the Exodus. At best, we have a text – the Tanakh – that exhibits a good grasp on a wide range of fairly standard aspects of ancient Egyptian realities. This is definitely something, and hardly to be sneezed at, but can we say still more? I believe that we can.

One of the pillars of modern critical study of the Bible is the so-called comparative method. Scholars elucidate a biblical text by noting similarities between it and texts found among the cultures adjacent to ancient Israel. If the similarities are high in number and truly distinctive to the two sources, it becomes plausible to maintain that the biblical text may have been written under the direct influence of, or in response to, the extra-biblical text. Why the one-way direction, from extra-biblical to biblical? The answer is that Israel was largely a weak

---

5. On the historicity of the Exodus, see James. K. Hoffmeier, *Israel in Egypt: The Evidence for the Authenticity of the Exodus Tradition* (New York: Oxford University Press, 1997); *Ancient Israel in Sinai: The Evidence for the Authenticity of the Wilderness Tradition* (New York: Oxford University Press, 2005). See also James K. Hoffmeier, Alan R. Millard, and Gary A. Rendsburg, eds., *"Did I Not Bring Israel Out of Egypt?" Biblical, Archaeological, and Egyptological Perspectives on the Exodus Narratives* (Winona Lake, IN: Eisenbrauns, 2016).

player, surrounded politically as well as culturally by much larger forces, and no Hebrew texts from the era prior to the Babylonian Exile (586 BCE) have ever been found in translation into other languages. Hence, similarities between texts in Akkadian or Egyptian and the Tanakh are usually understood to reflect the influence of the former on the latter.

Although the comparative method is commonly thought of as a modern approach, its first practitioner was none other than the Rambam in the twelfth century. As we saw in chapter 1, the Rambam tells us that he procured every work on ancient civilizations known in his time (Letter on Astrology). In his *Guide for the Perplexed*, he puts the resultant knowledge to service in elucidating the rationale behind many of the Torah's cultic laws and practices, reasoning that they were adaptations of ancient pagan customs, but tweaked in conformity with an anti-pagan theology.

The comparative method can yield dazzling results, adding dimensions of understanding to passages that once seemed either unclear or self-evident and unexceptional. As an example, consider the familiar biblical refrain that God took Israel out of Egypt "with a mighty hand and an outstretched arm."[6] The Tanakh could have employed that phrase to describe a whole host of divine acts on Israel's behalf, and yet the phrase is used *only* with reference to the Exodus. This is no accident. In much of Egyptian royal literature, the phrase "mighty hand" is a synonym for the pharaoh, and many of the pharaoh's actions are said to be performed through his "mighty hand" or his "outstretched arm." Nowhere else in the ancient Near East are rulers described in this way. What is more, the term is most frequently found in Egyptian royal propaganda during the latter part of the second millennium.

Why would the book of Exodus describe God in the same terms used by the Egyptians to exalt their pharaoh? We see here the dynamics of appropriation. During much of its history, ancient Israel was in Egypt's shadow. For weak and oppressed peoples, one form of cultural and spiritual resistance is to appropriate the symbols of the oppressor and put them to competitive ideological purposes. I believe, and intend to show in what follows, that in its telling of the Exodus the Torah appropriates

---

6. See Ex. 6:6; Deut. 4:34, 5:15, 7:19, 9:29, 11:26, 26:8.

far more than individual phrases and symbols – that, in brief, it adopts and adapts one of the best-known accounts of one of the greatest of all Egyptian pharaohs. [7]

Here a few words of background are in order. Like all great ancient empires, ancient Egypt waxed and waned. The zenith of its glory was reached during the New Kingdom, in roughly 1500–1200 BCE. It was then that its borders reached their farthest limits and many of the massive monuments still visible today were built. We have already met the greatest pharaoh of this period: Rameses II, also known fittingly as Rameses the Great, who reigned from 1279 to 1213.

THE KADESH BAS-RELIEFS AND THE TABERNACLE

Rameses's paramount achievement, which occurred early in his reign, was his 1274 BCE victory over Egypt's archrival, the Hittite empire, at the battle of Kadesh, a town located on the Orontes River on the modern-day border between Lebanon and Syria. Upon his return to Egypt, Rameses inscribed accounts of this battle on monuments all across the empire. Ten copies of the inscriptions exist to this day. These multiple copies make the battle of Kadesh the most publicized event anywhere in the ancient world, the events of Greece and Rome not excepted. Moreover, the texts were accompanied by a new creation: bas-reliefs depicting the battle, frame by frame, so that – much as with stained-glass windows in medieval churches – viewers illiterate in hieroglyphics could learn about the pharaoh's exploits.

Enter now a longstanding biblical conundrum. Scholars had long searched for a model, a precursor that could have inspired the design of the Tabernacle that served as the cultic center of the encampment of the children of Israel in the wilderness, a design laid out in exquisite verbal detail in Exodus 25–29. Although the remains of

---

7. This material is available in academic version in my "The Kadesh Inscriptions of Ramesses II and the Exodus Sea Account (Exodus 13:17–15:19)" in *"Did I Not Bring Israel Out of Egypt?" Biblical, Archaeological, and Egyptological Perspectives on the Exodus Narratives*, ed. James K. Hoffmeier, Alan R. Millard, and Gary A. Rendsburg (Winona Lake, IN: Eisenbrauns, 2016), 93–112, and in chapter 2 of my *Inconsistency in the Torah: Ancient Literary Convention and the Limits of Source Criticism* (New York: Oxford University Press, 2017), 35–61.

Phoenician temples reveal a floor plan remarkably like that of Solomon's Temple (built, as it happens, with the extensive assistance of a Phoenician king), no known cultic site from the ancient Near East seemed to resemble the desert Tabernacle. Then, some eighty years ago, an unexpected affinity was noticed between the biblical descriptions of the Tabernacle and the illustrations of Rameses's camp at Kadesh in several bas-reliefs.

In the image below of the Kadesh battle, the walled military camp occupies the large rectangular space in the relief's lower half:

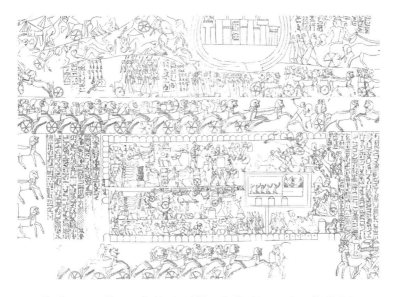

The throne tent of Rameses II with winged falcons flanking his cartouche at Abu Simbel.
W. Wreszinski, *Atlas zur altägyptischen Kulturgeschichte* (Leipzig: Hinrichs,1935), vol. 2, pl. 169.

The camp is twice as long as it is wide. The entrance to it is in the middle of the eastern wall, on the left. (In Egyptian illustrations, east is left, west is right.) At the center of the camp, down a long corridor, lies the entrance to a 3:1 rectangular tent. This tent contains two sections: a 2:1 reception tent, with figures kneeling in adoration, and leading westward (right) from it, a domed square space that is the throne tent of the pharaoh.

All of these proportions are reflected in the prescriptions for the Tabernacle and its surrounding camp in Exodus 25–27, as the two diagrams below make clear:

Battle Compound of Ramesses II

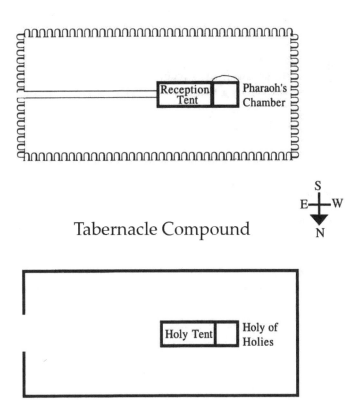

Tabernacle Compound

In the throne tent, displayed in tighter focus on the next page, the emblem bearing the pharaoh's name and symbolizing his power is flanked by falcons symbolizing the god Horus, with their wings spread in protection over him:

In Exodus (25:20), the ark of the Tabernacle is similarly flanked by two winged cherubim, whose wings hover protectively over it. To complete the parallel, Egypt's four army divisions at Kadesh would have camped on the four sides of Rameses's battle compound; the book of Numbers (chapter 2) states that the tribes of Israel camped on the four sides of the Tabernacle compound.

The resemblance of the military camp at Kadesh to the Tabernacle goes beyond architecture; it is conceptual as well. For Egyptians, Rameses was both a military leader and a divinity. In the Torah, God is likewise a divinity, obviously, but also Israel's leader in battle (see Num. 10:35–36). The tent of God, the divine warrior, parallels the tent of the pharaoh, the living Egyptian god, poised for battle.[8]

What have scholars made of this observation? All agree that no visual image known to us from the ancient record so closely resembles the Tabernacle as does the Rameses throne tent. Nor is there any textual description of a cultic tent or throne tent in a military camp that matches

---

8. This material is taken from Michael H. Homan, "The Divine Warrior in His Tent: A Military Model for Yahweh's Tabernacle," *Bible Review* 16, no. 6 (2000): 55, n. 12.

these dimensions. On this basis, some scholars have indeed suggested that the bas-reliefs of the Kadesh inscriptions inspired the Tabernacle design found in Exodus 25–27. In their thinking, the Israelites reworked the throne tent ideologically, with God displacing Rameses the Great as the most powerful force of the time. (For the Torah, of course, God cannot be represented in an image and requires no protection, and pagan deities have no standing, which is why, instead of falcons and Horus, we have cherubim hovering protectively over the ark bearing the tablets of His covenant with Israel.) Others suspect that the image of the throne tent initially became absorbed within Israelite culture in ways that we cannot trace and was later incorporated into the text described in Exodus, but with no conscious memory of Rameses II. Still others remain skeptical, considering the similarities to be merely coincidental.

THE KADESH POEM AND THE ACCOUNT OF
THE SPLITTING OF THE SEA (EX. 14–15)

Nonetheless, the *visual* similarities between the Tabernacle and the Rameses throne tent warrant a closer look at the *textual* components of the Kadesh inscriptions, to learn what they say about Rameses, the Egyptians, and the battle of Kadesh. The longest of these inscriptions, known as the Kadesh Poem, is some 335 lines long. What emerges is that the similarities extend to the entire plotline of the Kadesh poem and that of the Splitting of the Sea in Exodus 14–15. I believe it reasonable to claim that the narrative account of the Splitting of the Sea (Exodus 14) and the Song at the Sea (Exodus 15) may reflect a deliberate act of cultural appropriation. If the Kadesh inscriptions bear witness to the greatest achievement of the greatest pharaoh of the greatest period in Egyptian history, then the book of Exodus claims that the God of Israel overmastered Rameses the Great by several orders of magnitude, effectively trouncing him at his own game.

Let us see how this works. In the Kadesh poem and the account of Exodus 14–15, the action begins in like fashion: the protagonist army (of, respectively, the Egyptians and Israelites) is on the march and unprepared for battle when it is attacked by a large force of chariots, causing it to break ranks in fear. Thus, according to the Kadesh poem, Rameses's troops were moving north toward the outskirts of Kadesh when they were surprised by a Hittite chariot corps and took fright. The Exodus account opens in similar fashion. As they depart Egypt, the Israelites are described as an armed force (Ex. 13:18 and 14:8). Stunned by the sudden charge of Pharaoh's chariots, however, they become completely dispirited (14:10–12).

In each story, the protagonist now appeals to his god for help and the divine agent exhorts him to move forward with divine assistance. In the Kadesh poem, Rameses prays to Amun, who responds, "Forward! I am with you, I am your father, my hand is with you!"[9] In like fashion, Moses cries out to the Lord, who responds in Exodus 14:15, "Tell the Israelites to go forward!" promising victory over Pharaoh (vv. 16–17).

From this point in the Kadesh poem, Rameses assumes divine powers and proportions. Put differently, he shifts from human leader in distress to quasi-divine force, thus allowing us to examine his actions against the Hittites at the Orontes alongside God's actions against the Egyptians at the sea. In each account, the "king" confronts the enemy on his own, unaided by his fearful troops. Entirely abandoned by his army, Rameses engages the Hittites single-handedly, a theme underscored throughout the poem. In Exodus 14:14, God declares that Israel need only remain passive, and that He will fight on her behalf: "The Lord will fight for you, and you will be still." Especially noteworthy here is that this particular feature of both works – their parallel portrait of a victorious "king" who must work hard to secure the loyalty of those he saves in battle – has no match in the literature of the ancient Near East.

In each text, the enemy then gives voice to the futility of fighting against a divine force, and seeks to escape. In each, statements made earlier about the potency of the divine figure are now confirmed by the enemy himself. In the Kadesh poem, the Hittites retreat from Rameses: "One of them called out to his fellows: Look out, beware, don't approach him! See, Sekhmet the Mighty is she who is with him!" referring to a goddess extolled earlier in the poem. In this passage, the Hittites acknowledge that they are fighting not only a divine force but a very particular divine force. We find the same trope in the Exodus narrative: confounded by God in 14:25, the Egyptians say, "Let us flee from the Israelites, for *the Lord* is fighting for them against Egypt."

---

9. Throughout, translations of the poem are from Kenneth A. Kitchen, *Ramesside Inscriptions Translated & Annotated*, vol. 2 (Oxford: Blackwell, 1996), 2–14.

An element common to both compositions is the submergence of the enemy in water. The Kadesh poem does not assign the same degree of centrality to this event as does Exodus – it does not tell of windswept seas overpowering the Hittites – but Rameses does indeed vauntingly proclaim that in their haste to escape his onslaught, the Hittites sought refuge by "plunging" into the river, whereupon he slaughtered them in the water. The reliefs depict the drowning of the Hittites in vivid fashion, displayed here in panorama and closeup:

The corpses of the Hittite troops in the Orontes River as depicted on the second pylon at the Ramasseum. James Henry Breasted, *The Battle of Kadesh: A Study in the Earliest Known Military Strategy* (Chicago: Chicago University Press, 1903), pl. III.

As for survivors, both accounts assert that there were none. Says the Kadesh poem: "None looked behind him, no other turned around. Whoever of them fell, he did not rise again." Exodus 14:28 likewise states: "The waters turned back and covered the chariots and the horsemen... not one of them remained."

We come now to the most striking of the parallels between the two. In each, the timid troops see evidence of the king's "mighty arm," review the enemy corpses, and amazed by the sovereign's achievement, are impelled to sing a hymn of praise. In the Kadesh poem we read:

> Then when my troops and chariotry *saw* me, that I was like Montu, *my arm strong*... then they presented themselves one by one, to approach the camp at evening time. They found all the foreign lands, among which I had gone, lying overthrown in their blood.... I had made white [with their corpses] the countryside of the land of Kadesh. Then my army came to praise me, their faces [amazed/averted] at seeing what I had done.

Exodus 14:30–31 is remarkably similar, and in two cases identical: "Israel *saw* the Egyptians dead on the shore of the sea. And when Israel saw the *great hand* which the Lord had wielded against the Egyptians, the people feared the Lord." As I noted earlier, "great hand" here and "great arm" in 15:16 are used exclusively in the Tanakh with regard to the Exodus, a trope found elsewhere only within Egyptian propaganda, especially during the late second-millennium New Kingdom.

After the great conquest, in both accounts, the troops offer a paean to the king. In each, the opening stanza comprises three elements. The troops laud the king's name as a warrior; credit him with stiffening their morale; and exalt him for securing their salvation. In the Kadesh poem we read: "My officers came to extol my strong arm and likewise my chariotry, boasting of my name thus: 'What a fine warrior, who strengthens the heart/That you should rescue your troops and chariotry!'" And here are the same motifs in the opening verses of the Song at the Sea (Ex. 15:1–3): "Then Moses and the Israelites sang this song to the Lord.... 'The Lord is my strength and might; He is become my salvation...the Lord, the Warrior – Lord is His name!'"

In both the poem and in Exodus, praise of the victorious sovereign continues in a double strophe extolling his powerful hand or arm. The poem: "You are the son of Amun, achieving with his arms, you devastate the land of Hatti by your valiant arm." The Song (Ex. 15:6): "Your right hand, O Lord, glorious in power, Your right hand, O Lord, shatters the foe!"

And note this: the Hebrew root for the right hand (Y-M-N) is common to a variety of other ancient Near Eastern languages. Yet in those other cultures, the right hand is linked exclusively with holding or grasping. In Egyptian literature, however, we find depictions of the right hand that match those in the Song. Perhaps the most ubiquitous motif of Egyptian narrative art is the pharaoh raising his right hand to shatter the heads of enemy captives:

Relief of Seti I (thirteenth century BCE) with raised right hand, shattering the heads of his enemies, Hypostyle Hall at Karnak. The Epigraphic Survey, *The Battle Reliefs of King Seti I* (Chicago: Oriental Institute of the University of Chicago, 1986), pl. 15a. (Courtesy of the Oriental Institute of the University of Chicago.)

This Egyptian royal image endured from the third millennium down into the Christian era. In no other ancient Near Eastern culture do we encounter such portrayals of the right hand, which resonate closely with the Song and particularly with 15:6: "Your right hand, O Lord, shatters the enemy."

Continuing now: In the Kadesh poem, as the troops review the Hittite corpses, their enemies are likened to chaff: "Amun my father being with me instantly, turning all the foreign lands into chaff before me." The Song similarly compares the enemy with chaff consumed by God's wrath (Ex. 15:7): "You send forth Your fury, it consumes them like chaff." Again, no other ancient Near Eastern military inscription uses "chaff" as a simile for the enemy.

More parallels: In each hymn, the troops declare their king to be without peer in battle. The Kadesh poem: "You are the fine[st] warrior, without your peer"; the Song: "Who is like You, O Lord, among the mighty?" In each, the king is praised as the victorious leader of his troops, intimidating neighboring lands. The Kadesh poem: "You are great in victory in front of your army…O Protector of Egypt, who curbs foreign lands"; the Song (Ex. 15:13–15): "In Your lovingkindness, You lead the people You redeemed; in Your strength, You guide them to Your holy abode. The peoples hear, they tremble."

Nearing the end, the two again share main elements as the king leads his troops safely on a long journey home from victory over the enemy, intimidating neighboring lands along the way. The Kadesh poem: "His Majesty set off back to Egypt peacefully, with his troops and chariotry, all life, stability, and dominion being with him…subduing all lands through fear of him." The Song (Ex. 15:16–17): "Terror and dread descend upon them, through the might of Your arm they are still as stone – Till Your people pass, O Lord, the people pass whom You have ransomed." And the final motif is shared as well: peaceful arrival at the palace of the king, and blessings on his eternal rule. The Kadesh poem:

> He having arrived peacefully in Egypt, at Pi-Ramesses Great in Victories, and resting in his palace of life and dominion…the gods of the land [come] to him in greeting…according as they have granted him a million jubilees and eternity upon the throne

of Re, all lands and all foreign lands being overthrown and slain beneath his sandals eternally and forever.

The Song (Ex. 15:17–18):

You will bring them and plant them in Your own mountain, the place You made Your abode, O Lord, the sanctuary, O Lord, which Your hands established. The Lord will reign forever and ever!

The Kadesh poem is a much longer composition than the Exodus account, and it contains many elements without parallels in the latter. For instance, Rameses offers an extended prayer to his god, Amun, and issues two lengthy rebukes to his troops for their disloyalty to him. But appropriation of a text for purposes of cultural resistance or rivalry is always selective, and never a one-to-one exercise. The Exodus text focuses on precisely those elements of the Kadesh poem that extol the pharaoh's valor, which it reworks for purposes of extolling God's. Moreover, the main plot points – it is worth stressing again – are common to both. These are:

- The protagonist army breaks ranks at the sight of the enemy chariot force.
- A plea for divine help is answered with encouragement to move forward, with victory assured.
- The enemy chariotry, recognizing by name the divine force that attacks it, seeks to flee.
- Many meet their death in water, and there are no survivors.
- The king's troops return to survey the enemy corpses.
- Amazed at the king's accomplishment, the troops offer a victory hymn that includes praise of his name, references to his strong arm, and tribute to him as the source of their strength and their salvation.
- The enemy is compared to chaff, while the king is deemed without peer in battle.
- The king leads his troops peacefully home, intimidating foreign lands along the way.
- The king arrives at his palace, and is granted eternal rule.

This is the story of Rameses II in the Kadesh poem, and this is the story of God in the account of the sea in Exodus 14–15.

Just how distinctive are these parallels? Similarities between two ancient texts do not *automatically* imply that one was inspired by the other; common terms and images could be and were the intellectual property of many cultures simultaneously. Some of the motifs identified here, including the dread and awe of the enemy in the face of the king, are ubiquitous across battle accounts of the ancient Near East. Other elements, such as the king building or residing in his palace and gaining eternal rule, are typological tropes known to us from other ancient works. Still others, though unique to these two works, can arguably be seen as reflecting similar circumstances, or authorial needs, with no necessary connection between them. Thus, although few if any ancient battle accounts record an army on the march that is suddenly attacked by a massive chariot force and breaks ranks as a result, it could still be that Exodus and the Kadesh poem employ this motif independently.

What really suggests a relation between the two texts, however, is the *totality* of the parallels – largely in order – plus the large number of highly distinctive motifs that appear in these two works alone. No other battle account known to us either from the Tanakh or from the epigraphic remains of the ancient Near East provide even half the number of shared narrative motifs exhibited here.

To deepen the connection, let me adduce a further resonance between the Song at the Sea and Egyptian New Kingdom inscriptions more generally. A common literary motif of the period is the claim that the pharaoh causes enemy troops to cease their braggadocio. Thus, in a typical line, Pharaoh Seti I "causes the princes of Syria to cease all of the boasting of their mouths." This concern with silencing the enemy's boastings is distinctly Egyptian, not found in the military literature of any other neighboring culture. All the more noteworthy, then, that the Song at the Sea depicts not the movements or actions of the Egyptians but their boasts (Ex. 15:8–9): "The enemy said, 'I will pursue! I will overtake! I will divide the spoil! My desire shall have its fill of them, I will bare my sword, my hand shall subdue them!'" Thereupon, at God's command, the sea covers them, effectively stopping their mouths.

The similarities between these two texts are so salient, and so distinctive to them alone, that the claim of literary interdependence is wholly plausible. And so, a question: If, for argument's sake, we posit that the Exodus sea account was composed with an awareness of the Kadesh poem, when could that poem have been introduced into Israelite culture?

In theory, scholars could propose that the poem reached Israel in a period of amicable relations with Egypt, perhaps during the reign of Solomon in the tenth century or, still later, of Hezekiah in the eighth. Counting against this, though, is that the latest copies of the Kadesh poem in our possession are from the thirteenth century, and there are no explicit references to it, or any clear attempts to imitate it, in later Egyptian literature. Moreover, we have no epigraphic evidence that *any* historical inscriptions from ancient Egypt ever reached Israel or the southern kingdom of Judah, either in the Egyptian language or in translation. And this leaves aside the puzzle of what, in a period of entente, would have motivated an Israelite scribe to pen an explicitly anti-Egyptian work in the first place.

To determine a plausible date of transmission, we should be guided by the epigraphic evidence at hand. Egyptologists note that in addition to copies of the monumental version of the Kadesh poem, a papyrus copy was found in a village of workmen and artisans who built the great monuments at Thebes. As we saw earlier, visual accounts of the battle were also produced. This has led many scholars of ancient Egypt to argue that the Kadesh poem was a widely disseminated "little red book," aimed at stirring public adoration of the valor and salvific grace of Rameses the Great, and that it would have been widely known, particularly during the reign of Rameses himself, beyond royal and temple precincts.

Proofs exist in geometry, and sometimes in law, but rarely within the fields of biblical studies and archaeology. As is so often the case, the record at our disposal is highly incomplete, and speculation about cultural transmission must remain contingent. We do the most we can with the little we have, invoking plausibility more than proof. To be plain about it, the parallels I have drawn here do not "prove" the historical accuracy of the Exodus account, certainly not in its entirety. They do not prove that the text before us received its final form in the thirteenth century BCE. And they can and no doubt will be construed by rational individuals, lay and professional alike, in different ways.

Some might conclude that the plot line of the Kadesh poem reached Israel under conditions hidden to us and, for reasons we cannot know, became incorporated into the text of Exodus many centuries down the line. Others will regard the parallels as one big coincidence. But my own conclusion is otherwise: The evidence adduced here can be reasonably taken as indicating that the poem was transmitted during the period of its greatest diffusion, which is the only period when anyone in Egypt seems to have paid much attention to it – namely, during the reign of Rameses II himself. In my view, the evidence suggests that the Exodus text preserves the memory of a moment when the earliest Israelites reached for language with which to extol the mighty virtues of God, and found the raw material in the terms and tropes of an Egyptian text well known to them. In appropriating and "transvaluing" that material, the Torah puts forward the claim that God had far outdone the greatest achievement of the greatest earthly potentate.

THE HISTORICAL ACCURACY OF THE
TANAKH AND THE CULTURE WARS

In the previous chapter, I argued that to perceive how the Tanakh casts the events of the past, we have to distinguish between the pre-modern category of exhortation and the modern category of history. But to fully understand the academic critique of the Tanakh as a historical source, we need to grasp the issue from a second angle. We need to appreciate the way in which culture wars between liberals and conservatives color academic discussions of the issue.

An Academic Double Standard

Can the Tanakh be trusted on *anything* as a historical source? Should it be considered "innocent" (i.e., historically accurate) until proved "guilty" (i.e., erroneous), or "guilty" unless and until its claims can be corroborated by external sources? As a credible historical source, the Tanakh has many strikes against it. It contains materials like the Garden of Eden story that seem frankly mythical in nature. It recounts supernatural occurrences that a modern historian cannot accept as factual, and it regularly describes earthly actions as the results of divine causation. Many of its texts, scholars believe, were composed centuries after the events purportedly documented, and – as with the Exodus – few of those events can be corroborated by independent outside sources.

In short, the Tanakh in this view is a book of religious propaganda – "history" that suits its writers' purposes. And the view is well buttressed. But it is no less problematic for that, and the reason is simple: many other historical inscriptions from the ancient Near East – and elsewhere – are susceptible to the same charge. Cuneiform and hieroglyphic texts that tell of divine revelations to royal figures are found everywhere, overt propaganda on behalf of the kings of yore and the gods they served. Nor can most of the events recorded in these ancient records be corroborated by cross-reference to sources from other cultures. Frequently, the events themselves are miraculous. Often, the events occurred, if they occurred at all, centuries before the text's date of composition. Many of these characteristics are true, for example, of the Kadesh Poem of Rameses II. God speaks to the pharaoh. The pharaoh's diadem spews forth fire in miraculous fashion. Hittite accounts of the battle, brief as they are, do not corroborate the Egyptian accounts. Archaeological excavations of Tel Kadesh have produced no evidence of the battle.

Yet, to one degree or another, scholars routinely accept ancient Near Eastern texts as historically reliable. Literally dozens of scholars have attempted historical recreations of the Battle of Kadesh on the basis of Rameses's inscriptions alone.[10] Scholars today use the works of Livy to reconstruct the history of the Roman republic, founded several centuries before his lifetime, and all historians of Alexander the Great acknowledge as their most accurate source Arrian's *Anabasis*, which dates from four centuries later. Of course, they exclude the blatantly unrealistic elements, which they peel away from the remainder before crediting its reliability. By contrast, however, when it comes to biblical sources, the questionable elements are often taken as prima facie evidence of the untrustworthiness of the whole.

---

10. For bibliography, see Kenneth A. Kitchen, *Ramesside Inscriptions: Translated and Annotated, Notes and Comments*, 6 vols. (Oxford: Blackwell, 1993–2008), 2:3–5.

This is all the more remarkable (to put it mildly) in light of one significant difference between biblical literature and the writings of other ancient Near Eastern civilizations. Throughout, the Tanakh displays a penchant for judging its heroes harshly, and for recording Israel's failings even more than its successes. No other ancient Near Eastern culture produced a literature so revealing of fault, so realistic about the abuses of power, or so committed to recording those abuses for posterity. On this point, at least, there is universal agreement. Yet in academic precinct, recognition of this fact has not in the least improved the Tanakh's reputation as an honest reporter of historical events.

Here is a thought experiment: Imagine the Tanakh had never spoken about Hebrew enslavement or of an exodus from Egypt. Instead, a story much like it turned up in a first-millennium-BCE inscription from a dig in Transjordan, the land of the ancient Moabites. Telling of the earliest period of this people and their deity Kemosh, the inscription reports that the Moabites were slaves in Egypt but mighty Kemosh defeated Amun and Re at the sea, liberating the slaves and enabling them to set out homeward to Moab while their enemies perished under a storm of hail.

In the face of such an account, scholars would assuredly be skeptical of the theological and supernatural elements, but I suspect they would look for clues of an authentic core, especially if there were peripheral evidence of the kind I pointed to above in connection with the biblical account. They would be impressed, for instance, with the story's demonstrable familiarity with Egyptian names, its awareness of settlement patterns in the eastern delta and of the correct way of naming the pharaoh, and its cognizance of royal fortifications outside of Egypt and the geography of the Sinai Peninsula, the Negev, and Transjordan.

Would these hypothetical scholars also pounce on the lack of any mention of Moabite slaves in Egyptian sources? I doubt it. That so many of the account's details accord with our knowledge of the period would lead many to assess the source as trustworthy – especially in the absence of hard evidence to the contrary.

The reliability of ancient sources – extra-biblical as well as biblical – is a vexing issue. In the previous chapter I noted that in a wide variety of pre-modern and ancient sources we find embellishment and imagination layered upon a basis of fact. In any of these sources, where does reality end and the sculpting of events to produce a message begin? These questions are not easy ones to answer. But from an academic perspective, the Tanakh should be subject to criteria of analysis applied to other comparable ancient texts. The fact that it is not so treated – that a double standard is in operation – tells us something about the field of academic biblical studies, and about the academy itself.

Agendas on the Right and Agendas on the Left

The double standard applied to biblical texts is a key aspect of an ongoing power struggle within biblical studies, which as an academic discipline is somewhat anomalous within the humanities. The Bible is studied today in degree-granting institutions of all kinds, from the fully secular to the most dogmatically committed. But unlike Shakespeare, or the orations of Cicero, or the Gilgamesh Epic, or the Code of Hammurabi, the Bible is itself anomalous: not only a work that people read and study but, for many – Jews and Christians – a work that guides life itself, a work of sacred scripture.

It is of course appropriate for scholars to be wary of the encroachment of belief systems and religious doctrine upon the enterprise of critical analysis. But in the United States, as fundamentalist Christianity has grown, so has the level of defensiveness in certain sectors of the field. Indeed, for some the very word "Bible" seems to have become radioactive, if not taboo. In 1998, for instance, the American School of Oriental Research, a nondenominational academic organization, changed the name of its popular magazine *Biblical Archaeologist* to *Near Eastern Archaeology*. Recently, a prominent American Bible scholar even proposed that the Bible itself be given a new name and rebranded as "The Library of Ancient Judah."[11]

Within the guild, the fear of fundamentalist intrusion reached a crescendo in 2010 when the Society of Biblical Literature, the largest academic body in the field, started sending the following automated

---

11. See William H. C. Propp's comments on "Discussing Faith and Reason in Biblical Studies," https://www.sbl-site.org/membership/farewell.aspx.

notice to everyone submitting a proposal for a conference paper for its
annual meeting:

> Please note that, by submitting a paper proposal or accepting a
> role in any affiliate organization or program unit session at the
> annual or international meeting of the Society of Biblical Lit-
> erature, you agree to participate in an open academic discussion
> guided by a common standard of scholarly discourse that engages
> your subject through critical inquiry and investigation.[12]

One may safely assume that proposals to the Society for Neuroscience
do not merit similar warnings.

To an extent, again, one can appreciate the sense of alarm.
"Because the Bible says so!" and "Because God said so!" do not qualify
as academic arguments. Yet, if the ideal is "open academic discussion"
and "a common standard of scholarly discourse," overzealousness from
the other direction should be no less disturbing. In the drive to keep
fundamentalists at bay, some scholars have wound up throwing out the
Bible with the bathwater, preemptively downgrading its credibility as
a historical witness.

And that is not all. The power struggle within biblical studies is
also an aspect of the larger culture war that rages between liberals and
conservatives in the US (and, with different expressions, in Israel). In
that war, the place of religion in the public square is a major battleground,
with skirmishes over hot-button issues ranging from abortion and gay
marriage to public display of the Ten Commandments. The fight plays
itself out in the realm of law and public policy, in the media, and also
in the universities; in the last-named arena, whole fields of inquiry are
drawn into the fray. One larger-than-academic dispute is over the status
of evolutionary psychology as a science; another is over the status of the
Bible as a historical witness. Once ideology enters the picture, the stain
can spread. Attempts by Arab intellectuals and political leaders to deny
the Jews an ancient past in the Land of Israel may seem risible to some,

---

12. See the thread of discussion about these concerns, "Discussing Faith and Reason in
Biblical Studies," https://www.sbl-site.org/membership/farewell.aspx.

but they have been given an aura of respectability in works like *The Invention of Ancient Israel: The Silencing of Palestinian History*, by a scholar at one of the most prominent biblical studies programs in the UK.[13]

In recent years, two major academic conferences have been devoted to the historicity of the Exodus accounts, and their respective titles tell all. One, most of whose participants doubted that there was an Exodus, was titled "Out of Egypt: Israel's Exodus Between Text and Memory, History and Imagination."[14] The other, convened in explicit response to the first, was titled "A Consultation on the Historicity and Authenticity of the Exodus and Wilderness Traditions in a Post-Modern Age."[15] The "liberal" conference was held in California; the "conservative" one was in Texas. In brief: tell me a scholar's view on the historicity of the Exodus, and I will likely be able to tell you how he or she voted in the last presidential election.[16] There is great truth in the observation by archaeologist and Israel Prize winner Amihai Mazar that "the interpretation of archaeological data and its association with the biblical text may in many cases be a matter of subjective judgment…inspired by the scholar's personal values, beliefs, ideology, and attitude toward the [data]."[17]

In conclusion, we have seen that the Torah displays an intimate familiarity with the realia of late second-millennium Egypt. The visual parallels between Rameses's throne tent and the Tabernacle coupled

---

13. Keith W. Whitelam, *The Invention of Ancient Israel: The Silencing of Palestinian History* (London: Routledge, 1997).

14. For details, see "Exodus: Out of Egypt: Interdisciplinary Perspectives on Archaeology, Text and Memory," http://exodus.calit2.net/.

15. For details, see http://www.laniertheologicallibrary.org/wp-content/uploads/2014/01/program-bio.pdf. In the spirit of full disclosure: the present author presented the contents of this chapter at this conference.

16. Elsewhere I have expanded upon the corrupting role of culture and intellectual currents in influencing the field of biblical studies. See my essay, "The Corruption of Biblical Studies," *Mosaic*, July 10, 2017, available at https://mosaicmagazine.com/essay/2017/07/the-corruption-of-biblical-studies/.

17. Amihai Mazar, "On Archaeology, Biblical History, and Biblical Archaeology," in *The Quest for the Historical Israel: Debating Archaeology and the History of Early Israel*, by Israel Finkelstein and Amihai Mazar, ed. Brian B. Schmidt (Atlanta: Society of Biblical Literature, 2007), 31.

with the textual parallels between the Kadesh poem and the accounts of Exodus 14–15 are mutually reinforcing and attain a cumulative force. When we gather on the night of Passover to celebrate the Exodus and liberation from Egyptian oppression, we can speak the words of the Haggada with honesty and integrity: "We were slaves to a pharaoh in Egypt."

Chapter 4

Narrative Inconsistencies: The Book of Deuteronomy and the Rest of the Torah

O ne of the greatest challenges posed for Orthodoxy by critical study of the Bible concerns the coherence of the Torah. And nowhere is this more pressing than in the question of the relationship between the book of Deuteronomy – *Sefer Devarim* – and the earlier books of the Torah. In serial and wholesale fashion we find that the stories and laws related in this book seem to stand at odds with earlier versions of the same stories and same laws found elsewhere in the Torah. However, the question of the inconsistent narratives and the question of inconsistent laws are two discrete issues, and need to be addressed separately. In this chapter, I examine the narrative inconsistencies between Deuteronomy and the earlier books of the Torah. In the next chapter, I examine the phenomenon of inconsistencies within a single narrative account, focusing on the Flood narrative of Genesis 6–9. In chapter 6, I address the seeming inconsistencies of law within the Torah, focusing on the discrepancies between Deuteronomy and the previous four books.

Addressing the narrative inconsistencies between Deuteronomy and the other books requires extended discussion. Toward that end, let me explain up front what lies ahead in this chapter. First, I examine sample discrepancies between the narratives of Deuteronomy and the earlier books. I lay out why some find the approaches of our classical rabbinic exegetes unsatisfying. I then present the critical approach and lay bare the *academic* difficulties of that position. In chapter 1 of this book I presented the rabbinic sources that support and encourage understanding the Torah in its ancient Near Eastern context, and in chapter 2 we saw how the writing of "history" in the pre-modern world was really an exercise in exhortation. In the next part of this chapter, I introduce a particular genre of writing that is crucial for understanding the narrative discrepancies between Deuteronomy and earlier accounts in the Torah: the treaties between sovereign and vassal kings. I demonstrate that in this literature, the vassal would routinely receive from the sovereign king differing and conflicting accounts of the history of their relationship. I explain why this was so and how it sheds light on the relationship between the narratives of Israel's behavior in Deuteronomy and those contained in the earlier books.[1]

NARRATIVE INCONSISTENCIES: SOME EXAMPLES

I will take as my sample Deuteronomy chapter 1, which already reveals a slew of discrepancies. If you carefully review that chapter, covering the appointment of officers and judges at Sinai (compare with Exodus 18) and the account of the spies (compare with Numbers 13–15), you ought to come up with no less than fifteen discrepancies. Among the more striking ones:

1. When did Moses appoint judges at Sinai, before the giving of the Torah (Exodus) or after (Deuteronomy)?
2. Who chose the judges, Moses (Exodus) or the people (Deuteronomy)?

---

1. A full academic presentation of this approach is found in chapters 3 and 4 of my *Inconsistency in the Torah: Ancient Literary Convention and the Limits of Source Criticism* (New York: Oxford University Press, 2017), 63–103.

3. Who was it that declared the land to be good, Caleb and Joshua (Numbers) or all of the spies (Deuteronomy)?
4. What was Moses's response to the spies' defamatory report: silence (Numbers) or stern rebuke (Deuteronomy)?
5. Why was Moses denied entry into the land? Was he punished on account of his own shortcomings for hitting the rock (Numbers 20) or together with the rest of the people on account of the sin of the spies (Deuteronomy)?

By and large, our medieval rabbinic exegetes attended to these questions through strategies of *harmonization*. In their view, all accounts recorded were true and the discrepancies could be explained. Thus, in a well-known example, Numbers implies that it was God, or perhaps Moses, who decided to send the spies (Num. 13:2), while Deuteronomy (1:22) clearly states that the idea was initiated by the people. Rashi suggests that both are true: Moses capitulated to pressure from the people to endorse the expedition. Concerning the discrepancy surrounding the historical juncture at which judges were appointed, Abarbanel explains that the idea was raised prior to the giving of the Torah (as per Exodus 18) but implemented only following that event (Deuteronomy 1). Such explanations, however, often exhibit a dynamic reminiscent of the Dutch boy who sticks his finger in a hole in the dike to prevent the dam from bursting; no sooner is one hole plugged than another springs open. Having elegantly posited that Moses fulfilled Yitro's plan only after the Revelation at Sinai, Abarbanel must contend with Exodus 18:24–26, which seems to locate Moses's implementation of the plan right then – prior to Sinai. Abarbanel explains that those represent a telescoping in narrated time and actually depict events that occurred after the Revelation at Sinai.

I will leave it to the sensitivities of readers to decide how well these approaches resolve the questions raised. My own feeling is that in many cases they do. However, exegetical questions linger; while a canvass of the rabbinic exegetes will turn up resolutions to most of the questions, some have received no attention at all. Consider my fourth question above: According to the account in Deuteronomy, Moses offers stern rebuke to the spies and to the people immediately upon hearing their report. Yet, the account in Numbers seems to portray Moses as nearly impotent in his dealing with the spies. The strong sense there is that he left the "heavy lifting" of contending with the spies to Caleb and to Joshua, who, after all, were the only ones who really had credibility, because they had been there and had seen precisely what the others had seen. Why would the Torah portray Moses as nearly impotent in Numbers, if, in fact, he had issued stern rebuke and demonstrated such strong leadership as reported in Deuteronomy? I do not know of a classical exegete who relates to this question.

As I noted, some will find the attempts to harmonize the accounts more convincing, as multiple aspects of the same complex events. Others will be more skeptical of such attempts, or find the proposed answers simply fanciful. Abarbanel, for one, saw no harmonization possible with some of these questions. Consider his resolution of the question of who initiated the plan to send the spies, God or the people. For Abarbanel, it was God, as reported in Numbers. When Moses lays the onus on the people in Deuteronomy, says Abarbanel, he deliberately engages in falsification. For Abarbanel, had Moses shared with the second generation the fact that God had initiated the plan which had turned out so disastrously, it would have caused them to lose faith in Him. Moses, then, deliberately distorts the historical record "for the sake of Heaven," as it were. I bring this simply to demonstrate that not all rabbinic exegetes thought harmonization possible.

Even if one accepts the general harmonizing tendency taken by rabbinic exegetes, two questions still remain.

First, why is there a need to "cover" for so many seeming discrepancies in the first place? It is one thing to harmonize an occasional inconsistency. The narratives of Deuteronomy 1–11, though, exhibit such inconsistencies in wholesale fashion. Some maintain that these chapters are Moses's subjective voice. That is, they are not "the Torah" speaking, but Moses's address to the people. From a narratological point of view, this is true. And it may be that Moses here and there had his own slant on things, as we all do concerning major experiences that we have endured. In that case, though, the presence in the Torah of both the original "authentic" or "authorized" stories of Exodus–Numbers and Moses's subjective telling become problematic. What are later readers (like us) meant to take away from all this? Which version of events is real and which is subjective? If events really happened as depicted in the earlier four books, does that not undercut our opinion of Moses, who then emerges as somewhat of a fabricator? How much license did he have to "bend" the facts?

Second, consider all of the well-known differences between the Ten Commandments in Exodus 20 and Deuteronomy 5. The Talmud (Shevuot 20b) explains that divine speech cannot be heard in all of its complexity in a single hearing. But in light of all of the discrepancies that we have seen in Deuteronomy 1 alone, it would seem that the discrepancies exhibited between the two versions of the Decalogue are not exceptional (i.e., divine speech), but are part of some larger phenomenon whereby inconsistency is exhibited between Deuteronomy and the earlier books in many areas of narrative. Perhaps Moses could recast historical events, but did he have the license to "misquote," as it were, what God Himself had said? These questions may not defeat the harmonization approaches but. they require attention.

THE SOURCE-CRITICAL APPROACH
AND ITS PROBLEMS

Scholars often take these inconsistencies as signs of editing as they seek to recreate the history of the text's development. The inconsistencies, according to these scholars, are evidence that the Torah is composed of several preexisting sources. *Source criticism* is the attempt to identify and recreate those hypothesized preexisting sources. For source critics, the narratives of Deuteronomy were written by a historian who rewrote the earlier history he had received in line with his own ideological agenda. He had no interest in preserving the earlier – and to his mind, inferior – versions of the story, and thus no desire to harmonize the accounts. In one stroke, all of the discrepancies are accounted for.

Here is where we must take a closer look at the critical theory. Precisely from an *academic* perspective, the source-critical approach to the question at hand is subject to critique on six separate accounts. While I am only one scholar, I do not write here as an individual critiquing the consensus but as one writer summarizing a sustained scholarly critique of many in recent years.[2]

First, source criticism must give an accounting of the final shape of the Torah before us. If these are the works of competing and opposing historians, how and why were their conflicting histories sewn together? Could the hypothesized redactor of the Torah not see these problems as well? Why did he choose to retain multiple, conflicting accounts? It is often surmised that the Torah is an anthology of different traditions of Israel's history, and that the upheaval occasioned by the destruction of the Temple and the Exile forced Israel's leaders to bring these traditions together. This posits a form of composition that has no precedent anywhere in the ancient world. Nearly every ancient culture that we know of experienced cataclysm at one point or another in its history. Nowhere do we see that the embattled culture responds by assembling its conflicting historical traditions under one cover. The one distantly similar phenomenon sometimes cited as a model for this hypothesized form of redaction is in fact the most telling: In the second century, the church apologist Tatian combined the four accounts of the life of Jesus found in the gospels into a single work known as the diatessaron. Yet, as he did so, he took four often conflicting works and endeavored to produce a harmonious narrative. The source-critical approach posits exactly the opposite: originally integral and coherent narratives were combined producing disharmony.

Moreover, this theory of an anthology of histories has no external evidence. There is no epigraphic record (inscriptions or documents) from the Land of Israel, Babylon, or Persia that mentions this process. There is no epigraphic evidence of either the version of history found in Deuteronomy or of the alternative versions found in the other books as separate, independent works. Nor is there any evidence for this approach within the other books of the Tanakh itself. That is, we do not find any book outside of the Torah that seems to rely solely on the history found in Deuteronomy or solely on the version found in the other books. The

---

2. See, for example, this essay by British scholar David Clines, "Response to Rolf Rendtorff's 'What Happened to the Yahwist? Reflections after Thirty Years,'" Society of Biblical Literature, https://www.sbl-site.org/publications/article.aspx?articleId=551.

theory that the Torah represents an anthology of traditions of Israel's history stems solely from the supposition that these histories are contradictory. Once these discrepancies are interpreted as contradictory, a hypothesis must be adduced to account for their combination under one cover.

Second, it is unclear what motivates the so-called historian who is credited with having written the accounts of Deuteronomy. When someone wrote a history in the ancient world (and maybe also the not-so-ancient world), it was with an agenda in mind. The difficulty this presents for the standard source-critical approach is best understood with reference to a retelling of history elsewhere: the account of the two monarchies in the book of Chronicles as opposed to the account found in the books of Samuel and Kings. Chronicles reveals several consistent phenomena that distinguish it from Samuel and Kings. It recounts virtually no disparaging accounts of the life of David. It places much more emphasis on the Temple than is found in the earlier books. The book's writer demonstrates a clear agenda of promoting the Davidic dynasty and the Temple.

But what of the hypothesized historian who composed Deuteronomy? Here, it turns out it is difficult to identify a consistent agenda for the details provided across its several stories. It is not as though Deuteronomy is a "pro-Moses" account while the earlier versions are "pro-Aaron," or Deuteronomy "pro-David" while the earlier accounts are "pro-Saul." We would expect an altered history to reflect a consistently different theme than its rejected version.

Truth be told, there is one difference that runs throughout most of the accounts of Deuteronomy: Israel is portrayed more negatively in the stories of Deuteronomy than in the other accounts. For example, while God told Moses to send spies in Numbers, in Deuteronomy it is the people who push Moses to do so. Moses is punished for his own sins in Numbers but in Deuteronomy he is punished for the people's sin. This emphasis does not explain every detail but it is highly present in most of the retold narratives. But whose interest – priestly, Davidic, northern, southern, etc. – is served by retelling the stories in this way?

Third, it is difficult to understand why the hypothesized historian chooses to rewrite precisely these five or six stories. The author of Chronicles, too, retells history selectively, but he covers the whole period of the monarchy. In Deuteronomy, the historian inserts changes in wholesale fashion in every story he recounts. Yet, it is also clear that he is familiar with the Exodus from Egypt and with the patriarchs. Is it not strange that he saw fit to change so much about a seemingly minor story such as the appointing of judges but has nothing at all of his own to say about the Exodus from Egypt or the accounts of the patriarchs?

Fourth, the hypothesis of a separate and competing history is compromised by the fact that the accounts of Deuteronomy do not constitute a stand-alone work. Chronicles never refers the reader back to Samuel and Kings. Readers may make connections themselves between the texts but Chronicles never asks the reader to do so. From an academic perspective, one can read Chronicles as a stand-alone history to be read entirely in place of Samuel and Kings, and the story makes sense (even if Ḥazal, typically, did not read these books in this way). Crucially, this is not so of the accounts in Deuteronomy. Even as Deuteronomy introduces changes, it also relies on the reader's knowledge of the earlier versions. Deuteronomy presupposes the readers' ability to fill in details known to them only from earlier stories, such as the reference to Caleb's exemption from divine wrath (Deut. 1:36), the sin of Baal Peor (4:3), God's anger at Aaron (9:20), and the punishment that befell Miriam (24:9). The accounts of Deuteronomy, therefore, are not stand-alone alternative histories but rather supplements that refer back to the earlier versions it supposedly rejects, expecting the audience to be familiar with them. It is also worthy of note that, unlike the author of Chronicles, the author of Deuteronomy introduces no new stories of his own. He seems only to rework material that already appears in the books of Exodus–Numbers.

Fifth, the narratives of Deuteronomy have a peculiar narratological dimension about them. Most of the stories in the Tanakh are related in third person, by what is sometimes referred to in narratological terms as the "omniscient scribe." The "narrator" in most passages is detached and objective, representing God's view of things, as it were. Were the accounts of Deuteronomy the work of a competing historian, why would he present his version in the subjective voice of Moses? Consider, especially, the fact that Moses recounts his own failures within these narratives. These accounts are not presented as objective fact but as a call to recollection. Repeatedly, Moses tells Israel to recall what happened *ba'et hahi*, "at that time" – some nine times overall. Would this competing historian not want to portray his version in the same authoritative voice of the "omniscient scribe" as is found nearly everywhere else?

Sixth, and finally, why is this phenomenon of extended conflicting histories limited to the Torah? We have, it is true, two histories of the monarchy, Samuel/Kings and Chronicles, but those have come down to us as two separate works. Within the Torah we have two histories of the wandering in the desert – one in Exodus–Numbers and one in Deuteronomy. Why do we not have multiple versions of the accounts of the judges within the book of Judges? Or of the career of Saul within the book of Samuel? If there were, in fact, competing traditions of Israel's history that were all anthologized at a certain point in time, why are accounts retold in this fashion within a single work only in the Torah, and only with regard to a portion of the desert history?

Now, some readers might find some of these challenges more compelling than others. And some will maintain that the source-critical approach is still more compelling, religious belief aside, over the harmonizing strategies surveyed earlier. I would suggest that when the competing explanations before us are each problematic, a viable option is not to choose between them but to frankly admit that we do not have good options on the table in front of us.

What would a satisfying explanation look like? That explanation would include the following nine facets:

1. Rather than seeking to harmonize differences in piecemeal and sometimes forced fashion, it should recognize that the discrepancies are real.
2. It should explain how and why contradictory accounts are included together under one cover.
3. It should draw from a documented and existing precursor for such literary activity.
4. It should draw from a literary precursor that conceivably has some relation or connection to the time period and literary genres of the Torah (unlike, say, the diatessaron, discussed above).

5. It should explain why these wholesale contradictions are found not with regard to the entirety of history in the Torah but specifically with regard to the period of the wandering in the desert.

6. It should explain why the dominant thematic difference between the conflicting accounts concerns the degree of waywardness attributed to Israel during this time.

7. It should explain why this phenomenon is exhibited in the book of Deuteronomy and not other books of the Torah, or, even, other books of the Tanakh generally.

8. It should explain why the retold history (i.e., the Deuteronomy account) is not narrated in the standard third-person narration of the omniscient scribe but rather as a leader calling upon his followers to "recall" things they already know.

9. It should explain why the retold history differs widely from the earlier accounts and at the same time seems to rely on them (i.e., the reference to Caleb's exemption from divine wrath [Deut. 1:36], the sin of Baal Peor [4:3], God's anger at Aaron [9:20], and what befell Miriam [24:9]).

I will lay out an explanation that satisfies these nine criteria later in the discussion, but we have much work to do before that.

UNDERSTANDING *BRIT SINAI* IN ANCIENT NEAR EASTERN CONTEXT

There is a particular genre of ancient Near Eastern writing that is central to understanding how many parts of the Torah are composed and allows us to understand how and why the Torah offers multiple accounts of the same event. Taking a note from the writings of Ralbag that we saw in chapter 1, we will be open to the idea that even in the Torah, "the prophet expresses himself according to the convention of the time." Taking a note from the Rambam, we will be undaunted by the striking similarities that we see between various passages from the Torah and passages found in ancient writings. Rather, we will seek out – as the Rambam himself did – the continuities and the discontinuities between those foreign literatures and the Torah. We will aim to understand how the Torah appropriates and adapts foreign concepts and institutions and uses them in the service of bringing Israel to a higher theological understanding.

It is commonplace that the Torah speaks of a *brit* that was formed between God and Israel at Sinai. But just what is a *brit*? Translating *brit* into English, "covenant," is of little help, and merely begs the question, then, of what is a "covenant." More to the point, we should note the unusual dynamics present in this relationship. *Brit* seems to be a compact, contract, or pact between two parties. Yet, in modern times both sides to a contract freely enter the agreement and each side has the right to decline entering the agreement, if it wishes. While Israel at Sinai expressed her agreement – *naaseh venishma* – it is also plain that she had little choice but to do so. Put differently, what we have at Sinai is a form of agreement where the parties are unequal, and where the lesser side (Israel) is expected to agree to the terms dictated by the stronger side (God). On the other hand, it seems that the stronger side is not tyrannical or cruel, but seeks a genuine relationship with the lesser side – though on His terms. There is no modern counterpart to this type of relationship.

However, we do see precisely this type of relationship in political treaties of the late second millennium BCE, the proposed period of the bondage, Exodus, and settlement of the land. This type of relationship – bilateral but fundamentally between non-equals; dictated, yet while establishing a positive relationship between the parties – is found in what are known as the vassal treaties of the period, between stronger and lesser kings. The Torah articulates the relationship between God and Israel as one between a great king and a lesser king engaged in just such a treaty.[3] In the fourteenth and thirteenth centuries BCE, all nations around the eastern Mediterranean rim participated in these relationships. What I will show here are some of the ways in which the

3. The notes of convergence between vassal treaty modalities and the Torah have been well documented in the scholarly literature for more than sixty years, with more insights added on a regular basis. See the summary in my *Created Equal: How the Bible Broke with Ancient Political Thought* (New York: Oxford University Press, 2008), 28–44.

Torah adopts – and yet adapts – this idea, to help Israel understand the nature of her relationship with her Heavenly King. This will set the table for us to then examine the role of contradictory narratives both in the treaties and in the Torah.

ELEMENTS OF THE LATE SECOND-MILLENNIUM-BCE VASSAL TREATY

The Historical Prologue

The central part of the vassal treaty, as with any contract, is the stipulations it contains: the obligations to be undertaken by each of the parties. But this is not the first element that we find in these treaties. Almost universally, these treaties open with a historical prologue, which delineates the events that led to the establishment of the treaty between the stronger and lesser king. Oftentimes written at great length, it tells of the salvation rendered by the sovereign on behalf of the vassal that led the vassal to subordinate himself to the sovereign: a stronger king could send troops, thereby affording the lesser military salvation, or he could send food supplies in time of drought. Universally in these treaties, we find that the lesser king appeals to the stronger for assistance. The stronger king agrees to act on behalf of the subordinate, but does so without specifying conditions. Once salvation has been delivered, it is clear to all parties that the sovereign may now dictate the terms of an amicable relationship between the two, and that the lesser is expected to agree to those terms, in recognition of the salvation offered him. The stipulations put forth by the sovereign upon the lesser king always follow this prologue.

This helps us understand the *brit* at Sinai.[4] The account of the *brit* at Sinai in Exodus 19–24 is preceded by the story of the Exodus. Put differently, the Torah tells us about the beneficence of the sovereign toward the subordinate in a way that is similar to the vassal treaties. Strikingly, these treaties would begin with the formula, "The words of [name of the sovereign king]" followed by a delineation of the

---

4. Although the term *brit* is used to describe commitments made to Abraham, Noah, and Pinhas, it is clear that the extended bilateral nature of the *brit* between God and Israel is a distinct category of *brit*. This category alone is our subject here.

favor bestowed upon the subordinate. The Decalogue reveals such an introduction. Before the delineation of the laws themselves, we find the following introduction (Ex. 20:1–2): "God spoke all these words, saying: 'I the Lord am your God who brought you out of the land of Egypt, the house of bondage.'" Notice the basis upon which God enjoins Israel. He identifies Himself not as the God who created heaven and earth, but as the God who bestowed a great favor upon the "kingdom" of Israel (cf. Ex. 19:6), and is thus deserving of its subordinate loyalty. Note that the phrase "I the Lord am your God who brought you out of the land of Egypt, the house of bondage" is surely unnecessary after nineteen chapters of exodus and delivery that clearly delineate that this is so. At this juncture in time, however, God is entering into "treaty" with the Israelites, and hence the formal need within the written contract for the grace of the sovereign to be documented.

As noted earlier, the vassal treaties usually indicate that the relationship between the two kings would be initiated by the subordinate king, appealing to the sovereign king for assistance. This pattern emerges from the narrative of the early chapters of the book of Exodus. The process of divine salvation begins only after Israel cries out (Ex. 2:23). The Torah then notes that God indeed heard their cry (2:24–25), a detail which He repeatedly underscores as He tells Moses of His intention to deliver them from bondage (3:7, 9).

Treaty Stipulations

Following the historical prologue, the vassal treaties typically enumerate the stipulations imposed upon the subordinate by the sovereign that were to be the expressions of his loyalty. Many of the treaties restrict the political activity of the subordinate king. He may enter into an alliance only with the sovereign. One treaty warns the vassal of punishment: "If you seek the well-being of another [king] ... thereby you will break the oath."[5] Such clauses add new dimensions to readily familiar passages in the Torah. The opening stipulation of the Ten Commandments, "You

---

5. Treaty between Suppiluliuma and Aziru § 15 (iv.21–26; *CTH* 49) in Itamar Singer, "The Treaties Between Hatti and Amurru," in *The Context of Scripture II: Monumental Inscriptions from the Biblical World*, ed. William W. Hallo (Leiden, Netherlands: Brill, 1997), 95.

shall have no other gods beside Me" (Ex. 20:2; Deut. 5:6), is readily understood to a contemporary reader from an epistemological perspective: God, who took Israel out of Egypt, is the only true god. All other "gods" are false. Yet the command takes on a different light when seen in the context of ancient Near Eastern treaty formulations. God is the sovereign, Israel the subordinate. When Israel reveres another god she violates a relationship; she expresses ingratitude in light of the favor and grace bestowed upon her by God the sovereign, as laid down in the "historical prologue" of the Decalogue, indeed, as laid out in the entire narrative of the book of Exodus to that point (cf. Ex. 34:12, 15). For the subordinate king to establish treaties or other ties with another power would be tantamount to treason.

One term found in the treaty literature elucidates the identity of Israel as a chosen people. The biblical term for "chosen" people is *segula* (Ex. 19:5). In one document, a favored vassal of the king of Ugarit is called the *sglt* of his sovereign. Importantly, the term implies both subordination and yet also distinction. Indeed, this tension between distinction on the one hand and subordination on the other seems to be implicit in the first reference to "chosenness" in the Torah. It is in the opening verses of the *brit* narrative of Exodus 19: "Now, then, if you will obey Me faithfully and keep My covenant, you shall be My treasured possession (*segula*) among all the peoples, for all the earth is Mine" (19:5). Entering into covenant renders Israel a subordinate. But she is promised favored status among God's subordinates, when faithful to the terms of the subordination treaty.

Some of the treaty stipulations have remarkable parallels in the Torah. In some treaties we find that the subordinate king must make regular appearances before the sovereign. One treaty states that the vassal king "must come before His Majesty and *look upon the face of His Majesty. As soon as he comes before His Majesty, the noblemen of His Majesty (will rise) from their seats. No one will remain seated above him."[6] Note that the visit of the vassal is a state visit replete with honor,

---

6. Treaty between Tudhaliya II of Hatti and Sunashshura of Kizzuwatna § 9 (A i 38–44; *CTH* 41 – Hittite; *CTH* 131 – Akkadian). The Akkadian version is translated in Gary Beckman, *Hittite Diplomatic Texts*, ed. Harry A. Hoffner Jr., 2nd edition, Society of Biblical Literature Writings from the Ancient World Series 7 (Atlanta: Scholars Press, 1999), 19.

as the sovereign king's nobles must rise in his presence. The visitation is an act of "looking upon the face of His Majesty," a term used throughout the Torah to refer to a court appearance (e.g., Gen. 43:3, 5, 23; Ex. 10:28–29). We find similar language in the stipulations of the *brit* narrative of Exodus 19–24. In 23:17, we read, "Three times a year, all of your males shall be seen *by the face of the Lord* – Hashem" (cf. Ex. 34:23; Deut. 16:16). The mitzva of *aliya laregel*, pilgrimage on the festivals, is a call to the vassal Israel to pay a visit of homage to the sovereign King of Kings.

The treaties routinely mandate the periodic reading of the treaty within the subordinate king's court. In one treaty, the vassal is told, "[This tablet which] I have made [for you], shall be read out [before you three times yearly]."[7] Once again, we see a parallel stipulation in the Torah, but one that is extended to include all members of Israel. In the vassal treaty the subordinate king is ultimately responsible to execute and follow the terms of the treaty, and thus he personally must hear its provisions read. But the covenant between God and Israel is consecrated with each and every person, and thus each and every person must hear it read, because each and every member of the people is responsible for its faithful implementation. We find, in fact, that "treaties," or the terms of the covenant between God and Israel, are read out before the whole people on a number of occasions: at Sinai (Ex. 24:3–4, 7–8), and at the mitzva of *Hak'hel* (Deut. 31:10–13).

Deposit of the Treaty in the Temple

The next typical element of the vassal treaty called for a copy of the treaty to be deposited within the temple of the subordinate's deity. This would demonstrate and affirm that the local deity of the subordinate was interested in the fulfillment of its terms. It also sent an implicit message to the inhabitants of the subordinate state that the treaty was now to occupy a central place within their value system. The Torah adopts this same idea, but transforms it to help Israel realize its "treaty" obligations. The text of the "treaty," or at least a part of it – the Tablets of Testimony (*Luḥot HaBrit*) – was deposited within the Ark of the Covenant (*Aron HaBrit*) within the Holy of Holies,

---

7. Treaty between Mursili II of Hatti and Kupanta-Kurunta of Mira-Kuwaliya § 28 (I iv 1'–8'; *CTH* 68); see Beckman, *Hittite Diplomatic Texts*, 81.

the *Kodesh HaKodashim* (Ex. 25:21; 40:20; cf. Deut. 31:26). In this fashion, Israel the subordinate would symbolically recognize the place of the treaty with the divine sovereign within their own value system. Notice specifically that within the book of Exodus the tablets are called *Luḥot HaEdut*, the Tablets of Testimony, and the ark is called the *Aron HaEdut*, the Ark of Testimony. The ark and its tablets bear testimony that Israel is obligated to fulfill the stipulations written on the tablets. Within the pagan logic of the vassal treaty, the vassal deposited the tablets of the treaty into the temple of his own god, demonstrating that that god attested to the binding nature of the treaty. At Sinai, of course, the "deity" of the subordinate king is none other than the sovereign king, the Almighty.

From the treaty literature we learn that if the tablet inscribed with the text of the treaty was lost or stolen, it would need to be replaced. The apparent need for a replacement copy of a treaty tablet is well attested in the Torah as well; the breaking of the tablets by Moses necessitates the drafting of a new set of tablets (Ex. 34:1–4). A sovereign king would grant the vassal treaty tablet royal legitimation by sealing it with his seal. The Tablets of the Covenant are consecrated by the fact that they are inscribed by God Himself (Ex. 32:15–16; 34:1, 28; Deut. 10:1–4).

Expanding our focus from the Sinai narratives of the book of Exodus to the structure of the book of Deuteronomy, we see that the treaty elements we have identified are best represented within that book. The book opens with a pedagogic history (chs. 1–11) followed by extensive stipulations (chs. 12–26). There were, however, two other typical elements of the vassal treaty form – elements found always at the end of those treaties – that come into play in the final chapters of Deuteronomy: witnesses to the treaty and blessings and curses.

Witnesses to the Treaty

Vassal treaties typically included a long list of divine witnesses that were called upon to enforce the treaty and to punish the subordinate in the event of violation. These were often gods of the natural world. One representative text reads:

> The mountains, the rivers, the springs, the great sea, heaven and earth, the winds and the clouds. They shall be witnesses to this

treaty and this oath. All the words of the treaty and oath which are written on this tablet – if (name of vassal king) does not observe these words of the treaty and oath, but transgresses the oath, then these oath gods shall destroy (name of the vassal king).[8]

Similarly, the natural elements of the heaven and the earth bear witness to God's treaty with Israel (cf. Deut. 4:26, 30:19; 32:1).

Blessings and Curses

Finally, these vassal treaties concluded with blessings that would be bestowed upon the subordinate by the gods in exchange for his loyalty, and, conversely, curses that would befall him in the event of violation of the terms of the treaty. These were usually juxtaposed, and located at the end of the treaty, as in the following passage:

> If you ... do not observe the words of this treaty, the gods ... shall destroy you ... they will draw you out like malt from its husk.... And these gods ... shall allot you poverty and destitution.... Your name and your progeny ... shall be eradicated from the earth. The ground shall be ice, so that you will slip. The ground of your land shall be a marsh of [tablet broken] ... so that you will certainly sink and be unable to cross.
>
> If you observe this treaty and oath, these gods shall protect you ... together with your wife ... her sons and grandsons.[9]

Both in Leviticus 26 and Deuteronomy 28, similar conventions are employed. A series of blessings of prosperity and bounty open with the phrase, "If you heed ... then ..." (Lev. 26:3; Deut. 28:1), followed by a longer, more elaborate series of curses, which likewise opens with the phrase, "If you do not heed ... then ..." (Lev. 26:14; Deut. 28:15).

---

8. Treaty between Suppiluliuma I of Hatti and Tette of Nuhashshi § 17 (A iv 44'–57'; *CTH* 53); Beckman, *Hittite Diplomatic Texts*, 58).

9. Treaty between Suppiluliuma I of Hatti and Shattiwaza of Mittanni §§ 15–16 (A rev. 58–75; *CTH* 51); see Beckman, *Hittite Diplomatic Texts*, 48.

Israel's Familiarity with the World of Treaty

To summarize: We have seen only some of the ways in which the Torah portrays the relationship between God and Israel as that between a vassal and his sovereign king.[10] Following the Rambam's approach to sacrificial worship, we have explored the continuities and the discontinuities that the Torah displays with respect to the original, pagan institutions. We have noted how it adopts those concepts even as it adapts them. We can see within this use of the vassal treaty model the manner in which the Torah introduced Israel to the idea of the kingship of God. Moreover, the Torah uses this model to help concretize for Israel what it means to be in a relationship with God, using a model that was readily familiar throughout the region at that time. We have always known that the Torah portrayed God as a sovereign, a king. The vassal treaty literature allows us greater definition in our understanding of God as king and we as His servants.

The striking similarity between these ancient treaty forms and various passages of the Torah raises an understandable question: Does this mean that all members of Israel were presumed to have advanced degrees in Hittitology and Ugaritic? And if not, would they not have been as clueless about all this as are most laymen today?

It is unlikely that many in Israel had a rich knowledge of ancient languages. At the same time, all possessed a much, much richer familiarity with ancient culture than we have today. Many of the elements found in the vassal treaties and in the Torah are taken from the warp and woof of day-to-day life in the ancient world. Everyone knew that "to see the face" of a king meant to pay a court visit, just like all of us know what "swearing in" or "death row" means. You do not need a degree in political science or criminology to understand those phrases; they are simply common stock phrases of our culture. Natural bodies were invoked as witnesses for all sorts of things in the ancient world, and blessings and

---

10. The language and structure of what Ḥazal called the passages of *mesit umediaḥ* (inciting for idol worship) and *ir hanidaḥat* (a wayward city) (Deut. 13:7–19) are remarkably similar to those found in the clauses of treason in one of these treaties. The language of treason against the king is transformed in the Torah to the language of apostasy against God. See my "CTH 133 and the Hittite Provenance of Deuteronomy 13," *Journal of Biblical Literature* 130, no. 1 (2011): 25–44.

curses were bestowed to encourage compliance with commitments of all kinds. What we understand today is that these are brought together in the Torah in a constellation that we can recognize as a reflection of the idea of the relationship between vassal and sovereign. These forms of relationship between cities and states existed far and wide during this time. I suspect that local residents in a vassal state knew that their state was subservient to a larger empire. Indeed, the Tanakh speaks at length about such arrangements (e.g., Is. 30–31), so the general idea was readily known to anyone who heard the prophets. The more literate and knowledgeable may have understood these parallels more deeply. But it has always been the case that the Torah and the Tanakh communicate both to more learned and literate audiences on one level as well as to simpler folk.

While all of this is fascinating in and of itself, we engaged the form of the vassal treaty and its relationship to the idea of *brit* in the Torah with a single purpose in mind: to prepare ourselves to investigate the issue of seemingly conflicting narratives between those found in Deuteronomy and the parallel narratives found in the other four books of the Torah. We have seen that the vassal treaties in question wrote at length about the events that led up to the establishment of vassalage between the lesser and greater king, in what I termed the historical prologue to the treaties. To understand the conflicts, however, between the stories in Deuteronomy and elsewhere in the Torah, we will now need to take a closer look at the genre of the historical prologue, and ask what type of writing it is, what its purpose was, and for whom it was composed.

The Historical Prologue of the Vassal Treaty as Diplomatic Signaling

The vassal treaty was essentially a contract between sovereign and vassal, and many of the basic elements of our contracts are found in these treaties. Just as they listed stipulations that obligated each side, so do the contracts that we draw up today. They imposed penalties for breach of contract – through the form of curses – and so do we, through fines. They sought outside authority to back up the clauses – through divine witnesses – and so do we through a notary.

However, there is one element of the ancient treaty form that finds no parallel in the contracts that we write: the historical prologue which described the events that led to the establishment of the treaty. When my wife and I purchased our current home, we bought from a man in my community for whom I had long had great respect. But there's no mention of that in the contract that transferred title to me. After a month of dating Michal, I knew that we would eventually get engaged. But our *ketuba* makes no mention of that. Our contracts today are "strictly business." Why do these ancient contracts go to length to tell of the events leading up to the treaty?

More background is necessary to understand the function of these compositions. The world in which these treaties arose – the eastern Mediterranean rim of the fourteenth and thirteenth centuries BCE – is the first in which we find an *international order*. Think of the geopolitical situation today. No country exists in isolation. All countries seek alliances. Countries, of course, are primarily concerned with their immediate neighbors. But all countries today recognize that there is strength that comes by creating alliances with a group or groups of other countries. This is what political scientists call an international order.

Now, long, long ago, there were no such alliances with countries afar. The centuries in question mark the first time that city-states in this region were acutely aware that they would be much better off establishing alliances with even distant neighbors than merely trying to go it alone. During this period, there were two regional powers: the Hittite empire, based in modern-day Turkey, to the north, and Egypt, a perennial powerhouse, to the south. At this time, the Hittite empire and Egypt played the roles of the sovereign. A large assortment of small city-states throughout the Levant – modern-day Israel, Lebanon, and Syria – would sign on as vassals to these larger states.

Although the Hittite empire and Egypt were the largest and strongest players in the region, they were not superpowers. They did not rule by the grip of fear, say, in the way the Kremlin dominated Soviet bloc countries during the Cold War, or the way that the Nazis installed puppet regimes throughout occupied Europe during World War II. The Hittites, whose records have been remarkably preserved, sought to leverage their advantage over the smaller, weaker states around them.

They sought to form amicable alliances in which they could get the best terms possible. The smaller states, for their part, were trying to do the same thing. Sometimes they would ally with one another; at other times they would jockey for position and try to play off the Hittites against the Egyptians – just as modern states do. Think of how Egypt jumped ship from the Soviet orbit to the American orbit in the wake of the Camp David Accords in 1978.

Today, we have news reports around the clock and instant communication. Nations today always know what is going on around them. But back then, of course, things were different. All of the political entities of the time were in a constant state of jitters about their relationships: Will my "ally" really be there for me if I face a crisis? Is he backstabbing me at this very moment? For this reason, vassals and sovereigns were in continuous written correspondence with one another and constantly sending token gifts to one another as a way of stating, "Do not worry about me; our deal is still on." We know all of this from a cache of more than three hundred such letters from vassals to the king of Egypt in the fourteenth century, known as the El Amarna letters.

This brings us to the historical prologue of the Hittite empire vassal treaties. When court scribes of the Hittite kings wrote these brief histories, they certainly were not doing so for the sake of historians who would live today, 3,200 years later. They did so for the purpose of *diplomatic signaling*, of setting a tone for the relationship with the vassal. Leaders today do it as well. When a leader visits another country, there may well be contracts signed and deals made. But part of what goes on in such a visit is to establish a tone for the relationship. The visiting leader will give public addresses. Usually, he or she will reflect on some aspects of the history of the two countries. If there is a history of tension between them, the public address might hint at what needs to change to further cement the relationship.

In the fourteenth and thirteenth centuries BCE, this type of diplomatic signaling between states was a critical component of statecraft. If I am a Hittite king, I am looking to establish a relationship with a potential vassal on the best terms possible. I find a vassal who is willing to sign with me, and we conclude a treaty with one another. Now the question becomes: What messages do I want to convey to the vassal about our relationship? It is always a delicate balance of carrot and stick. These diplomatic correspondences are always written from the first-person perspective of the Hittite king as a direct address to the vassal king. Sometimes I feel that I will be able to best cement the relationship and get what I want from my vassal by being highly complimentary to him and by addressing him in a fashion that instills confidence that I am there for him. And indeed, we find that some of these historical prologues are highly laudatory. Other times, though, I, as Hittite king, might feel that I can get the most out of this vassal by intimidating him. In fact, in some of the prologues we find statements like, "Thus says Suppiluliuma, King of Hatti: I have now elevated you, Huqqana, a lowly dog, and have treated you well."[11] The historical prologue, then, was the "speech" through which the Hittite king set the tone for the relationship that was now being established. None of this should surprise us, however. We saw in chapter 2 that all over the world in pre-modern times, people spoke and wrote about the past for the purpose of *exhortation*. The historical prologues of the late second-millennium vassal treaties were merely one instance of this. Both the Hittite and vassal kings knew what had transpired between them. But when the Hittite sovereign addressed his vassal in the historical prologue of the vassal treaty, he was putting just the right spin on what had transpired so as achieve his goals of exhortation – the right mix of rhetorical carrot and stick.

The Renewal Treaty and Discrepancies with the Original Treaty

Hittite kings wished their treaties to be long-lasting. Therefore, when a vassal king died, the Hittite king would establish a renewal treaty with his successor. The idea was to stress continuity. The renewal treaty was a way for the Hittite king to say, "Until now I had a treaty with your father, and now I will continue that treaty with you." The record shows that sometimes the stipulations remained the same, and sometimes they reflected new realities, or a changed political situation. The river never does stand still in the balance of power politics. When a Hittite king would pen such a renewal treaty, he would, of course, begin the text of

---

11. Treaty between Suppiluliuma I of Hatti and Huqqana of Hayasa (*CTH* 42 § 1 [A I 1–5], translated in Beckman, *Hittite Diplomatic Texts*, 27).

the treaty with a historical prologue of how the parties got to where they were. And if he was penning a renewal treaty, then he would rewind the historical review back to the beginning: how the present vassal's father or grandfather had originally come to accept vassalage to the Hittite throne.

One series of treaties is between the Hittite kings and the rulers of a city-state called Amurru – possibly the Torah's *Emori*. Here we find the original treaty and an additional three rounds of successive renewal treaties between these two parties. The original treaty, between Suppiluliuma of Hatti (the Hittite capital) and Aziru king of Amurru, tells of how Aziru came to submit to the Hittite king. And all of the subsequent three renewal treaties across a span of more than a century also retell that story. It is here that we see an astonishing phenomenon: each and every one of those tellings is different. From treaty to treaty, the "facts" behind the initial treaty between Suppiluliuma and Aziru change. Moreover, the spirit through which Aziru came to Suppiluliuma is cast differently as we move from treaty to treaty. Some of the treaties describe the great joy that Suppiluliuma felt when Aziru joined him. Others suggest Suppiluliuma was merely having compassion on him. In fact, when we look across all of the Hittite treaties with their vassals we see the same phenomenon: when we find an original treaty and then a renewal treaty between the Hittite king and a given vassal, the story of how the original vassal king came to submit to the Hittite throne is never told the same way twice. In most cases, the various versions are incompatible. Why is this?

The explanation is rooted in the identity we stressed earlier, in which the historical prologues are seen as diplomatic signaling, a form of exhortation, a way of indicating to the vassal how the sovereign views him. At all times, the Hittite kings composed their versions of the history of the relationship with the vassal with one aim in mind: to project a message, an impression for the present. At all times the past was a resource that the Hittite king could use to shape the present. In the first treaty between Hatti and Amurru, it would seem that the Hittite king, Suppiluliuma, was genuinely grateful that Aziru was abandoning an Egyptian coalition and joining forces with him. In the third treaty between them, some eighty years later, we see the sharpest differences in the account. At this point in time, Amurru had already rebelled once. The current Hittite king, Hatusili, now found it politically expedient to resuscitate the relationship, and thus forged a renewal treaty with the Amurru king, Bentesina, who was being reinstated almost as a puppet. The tone that Hatusili takes toward him is paternalistic and condescending. When Hatusili describes the conditions under which Aziru had initially submitted to Suppiluliuma, he makes no mention of Suppiluliuma's celebration and appreciation as had been expressed in the prologue to the first treaty between the kingdoms. Instead, the relationship between Suppiluliuma and Aziru is made to sound a lot more like the current relationship between Hatusili and Bentesina.

Put differently, the purpose of telling the past is only to help shape the present. In fact, Hatusili even says to Bentesina that in spite of Amurru's insurrection in the interim, he is prepared to offer him the same terms that Suppiluliuma had offered Aziru some eighty years earlier. It is apparent from the text that Hatusili has a copy of that text, and expects that Bentesina does as well. Archaeological evidence from across the region demonstrates that old copies of treaties were not discarded, but rather archived for further reference. We possess copies of that earlier treaty and can see that Hatusili was being true to his word: the stipulations that he offers Bentesina are those that Suppiluliuma offered to Aziru. Yet if Bentesina had compared the historical prologue of the earlier treaty with the one found in the renewal treaty he was now entering with Hatusili, he would no doubt have noticed the divergent accounts of how Aziru accepted subjugation to Suppiluliuma. What was he supposed to make of that? Did Hatusili not realize that he would be caught in a lie?

The answer, once again, can be grasped by seeing these "histories" as subordinate to the art of diplomatic signaling, of exhortation. A contemporary example illustrates the point: When a spokesperson for the United States Department of State says concerning an adversary that "the military option is still on the table," that statement – that diplomatic signaling – only has meaning in the context of previous dispatches on the issue. If the spokesperson had commented in an earlier release, "We are sending the US Seventh Fleet to the region," then the newer statement, "The military option is still on the table," signals a moderate, more restrained tone, even as it keeps the pressure on. By contrast, if the spokesperson had previously said, "All options are still on the table," then the newer statement, "The *military* option is still on the table," represents a ratcheting-up of the rhetoric by a notch. The point of this example is that diplomatic signaling always takes place within the context of the codes that both sides understand, and most pointedly, the context of previous communications on the issue. Past communications provide a baseline for understanding the nuance and import of a given diplomatic statement.

This observation allows us to return to the question of twice-told histories in the Hittite historical prologues. Neither sovereign nor vassal had any expectation that these narratives would dutifully reflect history "as it really had been." All sides understood that these were exercises in diplomatic signaling. The Hittite kings "updated" the past to serve the needs of the moment. Crucially, however, to write new history here was expressly *not* a process of erasure. There was no desire to forget how the story had been told in earlier generations. Rather, the retention of the previous telling of the history was crucial, even as that history was rewritten. Diplomatic statements today can be construed properly only against the grid of what has been said previously on the issue. The same was true for the vassals as they read the historical narratives of the vassalage sent them by the Hittite kings. Only by accessing the previous version of the history between the two kings would the vassal fully grasp the nuance of the new version of those events and properly digest the diplomatic signaling inherent in the telling. The whole point of retelling the story is to highlight those differences, to make some comment to the current vassal about the nature of his own relationship with the sovereign here and now. Every change in nuance between the accounts was carefully measured.

To illustrate just how closely the parties read these correspondences and how much was at stake in even the simplest formulation, consider the following passage from one of the El Amarna letters I referred to earlier (EA 42). The communication is written by Suppiluliuma I of Hatti – the very same Hittite king who entered into a treaty with Aziru of Amurru – and responds to a letter he had received from the Egyptian king. Suppiluliuma takes umbrage with the formulation of a sentence in the pharaoh's letter in which the pharaoh's name appears above his own:

> As to the tablet that [you sent me], why [did you put] your name
> over my name? And who [now] is the one who upsets the good
> relations [between us], and is su[ch conduct] the accepted prac-
> tice? My brother, did you write [to me] with peace in mind? And
> if [you are my brother], why have you exalted [your name], while
> I, for [my part], am thou[ght of as] a [co]rpse?[12]

Suppiluliuma's letter demonstrates that when a king received a diplomatic document – sent by royal courier, carefully engraved by an offi-
cial scribe – he read it and interpreted it with the greatest of scrutiny.
In contemporary times, leaders converse nearly at will. In the Amarna
Age, by contrast, a king needed to weigh carefully the words that would
be inscribed in the correspondence, as letters could take weeks or even
months to transmit.

Across the rich record of documentation in our hands from the
period, we find kings expressing their displeasure with one another
over a host of issues. We never find, though, a vassal complaining that
the Hittite king's account of events was incorrect. This is the case even
when the Hittite king himself offered conflicting accounts of that history.
Both sides, I suggest, understood that the historical narrative offered
in the prologue was an exercise in diplomatic signaling and read it and
considered it on those lines only.

THE RETELLING OF HISTORY IN DEUTERONOMY

The dynamics of history writing in the Hittite treaty tradition can help
us make sense of the historical introduction of Deuteronomy. The sovereign king, God, looks to renew the treaty with his rebellious vassal,
Israel, as a new generation has supplanted the old. As noted, Deuteronomy is constructed along the lines of a treaty: historical prologue
(chs. 1–11), stipulations, or mitzvot (12–26), and witnesses and curses
at the end. Deuteronomy retells history in the fashion in which it is
retold in the vassal renewal treaties. The accounts of appointing judges,
of the spies, of the conquests of the area of the Transjordan are all told

---

12. EA 42: 15-24 translated in William L. Moran, ed., *The Amarna Letters* (Baltimore:
Johns Hopkins University Press, 1992), 115.

anew and given new agendas. Yet, this is not a process of erasure or denial of the earlier versions of those stories. We saw how a later king of Amurru could read the varying accounts of how his forefather, Aziru, had submitted to Suppiluliuma and note how those varying narratives reflected the nature of the bond between vassal and sovereign in each generation. Far from erasing the past and deceiving the servant kings, the Hittite kings intended the vassals to note the ways in which the history had been reworked. The changes that the vassal could plainly see for himself were to serve as an index of change in the sovereign king's disposition toward him.

So, too, we are to read the differing historical accounts in the earlier books of the Torah and in Deuteronomy. We, as the audience of the Torah, are descendants of the earliest vassal, the generation of the wilderness. We are meant to discern the unilaterally more critical depiction afforded Israel in the accounts of Deuteronomy. This reproachful thread is a signal that as the rebellious vassal Israel renewed her covenant on the plains of Moab, she was now on different terms with her sovereign Lord, Hashem. At Sinai, there had been hope that all would go well. After forty years, Israel had strained that relationship severely. The retold history of the period with its alterations and emphases communicates that idea emphatically.

At the outset of this chapter, I presented and critiqued both the harmonizing approach of the classical medieval exegetes and the source-critical approach of competing histories. I would like now to examine the relative strength of the approach presented here. By reading the historical accounts of Deuteronomy in the context of vassal treaty history telling, there is no longer any need to harmonize details. In fact, quite the opposite is so. The stories are retold precisely because the discrepancies are an index of change in God's disposition toward Israel following her faithlessness as a vassal in the desert.

The treaty history approach I have developed here has several advantages over the source-critical approach of mutually exclusive and competing histories. That approach had to explain the combination of purportedly contradicting histories together in the text of the Torah that we have received. It did so with recourse to a theory of anthology that has no ancient precedent. By contrast, the treaty history approach presented here is well attested in the vassal treaties and joins a long list of other elements shared between that tradition and the Torah.

The competing histories approach was at pains to explain why the author of Deuteronomy had nothing of his own to say about the patriarchs or the Exodus. For the treaty history approach, however, the choice of stories in Deuteronomy is clear. This is not a general history. It is strictly a history of the relationship between sovereign and vassal – God and Israel after Sinai – and hence covers the period of the wandering only.

The competing histories approach was at pains to explain why this extended retelling of stories is found only in the Torah, but not with regard to any other segment of Israel's history. The vassal treaty approach well explains this. The Hittite empire collapsed in the early twelfth century, and no remnant of its treaty formulae survived thereafter. Only the Torah, whose narrated time covers the Late Bronze Age (fifteenth–thirteenth century BCE), employs that literary model. Books written many centuries later would have been penned by authors who had no knowledge of this convention. In time, this phenomenon of conflicting accounts within a single work would be looked upon with embarrassment, as something that needed to be fixed.

Although most history in the Tanakh is reported through the voice of the authoritative, omniscient scribe, history in Deuteronomy is reported as an exhortation *to recall* what had happened "at that time" (Deut. 1:16, 18; 2:34; 3:4, 8, 12, 18, 21, 23). The competing histories approach offers no reason why its author would choose to vary from the norm and employ first-person narration. The vassal treaty approach well explains this. The narratological tone is highly similar to that which we encounter in the vassal treaties: the sovereign essentially mandates the vassal to recall events that putatively are known to both sides and to draw the appropriate lessons; he does so from his position of relative authority. In Deuteronomy, Moses does so as well, as the representative of the sovereign king, the Almighty.

Competing histories – as we find in Chronicles, in distinction from the accounts of Samuel/Kings – are normally composed with an ideological agenda in support of some group or institution. Yet the narratives of Deuteronomy seem to revolve around a single editorial line – greater criticism of Israel than is found in the earlier versions.[13] The competing histories approach is at pains to explain why no group or institution emerges at the focus of this reworking. By contrast, the vassal treaty approach well explains this. When the vassal has been unfaithful, we saw, the reworking of history reflects that. Episodes that once had been narrated in a relatively positive light now are retold with a more reproachful bent, reflecting the needs of the moment and the current state of the relationship between sovereign and vassal.

We noted that Deuteronomy calls upon its readers to access accounts that we find in the other books of the Torah, such as the reference to Caleb's exemption from divine wrath (Deut. 1:36), the sin of Baal Peor (4:3), God's anger at Aaron (9:20), and what befell Miriam (24:9). For the competing histories approach this presents a challenge: Why would the author of the new history call upon his audience to access and acknowledge what was in his mind a flawed version of history, one that needed to be replaced? For the vassal treaty approach this provides no challenge at all. The accounts in Deuteronomy are changed in many ways. But they do not supplant the earlier accounts. They only make sense if the reader is familiar with those earlier accounts. It is therefore eager to instruct the reader to reread those earlier accounts.

As I mentioned earlier in this chapter, I do not assume that all of Israel had an intimate understanding of diplomatic treaty formulations. My assumption is that the practice of retelling accounts in those treaties is a reflection of what was common practice: when an authority figure – a king in a treaty or a bard in a village – retells a story, his audience focuses on how the message had changed, and not on the strict factual nature of the claims.

We have proof for this from another set of texts, which have nothing to do with treaties and their prologues. In chapter 3 we examined at some length the Kadesh poem of Rameses II. While the Kadesh poem was the longest account that Rameses promulgated concerning the Battle of Kadesh, it was not the only one. In fact, at several sites across Egypt,

---

13. The exception to this is the recounting of the Revelation at Sinai in Deuteronomy 5, which is more laudatory of Israel than the parallel accounts of Exodus 19–24. On this point, see my *Inconsistency in the Torah*, 91–103, specifically p. 99.

Rameses charged his workers to carve three accounts of the battle. One was primarily poetic in form. Alongside that we find another, shorter account in prose. And alongside both of these we find a third account of that battle, the bas-reliefs with captions that we saw in chapter 3. The remarkable thing about these three accounts is that they are irreconcilable in their details. The battle unfolds differently in each in ways that are not easily harmonized. Yet when seen as agents of exhortation, they may be understood as complementing one another. Each account bears its own focus. The poem focuses on the salvation granted Rameses by his god Amun; the prose version of the story emphasizes Rameses's own valor in battle; the reliefs highlight the courage of a particular brigade in Rameses's chariotry corps. One cannot discern from these inscriptions a clear picture of the chronology of the Battle of Kadesh. But one can certainly discern the three lessons that Rameses wished to promulgate by having these three inscriptions carved at multiple sites across Egypt.[14]

SCHOLARSHIP AND LUCK

I should like to conclude with a note about biblical scholarship and plain luck. There is much that we know today about the ancient world. There is also much that we do not. How much we do not know is hard to say. The argument that I have made in this chapter concerning the hortatory nature of history telling in treaty literature highlights for me how far removed we are from ancient ways of thinking and writing, and how much luck played into developing these ideas.

Much of the material that forms the basis for this theory was recovered from the archives of the great palace at Hatti. Unlike most other major capitals of the ancient world, Hatti was never ransacked. The empire crumbled and was abandoned in the early twelfth century BCE amid drought and famine. That meant the archives were left largely intact, revealing a treasure trove for archaeologists and scholars 3,200 years later. That is good luck.

Most of the kingdoms of old that were situated in modern-day Syria have never been excavated. But in 1929, a farmer set his plow into the plateau at Ras Shamra overlooking the Syrian coast and accidentally

---

14. See further my analysis of these inscriptions in *Inconsistency in the Torah*, 19–34.

discovered the ancient kingdom of Ugarit. Much of the supporting material for this approach (which I did not bring here, but is available in my broader academic study) stems from those excavations. That is good luck.

Late Bronze-Age Hittite vassal treaties are an arcane field of study in which only a handful of scholars have major competence. But in 2004, the late Israeli historian Amnon Altman composed his magnum opus, a study of all of the historical prologues of these treaties, in comprehensive fashion.[15] That allowed me to engage these materials in a way that would not have been possible otherwise. That was my good luck.

Without the confluence of all three of these strokes of luck, the approach presented here would be hidden today. There is no way that a modern mind could possibly adduce such a theory without them. Scholarship aims to offer the best answers it can with what we know. When the answers provided seem strong and unimpeachable, that is a sound way to proceed. When the answers, however, are problematic, perhaps that is because there is so much that we still do not know. Methodological modesty mandates us to always keep that in mind.

In this chapter we addressed the issue of inconsistencies between stories in the Torah. But what are we to make of stories that bear repetition and inconsistencies within themselves? Perhaps the most glaring example of this is the Flood account of Genesis 6–9. Appreciating the Torah in its ancient context can give us insight into texts like this, and can raise questions about the validity of methods that source-critical scholars have engaged in analyzing them. To this we turn in the next chapter.

---

15. Amnon Altman, *The Historical Prologue of the Hittite Vassal Treaties* (Ramat Gan: Bar-Ilan University Press, 2004).

Chapter 5

Critiquing Source Criticism: The Story of the Flood

Narrative inconsistencies in the Torah are not limited to the discrepancies we find between the accounts of the book of Deuteronomy and the earlier books of the Torah. Indeed, they may be found throughout the Torah. Source critics often take these inconsistencies as signs of editing as they seek to recreate the history of the text's development. More than any other branch of biblical studies, it is this pursuit of the history of the composition of the biblical texts that has dominated the agenda of biblical studies for more than two centuries. The well-known hypothesis that the Torah constitutes the editing – or redaction – of four separate documents, pioneered in the mid-nineteenth century, is but one iteration of the source-critical approach. Many find source criticism satisfying because it strives to make sense out of passages that are difficult to understand. But how reliable is this type of inquiry? Increasingly, scholars are calling into question whether it is really possible to work back from a received text, such as the Tanakh, and recreate its prior stages of development without the help of any external corroborating evidence.[1]

Consider this: In biblical studies, scholars are faced with texts – the texts of the Tanakh – that are but copies of copies. Our earliest texts are those of the Dead Sea Scrolls from the first and second centuries BCE. But even these are clearly centuries removed from the original compositional dates of the biblical texts themselves. We have in our possession no "original" texts from the biblical period, nor even epigraphic finds from that period with which to assess the received text before us. Now, this situation is true as well of many other scholarly fields that focus on ancient texts, such as Assyriology, Egyptology, and Classics. In these disciplines, too, scholars oftentimes can study only copies of copies of very old texts, where the actual texts written by the authors themselves are no longer extant. Yet, today, it is in biblical studies alone that scholars remain convinced that they can reliably recreate the history of the texts' composition solely on the basis of the form of the texts before them. In the eighteenth and nineteenth centuries, for example, classicists believed that what appeared to them to be inconsistencies in Greek and Roman compositions could be the clues to retracing the compositional history of those texts. In the twentieth century, however, classicists largely gave up the task as lacking in rigor. The pursuit of the "prehistory" of the text on the basis of the received text before us – the Tanakh – remains widely practiced in biblical studies alone.

The parade example of the so-called achievements of this approach to the biblical text is found in the scholarship to the story of the Flood in Genesis 6–9. And yet it is precisely here that we can see all of the faults of the source-critical approach on display.[2]

---

1. See the collected essays in Raymond F. Person Jr. and Robert Rezetko, eds., *Empirical Models Challenging Biblical Criticism* (Atlanta: SBL Press, 2016).

2. The following is a summary account of the material I present in chapter 13, "Source Criticism and Its Biases; The Flood Account of Genesis 6–9," in *Inconsistency in the Torah: Ancient Literary Convention and the Limits of Source Criticism* (New York: Oxford University Press, 2017), 236–68.

A SOURCE-CRITICAL READING OF
NOAH AND ITS DIFFICULTIES

The attempt to separate the Flood story into two strands stems from seemingly reasonable observations. A linear or synchronic reading of this passage reveals many difficulties, as the Flood account seems riddled with doublets and inconsistencies. To recount the most significant of these, it alternates between two divine names, Hashem and Elokim. Some passages speak of a downpour lasting forty days and forty nights (Gen. 7:4, 12, 17a), while others speak of a cosmic deluge whose waters crest for 150 days (7:11, 24). One passage instructs Noah to gather a pair of every living creature (6:19–20), while another differentiates between clean animals, of which seven pairs are to be taken, and unclean animals, where a single pair of each will suffice (7:2–3). The source-critical solution to these and other similar inconsistencies and redundancies has been to identify within the account the interweaving of two versions of the story, usually referred to as the Priestly (or, simply, "P") and non-Priestly ("non-P") accounts. The strength of the approach is in its cumulative power, because the presence of so many details that coalesce so neatly along these lines suggests that what we see here is more than just a coincidence.[3] The devil, however, is in the details, and as we shall see, the theory yields to scrutiny on eight points of methodology.

1. A double standard for determining doublets

The great appeal of the source-critical approach was that it supposedly produced two accounts of the Flood that would read cleanly, without the repetitions and doublets that seem to plague a reading of the full Genesis text. However, neither the proposed P text nor the proposed non-P text achieves this. Consider that within the non-P account we find the following reconstruction of our Genesis text: "(7:12) And the rain was upon the earth forty days and forty nights. (7:16b) And God

---

3. See the synoptic table of these parallels in David M. Carr, *Reading the Fractures of Genesis: Historical and Literary Approaches* (Louisville, KY: Westminster John Knox, 1996), 52–55. For a color-schemed breakdown of the Genesis Flood account along the lines of the proposed P and non-P accounts, see "A Textual Study of Noah's Flood," https://thetorah.com/textual-study-of-noahs-flood/.

sealed him therein. (7:17) And the deluge was forty days upon the earth, and the waters increased and lifted the ark so that it rose above the earth." The note in verse 17a that the deluge was forty days long is glaringly superfluous following the exact same claim two verses earlier in the non-P version.

The fact that source critics are willing to overlook this doublet and others like it calls into question the criterion of doubling that is the basis for the hypothesis of two strands. The criterion does not seem to be applied rigorously and consistently. Rather, it seems that source critics see doublets when these will fit into the procrustean bed of two separate sources, but overlook doublets when they remain within the hypothesized versions.

2. Creating false doublets

Further, the two-source theory is foisted upon the text; it produces dichotomies and doublets that are of its own creation and not inherent in the text. One such "imaginary" difficulty and contrived doublet concerns the source of the deluge. For source critics, the P version claims that God allowed the waters of the depths and the heavens to flood the earth (Gen. 7:11; 8:2) whereas the non-P source maintains that the deluge was rainfall (7:4, 12; 8:2).[4] The difference and distinction between the two founts of the deluge are presented as if they are mutually exclusive.

Logically, of course, there is no reason why the deluge could not have emanated from both rainclouds and heavenly and earthly wellsprings. There is no contradiction between the two. Moreover, the notion of divine deluge stemming from these two sources is a common trope. In fact, consider the sources of the deluge in the Mesopotamian account of the flood story, which is caused both by rainfall and opened dikes:

> I gazed upon the appearance of the *storm,*
> The *storm* was frightful to behold! ...
> A black cloud rose up from the horizon,
> Inside [the cloud] Adad was thundering ...

---

4. See, e.g., Carr, *Reading the Fractures*, 52–55.

Erregal tore out the *dike* posts,
Ninurta came and brought with him the *dikes*.[5]

Divine deluges that stem from both from cloud rain and from the well-springs of the earth are a familiar trope in the Tanakh (Ps. 77:17–18; Prov. 3:20). Moreover, the Genesis Flood account mentions these two founts together in two places (Gen. 7:11–12; 8.2). However, were source critics to adopt a reading whereby the Genesis Flood derived both from cloud rain and from other wellsprings together, it would no longer be possible to bisect the text into two accounts. Source critics *must* ignore the attested trope in the Mesopotamian version of the flood story and the other biblical sources of divine deluge from rain and from other wellsprings, so that each of the putative versions of the story will have a flood unto itself. When critics separate the founts of the deluge, they do so not because the theory solves a problem in the text; rather a problem in the theory gives rise to an unnecessary and forced distinction in the text.

3. Irrational non-sequiturs in the putative sources

In addition to creating unnecessary and unwarranted dichotomies, the source-critical reading also produces non-sequiturs in the putative sources that it claims to recover. Consider the Masoretic Text's version of Genesis 7:15–16: "[The animals] came unto Noah, unto the ark, two by two, from all of the living creatures. They were male and female of all creatures, as Elokim had commanded him. And Hashem closed him in."[6] The final phrase of verse 16, "And Hashem closed him in," follows directly from the previous elements in verses 13–16. Noah and his family enter the ark, the animals enter the ark, and, to conclude, Hashem "shuts the hatch" as it were, and closes Noah in. However, in the putative non-P source, the following text is hypothesized: "(7:10) And after seven days, the waters of the deluge were on the earth. (7:12) The rain was on

---

5. Tablet XI of the Gilgamesh Epic (XI:98–103). Translated by Benjamin Foster in William Hallo, *Context of Scripture*, vol. 1 (Leiden, Netherlands: Brill, 2003), 459.

6. Elsewhere in this book, I have translated the divine names into accepted English equivalents. However, because source-critical approaches to this story have placed such a great emphasis on the so-called "names" of God, I have rendered these here according to colloquial Hebrew pronunciation.

the earth forty days and forty nights (7:16b) and Hashem shut him in." Source critics splice the text in this fashion because verse 16b refers to God as Hashem, and thus must be assigned to the non-P source, which they reckon refers to God exclusively as Hashem. However, this reading is deficient on two grounds. In the first place, it creates a non-sequitur as it implies that it had been raining already for forty days and forty nights *before* God enclosed the ark![7] Secondly, it removes verse 16b, the notice of God shutting in Noah, from the simple context of the verses in which it is organically found in the Genesis text, following the embarking of Noah, his family, and the animals.

4. Hiding problems with the theory in the work of the "redactor"

Other seemingly needless repetitions abound in the Flood narrative, such as the extended repeated report of Noah's entry into the ark in the hypothesized P version (Gen. 7:8–9, 11, 13–16). Difficulties such as the unnecessary and juxtaposed repetition of the duration of the rain in non-P, and the wholesale repetition of the boarding of the ark in hypothesized P, might have been the types of literary phenomena that could have called into question the very suggestion that we have here two conflated sources. Splitting the text clearly does *not* provide us with two accounts, each free of repetition and free of incongruities. And yet rather than walking back from the hypothesis, source critics have sought to buttress their hypothesis by resorting to a series of redactors, who are the agents responsible for the disruptive passages.

The recourse to redactors and the claims that various words and verses are later additions are made solely so that scholars will be able to preserve the integrity of the two sources, purportedly identified in the remaining verses of the narrative.[8] The strategy is reductive in that

---

7. Note that the *vayiktol* form of the verb, *vayisgor*, cannot have the connotation of the past perfect, "had closed in."

8. Similar "quarantining" of bad data by assigning it to a redactor is exhibited in Genesis 7:8–9. Verse 7:2 speaks of a distinction between clean and unclean animals, a distinction which source critics believe is exclusive to the non-P source. However, the narrative of 7:8–9 speaks of pairs of animals boarding the ark, in accordance with the verses assigned to the P source (cf. 6:20). It is unclear therefore how clean and unclean animals (as per the non-P source) and pairs of animals (as per the P source) can be combined in these verses.

it ensures that the underlying premise of two sources will always be preserved. For the source critic, data that complicates the split into two sources is not allowed to undermine the theory. Instead, "bad" data – data that are incongruous with the two-source theory – are isolated from the "good" data, and are assigned to redactors, often with no explanation as to why a redactor would add such sloppiness to the text. The theory of two sources is thus always sustained. The source critical approach takes as axiomatic that the scholar has the full capacity to determine the text's compositional history. This strategy of the textual "quarantine" of inconvenient passages and assigning them to later hands empowers scholars to propose a clean history of the text's composition. However, it would be methodologically more prudent to arrive at the sober conclusion that, in fact, the "bad data" complicates our capacity to account for the present shape of the text.

5. The mistaken presumption of preserved sources

The source-critical approach rests on the foundational assumption that the biblical redactors faithfully preserved their sources and that these sources, therefore, can be recreated by properly analyzing the received, redacted version we have today. However, this assumption is challenged both by contradictions within the source-critical approach itself and by the evidence we now have of editorial practices of scribes in ancient Israel and in the ancient Near East.

The source-critical approach rests on an internal contradiction in its claims. Source criticism does not produce two complete stand-alone accounts of the Flood when the fourteen snippets of hypothesized P and the thirteen snippets of non-P are separated and reconstructed. The P account may be considered a full account, but not so the non-P account, where two omissions are notable: First, it lacks a command to build an ark. Moreover, the non-P account does not report the exit from the ark by Noah and the animals. Source critics are forced to concede that the final redactor does *not* retain full fidelity to the putative original version of this account but has borrowed from it selectively. Source critics claim that material from an original source may be missing, but what is preserved is derived *word for word* from the original source and can be recovered. Yet, if, as we have seen, the redactor could violate the integral nature of the original version by omitting sections of it, by what right may we assume that he has not supplemented and otherwise altered other phrases in his creation of the final version of the text before us?

Source critics retort that the redactors sought to conflate the original sources as fully as possible so as to create a relatively seamless whole and tried to tamper with the original text as little as possible. But the very repetitions and inconsistencies noted by source critics in the biblical text before us undermine that claim. For their theory to account for the unevenness of the Flood narrative as found in Genesis 6–9, source critics must uphold three claims: (1) that the redactor worked tirelessly to disassemble the original sources and then conflate them, combining a total of twenty-seven snippets, some no longer than a phrase; (2) that the redactor freely omitted material from the non-P source, and yet with no clear explanation of why he would or could do so; (3) that in the end the redactor(s) had free reign to tamper with the text, and yet performed his (their) task in sloppy fashion, or that later accretions are responsible for the unevenness seen in passages such as the accounts of Noah's embarking the ark, discussed earlier. Had both versions been fully preserved, perhaps one could believe that the redactor's need to preserve the wording of both texts in their entirety leads in the end to unevenness in the text. But source critics freely admit that material from non-P is missing in the final version.[9]

The stakes here for the field of critical biblical studies are enormous. The very enterprise of tracing the history of composition of the biblical texts rests on the assumption that the earlier sources are recoverable solely on the basis of the so-called clues and evidence within the received text, and without supporting textual witnesses or epigraphic evidence. But those putative sources are available only if we assume that redactors and editors never altered or augmented their sources. Were

---

9. Other versions of the source-critical approach to the story see the non P version as a later accretion to the earlier P text, claiming that this accretion did not comprise a complete version of the story; however, they are at a loss to explain why the editor who added these accretions would do so for some parts of the story and not others. See, e.g., the discussion in Jean-Louis Ska, "The Story of the Flood: A Priestly Writer and Some Later Editorial Fragments," in *The Exegesis of the Pentateuch: Exegetical Studies and Basic Questions* (Tübingen, Germany: Mohr-Siebeck, 2009), 1–22.

source critics to concede the possibility that earlier sources had under-
gone alteration or augmentation, their concession would effectively shut
down the quest for the compositional history of the text; it would no
longer be possible to work backward from the received text and to iso-
late the earlier source texts. Scholars committed to tracing the history
of the text, therefore, have a vested interest in upholding the axiom that
original sources were neither altered nor augmented during redaction.

Source critics, however, are additionally challenged to demonstrate that the original sources have been preserved word for word
in light of what we now know about compositional practices in the
ancient Near East. Recent scholarship has amply demonstrated that
when ancient writers edited and redacted hallowed texts, they did *not*
display fidelity to their original texts as they incorporated them into new
creations. There is not a single documented case of this either within
biblical literature or outside of it. Consider, for example, the work of
the author(s) of the book of Chronicles. It is clear that this author
composed the book of Chronicles by drawing heavily on the history of
the divided kingdoms found in the book of Kings. And yet even when
the account found in Chronicles closely matches that found in Kings,
it is never identical, and often displays great variation. The author of
Chronicles clearly feels himself free to add or delete or otherwise alter
entire passages that he found in the earlier text of the book of Kings.
This dramatically weakens the claim of source critics that based on the
text before us alone they can confidently recreate what the earlier versions of the story looked like.

Only in the postbiblical period do we find something akin to what
source critics propose. As we saw in the previous chapter, in the second
century CE, employing Greek notions of literary unity unknown in the
ancient Near East, the church father Tatian sought to harmonize the
four books of the Gospels. He culled verses from all four and created a
composite narrative of the life of Jesus of Nazareth. But this example is
telling: its author produced a composition that bears virtually no inconsistencies – that was the very purpose of the exercise in the first place.
By contrast, the Torah, if source critics are to be believed, represents
the work of a redactor who leaves contradictions in his work in great
quantity and with great conspicuousness.

To highlight the futility of the search for the compositional history of biblical texts consider the following challenge: Take half of the book of Chronicles and subject it to a careful analysis vis-à-vis its source in Samuel and Kings. On the basis of the evidence, adduce a literary algorithm that explains what the author of Chronicles does to the texts of Samuel and Kings to produce what we see in the first half of the book of Chronicles. This literary algorithm will tell us how that author systematically adopts or adapts, adds or deletes material relative to the sources of Samuel and Kings. Now move to the second half of Chronicles and apply the algorithm to the second half of the book. Based on that algorithm, can you now faithfully recreate the corresponding sections of the book of Kings? You cannot. In fact, no scholar has ever attempted – let alone succeeded in – doing so.[10] It is unclear, then, why scholars should have confidence that they can indeed recreate the earlier forms of any biblical text in the absence of corroborating epigraphic evidence.[11]

---

10. One of the Dead Sea Scrolls, known as the Temple Scroll, rewrites many passages of the Torah in a fashion similar to the way the book of Chronicles rewrites Samuel and Kings. In an oft-cited article, Stephen A. Kaufman ("Temple Scroll and Higher Criticism," *Hebrew Union College Annual* 53 [1982]: 29–52) says that he began to try to do an experiment with the Temple Scroll and the Torah similar to the one I have outlined here, eventually discovering that it was "a consummately fruitless endeavor" (p. 29).

11. A further methodological flaw of source criticism is worthy of note here. Source critics believe that simply by looking at the text they can identify the inconsistencies and fissures that are the keys to recovering and recreating the putative sources of the Torah. They assume that our notions of literary unity and what constitutes an inconsistency in the text are universal and obvious. But they are not. Consider the biblical criticism of one of Islam's most celebrated theologians, Ibn Hazm the Andalusian, who lived in Cordoba in the eleventh century. He hated Jews and hated Judaism, writing a one-hundred-page critique of Genesis in which he demonstrated that it could not possibly have been written by Moses alone and must have had multiple authors, owing to all of the inconsistencies in it. Although Ibn Hazm identifies many of the inconsistencies flagged by modern scholars, repetitions do not bother him in the least. Two accounts of Creation, two times Noah boards the ark, etc. these are textual phenomena that Ibn Hazm never flags as signs of multiple authorship. It is no coincidence; medieval Islamic literature revels and delights in repetitions of all sorts. From this we can clearly see that canons of literary unity are not universal but culturally dependent. Our modern, Western notions of consistency are actually those of Aristotle. Can we be certain that the authors of biblical Israel shared our Aristotelian notions of what a consistent text looks like? Put differently, the burden

6. Disregard for Mesopotamian parallels

The source-critical approach to the Flood narrative is also challenged by the fact that the Genesis version of the Flood story hews closely to the plotline of its Mesopotamian parallel.[12] Scholars have highlighted the common plot structure found both in Genesis 6–9 and in the Mesopotamian flood account of Tablet XI of the Gilgamesh Epic.[13] They identify seventeen plot elements common to both, which appear in precisely the same order in both traditions:

	Motif	Genesis Flood Account	Gilgamesh Tablet XI
1	Divine decision to destroy mankind	6:6	ll. 14–19
2	Warning to the flood hero	6:13	ll. 20–23
3	Divine command to build ark with dimensions	6:14–21	ll. 24–31
4	Hero complies with command	6:22	ll. 3–85
5	Command to board the ark	7:1–4	ll. 86–88
6	Hero boards the ark with family and animals	7:5–16	ll. 89–93
7	Closing the door of the ark	7:16	l. 93
8	Description of the flood	7:17–24	ll. 96–128
9	Destruction of life	7:21–23	l. 133
10	End of rain, etc.	8:2–3	ll. 129–131

---

of proof falls upon source critics to demonstrate that they truly bear all of the keys necessary to identify inconsistencies in the ancient text. For more, see my "The Biblical Criticism of Ibn Hazm the Andalusian: A Medieval Control for Modern Diachronic Method," *Journal of Biblical Literature* 138, no. 2 (2019): 377–90.

12. See above, p. 11, where we saw that Rabbi Abraham Isaac HaKohen Kook embraced the existence of ancient Near Eastern versions of the Flood story similar to that found in the book of Genesis.

13. Gordon J. Wenham, "The Coherence of the Flood Narrative," *Vetus Testamentum* 28 (1978): 346–47; cf. Gary A. Rendsburg, "The Biblical Flood Story in Light of the Gilgamesh Flood Account," in *Gilgamesh and the World of Assyria*, ed. Joseph Azize and Noel Weeks (Leuven, Belgium: Peeters, 2007), 115–27.

	Motif	Genesis Flood Account	Gilgamesh Tablet XI
11	Ark grounding on mountain	8:4	ll. 140–144
12	Hero opens window	8:6	l. 135
13	Reconnaissance of the dove and raven	8:6–12	ll. 145–154
14	Hero exits ark	8:15–19	l. 155
15	Hero offers sacrifices	8:20	ll. 155–158
16	Divinity smells sacrifices	8:21–22	ll. 159–161
17	Divinity blesses flood hero	9:1 ff	ll. 189–96

The broad similarity in plot is unmistakable. Neither of the two hypothesized sources, P and non-P, comes close to having all of the plot elements that are shared in sequence by Genesis 6–9 (Masoretic Text) and Tablet XI of the Gilgamesh Epic. If the two-source theory is correct then, following one scholar, "we are supposed to believe that two separate authors wrote two separate accounts of Noah and the Flood, and that neither of them included all the elements found in the Gilgamesh Epic, but that when the two were interwoven by the redactor, *voila*, the story paralleled the Gilgamesh flood story point by point."[14] How is it that there are six elements in the Epic absent from hypothesized P that just happen to be present in hypothesized non-P?[15] The coincidence here is too great.

The conclusion from this should be clear. Rather than claiming that the Genesis Flood account represents the redaction of two preexisting sources, we should maintain that the Torah's account represents a significant reworking of a well-known Mesopotamian template, but now in accordance with the Torah's ideology. The Mesopotamian flood traditions maintain that the gods annihilated mankind because overpopulation of

---

14. Rendsburg, "Biblical Flood Story," 116.
15. Likewise, the account of the recreation of the world in the second half of the Flood story (Gen. 8:1–9:17) follows, step by step, the account of the seven days of creation in Genesis 1. But this pattern emerges only when the Masoretic Text's Flood story is read as a whole. See further in my *Inconsistency in the Torah*, 255–60.

the world resulted in excessive noise that disturbed their sleep. The Torah maintains that God annihilated mankind because of corrupt behavior. The Mesopotamian traditions conclude the story of the flood with a series of divine decrees designed to limit mankind's reproductive capacity. The Torah's Flood story ends with a ringing endorsement of the value of every human life: a call to be fruitful and multiply and to fill the earth (Gen. 9:1).[16]

By contrast, the source-critical approach to the Genesis Flood account cannot allow that the Genesis text hews closely to the plot of the flood tale in Tablet XI of the Gilgamesh Epic. For if this is allowed, then the source-critical approach is delegitimated, because this pattern requires one to read the final form of the account and not its putative sources.

There is another telling pattern that emerges from the Masoretic Text's version of the Flood account that is worth mentioning at this point. The Flood account of Genesis 6–9, for all of its repetitions, forms an elaborate chiastic structure (see next page).

There are several aspects of this structure that are worthy of note. Note that it centers around Genesis 8:1: "And God remembered Noah and all of the animals that were with him in the ark." This is the turning point of the story. All that precedes this verse is death and destruction. All that follows is rebirth and recreation. It is exactly the verse we would expect to find right in the middle of the structure. We ought to note as well that this is an extremely tight and elaborate structure. By "tight," I mean that it has no major gaps anywhere in the three chapters it covers. By "elaborate," I mean that it covers matching pairs of seventeen motifs and elements. But most significant is this: Every matching pair is much more than a deliberate repetition. Rather, each pair is a report of an event of destruction and its matching event of recreation. Thus element A is a divine pledge to destroy all flesh, while A' is a divine pledge to preserve all flesh; element B tells that the Flood will destroy all flesh, while B' tells that never again will a flood destroy all flesh, etc. This structure is found only when the entire Flood account of Genesis 6–9 is read in order.

---

16. These insights are found in Tikva Frymer-Kensky, "What the Babylonian Flood Stories Can and Cannot Teach Us About the Genesis Flood," *Biblical Archaeological Review* 4, no. 4 (1978): 32–41, available online at http://cojs.org/what-the-babylonian-flood-stories-can-and-cannot-teach-us-about-the-genesis-flood/.

A. Elokim pledges to Noah to destroy all flesh (6:13)
  B. Flood to destroy all flesh (6:17)
    C. Covenant to sustain Noah and his animals (6:18–20)
      D. Command to gather food while world is destroyed (6:21)
        E. Command to enter the ark + fulfillment (7:1–5)
          F. Year 600 – beginning of the Flood (7:6)
            G. Birds enter the ark (7:8)
              H. Seven days waiting for Flood (7:10)
                I. Rain on the earth (7:12)
                  J. Birds enter the ark (7:14)
                    K. Hashem shuts Noah in (7:16)
                      L. Forty days of Flood (7:17a)
                        M. Waters increase (7:17b–18)
                          N. Mountains covered (7:19–20)
                            O. 150 days when waters prevail (7:24)
                            God remembers Noah (8:1)
                          O'. 150 days when waters abate (8:3)
                        N'. Mountaintops visible (8:4–5)
                    M'. Waters abate (8:5)
                  L'. Forty days of receding waters (8:6a)
                K'. Noah opens window of ark (8:6b)
              J'. Raven and dove leave ark (8:7–8)
            I'. Water on the earth (8:9)
          H'. Seven days waiting for water to subside (8:10)
        G'. Dove leaves the ark (8:10b–12)
      F'. Year 601 – the earth dries (8:13)
    E'. Command to leave the ark + fulfillment (8:15–19)
    D'. Commands regarding food in the new order (9:1–5)
  C'. Covenant to sustain all flesh (9:8–10)
  B'. No flood will destroy flesh (9:15)
A'. Elokim pledges to Noah to preserve all flesh (9:17)

7. A theory that creates the text, instead of the text creating the theory

Another critique of the source-critical method concerns the relationship between theory and text: Should theory stem from the textual data? Or should theory dictate how to split up the text? An illustration will clarify the question. The impetus to separate the Genesis Flood account into two strands stemmed from the difficulties the received text presents us. At its best, from an academic perspective, the theory of two versions stems *from* the text and the difficulties it presents. It is indisputable that the source-critical approach to the Flood story well accounts for several of these irregularities, such as the seemingly conflicting numbers of animals to be rescued on the ark (cf. Gen. 6:19–20; 7:2–3) and the repeated narrations of Noah's entry into the ark (cf. 7:7; 7:13). Indeed, in a scientific inquiry the data should drive the theory; when scholars point to difficulties in the text and adduce a theory of sources to explain those difficulties, they are remaining loyal to this axiom.

However, the source-critical approach to the Genesis Flood narrative violates this principle at several junctures, when it takes the theory as a given, and uses it – perhaps *abuses* it would be a better word – to recreate the text, when the received text itself is entirely unproblematic. Consider the source-critical approaches to Genesis 6:7: "The Lord said, 'I will blot out from the earth man whom I created, from man to the beasts to the creeping things to the birds of the sky, for I regret that I made them.'" The verse itself is coherent and clear. It functions well as a whole: man is the pinnacle and raison d'être of the universe. If man is to be destroyed there is no point in sustaining the world created for his benefit. Indeed, the fate of all of creation is linked to that of man elsewhere in the Flood account as well (Gen. 8:1, 21; 9:15). There would appear to be no reason to aggressively bisect this verse, assigning parts of it to one source and parts of it to another. And yet this is what critics have increasingly proposed.[17] For these scholars, the words "from man to the beasts to the creeping things to the birds of the sky" are a later

---

17. See, e.g., Carr, *Reading the Fractures*, 57; Ska, "The Story of the Flood."

insertion of P language from Genesis 1 into the original form of Genesis 6:7. But why do source critics propose this, if there is no repetition or inconsistency in the verse as it stands?

Source-critical scholars realize that lining up seeming doublets and contradictions in parallel columns is insufficient. There must be a fundamental ideological divide between the two accounts that justifies their original composition and preservation as distinct traditions. It is inconceivable that two ancient communities within Israel would preserve two separate accounts of the Flood if the differences between them were purely a question of a few random details here and there. One of the greatest ideological dividing lines that scholars try to wedge between the two hypothesized versions of the Flood concerns the scope of God's wrath. For source critics, the P version maintains that God wished to destroy all that He had created, while non-P maintained that God wished to annihilate man alone. Moreover, the P version should, ideally, resonate with and echo the language of the account of Creation in Genesis 1, which they consider a P text. But this ideological divide is entirely dependent on splicing the verse in question, Genesis 6:7. The received version of the verse does not square with the ideological wedge that source critics hypothesize. Verse 6:7 is found in the midst of the hypothesized non-P version's introduction to the Flood story. And yet, the verse calls for the destruction of all of Creation – supposedly P's ideology – and even invokes the language of the fifth and sixth days ("from man to the beasts to the creeping things to the birds of the sky") from the account of Creation of chapter 1, theorized to be a P chapter. If the entire verse is retained as emanating from hypothesized non-P, a major ideological divide between the two versions is itself "blotted out," as it were. This would represent a challenge to the source-critical theory, for it would eviscerate the ideological distinction between the two versions, calling into question why two separate versions had been maintained in the first place. It would also challenge the accepted view that the account of Creation in Genesis 1 is the exclusive purview of the P source. Excising the catalog of animals from Genesis 6:7 secures for the source critic the ideological wedge that he or she needs to legitimate the presence and ideological distinction of the two sources. Note well: here there is no difficulty in the text that gives rise to the theory; rather a difficulty in the theory is then read back into the received text, whose words must now be reassigned in a manner that will conform to the source-critical theory. Critics could have read Genesis 6:7 and concluded that there is no great ideological divide between the two sources, though that would have undercut the very argument for their existence. By positing the catalog of animals in Genesis 6:7 as an insertion of P language by a late editor into a non-P text, critics choose the one path that will preserve the paradigm of the source-critical approach: that there are two separate sources interwoven in the text. The damning evidence of so-called P terminology square in the middle of a so-called non-P passage is not allowed to undercut the hypothesis. Rather, it is "quarantined" under the guise of editorial insertion, and disallowed rhetorical and hortatory contact with the rest of the passage, lest it contaminate that source's hypothesized ideological purity and distinction from the P source. And thus a perfectly coherent verse is aggressively torn asunder. The needs of the theory – wrongly – are allowed to determine the text.

8. A foundational epistemological error

My final critique of the source-critical approach concerns an epistemological fallacy – that is, a fallacy about what constitutes a justified belief – that has long dominated compositional theory of the Torah in general and scholarship on the Flood story in particular. Consider the following comment by one scholar in a widely cited study defending the source-critical approach to the Flood narrative and the difficulties found in that text: "If a scholar thinks he can advance a better, or even an equally satisfactory, explanation, then he may offer it as an improvement on, or substitute for, the hypothesis of a redactor (and if he cannot, he had better refrain from finding fault with it)."[18] Let us focus attention on the parenthetical statement at the end of this citation. For this scholar, the source-critical approach provides us with a reasonable solution for many of the problems raised by a synchronic reading of the text. He believes, however, that scholars may challenge this approach only if they believe they have "a better, or even an equally satisfactory, explanation." For this

---

18. John Emerton, "An Examination of Some Attempts to Defend the Unity of the Flood Narrative in Genesis: Part I," *Vetus Testamentum* 37 (1987): 402.

scholar, we *must* adopt a hypothesis to account for the growth of the text. Note well, however, that the source-critical approach is measured only against other alternative hypotheses. For this scholar, if source criticism offers a fuller explanation of the data than any other theory, we do not subject it to scrutiny on its own terms. There is no possibility of delegitimizing the source-critical approach unless and until we propose an alternative hypothesis to account for the data that is more compelling. This, I would maintain, is a profound methodological flaw. Epistemologically, this writer – and with him most source critics – assumes that scholars have the keys to unlock the difficulties of the text. All that we must do is choose between the competing hypotheses offered to explain the difficulties within the text. For source critics, there does not seem to be an option of maintaining that the compositional history of the text might be beyond our reach.

The possibility that our understanding of the prehistory of the text may be partial at best is not entertained. Methodological rigor, however, demands that a hypothesis must withstand scrutiny and stand on its own, regardless of whether competing hypotheses fare worse. It may well be that the hypothesis of two sources explains more textual data than any other scholarly hypothesis available to us today. The two-source hypothesis, however, should be rejected entirely on academic grounds, because it collapses under the weight of its own deficiencies, eight of which I have identified here.

Additionally, source critics differ on a wide array of questions about the compositional history of the Flood story. They differ on the question of whether to assign certain troubling verses or even phrases to the P or non-P strand; they differ on whether the non-P strand should be considered part of a larger non-P source that runs throughout the narrative of the Torah; they differ as to the chronological priority of one strand over the other; they differ as to whether the two versions have been redacted together, or whether one is derived from the other. Remarkably, though, source critics are nearly unanimous in their belief that scholars possess the tools to offer a complete accounting of the history of the text. Nearly all source-critical analyses of the Genesis Flood narrative account for all of the verses found in Genesis 6–9. The analyses are total in nature. We might have expected that more source-critical scholars would leave chunks of the passage as unresolved problems, or as passages whose provenance is unclear. The fact that source critics differ with one another on a variety of issues but claim nearly unanimously that the entire textual puzzle may be solved speaks volumes to the overconfident epistemology that undergirds the source-critical approach.[19]

This chapter, like the one before it, highlights the necessity of examining the literary conventions of the Torah in light of those of the ancient Near East. The eighteenth and nineteenth century scholars who invented source criticism did so with no recourse to the writings of the ancient Near East, because these were unknown until the late nineteenth century. Perforce, they examined the text of the Tanakh with the only notions of literary unity they knew – their own. But findings such as the Gilgamesh Epic and the discovery of chiastic structure in a wide array of ancient texts open our eyes to the realization that we read texts from within the fishbowl of our own literary assumptions. These ancient resources demand of us intellectual modesty. They demand of us that before we pass judgment on a text, we had better first check our own assumptions and do all we can to master the thought and writing of ancient writers, so as to read the text as best as we can within the literary canons of ancient times rather than our own.

These last two chapters have shown us the dramatic new insights that we can gain into what seemed like contradictions in the narrative portions of the Torah. But this lens affords us insights no less dramatic into the seeming contradictions within the Torah's laws, to which we turn in the next chapter.

---

19. Elsewhere I trace the ways in which the Enlightenment, German Historicism, Romanticism, and, more recently, Liberalism have corrupted the scientific pursuit of biblical study. See in long form, chapter 11 of my *Inconsistency in the Torah*, "A Critical Intellectual History of the Historical-Critical Paradigm in Biblical Studies," 201–226, and online in abbreviated essay form, "The Corruption of Biblical Studies," *Mosaic*, https://mosaicmagazine.com/essay/2017/07/the-corruption-of-biblical-studies/.

Chapter 6

Legal Inconsistencies: The Book of Deuteronomy and the Rest of the Torah

I turn now to the vexing question of the seeming discrepancies between laws in the Torah. My focus here will be on the mitzvot found in the book of Deuteronomy, where many commandments given earlier in the Torah are repeated; as we shall see, sometimes they are repeated in ways that seem incommensurate with the earlier versions of the mitzva elsewhere in the Torah.[1]

I discuss the issue here with the same methodological suppositions that governed my analysis of seeming contradictions in the Torah's narratives: in order to understand how the Torah coheres as a unified whole, we must identify and shed the anachronistic assumptions that

---

1. This chapter is a summary presentation of my discussion of law in the Torah and in the ancient Near East as found in my *Inconsistency in the Torah: Ancient Literary Convention and the Limits of Source Criticism* (New York: Oxford University Press, 2017), 107–200.

we bring to our reading of the Torah. Moreover, we must recapture the modes of thinking and writing that were prevalent in the ancient world. Only by reading the *peshat* of the Torah in its ancient Near Eastern context, as its first audience understood it, can we hope to grasp its message. Here, too, the questions cannot be satisfactorily explained in a few short paragraphs. I therefore offer up front a sense of where I am going in the argument that follows.

First, I will survey the approaches within rabbinic sources to the questions of legal discrepancies between the book of Deuteronomy and the other books. Here I will also address why many people do not find these approaches satisfying. I will then present the source-critical approach to the issue, and note the problems inherent in that approach from within its own frames of reference – from an *academic* perspective.

In the second part of the discussion, I will claim that we today use the word "law" and think of legal texts in ways that are distinctly modern. These highly intuitive ways of thinking about law and legal texts are anachronistic when applied to "law" and "legal texts" in the ancient Near East and in the Torah. Here I will examine legal writings from the ancient Near East and recapture what the word "law" meant back then, and how people wrote and understood "legal texts."

From there, I will move to law in the Tanakh generally. Using ancient legal writings as a guide, I will delve into the ways in which laws shifted within the biblical texts and the evolution of halakhic interpretation over time. We will see provocative comments made by the Netziv (Rabbi Naftali Tzvi Yehuda Berlin, 1816–1893) about the fluid and changing nature of halakha and, looking specifically at the Deuteronomic law's divergences from the other Pentateuchal books, reach conclusions that were already anticipated in the writing of Rabbi Tzadok HaKohen Rabinowitz of Lublin (1823–1900).

Finally, I will discuss the implications of this understanding of the fluidity of legal practice in biblical times for an understanding of halakha as we practice it today. Fluidity and change in halakha are very threatening propositions today, and for good reason. But it is important to understand how and why the halakha evolved from a more fluid system to one that is more resistive of change, and the concepts developed in this chapter help us understand this evolution in how halakha works.

A Signature Example of the Problem: The Law of
the Firstborn Animal – Ḥazal's Approaches

To illustrate the problem at hand, I will turn to one specific biblical case: the mandate to dedicate and sanctify the firstborn animal. This mitzva appears in several places in the Torah and is one of the clearest examples of how irreconcilable two formulations of a mitzva can be when read on the level of *peshat*.

In Numbers 18:14–18, God addresses Aaron and issues the following promise to him and his descendants, the *kohanim*:

> Every devoted thing in Israel shall be yours. The first issue of the womb of all creatures, human and animal, which is offered to the Lord, shall be yours; but the firstborn of human beings you shall redeem, and the firstborn of unclean animals you shall redeem. Their redemption price, reckoned from one month of age, you shall fix at five shekels of silver, according to the shekel of the Sanctuary (that is, twenty gerahs). But the firstborn of a cow, or the firstborn of a sheep, or the firstborn of a goat, you shall not redeem; they are holy. You shall dash their blood on the altar, and shall turn their fat into smoke as an offering by fire for a pleasing odor to the Lord; but their flesh shall be yours, just as the breast that is elevated and as the right thigh are yours.

Note that here the flesh of the firstborn kosher animal is expressly given over to the *kohen*, and is considered as much his as the other priestly entitlements (*matnot kehuna*) enumerated in the opening chapters of Leviticus (Num. 18:18). The *kohen* is called upon to dash the blood on the altar (18:17). Because these animals have *Kedusha*, sanctity, it would be expressly forbidden for a *Yisrael* to partake of them. Compare this, however, with what the Torah says on the subject in Deuteronomy 15:19–23:

> Every firstling male born of your herd and flock you shall consecrate to the Lord your God; you shall not do work with your firstling ox nor shear the firstling of your flock. You shall eat it,

> you together with your household, in the presence of the Lord
> your God year by year at the place that the Lord will choose. But
> if it has any defect – any serious defect, such as lameness or blind-
> ness – you shall not sacrifice it to the Lord your God; within
> your towns you may eat it, the unclean and the clean alike, as
> you would a gazelle or deer. Its blood, however, you must not
> eat; you shall pour it out on the ground like water.

Here it is clear that the firstborn animal is to be consumed by its owner, a *Yisrael* (Deut. 15:20). *Ḥazal* were aware of the discrepancy between the two sources and resolved it through a strategy of harmonization. Rashi on Deuteronomy 15:20 invokes the solution of the *Sifrei*: Indeed, the owner of the animal must bring it to the Temple, as is suggested by Deuteronomy 15:19. However, when verse 20 states, "*You* shall eat it," that must refer to the *kohen*, because Numbers 18 clearly states that the *kohanim* alone may consume these animals. This reading, however, is difficult to maintain as a *peshat* reading of Deuteronomy 15. The same addressee ("you") who consecrates the animal (15:19) – presumably the *Yisrael* owner – and who must take it home to consume it if it is blemished (15:22) and must properly dispose of its blood (15:23) is the addressee commanded, "*you* shall eat it" in verse 20. In fact, verse 20 suggests the addressee here is someone who comes from afar to the Temple only periodically, and not someone who is there on a more regular basis, as a *kohen* would be. The implication is that this verse, too, is referring to a *Yisrael* and not to a *kohen*.

Abarbanel offers one of the most comprehensive rabbinic medi-tations on the issue of discrepancies between the laws of Deuteronomy and the laws found in the previous books of the Torah. The present case, however, highlights the weakness of his approach. Indeed, he notes, laws in Deuteronomy are presented differently than they are earlier in the Torah. This, he explains, is because Moses expanded and added to the laws already given, in anticipation of the needs of a new generation settling in the land. In some places he refers to these addenda as *toladot*, a term familiar to us from the laws of Shabbat, which suggests a "corollary" or "ancillary" to the core law given earlier. Thus, when the Torah repeats the law of manu-mission (*eved ivri*) – already given in Exodus 21:1–6 – in Deuteronomy

15:12–18, it adds the mandate for the owner to release the servant with severance gifts to help him get on his financial feet (Deut. 15:13–14). This addition does not contravene the law in Exodus 21, but adds to it. Moses adds to it, says Abarbanel, because some Israelites are about to become wealthy landowners, and it behooves them to behave in a charitable way.

Abarbanel's approach has value, and I shall review it more closely later in the discussion. But it is also limited as a solution to the problem of discrepancies between law in Deuteronomy and elsewhere. The notion that some of the mitzvot in Deuteronomy may represent extensions, corollaries – *toladot* – of some earlier mitzvot is well and good. It does not, however, help us reconcile the law of the firstborn in Numbers 18 and in Deuteronomy 15. Here, there is no way to see the law in Deuteronomy as an extension or a *tolada* of the law in Numbers 18. The law in Deuteronomy 15 directly contravenes the law given in Numbers 18. Abarbanel was aware of this discrepancy, but does no more than to cite the harmonistic solution of the *Sifrei* mentioned above.

The Hypothesis of Competing Legal Traditions – A Critical Evaluation

Critical study of the Bible proposes a simple solution for the discrepancy: the laws of Deuteronomy and the laws of Numbers are from two separate law codes. They were not originally written to coexist in one text. The two codes are mutually exclusive. This source-critical approach maintains, in fact, that the Torah contains four distinct law codes: the Covenant Code, comprised essentially of Exodus 21–23; the Priestly Code, which includes the Torah's cultic laws; the Holiness Code, which is comprised of the laws governing life in the land, contained in Leviticus 17–26; and, finally, the Deuteronomic Code, containing the laws found in the book of Deuteronomy. These codes, it is said, were successively composed with the intent of replacing the law found in an earlier code. Thus, for example, Deuteronomy offers its own version of the law of manumission (*eved ivri*) in chapter 15, because its author rejected the formulation of the law found in Exodus 21:1–6.

The hypothesis of four codes of law is born out of the reasonable premise that no single agent would compose a work so fraught with contradiction in its laws. Advocates of the hypothesis must explain, however, how these disparate law corpora came together. The proposed solution essentially kicks the ball downfield. The bringing together of these materials is not the act of an author but of an editor, or redactor. Scholars, however, must then explain why an editor would bring together material in a way that an author would not. The standard explanation is that the redactor did so out of duress. With the pressures of the Destruction and Exile, there was a need for Israel's disparate subcommunities and traditions to unite together around a compromise document, and that document is the Torah.

This hypothesis of mutually exclusive codes brought together under duress in a compromise is subject to critique from a strictly academic perspective on six accounts.

First and foremost, it is difficult to see how the Torah in its present form could satisfactorily be termed a "compromise document." There may well have been subcommunities within Israel at the time of the Destruction. And joining forces and reaching compromise may well be a wise strategy for survival. But the discrepancies within the Torah render it the antithesis of a compromise document. A document reflecting compromise between competing agendas is one in which each side gives ground on its original positions and a middle ground is found. Alternatively, one side will get its way on a given issue and the other side its way on another. Where draftsmen truly find no common ground, they may employ creative ambiguity, or skirt the issue altogether. The sine qua non of a compromise document, however, is that it will iron out conflict and contradiction so that the community can proceed following one authoritative voice. What compromise is there in the competing laws of the firstborn animal? If anything, the Torah would seem to guarantee a state of anarchy, with *kohanim* insisting that the law should follow the formulation of Numbers 18, and landowning *Yisraelim* pointing to the formulation in Deuteronomy 15 as the right way to go.

Second, the theory that the Torah is a compromise document has no external control to validate it. There were actually a number of law codes composed in the ancient Near East, the Code of Hammurabi being the most famous of them. Nonetheless, nowhere else in this vast region do we see that a culture faced with catastrophe suddenly merged its competing strands of thought and law into such a so-called "compromise document." This is so even though in the annals of ancient Near Eastern history, Israel hardly stood alone in experiencing dislocation and disaster. Nor is there any attestation to this process of assembling the Torah in this fashion either from extra-biblical sources or from anywhere in the Tanakh itself.

Third, the notion that the various law codes compete with one another and were not intended to be combined is challenged by evidence within the Torah itself. Deuteronomy makes no claim to its own sufficiency as a source of law and calls upon Israel to fulfill precepts "as I have commanded you" elsewhere (Deut. 12:21; 18:2; 24:8; cf. also 5:12, 16), seemingly referring to passages contained in one of the other so-called codes.

The fourth complication for this hypothesis stems from the peculiar authority that Deuteronomy ascribes to its laws. In the earlier books of the Torah, the laws are commanded to Moses by God Himself. In Deuteronomy, however, the laws seem to be *given* – not merely transmitted – by Moses himself. Abarbanel noted that nowhere in Deuteronomy does the Torah say that the laws contained in that book were dictated by God to Moses. In fact, at several junctures Moses explicitly states that these are the laws that *he* is giving to Israel (e.g., Deut. 4:44–45; 5:1; 6:6). Moreover, none of the mitzvot found in Deuteronomy are prefaced by the introduction ubiquitously found elsewhere in the Torah, "And the Lord said to Moses saying, 'Command the children of Israel.'" This is what led Abarbanel to his theory that the laws in Deuteronomy represent *toladot* or corollaries to the earlier laws. Moses, for Abarbanel, could not make new laws, but he could add stipulations that would buttress the earlier laws and support their spirit. We noted that this theory breaks down when we come to discrepancies like the ones exhibited in the various iterations of the law of the firstborn animal. That Deuteronomy maintains that its laws emanate from Moses is problematic for the hypothesis of competing sources of law. Many scholars maintain that law in Deuteronomy comes to replace the law in the Covenant Code of Exodus 21–23. Yet those laws are said in God's name. Why would the later author of Deuteronomy compose laws designed to replace laws spoken by God in Exodus, and replace them with laws whose authority is only that of Moses?

Fifth, were these so-called schools truly inimical to each other, we would expect the warfare over the law to spread to many other books of the Tanakh. Indeed, scholarship routinely maintains that Deuteronomic, or Priestly, or Holiness, editors were largely responsible for the redaction of many of the books of the Tanakh. The other books of Scripture touch upon literally dozens of areas of law. Yet, nowhere in the rest of Tanakh do we find a prophet, *kohen*, king, or narrator who argues in explicit fashion for the legitimacy of one version of a law over another. Nowhere in the Tanakh do we find a book or a prophet who can be classified as purely following Deuteronomy, or the Holiness Code. In fact, quite the opposite is true. Nearly all the books of the Tanakh resonate with passages from all so-called sources of law. Often, biblical writers will weave together purportedly "competing" law sources. Nehemiah does this with the very laws we have taken as our case study – the laws of the firstborn animal – in his discussion of practice in his day (Neh. 10:35–37). In fact, scholars have long recognized that such legal blends are legion in post-exilic biblical literature such as Ezra-Nehemiah and Chronicles. I would note that the phenomenon is hardly limited to post-exilic books. Jeremiah censures the elite for failing to release their debt-servants. His rebuke weaves references to the laws of debt-servitude from Leviticus and Deuteronomy (cf. Jer. 34:12–16). At least a half dozen more examples can be adduced from books that are not clearly post-exilic.[2] Put succinctly, while the source-critical approach sees the different law collections as mutually exclusive, all sections of the Tanakh, from the Torah and on into the other books, seem to put them together. In the Torah we find these laws all united under one cover, and in the other books we see references to these law codes woven and cited with no sense that affinity to one comes at the expense of the standing of the other.

Sixth, I take a page from the history of the critical study of the Torah. When we look at the early major figures of this movement, we see a curious trend. Until the mid-nineteenth century, scholars attended solely to contradictions within the narrative portion of the Torah. I am speaking of figures like Benedict Spinoza, Jean Astruc, Johann Gottfried Eichhorn, Wilhelm Martin Leberecht de Wette, and Heinrich

2. See my *Inconsistency in the Torah*, 148–70.

Ewald. These figures read the *narratives* of the Torah with a keen eye, and looked for every slight indication of difference as evidence of independent sources. These are the figures that, for example, hypothesized a J source and a P source for the stories of the Torah. Yet, remarkably, their work never makes mention of the contradictions within biblical law. That enterprise began in earnest only in the second half of the nineteenth century. Why were earlier scholars oblivious to problems in the text that would be so obviously troublesome to later scholars?

All of this suggests that we should look for an alternative explanation. Here, then, is a "prospectus" of what a satisfactory hypothesis would include to explain the discrepancies between law in Deuteronomy and the earlier books. This theory should explain what seems a Gordian Knot: On the one hand, many laws in the Torah seem to be mutually exclusive – such as the laws of the firstborn animal. And yet at the same time, the literature in which these laws are found – the Torah and the Tanakh generally – seems to relate to them as compatible. It should explain why Deuteronomy ascribes the laws to Moses when the other books of the Torah ascribe them to God Himself. It should explain why Deuteronomy seems to approve of prior versions of the laws in the Torah, beckoning Israel to follow certain laws "as I have commanded you," and yet at the same time often gives a divergent formulation of the law. Finally, our solution should explain why scholars before the mid-nineteenth century rarely, if ever, saw contradiction within the laws of the Torah, whereas these contradictions have been obvious to scholars working in the last century and a half.

That solution, I maintain, is available. Its root lies in identifying our anachronistic understanding of the word "law" and how legal texts are to be read. It lies in recovering how people thought about "law" and legal texts in pre-modern times. To this we now turn.

THE CONCEPT OF LAW IN THE ANCIENT WORLD

The difficulties that many sense in the law collections of the Torah stem from anachronistic notions of how law functions and of what a legal text is. Here I lay out the difference between modern and ancient notions of law. This will enable us to comprehend anew a host of questions concerning law in the Tanakh, and gain a greater appreciation of the relationship between *Torah Shebikhtav* and *Torah Shebe'al Peh*, usually translated as "Written Law" and "Oral Law." I begin by laying out the assumptions we bear when we speak about law today.

Common Law vs. Statutory Law

What do we mean when we use the word "law"?

Consider the following common usages of the word *law*: "uphold the law," "comply with the law," "the letter of the law," "pass a law," "against the law." These statements share a basic assumption: the "law" in question is a written formulation and is found in a law code. However, the intuitive notion that by "law" we mean written law found in a law code is itself a relative newcomer in the history of legal thought. Once upon a time, the norms of society were not written. There were no codes. This is the story of the evolution of the word "law" and how it came to take on the modern meaning of law written in a law code. More profoundly, this is the story of how our modern use of the term "law" has put us out of touch with the way law worked in the time of the Tanakh.

When most people today think of the word "law," they have in mind what legal theorists call *statutory law*. Law, within this conception, is contained in a *codified* text. Only what is written in the code is the law. The law code supersedes all other sources of norms that preceded the formulation of the code. No other sources of authority have validity other than the code itself. Therefore, the courts must pay great attention to the wording of the text and cite the text in their decisions. Where the code lacks explicit legislation, judges must adjudicate with the code as their primary guide. For many of us today this *statutory* approach to law is intuitive and even unremarkable. Yet as recently as the early nineteenth century the vast majority of Germans, Englishmen, and Americans thought about law in very different terms. The prevailing view for them was a *common-law* approach to jurisprudence.

For common-law theorists, the law is not found in a written code which serves as the judges' point of reference and which delimits what they may decide. Instead, a judge arrives at a judgment based on the mores and spirit of the community and its customs. Norms develop gradually through the distillation and continual restatement of legal doctrine through the decisions of courts. When a judge decides a particular case, he or she is empowered to reconstruct the general thrust of these norms in consultation with previous judicial formulations. Critically, the judicial decision itself does not create binding precedent. *No particular formulation of these norms is final. There is no authoritative text called "the law" or "the law code."* As a system of legal thought, the common law is consciously and inherently incomplete, fluid, and vague.

When decisions and precedents were collected and written down, these texts did not become the *source* of law, but rather a *resource* for later jurists to consult. Every decision became "a datum from which to reason," in the words of the early-nineteenth-century common-law theorist John Joseph Park.[3] Within this conception judges address new needs and circumstances by reworking old norms, decisions, and ideas. Although the common law attached great importance to the venerated customs of the past, the key was not the unchanging identity of its components but a steady continuity with the past.

By the end of the nineteenth century, legal codes were being drafted across the Western world, from Germany to America. The statutory approach had won the day. But why? What was it that led sensibilities about jurisprudence to shift so dramatically in the second half of the nineteenth century from a common-law approach to a statutory approach? Why do we think of law as *statutory law* today?

Common-law thinking flourishes in homogeneous communities where common values and cultural touchstones are nourished and maintained by all. Where cohesion breaks down, however, it is difficult to anchor law in a collective set of mores and values. Nineteenth-century Europe witnessed large-scale urbanization and the rise of the modern nation-state. Great numbers of disparate individuals were coalescing in social and political entities of ever-larger scope. A clearly formulated set of rules could unite a heterogeneous populace around a single code of behavior. The earliest known instance of codification reflects the same political logic: The first written Greek laws date to the middle of the seventh century BCE, and proliferated at just the period when Greek

---

3. John Joseph Park, *A Contre-Projet to the Humpheresian Code* (London, 1827), 21, 25, cited in Michael Lobban, *The Common Law and English Jurisprudence 1760–1850* (Oxford: Clarendon Press, 1991), 220–21.

city-states were in a process of state formation and developing more formal political systems.

Today, we are citizens of large, polyglot political entities, far removed from the spirit that animated common-law jurisprudence in the pre-modern period. But to appreciate the vitality of the common-law system within a local, homogeneous environment, we need look no further than our own homes and the dynamics of the nuclear family. At home we certainly do set the bar high in terms of expected behavior, but we do not typically run the house on the basis of "laws." Children may be reminded not to jump or eat on the couch – but there are no "laws of the couch" posted on the side of the refrigerator. At home, proper behavior and attitudes are modeled by parents and neighbors. Cues suggesting how a child should behave, think, and feel are all interwoven in and inculcated through the gestalt of the environment created by the home and its surroundings. Here parental discipline is exercised in a fluid and changing manner. Parents may address a child's misdeed one way on one day and in an entirely different way with another child at a different time. The broad set of goals and ideals remains the same – but their implementation and expression are in a constant state of flux.

This is a good model for understanding the dynamics of law in much of the pre-modern world. Villages were small and homogeneous. Families typically had lived in the same village for generations and could assume that continuity for the future. Village members shared a common language, religion, and heritage, common enemies, and common economic opportunities. There was no need for societal norms to be legislated by a formal body, let alone written. What was expected of a person in attitude and behavior was part of the warp and woof of day-to-day life, much as is the case with family life for us today. When a member of the village violated those norms the elders convened and decided the appropriate remedy. There were no "jurists" as a professional guild. Village elders possessed the wisdom of the ages and determined on an ad hoc basis the best redress for the situation at hand. When the continuity and homogeneity of small community are torn asunder, however, the statutory approach to jurisprudence serves to bridge the chasm that separates the behavioral and attitudinal differences of constituent citizens.

Lessons about "Law" from Hammurabi

The dichotomy between a statutory system of law and a common-law system is essential to an understanding of the idea of law in the ancient world.

In the ancient Near East there was no "law" in the sense of a statutory code. Moreover, as I will proceed to demonstrate, there was no such "law" in the Torah either. Indeed, there was no such law *anywhere* in the ancient world. I would like to demonstrate this by laying out a series of observations that scholars have made about what some erroneously call "history's first law code" – the Code of Hammurabi. This is an excellent place to begin our discussion of statutory law in the ancient world because the "Code" of Hammurabi, it turns out, is no code at all. Following how scholars reached this conclusion offers important context for understanding the nature of law in the Torah. A series of startling observations about this famous document speaks volumes about the so-called "law codes" of the Torah.

French archaeologists discovered the Code while digging in 1901 at Susa – ancient Shushan. They unearthed an imposing seven-foot-tall stele of black diorite inscribed with cuneiform writing on all sides that today stands as the marquee holding of the Louvre in Paris. Scholars quickly translated the Akkadian, written circa 1750 BCE, and saw that it contained provisions – 282, to be exact – that read like this:

> [55] If any one opens his ditches to water his crop, but is careless, and the waters flood the field of his neighbor, then he shall pay his neighbor corn for his loss.

Or like this:

> [229] If a builder builds a house for someone, and does not construct it properly, and the house which he built falls in and kills its owner, then that builder shall be put to death.

As scholars sought to uncover the meaning of this text, however, the intellectual shovels at their disposal were not equal to the task. Recalling their lesson from the study of proverbial ducks, as it were, scholars concluded that if it looks like a law code, and reads like a law code – it must be a law code! This was, after all, the early twentieth century, and every civilized country in Europe was now incorporating jurisprudence that championed statutory law.

Scholars are always quick to identify evidence in support of their hypotheses, and sure enough, evidence was quickly found supporting the understanding of this text as a statutory code. In time, more than fifty fragments of the "Code" of Hammurabi were found all across the Mesopotamian region. Moreover, these copies or fragments had been copied over a period that spanned more than 1,500 years. Most remarkably, these fragments revealed virtually no editing of content over that time. For half a century, scholars considered it an assured result: The Code of Hammurabi (or CH, as scholars refer to it in shorthand) had canonical status throughout Mesopotamia and was unrivaled as the source of law.

Around mid-century, however, scholars started to identify cracks – not in the stele, but in the theory that the Code of Hammurabi was a statutory code. Scholars were puzzled: Wild fluctuations of inflation and deflation were well known throughout the ancient Near East. Nonetheless, the fines that the Code of Hammurabi mandates for various offenses remain unchanged across the 1,500-year epigraphic record. Had the Code of Hammurabi served as a statutory code, those fines would surely have been adjusted over time. Scholars were further puzzled: Significant areas of day-to-day life receive no attention at all in the Code. There are no stipulations relating to inheritance, for example. This is inexplicable if, indeed, the Code of Hammurabi was the binding law code of a culture. Puzzling even further was the evidence from the archaeological record. Archaeologists have discovered copies of the Code of Hammurabi in royal archives and in temples, but never at the sites of local courts, and never together with the literally thousands of court dockets that have come to light from Mesopotamia. Were the Code statutory law, we would certainly expect to find it well represented in court settings. But most puzzling to scholars was this: Not one of these thousands of court dockets ever refers to or cites the Code of Hammurabi as a source of law. In fact, *not a single court docket from anywhere in the ancient Near East ever refers to any ancient law collection as a source of law*. The practice of citation is strikingly absent from the record. Think of that in modern – or even in halakhic – terms. Today a judge must cite sources when he or she delivers a decision, just as a *posek* must cite his sources in a responsa. Finally, and most crucially, many court dockets from ancient Mesopotamia record proceedings of cases whose remedy the Code of Hammurabi directly addresses. Nonetheless, in many of these, the judge rules *counter* to the prescription offered in the Code. If this text was the "law code" of Mesopotamia, how could a judge rule contrary to it? These complications raised two enduring and interrelated questions: If seeming "law collections" such as the Code of Hammurabi did not contain the law, where could the law be found? Where was it written? And, secondly, if texts like the Code of Hammurabi were not statutory codes, then what were they?

Where was the law written in Mesopotamia? The answer is that it was not. A judge would render a decision at the moment of adjudication by drawing on an extensive reservoir of custom and accepted norms. It would continually vary from locale to locale. One could not point to an accepted text of the law – neither the Code of Hammurabi nor any other text, for that matter – as the final word on what the law was or prescriptively should be. Philology here speaks volumes: In ancient Greece the word for written law was *thesmos*, and later, *nomos*. But that was Greece. Nowhere in the cultures of the ancient Near East is there a word for written law. The very concept does not exist.

If the Code of Hammurabi, though, was not a collection of "laws," what was it? These collections, instead, are anthologies of *judgments* – snapshots of decisions rendered by judges, or perhaps even by the king himself. The domain of these texts was the ivory tower of old, the palaces and the temples, the world of the court scribe, the scholars of ancient times. Collections like the Code of Hammurabi were a model of justice meant to inspire, a treatise with examples of the exercise of judicial power. They were records of *precedent*, but not of *legislation*.

Scholars have long noted that the style – if not always the content – of law in the Torah resembles the legal writings of the ancient Near East, such as the so-called "Code" of Hammurabi. The lessons scholars learned about the Code of Hammurabi as essentially common law as opposed to statutory law shed great light on law in the Torah and elsewhere in the Tanakh.

What can this distinction tell us about the nature of law in the Tanakh generally and in the Torah specifically? To my mind, it can tell us a whole lot, especially when we see the same law presented in highly divergent ways. The conclusions that I will draw about how law functioned in the time of the Tanakh may surprise some. Following my main presentation, therefore, I will turn to remarks by the Netziv about the development of halakha that support these conclusions.

LAW IN THE TANAKH:
COMMON LAW, NOT STATUTORY LAW

Our earlier distinction between common law and statutory law throws great light upon what we call "law" in the Torah. Intuitively, we read the legal portions of the Torah through the lens of statutory law because all law in the world we live in is statutory law. Yet, law in the Tanakh follows a common-law conception of how law and legal writing work, as does ancient Near Eastern law generally. This explains why the Tanakh never instructs judges to consult written sources, even as it speaks about how they go about their task of judging.[4] Narratives of adjudication, such as Solomon's "split the baby" trial (I Kings 3), likewise make no reference to written sources of law. No single collection of Torah "laws," such as the Covenant Code (or "Book of the Covenant"; cf. Ex. 24:7) in Exodus 21–23 or the "laws" of Deuteronomy (12–26), displays an attempt to provide a comprehensive set of rules to be applied in judicial cases. Here, as in the Code of Hammurabi, we find critical aspects of daily life that receive no legal attention. The Torah clearly endorses and sanctifies the institution of marriage. Yet, if you want to marry a woman, just what do you have to do, ritually or contractually? The Torah nowhere says. That would be unthinkable in a work of statutory law. Biblical "law" is not "law" at all – in the sense of *statutory* law.

Let us look at two examples of how law in the Tanakh is negotiated through a common-law mentality. Recall the parable of the poor man's ewe in II Samuel 12:1–4. David has slept with Batsheva, the wife of Uriah, one of his soldiers on the battlefront. The prophet Nathan wishes to bring the errant king to an awareness of his misdoing. He brings a

---

4. Cf. Ex. 18:13–26; Deut. 1:16–17, 16:19–20; II Chr. 19:4–7.

fictitious case to the king for adjudication in which a man blessed with large flocks steals and slaughters the ewe of his neighbor, a poor man who owns nothing but the ewe, which he loves very much. The king does not realize that the parable is a metaphor for his own lustful misdeed. Significant for our purposes here is the punishment that David imposes upon the thief. What should be the ruling here? If Torah law is statutory law, then the answer is simple: David needs to look no further than Exodus 21:37: "If a man steals an ox or a sheep and slaughters it or sells it, he shall pay five oxen for the ox and four sheep for the sheep." David, however, deviates from this ostensible "statute." He indeed obligates the thief to fourfold restitution – as per the "law" in Exodus – but also sentences him to death (II Sam. 12:5–6)! From a statutory perspective, David's actions are out of line. A cardinal tenet of statutory law is the principle of strict construction – interpreting the law as literally as possible. If the Torah calls for fourfold restitution and no more, then no harsher sentence may be leveled.

Torah "law," however, is not statutory law; it is common law, which is to say situational and ad hoc. When the Torah proposes that a thief who slaughters a stolen sheep should pay fourfold restitution, that is not a prescriptive, statutory law. It is, rather, an *example* of justice. In most instances in which a man steals a sheep and slaughters it, he does so because he lacks means and wishes to provide for his family. It is relatively easy to pilfer a sheep from the pasture, and so the Torah prescribes a harsh financial penalty. David, clearly aware of the proposition in Exodus 21:37, applies that teaching to the specifics of the case at hand. In the case brought to him by the prophet, the thief's actions are flagrant and contemptible in the extreme. The thief here was neither hungry nor desperate. The aggrieved – the poor man – was denied his only, beloved possession. The prescription found in Exodus 21:37 will simply not do here; the thief's avarice and callousness warrant his death. From the anachronistic perspective of statutory jurisprudence, the law in Exodus is plain and literal. Going beyond the letter of the ostensible "statute," David performs a miscarriage of justice, even as he paraphrases the verse in question. However, from the perspective of common-law jurisprudence, David utilizes the case in Exodus as "a datum from which to reason" and applies justice to the specifics at hand in front of him.

The idea that divine law can be as malleable as human law is counterintuitive to some. It is one thing to posit that laws of human origin evolve in a common-law fashion. Humans are fallible and limited in their perspective. But surely, some will say, divine law is different. God's wisdom is infinite and thus His laws cannot be altered. This intuition, however, misunderstands common-law thinking. The fluid nature of the common law stems only partially from the limitations of the human jurist. The common law insists on fluidity because society itself is in constant flux as well. Even divine law requires adaptation to the changing needs of society.

This view of biblical law as common law is substantiated when we examine how law is approached broadly across the Tanakh. Laws in the Tanakh do not assume a single, immutable form. Rather, the basic institution undergoes restatement and receives new expression across the ages. This is seen with regard to the laws of Shabbat, Passover, *yibum* (levirate marriage), and many other commandments. Just consider a well-known example: levirate marriage (*yibum*) in the Book of Ruth. The prescription in Deuteronomy 25:5–12 speaks solely of the obligation of a brother-in-law to his deceased brother's widow. The Book of Ruth, however, insists that Boaz has an obligation to marry Ruth (Ruth 3:9), even though Boaz was but a distant cousin of her deceased husband. Boaz, in turn, reveals that there is an obligation to redeem the land of the deceased, when a man performs *yibum* (4:5–6). This is nowhere hinted at in the laws of land redemption in Leviticus 25, nor in the laws of *yibum* in Deuteronomy 25. What the Book of Ruth shows us is a common-law reapplication of the institutions of *yibum* and land redemption as they were practiced in Boaz's time. The manifestations of these mitzvot in his time were different from what the Torah had originally specified, and differed also from the halakha that Ḥazal would spell out on these matters.

The prophets of Israel censured Israel for many failings: theft, murder, idolatry. Nowhere do the prophets "throw the book" at the people with the claim that they were performing the law, but doing so in the wrong fashion by failing to adhere to a strict reading of a passage. Modern statutory jurisprudence mandates that judges adhere to the exact words of the code because the code by definition is autonomous and exhaustive. As we have seen, however, the ancient Near East knew no notion of statutory law. Hence, when Boaz performed a form of *yibum* that varied from a strict reading of Deuteronomy 25:5–10, no one thought that he was contravening that passage. That passage was an example of proper practice, reapplied anew in every generation.

I have presented here a fluid notion of legal practice – certainly more fluid than we find in talmudic writings, and much more fluid than we find in normative halakha today. Yet some of the greatest rabbinic figures envisioned that once upon a time, law did evolve much more fluidly than it does today. One such voice was the Netziv, Rabbi Naftali Tzvi Yehuda Berlin (1816–1893).

The Changing Nature of Halakha in the Thought of the Netziv

In his important work, *How Do We Know This?*,[5] Jay Harris reveals that the rabbinic tradition had always been of two voices concerning the continuity of the halakha. One voice is more familiar to most Orthodox Jews today and claims continuity of tradition: little has changed, and much of the *mesora* can be traced all the way back to Sinai. A flagship source for this opinion in the tradition is the statement in Berakhot 5a that Mikra, Mishna, and Talmud were all given to Moses at Sinai. At the opposite end of the spectrum, Harris notes, one can cite the aggada in Menaḥot 29b that when Moses sat and witnessed R. Akiva teaching a halakha to his students, he was dismayed that he did not recognize the law that R. Akiva was teaching, and was heartened only when R. Akiva explained that this law was, in fact, *halakha leMoshe miSinai*. The suggestion is that even Moses himself might not have been familiar with the laws later granted status of *halakha leMoshe miSinai*. The issue here is not which approach to halakha is historically correct, or even which is theologically correct. It is certainly the case that the former position has wider currency in our day. But the latter position is well represented in the sources.

In particular, I would like to bring attention to comments of the Netziv about the changing nature of halakha and the Oral Law. Consider his comments on Deuteronomy 5:1:

---

5. Jay Harris, *How Do We Know This? Midrash and the Fragmentation of Modern Judaism* (Albany: SUNY Press, 1994).

> "Listen, Israel, to the *ḥukkim* and *mishpatim* which I teach you today": *Ḥukkim* – these are the rules of interpretation, such as the thirteen rules [of R. Yishmael], through which the Torah is interpreted, down to each and every letter. *Mishpatim* – these are the actual laws derived from the rules of interpretation, thereby generating new laws…. Moses our teacher taught Israel several *ḥukkim* and *mishpatim* which he had derived from his powers of induction, with the intent that they, too, should do the same in each and every generation.[6]

Elsewhere (commentary on Lev. 25:18), the Netziv underscores that the process of deducing rules of interpretation is ongoing, as is the process of deriving through them actual laws throughout history. He notes that Hillel the Elder had his seven rules in his generation (Tosefta Sanhedrin 7:5) and later R. Yishmael derived his thirteen. The Netziv's approach raises many fascinating questions: Just what were the rules of interpretation in each generation prior to the rabbinic period? Who was it that was empowered to derive these rules? Why did this process of identifying new rules of interpretation slow down, or cease altogether? Why do we seem to have little record of this activity as part of the *mesora*? While all of these are worthy questions, they are not my concern here.[7] Instead, I wish to draw several conclusions about the Netziv's thinking:

1. Interpretation of the Torah law changed with some degree of frequency in the pre-rabbinic period.
2. Because the principles of interpretation – the *ḥukkim* – changed, perforce the actual practice of law changed in this time as well.
3. Rules of interpretation in one generation likely produced a practice that was at odds with the practice determined by a different rule of interpretation in a different age.
4. Presented with this historical development, there was no place to see in all this "contradiction." The system as a whole was meant to

---

6. The translation is my own.
7. See the Netziv's introduction to his commentary on *She'eiltot* for his lengthy treatment of this topic.

be fluid and changing. This, of course, raises the question of when and why the halakhic system endorsed codification, as found in Rambam's *Mishneh Torah* or in the *Shulḥan Arukh*, which I shall return to at the conclusion of the chapter.

The Netziv nowhere uses the language of common law vs. statutory law, as I have here. Yet his notion of the changing nature of the rules of interpretation suggests that the Torah, in his opinion, was not a statutory code. From here we address our original and primary question: Why do laws in the Torah seem to contradict each other?

Legal Discrepancy in the Torah within the Thought of Rabbi Tzadok of Lublin

Here I suggest a new approach to the presence of contradictory law within the various legal passages of the Torah, based upon the ideas presented earlier about the history of law in general and within the ancient Near East in particular. Because my conclusions may seem radical to some, I would like to create a theological space for my analysis by opening with remarks by a seminal rabbinic thinker, Rabbi Tzadok HaKohen Rabinowitz of Lublin. In the following passage, Rabbi Tzadok takes up the age-old question of the discrepancies found between the version of the Decalogue found in Exodus 20 and that found in Deuteronomy 5:

> The latter version of the Decalogue, that in the book of Deuteronomy, was said by Moses, on his own account. Nonetheless, it is part of the Written Law. In addition to the mitzvot themselves that Moses had already received at Sinai by the word of God, these words as well [in the book of Deuteronomy], which were said on his own account, which are not prefaced with the statement, "And God said," these, too, are part of the Written Law. For all of his [i.e., Moses's] are also a complete "torah," just like the dialogues of the patriarchs and other similar passages are considered part of the Written Law. But the material that begins, "And these are the things" [i.e., the first verse of the book of Deuteronomy and the rest of the book that follows], material that was said on his

own account, represents the root of the Oral Law, the things that the Sages of Israel say of their own account.[8]

For Rabbi Tzadok, the Torah contains material that is divine in origin, such as the mitzvot given to Moses at Sinai. The Torah, however, also contains material that is human in origin. This is what he refers to as "the dialogues of the patriarchs." That is, the words spoken by the *avot* (patriarchs) that are preserved in the book of Genesis are actual, human utterances that the Torah chose to preserve. Their origin is human, and nonetheless they have the same status as God's utterances at Sinai and are on equal footing as part of the Written Law. Rabbi Tzadok applies this same logic to everything found in Deuteronomy. When Deuteronomy opens with the statement, "These are the things that Moses spoke," Rabbi Tzadok takes that quite literally: God may have given His imprimatur for the book of Deuteronomy, but its content originated with Moses, not God. As I pointed out earlier, numerous statements throughout Deuteronomy – such as Deuteronomy 4:44–45 and 5:1 – support this understanding, and this is what led Abarbanel to the same conclusion.[9] Nowhere in Deuteronomy do we find the typical introduction to a mitzva found in the earlier books of the Torah, "And God spoke to Moses saying, 'Command the children of Israel.'" Rabbi Tzadok's position is unique because he employs this principle to explain the discrepancies between the version of the Ten Commandments found in Exodus 20 and the version found in Deuteronomy 5.

For Rabbi Tzadok, the version found in Deuteronomy 5 constitutes Moses's words. But how could this be? After all, in Deuteronomy 5:4, Moses himself says that *God* spoke the words of the Decalogue that

---

8. Rabbi Tzadok HaKohen of Lublin, *Pri Tzadik, Kedushat HaShabbat,* article 7. The translation is my own.
9. It is true that from Deuteronomy 5:28–6:2 it would seem that Moses claims that the commandments of Deuteronomy were given to Moses already at Sinai. However, this is complicated by the prohibition against allowing Ammonites and Moabites to join the people of Israel (Deut. 23:4–7). The Torah's reasons for this prohibition concern events that happened after Israel had left Sinai. Perforce, we must say that when Moses ascribes the commandments of Deuteronomy to Revelation at Sinai, he does not preclude his own adaptation and retelling of those commands.

follow (Deut. 5:6–18). Here we see Rabbi Tzadok's revolutionary leap. For Rabbi Tzadok, the words that Moses speaks throughout Deuteronomy are an exercise in *Torah Shebe'al Peh* – exegesis and reinterpretation of God's law. In fact, says Rabbi Tzadok, Moses's own exercise in such reinterpretation constitutes the paradigm – the "root" to use his term – for all subsequent such activity by the sages of Israel across the ages. The version of the Decalogue in Deuteronomy diverges from the version told in Exodus 20 because it is a *Torah Shebe'al Peh* retelling of the earlier version. For Rabbi Tzadok, Moses's statement in Deuteronomy 5:4, that God spoke "these words," is not a statement that what follows is a word-for-word transcript of divine speech. Rather it is a faithful interpretation and reapplication of those words.[10] No mitzva, then, in Deuteronomy will be identical to its precursor in the other books. The entire purpose of Moses's retelling of the mitzvot is to present an updated version and application of God's commands on the eve of the entry into the land.

Common-Law Development within the Torah Itself

Rabbi Tzadok's approach to law in the Torah dovetails well with the conceptual framework developed earlier. For Rabbi Tzadok, the mitzvot contained in the earlier books of the Torah cannot be read as divine statutory law. Were that the case, there would be no room to stray from a strict and close reading of the formulations of those laws. There would be no license for Moses to reinterpret those mitzvot; indeed, there would be no license for later rabbis to interpret the language of those mitzvot either. The entire enterprise of *Torah Shebe'al Peh* would be invalidated. We would be bound to strictly follow the literal meaning of those prescriptions.

Instead Rabbi Tzadok advocates a way of looking at those legal statements as binding, yet as fluid in their application. Put differently, Rabbi Tzadok looks at those prescriptions as common law, not statutory law. For common-law thinking, determination of the law is situational; the law is not found in an immutable text, but adapts with an

---

10. Ibn Ezra likewise sees the version of the Decalogue in Deuteronomy as Moses's commentary on what God had commanded at Sinai. See his introduction to the Ten Commandments in his long commentary on Exodus 20.

awareness of the changing historical situation.[11] The book of Deuteronomy presents a record of Moses's common-law application of earlier teachings. God spoke at Sinai to a people just released from bondage. With the people poised to enter the land, Moses reinterprets God's earlier words and applies the laws to an array of challenges posed by life in the Land of Israel.

This well explains the case studies of legal divergence that we examined earlier. We noted that the institution of manumission (*eved ivri*), first stated in Exodus 21, is restated in Deuteronomy 15 with the prominent addition of the mitzva of severance pay for the released servant. This is a good example of how Moses openly reworks the mitzvot of the Covenant Code (Ex. 21–23), yet without negating it. The laws of Deuteronomy address Israel as she is poised to assume a new condition of a landed people with a central temple and a more developed government. This is why the law of manumission (*eved ivri*) in Deuteronomy 15:12–18 addresses the master and his feelings and experiences as he derives benefit from the debt-servant. This focus is far less noticeable in the Covenant Code, which appears at the beginning of the trek in the wilderness. This way of viewing Moses's revision of the Covenant Code in Deuteronomy reflects a common-law approach to jurisprudence wherein changed historical circumstance leads to the evolution of the law, yet without the need of jettisoning earlier, revered texts. Revision of an earlier law does not entail a rejection of the text bearing that earlier law. We may invoke the words we cited earlier of John Joseph Park, the nineteenth-century common-law theorist, who noted that texts within the common-law tradition always remain "a datum from which to reason." Even as Moses in Deuteronomy interprets and reapplies the teachings of the Covenant Code, the Covenant Code remains on the books for later consultation, "as a datum from which to reason." Neither the Covenant Code nor the mitzvot found in Deuteronomy are statutory codes. They are sets of teachings. Deuteronomy borrows from the language of the Covenant Code because, in legal terms, it is a restatement and a new application of the older teaching.

---

11. This is a cardinal tenet in Rabbi Tzadok's writings. See his arguments about the need for growth and change within halakha in *Tzidkat HaTzaddik* 90 and in *Resisei Layla* 56.

This also explains the explicit contradiction between the law of the firstborn found in Numbers 18 and the version of the law found in Deuteronomy 15. When the laws of the priestly gifts are first presented (Leviticus 2), firstborn animals are not listed. The law in Numbers 18 itself is an ad hoc exigency. The Korah rebellion necessitated legislation that would buttress the standing of the priesthood of Aaron and his descendants. One measure that God orders is that the firstborn now be consecrated for the benefit of the *kohanim* alone. The law in Deuteronomy 15:19–23 restores the status of the firstborn animal to what it had been before the Korah crisis – the property of the owner. As with many laws in Deuteronomy, the law of the firstborn seeks to ensure that cultic activity only occur at the place that God chooses (eventually, Jerusalem and the Temple); a person must bring it to the central Sanctuary where he may consume it.[12]

To be sure, this is not the halakha as we have it today, based on the harmonization of the passages in the *Sifrei*, as we noted at the outset of this chapter. However, this should not cause any theological concern. As noted earlier, we see in the Book of Ruth forms of levirate marriage and land redemption that are at variance both with the provisions in the Torah and with the halakha as later determined by the rabbis. The comments of the Netziv that we saw earlier and the approach of Rabbi Tzadok of Lublin discussed above provide us a theological basis with which to comprehend the fluidity of practice during the biblical period. These luminaries did not state their opinions apologetically as some sort of concession to the findings of critical study. They stated their opinions as a celebration of the evolving human process of *Torah Shebe'al Peh*, a process which for both of them began with Moses himself. As we saw earlier, the tradition empowers *Ḥazal* to develop the Torah and derive biblical (*deoraita*) obligations, limitations, and conditions. The writings of Rabbi Tzadok of Lublin and the Netziv suggest that Moses, too, was invested with these powers.

---

12. For several more examples of how the laws of the Torah update each other see the fine collection of essays contained in Hezi Cohen and Aviad Evron, eds., *Gishat HeTemurot: Shita Ḥadasha BeParshanut HaTorah* (Jerusalem: Maggid, 2019).

Three Misunderstood Terms: *Ḥok Olam, Mishpat,* and *Lo Tosif*

Proponents of the statutory approach to law in the Torah often point to three terms as evidence that the Torah's laws are immutable, and must be kept precisely as stated. Below I review these terms, demonstrating that they are routinely misunderstood and do not suggest a statutory understanding of biblical law.

Some mitzvot are termed *ḥok olam*. This is often translated as "an everlasting statute." Clearly, if a mitzva is, indeed, termed "an everlasting statute," then its form is immutable, and it must be performed precisely as stated. The translation of *ḥok olam* as "everlasting statute" is a fine one, except for two problems: "everlasting" and "statute." Let us begin with the first term, *ḥok*. The root of this word is Ḥ-K-K, which means "inscribed." Something, then, that is called a *ḥok* is simply something that must be inscribed as a matter of importance. *Olam* is mistakenly translated as "everlasting" and therefore immutable. However, the biblical term for "forever" or "everlasting" is not *olam*. Rather, "eternal" or "forever" are expressed through more emphatic terms such as *olam va'ed*, or *me'olam ve'ad olam*, or *olamim*.[13] The term *olam* on its own means "open-ended," or "without fixed termination point." This is clearly the meaning in Exodus 21:6, where the freed debt-servant reneges on his freedom, and is told that he will therefore serve *le'olam*. The servant is mortal, and thus obviously cannot serve eternally. Instead of having the automatic release after six years, his servitude will continue; it will be "open-ended." This is also evident from the censure of Eli the *kohen gadol* in I Samuel 2:30–31: "Therefore the Lord, the God of Israel, declares: 'I promised that your house and the house of your father should go in and out before Me *le'olam*,' but now the Lord declares: 'Far be it from Me, for those who honor Me I will honor, and those who despise Me shall be lightly esteemed.'" If we assume that *le'olam* means something eternal, then God undermines Himself by reneging on His promise. Rather, God had promised that these *kohanim* would rule *indefinitely*. Indefinitely, however, does not guarantee eternity, and when their behavior warrants their removal, there is no barrier to doing so. Note that no commandment in the Torah is referred to using the formulae referred to above

---

13. The Rambam notes this distinction. See *Guide for the Perplexed*, II:28.

to connote something eternal or everlasting. Were the meaning of the phrase *ḥok olam* in fact "eternal statute," we would do well to ask why only a handful of commandments have that designation. What would that say about the rest?

Mishpat is sometimes translated as "law." That is certainly the case in Modern Hebrew. However, from many sources in the Tanakh we see that the proper translation is "justice." Abraham's descendants will perform *tzedaka umishpat* – "righteousness and justice." Proverbs uses the word *mishpat* solely in the sense of justice (cf. Prov. 12:5; 21:7; 28:5). This is also its meaning at the beginning of *Parashat Mishpatim* (Ex. 21:1): "These are the *mishpatim* that you shall place before them." The prescriptions contained there are not given to judges; they are examples of justice given to the children of Israel as examples of just living. This is why David could reapply what was said about the penalty for stealing a sheep, in light of the circumstances at hand, as we explained earlier.

Finally, many will point to a pair of verses in Deuteronomy that seem to insist that the law is precisely what is written and nothing else: Deuteronomy 13:1 states, "The entire word that I command you, shall you take to perform. Do not add to it, and do not subtract from it" (cf. Deut. 4:4). However, the phrase "do not add to it, and do not subtract from it" must be seen for what it is: a common idiom in the writings of the ancient Near East. When kings commissioned diplomatic correspondences, they were concerned that the text of the letter reach the recipient exactly as dictated. Typically, such correspondences would include a curse upon anyone who tampered with the text of the correspondence. When someone said with regard to a text of any kind, "Do not add to it and do not subtract from it," the exclusive meaning of that phrase was to ensure textual integrity. The *text* could not be changed.

The Advantages of the Common-Law Approach to Biblical Law

To summarize and conclude this approach to legal inconsistency between laws in Deuteronomy and the rest of the Torah, I list the advantages of viewing the discrepancies within Torah law as common-law development as opposed to statutory contradiction, from an *academic* perspective.

1. When viewed as statutory law, the law collections of the Torah are taken to be mutually exclusive. This led scholars to adduce a hypothesis to explain how these collections came to be incorporated in a single work. That gave rise to the notion of the Torah as a compromise document. As we saw, however, the law collections are too contradictory to be deemed a compromise. Moreover, there is no extra-biblical example of a legal document that works this way; indeed, there are no examples of statutory systems of law anywhere before fifth-century-BCE Greece. When viewed as common-law examples of justice, the Torah's laws emerge as reapplications of one another. All formulations are preserved because they have value as "data from which to reason" in the future.

2. Moses in Deuteronomy refers back to previous law collections, "as I have commanded you" (e.g., Deut. 12:21; 18:2; 24:8). If the law collection of Deuteronomy was composed to displace earlier formulations of these laws, it is unclear why its author would give credence to those collections at all. If law in the Torah is common law, however, the prescriptions in Deuteronomy do not stand in competition with the earlier laws.

3. If the laws of Deuteronomy were written to compete with earlier formulations of the laws, it is unclear why the author of this book would choose to make Moses the authority of the laws rather than God, as is the case in the laws contained in the other books of the Torah. If Torah law, however, is common law, the switch in authority is well understood. In Deuteronomy, Moses reinterprets and reapplies the principles and examples that God had given earlier, in light of the impending entry into the land.

4. Were the law collections of the Torah mutually exclusive and in competition with one another, we would expect to find evidence of this elsewhere in the Tanakh, because it is widely held that authors and editors adopting the worldview of one collection or another are responsible for composing or editing many of the other books of the Tanakh. In fact, we find no book that aligns with a single collection of law. Rather all the other books resonate with more than one of the law collections, and sometimes all of them. No king, *kohen*, prophet, or biblical narrator ever argues for

the validity of one version of the law over another. Because the law collections of the Torah are common-law reiterations of one another, other biblical writers freely sought inspiration from any or all of them. Even when discussing points of actual law, we find "legal blends" of phrases from several different law collections.

5. The early critics of the Pentateuch focused on narrative and scarcely ever noticed discrepancy in the laws of the Torah. This is because in the history of ideas, the idea of statutory law rises to the ascendancy only in the middle of the nineteenth century, and it is only from this period on that scholars began to read the Torah's law collections as standing in contradiction with one another.

The understanding of law in the time of the Tanakh that I have painted here is one in which the law is fluid and seemingly poles apart from how we think of halakha today. For us, halakha changes very slowly, if at all. Moreover, for us, halakha is contained first and foremost in codes of law – such as the *Shulḥan Arukh*. When we want to know the halakha, we "look it up." How and why did the world of halakha move toward a statutory understanding of the halakha? What are the implications of this move for our understanding of how the halakha evolves in our own time? To these critical issues I now turn.

THE EVOLUTION OF HALAKHA FROM
COMMON LAW TO STATUTORY LAW

Jewish jurisprudence retained its common-law nature from the close of the biblical period and into the beginnings of rabbinic history. Through varied systems of interpretation (Midrash) the rabbis continually engaged anew with Scripture and tradition in a fashion that allowed law to develop over time in response to the needs of the day. Codification of the halakha was expressly discouraged. Several talmudic Sages actually prohibit the commitment of halakhic decisions to writing. In the words of one, "Those who write down halakhot are like those who set fire to the Torah."[14] These voices understood the great reverence that Israel

---

14. See Temura 14b; Gittin 60b.

has for its Sages. Were a great Sage to formulate the halakha in written form, pious Jews thereafter would be loath to rule otherwise, and the fluid nature of the halakhic system might become ossified.[15]

How then did Judaism come to embrace the legal codes of the Rambam and Rabbi Joseph Karo (1488–1575)? When and why did Jewish jurisprudence turn toward statutory law?

As we saw earlier, the move to codify the law began in Greece in the seventh century BCE; it began in widespread fashion in nineteenth-century Europe, driven by an underlying goal to achieve an elusive unity. The impetus within Judaism has been the same, whether we look at the redaction of the Mishna by R. Yehuda HaNasi (circa 220 CE), the Rambam's *Mishneh Torah*, or Rabbi Joseph Karo's *Shulḥan Arukh*. At the same time, since each figure confronted a distinct social and religious landscape, each employed codification as a means toward a distinct end.

The Mishna itself, properly speaking, is not a code. It is at most a skeletal outline of Jewish law. Entire areas – the laws of tefillin (phylacteries), Ḥanukka, and conversion – are omitted, and only in some instances are prescriptive conclusions reached. Some scholars maintain that the Mishna was not even written down until well into the talmudic period. Nor do we have a firsthand account from R. Yehuda HaNasi of his reasons for formulating this text. It would appear that, rather than compiling a definitive code, he sought to preserve and disseminate a record of protocols and deliberations – a need occasioned by the upheaval and displacement wrought by the Destruction of the Second Temple in 70 CE and the aftermath of the failed Bar Kokhba Revolt in 135 CE.

The Babylonian Talmud is likewise a record of discussions and cannot be considered a code of any kind. Indeed, throughout the talmudic period, Jewish law retained its fluid character. During much of this time, the competing needs of continuity and change were mediated by the Sanhedrin, the universally recognized legal authority. Following

---

15. See Menachem Elon, *Jewish Law: History, Sources, Principles* (*Ha-Mishpat Ha-Ivri*), trans. Bernard Auerbach and Melvin J. Sykes, vol. 3 (Philadelphia: Jewish Publication Society, 1994), 1374–85. Elon notes that two great sages of fifteenth-century Polish Jewry, Rabbi Yaakov Pollack and Rabbi Shalom Shahna, refused to put their rulings to paper, precisely on account of their great stature, so as not to shackle the freedom and judgment of future *posekim*. See in this spirit Rambam, *Hilkhot Mamrim* 2:1.

the Sanhedrin's dissolution in 358 and the close of the talmudic era, the Geonim of Babylonia (seventh–eleventh centuries) penned digests of specific areas of law. To be sure, many rituals by this time had become accepted as standard practice, but these had not yet been written down with precise formulations that would be widely disseminated and accepted.

Not until the Rambam did anyone truly codify the halakha. Not only did his *Mishneh Torah*, completed in 1180, have no precedent in the annals of Jewish law; it had no precedent in the history of legal codification worldwide. When Greeks and Romans and others codified their laws, they did so, as we saw, in order to unite disparate peoples and incorporate them into new and large polities. The Rambam wrote his code to achieve the converse: to preserve the unity of a single people facing ever-greater dispersion. Keenly aware of the original nature of his work, he explained its historical impetus in just these terms.

So long as the great yeshivas of Babylonia flourished, the Rambam writes in the introduction to the *Mishneh Torah*, Jewish learning and knowledge were at their height; in his own day, however, these institutions were but a distant memory. Now the Jewish people faced unprecedented dispersal, compounded by political instability. For the Jews of these newly far-flung communities, mobility and communication were severely limited, and hence ignorance soared. The Rambam conceived of his code as a solution. If Jews could not gravitate to centers of learning, the code would come to them, providing clear instruction in all spheres of halakhic life.

What was the fate of the Rambam's bold innovation? Some communities, such as the community of Yemenite Jewry, embraced his *Mishneh Torah* as a statutory code. Many others came to regard it as a source to consult while electing to retain autonomy of rule and practice. It took another four centuries and the composition of Rabbi Joseph Karo's *Shulḥan Arukh*, completed in 1563, for codification to reach its apex.

Rabbi Karo – often referred to simply as the *Meḥaber*, or "author" – had personally experienced the expulsions from Spain in 1492 and Portugal in 1497. In his introduction to the *Beit Yosef*, the longer work of which the *Shulḥan Arukh* is a condensation, Rabbi Joseph Karo reveals that he wrote the code to save Judaism from an unanticipated threat – namely, Judaism itself. For seven centuries, commentaries on the talmudic sources had flourished along with the expansion and application of the Talmud's legal discussions. In Spain, Germany, and France, great traditions of learning had emerged, each with its own interpretations of the Talmud and its rulings. The printing press, now a century old, allowed access to the plethora of these commentaries and interpretations.

If the Rambam composed his code to grapple with the spread of ignorance, Rabbi Joseph Karo composed his to grapple with the spread of knowledge and conflicting interpretation. "It is not that we have today two Torahs," he wrote. "Today we have an infinite number of Torahs" – a blessing in itself but one that threatened the future cohesiveness of Jewish practice. Aware of his enormous personal stature and the sway his work would have, Rabbi Joseph Karo offered a homily on his given name in the introduction: "[The biblical] Joseph saved an entire populace, providing them nourishment of the body. I do the same, providing nourishment of the soul." It is interesting to note that Rabbi Karo embarked on his magnum opus following the collapse of the movement in Safed to reconvene the Sanhedrin in the mid-sixteenth century. A Sanhedrin would have enabled Israel's halakha to develop with a unified voice, and with an ultimate arbiter and authority. Moreover, the great stature that a Sanhedrin would possess would mean that the halakha could more easily and fluidly adapt to the needs of the times. We may speculate that when this effort failed, he began work on his alternative vehicle to bring unity to the world of halakha: his code would serve as that unifying element.

Joseph Karo's hopes for the reception of his code were well placed. Many today would define an Orthodox Jew as someone who adheres to halakha as laid down in the *Shulḥan Arukh*. Yet, in the first decades following the work's publication, the reception was far from uniformly enthusiastic. Rabbinic luminaries like Rabbi Yehuda Loeb ben Betzalel, the famed Maharal of Prague (c. 1520–1609), and the eminent talmudist Rabbi Shlomo Luria, known as the Maharshal (Lublin, 1510–1573), regarded Rabbi Joseph Karo's reform as radical and misguided.[16] They

---

16. See the caustic comments of the Maharal of Prague in his *Sefer Derashot Maharal MiPrague: Derush al HaTorah* (London, 1964), 48.

clung to a common-law view of the halakhic process as a continuing conversation among authorities applying principles articulated in the Talmud to an array of dynamic and changing situations. To them, the often indeterminate nature of talmudic discourse was a wellspring of elasticity. The rule of the code, they warned, would end all this, while also placing in jeopardy the privileged status of local custom rooted in tradition.[17]

What about the danger of Judaism's becoming subject to "an infinite number of Torahs," as Rabbi Joseph Karo warned? To the contrary, wrote Luria, the multitude of opinions was to be celebrated. The souls of Israel are each endowed with different capacities, he observed, and each may be considered to bear an aspect of a larger truth.[18] Halakha, in this thinking, positively resists unity of expression.

The battle lines were now drawn, and the debate raged for several decades. Within a century, however, the *Meḥaber*'s code became accepted as *the* benchmark of Jewish law. It would, however, be a mistake to state that halakha since that time has followed strictly statutory jurisprudence. As we can see on any printed page of the *Shulḥan Arukh*, we find the codified text is surrounded by its critics and commentators. Implicitly, these have bucked the call for unifying Jewish practice and continued to disagree, quote conflicting opinions, and add new laws and customs. Then, of course, there are well over 300,000 responsa – written from circa 500 CE until today – which are couched largely in the medium of common law. The responsa do cite the major codes, but frequently rely directly on the Talmud, the *Rishonim*, and previous responsa – often contradicting the rulings of the standard codes of Jewish law. In practice, however, only on rare and extreme occasions do today's *posekim* rule contrary to the codified prescriptions found in the *Shulḥan Arukh* or in the glosses to it by Rabbi Moshe Isserles (1520–1572) reflecting the customs of Ashkenazic Jewry.

---

17. On opposition to the codification of halakha by Rabbi Joseph Karo see the fine essay by Leon Weiner Dow, "Opposition to the 'Shulhan Aruch': Articulating a Common-Law Conception of Halacha," *Hebraic Political Studies* 3, no. 4 (2008): 352–76, available at http://www.hpstudies.org/20/admin/pdfs/29454988-f1ca-4255-93e9-341c2ab955e5.pdf.

18. Rabbi Shlomo Luria, *Yam Shel Shlomo*, introduction to Tractate Bava Kama.

NEGOTIATING A DUAL LEGACY

Under the seminal influence of H. L. A. Hart's *The Concept of Law*,[19] modern jurisprudence in general has sought a balance between the two poles of statutory and common law. In Judaism, however, consensus over how to achieve such a balance has proved elusive. We are today the heirs of two opposing modes of jurisprudence: in our earlier collective history – the biblical period and early rabbinic period – the determination of halakhic norms was fluid. Certainly from medieval times onward, we have witnessed a greater reliance on codes and a growing tendency toward rigidity as essential to safeguard the unity of the Jewish people and of Judaism itself. How shall we balance these two tendencies?

There are routine calls for halakhic change, harkening to the earlier period of Jewish jurisprudence. To reach a decision based on the Talmud rather than by rigidly following the codes is to follow in the best tradition of Jewish jurisprudence, arguably from Sinai until the medieval period; today, just as in the past, such an approach can infuse halakha with contemporary vitality. Yet, if Jews four centuries ago had followed the lead of the Maharal of Prague and of Rabbi Shlomo Luria, where would we be today if not face to face with "an infinite number of Torahs"? Would there not be one Judaism on the Upper West Side of Manhattan, another in the Bronx, several more in Brooklyn, and still many more in Jerusalem?

It is true that in ancient times, Beit Hillel and Beit Shammai issued widely divergent rulings and yet retained their standing as partners in a unified Jewish people. But back then there were only "two Torahs," and adherents of those schools lived in integrated communities. Such ancient precedents have little relevance to the religious and demographic complexity of the contemporary Jewish world. Unfortunately, there is scant recognition or discussion of this dilemma among advocates of far-reaching halakhic change. Perhaps they believe that Jewish unity has been irreparably shattered, and that the best we can hope for is to adjudicate according to the needs of our respective communities. Or, conversely, perhaps they believe that greater jurisprudential freedom will itself guarantee Jewish unity and that only a more inclusive halakha can succeed in

19. Oxford: Oxford University Press, 1961.

retaining Jews who are today only marginally affiliated with organized Judaism. Both of these positions are open to criticism.

This raises the question of how and when innovation in the halakha may emerge. At many junctures, this happened as the result of a bold decision on the part of giants of halakhic erudition like Rabbi Moshe Feinstein (1895–1986), figures whose broad shoulders and widely accepted authority allowed them to adopt and propagate rulings that lesser authorities could not. Today, however, such figures appear to be a dying breed. In the post-World War II period, one is hard put to name a halakhic leader of towering eminence who has been succeeded within his community by someone of equal stature. This is true across all lines in the halakhic world; as true in the United States as in Israel; as true among Sephardim, especially after the passing of Rabbi Ovadia Yosef, as among Ashkenazim; as true for the *haredim* as for the Modern Orthodox.

Is there something about the modern condition itself that has engendered this surprising trend? Is it that today's scholars live in an age of unprecedented prosperity, with unprecedented access and exposure to the world outside the study hall and unprecedented freedom of choice – all, arguably, inimical to achieving greatness in Torah scholarship at the highest level?

Or, alternatively, is it that thanks precisely to the blessings of modernity, which have encouraged unprecedented numbers to engage in classical Torah study, it has become much more difficult for any one individual to stand out? In previous generations, a scholar would achieve acclaim within his city or region, and from there his reputation might spread. Today, when the halakhic world partakes of the global village, reputations have little chance to develop incrementally, and the very word "local" has become a vestige of a long-gone past. Whatever may be the causes of this trend, by now it has been in place for six decades. If it continues, and if leaders do not emerge to command a broad following as in the past, then the bias toward sticking with what has been done until now will become all the more ingrained.

It would seem that for innovation to take place in this environment, the authority supplied in previous generations by recognized and accepted Torah giants will now stem from consensus. But in order for the consensus to have validity, it will need to be a consensus of accomplished halakhic authorities – individuals who have published responsa covering a broad cross-section of law and who also serve as community leaders, accepted by their peers and the public within their own local sphere and beyond. The call for change can come from academics, educators, speakers, and clergymen. But the change will only be valid when it is adopted by a consensus of recognized halakhic authorities.

What is clear is that halakhic adaptation to changing circumstances is today a very slow process. Indeed, some would argue that it is only getting slower; in a seminal essay, Haym Soloveitchik has traced the process by which, in recent decades, the statutory nature of halakha has produced an ever-greater rigidity.[20] Indeed, some would say that affirming the view that halakha stands outside society has itself become a central tenet – and boundary marker – of Orthodoxy.

Consider this: In fifteenth-century Germany, halakhic authorities ruled for the first time that during Passover, a Jew could retain possession of leavened items (*hametz*) in his property by formally selling them to a non-Jew prior to the holiday. At the time, the ruling was considered revolutionary. It could take hold only because communities lived in relative isolation and autonomy. German Jews accepted it even as Jews of other Ashkenazic lands did not; in the fullness of time, it became accepted by most.

By contrast, halakhically observant Jews today are at once ever more divided from one another and ever more connected. Ever more divided, because of competing visions of Judaism in general and of Jewish law in particular; ever more connected, because of the global village that is the internet. When a halakhic authority issues a ruling, he no longer does so in isolation; the speakerphone, so to speak, is on. If his opinion is even slightly controversial, in nanoseconds the filibuster in cyberspace will begin to block its adoption. There is never time and space for innovation to take hold on the local level, to demonstrate its merits, and then to become slowly adopted (or not) by others. In this environment, halakhic reform can most likely succeed only by slowly building a prior consensus for change.

---

20. Haym Soloveitchik, "Rupture and Reconstruction: The Transformation of Contemporary Orthodoxy," *Tradition* 28, no. 4 (1994): 320–76.

There is no denying that for many, the situation I have been describing is imperfect and unsatisfying; to my knowledge no one within Orthodoxy has formulated a satisfying approach to it. As we try to negotiate the dual legacy of Jewish jurisprudence, we remain caught between the ideal of unity and the ideal of relevance, between continuity and change, and between Judaism's common-law and code-based approaches to halakhic jurisprudence. At the very least, gaining a fuller appreciation of how those tensions have played out in the past might help us think creatively about how the same currents and counter-currents could play out differently in the future.

Minimally, an awareness of this dual legacy allows us to read the seemingly contradictory legal portions of the Torah with new eyes. Our halakha today is largely codified. An awareness of how our jurisprudence has evolved allows us to understand how we err when we try to read the legal portions of the Torah as "*Shulḥan Arukh* 1.0," that is, the earliest formulation of Israel's statutory codes. Across the Torah, these passages do indeed present us with differing prescriptions for the same law. But only with modern, anachronistic eyes do these differences constitute contradiction. They are, rather, an early record of Israel's common-law evolution from Sinai to the end of the trek in the wilderness.

Chapter 7

But Is It Divine? How the Torah Broke with Ancient Political Thought[1]

F or some, the proposition that the Torah needs to be understood in its ancient context seems to diminish from the sacredness and divinity of the text. Indeed, in these chapters we have seen that how the Torah relates history, the way it thinks about law, and the very ways in which it expresses ideas are all in line with the way real, live, ancients thought and wrote about these things. Where, then, is the Torah's divinity evident in all this? It turns out it is precisely through appreciating the Torah in ancient context that we can arrive at a set of illuminating insights into how the Torah stands out from that context and reveals its divinity, and this is through its approach to political thought.

---

1. This chapter is a concise presentation of the arguments I make in my monograph, *Created Equal: How the Bible Broke with Ancient Political Thought* (New York: Oxford University Press, 2008).

In ways that were astonishingly new and counterintuitive, in ways that served the purposes of no known interest group, the political philosophy of the Torah rose like a phoenix out of the intellectual landscape of the ancient Near East. Throughout the ancient world the truth was self-evident: all men were *not* created equal. It is in the five books of the Torah that we find the birthplace of egalitarian thought. When seen against the backdrop of ancient norms, the social blueprint espoused by the Torah represents a series of quantum leaps in a sophisticated and interconnected matrix of theology, politics, and economics.

EQUALITY: A BRIEF HISTORY

To appreciate the claim that the Torah represents the dawn of egalitarian thought, let us set the idea in historical perspective. It is only in the European revolutions of the eighteenth and nineteenth centuries that we find the rejection of the privileges of rank and nobility that resulted in the delegitimation of entrenched caste, feudal, and slave systems. Greece and Rome had known their respective reformers, yet nowhere in the classical world do we find a struggle to do away with class distinctions. Nor do we find this articulated as a desideratum by any of the ancient authors in their ideal systems. "From the hour of their birth," wrote Aristotle, "some are marked out for subjection, others for rule."[2] It was assumed that some would be rich and that many, many more would be poor – not simply because that was the way things were, but because that was the way things were actually supposed to be. Justice, for Aristotle, meant that equals would be treated as equals and unequals as unequals. The Greeks and Romans possessed an overwhelming belief in the harmony of various classes.

The medieval mindset, too, believed that an ordered society was one in which each socioeconomic class performed its tasks for the common good. Social stratification was likewise endemic to the empires and lands of the ancient Near East. Nowhere in the region is there articulated the ideal of a society without class divisions founded on the control of economic, military, and political power. It is not merely that the notion

---

2. Aristotle, *Politics* BK1 1254a20, trans. Benjamin Jowett, available at http://classics. mit.edu/Aristotle/politics.1.one.html.

of social mobility was unknown to the ancient world; it would have been unthinkable. These cultures believed that the only way that a society could function was if everyone knew their station in life. The modern ideas of free choice and equal opportunity would have struck them as surefire recipes for anarchy and chaos. It is in the books of the Torah that we find the world's first blueprint for a social and religious order that seeks to lessen stratification and hierarchy and to place an unprecedented emphasis on the well-being and status of the common person.

RELIGION AND CLASS IN THE ANCIENT WORLD

The Torah's revolution of political thought begins with its theology. The attempt to treat things political as distinct from things religious is a thoroughly modern notion; in not a single culture in the ancient Near East is there a word for "religion" as distinct from "state." To appreciate the ancient mindset and the conceptual default settings that it supplied, imagine that we are archaeologists digging up an ancient culture called "America." Deciphering its religious texts, we discover that the paramount god of the pantheon bore the title "Commander in Chief," resided in a heavenly palace called "White House," and would traverse the heavens in his vehicle, "Chariot One." We further discover that Commander in Chief had a consort known as "First Lady" – herself a goddess of apparently meager powers, yet assumed by some to be a barometer of desirable values and fashionable dress. In the heavens was another palace, this one domed and populated by 535 lesser, regional deities, who routinely schemed and coalesced into partisan groupings, and who were known, on occasion, to have been able to depose the Commander in Chief.

Put differently, what we would discover is that the institutional order "down below" manifests the divine order of the cosmos "up above." This phenomenon, wherein the political structure of the heavens mirrored that of the earthly realm, was widespread in the ancient world, and it is easy to see why. Political regimes are, by definition, artificial, constructed, and therefore tenuous. Always implicit is the question: Why should *he* reign? The imposed institutional order can receive immeasurable legitimation, however, if the masses underfoot believe that it is rooted in ultimate reality and unchanging truth, that the significance of the political order is located in a cosmic and sacred frame of reference.

Ancient religion is the self-interested distortion that masks the human construction and exercise of power.

For example, we find that Enlil, the chief god of the Mesopotamian pantheon, utterly resembles his earthly counterpart, the king. Enlil, like his earthly counterpart, rules by delegating responsibilities to lesser dignitaries and functionaries. Like his earthly counterpart, he presides over a large assembly. He resides in a palace with his wives, children, and extended "house." Generally speaking, the gods struggled to achieve a carefree existence and enjoyed large banquets in their honor. Like kings, gods needed a palace, or what we would call a temple, where they, too, could reside in splendor in separation from the masses, with subjects caring for them in a host of earthly matters.

If a god wanted something – say a temple repaired, or the borders expanded – he communicated through various agents with the king, and the king was his focus. The gods never spoke to the masses, nor imparted instruction to them. Within ancient cosmologies, the masses served a single purpose: to toil and offer tribute. They were servants, at the lowest rung of the metaphysical hierarchy. The gods were interested in the masses to the extent that a baron or feudal lord would have interest in ensuring the well-being of the serfs that run the estate and supply its needs. Servants, no doubt, play a vital role in any monarchical order, but it is an instrumental role. From an existential perspective, it is a decidedly diminished and undignified role.

RELIGION AND CLASS IN THE TORAH

By contrast, the Torah's central accounts – the Exodus and the Revelation at Sinai – preempt claims of election and immanent hierarchy *within* the Israelite nation. The Exodus story effectively meant that no member of the children of Israel could lay claim to elevated status. All emanate from the Exodus – a common, seminal, liberating, but most importantly *equalizing* event. Although we normally think of the Revelation at Sinai in religious terms, its political implications are no less dramatic, and constitute the bedrock of the Torah's egalitarian theology. Elsewhere, the gods communicated only to the kings, and had no interest in the masses. But at Sinai, God spoke only to the masses, without delineating any role whatever for kings and their attendant hierarchies. The ancients had no problem believing that the gods could split the seas, or descend on a mountaintop in a storm of fire. Nevertheless, the stories of the Exodus and Sinai necessitated an enormous stretch of the imagination, because they required listeners to believe in *political* events that were without precedent and utterly improbable, even in mythological terms. Slaves had never been known to overthrow their masters. Gods had never been known to speak to an entire people.

As we saw earlier, the pact or covenant between God and Israel displays many common elements with what are known in biblical studies as ancient Near Eastern vassal treaties between a great king and a weaker one. As we noted, in these treaties, we typically find that the more powerful king acts on behalf of a weaker, neighboring king; sensing an opportunity to foster a loyal ally, he may send food during a famine, or soldiers to break a siege. In return, the lesser king demonstrates his appreciation to the powerful one by agreeing to a series of steps that express his gratitude and fealty. In these treaties the vassal king retains his autonomy and is treated like royalty when he visits the palace of the powerful king. Having been saved from Egypt by God, the children of Israel sign on at Sinai to a vassal treaty as sign of fealty, becoming junior partners to the sovereign king, God. The theological breakthrough of the Torah was the transformation of the metaphysical status of the masses, of the common person, to a new height, and the vitiation of nobles, royalty, and the like. The common man, in short, received an upgrade from king's servant to servant king.

Yet no less significant is the Torah's call that these stories should be promulgated among the people as their history. The point requires a note of context for us as moderns. Although there are over one million inscriptions in our possession from the ancient Near East, there is nowhere evidence of a national narrative that a people tells itself about its collective, national life, of moments of achievement or of despair, recorded for posterity. Stories abound in the ancient Near East – but they revolve around the exploits of individual gods, kings, and nobles. The most important audience of these materials was the gods themselves – as witnessed by the fact that these texts were often discovered in temple libraries, buried, or in other inaccessible locations. Myths were recited to remind the gods of their responsibilities. Details of a king's achievements on the battlefield were to constitute a report to a deity about the king's activities on his or her behalf; they were not composed for the masses. The Kadesh Inscriptions of Rameses II that we saw earlier were the exception that proves the rule: Those inscriptions were not only textual, but pictorial; and they were not only carved on stone, but copied and disseminated via papyri. However, most inscriptions of royal activity in ancient times were limited to monumental structures in writing that was inaccessible to the common person.

We may take a page from the history of technology of communication to understand the implication of the Torah's call to promulgate the accounts of Israel's early history. The distribution of printed texts in the early modern period is said to have occasioned the birth of modern citizenship within the nation-state. The vernacular languages that were now fashioned and standardized led to the creation of newspapers and novels designed for a mass readership comprised of people who were in disparate locales but could now envision themselves as a public sharing a common heritage, destiny, and range of interests religious, social, and political. People could now imagine themselves as a political collective, and thus was born the political "we."

It is in the Torah that we see for the first time the realization that the identity of a people may be formed around an awareness of its past. Indeed, the Hebrew Bible is the first literature before the Hellenistic period that may be termed a national history. Moreover, the Torah displays an attitude toward the dissemination of texts among the populace that is in sharp contrast to the relationship between texts and society that we find elsewhere in the ancient Near East. It is a contrast, further, that is a reflection of the egalitarian agenda that the Torah seeks to pursue, over against the entrenchment of class distinctions. In an age and place such as our own, where literacy is nearly ubiquitous, access to texts of many kinds and the knowledge they bear is unfettered and, in theory, available to all. But in the ancient world, physical access to written texts and the skills necessary to read them were everywhere highly restricted. Indeed, in the cultures of the ancient Near East as well as of ancient Greece, the production and use of texts was inextricably bound up with the formation of class distinctions: those who possessed the capacity to read and write were members of a trained scribal class who worked in the service of the ruling order.

The origins of writing in the ancient Near East were as a component of bureaucratic activity. Systems of writing were essential for the administration of large states. Indeed, the elite in these cultures had a vested interest in the status quo, which prevented others from gaining control of an important means of communication. Far from being interested in its simplification, scribes often chose to proliferate signs and values. The texts produced in Mesopotamia were composed exclusively by scribes and exclusively for scribal use – administrative or cultic – or for the training of yet other scribes.

The Cambridge anthropologist Jack Goody notes that a culture's willingness to disseminate its religious literature inevitably reflects an emphasis on the individual within that culture.[3] The comment sheds light on the Torah's agenda to establish an ennobled egalitarian citizenry, as we are witness to an impetus within the biblical vision to share the divine word with the people of Israel. Moses reads the divine word to the people at Sinai (Ex. 24:1–8). Periodically, the people are to gather at the Temple and hear public readings of the Torah (Deut. 31:10–13). It is telling that the Tanakh never depicts *kohanim* or scribes as jealous or protective of their writing skills, as is found in neighboring cultures.

In sum, we have seen something remarkable about the most basic, familiar aspects of the Torah. The idea of covenant, the story of the Exodus, the fact that the Torah is a written, publicized text – these are as significant politically as they are religiously. They each point to the equal and high standing of the common man in Israel.

THE TORAH'S RADICAL CONCEPTION
OF POLITICAL OFFICE

Turning from theology, we see that the Torah radically revamped regnant notions of political office and the exercise of power. What is most striking about the Torah's statements on political office are two radical ideas about how these offices are to be governed. First, we are witness here to the transition from the law of rule to the rule of law. Elsewhere in the ancient world, the kings composed and promulgated law, but were above

---

3. Jack Goody, *The Logic of Writing and the Organization of Society* (Cambridge: Cambridge University Press, 1986), 2.

it, not subject to it. Before the thinkers of Athens came along, the Torah arrived at the notion of equality before the law. All public institutions in the Torah – the judiciary, the priesthood, the monarchy, the institution of prophecy – are subordinated to the law. Moreover, the law is a public text whose dictates are meant to be widely known, thus making abuse of power more obvious and safeguarding the common citizenry.

Second, we may see that the most important body of authority in the polity envisioned by the Torah is none other than the people themselves. The Torah addresses the fraternal and egalitarian citizenry in the second person, "you," and charges them with appointing a king – if they desire one – and appointing judges. Put differently, the Torah specifies no nominating body for appointing leaders or representatives. Rather, the collective "you" – the common citizenry – bears ultimate responsibility to choose a king and to appoint judges. From American history we know how unthinkable it was only a few generations ago for many to contemplate the notion that persons of color or women should play a role in choosing who rules. For the royal monarchies of the ancient Near East, the notion that the masses – who elsewhere were serfs, servants – would hold any sway over those that ruled them was equally unfathomable.

If the people did elect to have a king, the Torah was determined that he should be but a shadow of what a king was elsewhere. Elsewhere kings played central roles in the cult. In the Torah he plays none. Elsewhere, the king aims to build a strong army. The Torah calls for him to have a limited treasury and to forgo a cavalry (Deut. 17:16–17), limitations that would leave him commanding only a small army. Moreover, were a royal chariot force to serve as the backbone of the nation's defense, it would inevitably emerge as an elite military class. The great jurist of Athens, Solon, extended preferred status to the members of the cavalry over other citizens. But what confers status in the Torah is citizenship in the covenantal community, and this is shared by all. Elsewhere, the king would consolidate his power through a network of political marriages. The Torah forbids the king from taking a large number of wives (Deut. 17:17).

Finally, we see in the Torah a page in the history of constitutional thought, one that would not be written again until the American founding. It pertains to a highly advanced notion of the separation of powers. Classical Greek political thought had already understood that in the absence of a strong center in the figure of a monarch or a tyrant, factionalism threatened the stability of the polity. It was inevitable that the population would contain rich and poor, nobles and commoners. The absence of homogeneity led classical theorists to balance power by ensuring that each faction within society would receive a share of the rule. Yet, the balance of power was not a balance of institutions of government, as we are accustomed to today. Rather, the balance was achieved by allowing each of the socioeconomic factions a functioning role within each seat of government. Thus, in Roman jurist Polybius's conception, the legislative branch of government in the republic was to consist of two bodies – the senate for the nobles and the assembly for the commoners – with each institution permanently enshrined in law.

The notion that the effective division of power was predicated upon its distribution across preexisting societal seats of power was one that would hold sway throughout most of the history of republican thought, from Roman theorists through early modern thinkers. It is central even to the thinking of Montesquieu, the father of modern constitutional theory, who is credited with proposing the separation of powers into three branches – executive, legislative, and judiciary – in his 1748 work, *The Spirit of the Laws*. Looking at the English model of his day, Montesquieu held that the legislative power should consist of a body of hereditary nobles and a body of commoners. He saw hereditary nobility not as a necessary evil, nor even as an immutable fact of life, but rather as a boon to effective government. The nobility, with its inherent wealth and power, would serve as a moderating force within government against the abuses of the monarch. Moreover, the fact that the nobility's strength was derived from its own resources would endow its members with a sense of independence. This, together with developed education and time for reflection, would enable the nobles to contribute to effective government in a way that members of the lower classes could not. Montesquieu could not conceive of a classless society and a regime in which the division of powers was purely institutional and instrumental, where the eligibility to hold office was independent of class.

Here the Torah stands distinct. For the first time in history we see the articulation of a division of at least some powers along lines of institution and instrument rather than of class and kinship, where office legitimizes preexisting societal seats of power. Anyone who is "among your brethren" (Deut. 17:15) is eligible to be appointed king. Moreover, the king is appointed by the collective "you" that we mentioned before. How that selection occurs, apparently, is an issue that the Torah deliberately left open so as to imply that there is no body that a priori has a greater divine imprimatur than any other. In this sense, the Torah's notion of offices that are entirely institutional and instrumental is an idea that would again appear only with the American Founding Fathers.

The same is true with regard to the judiciary, as outlined in the book of Deuteronomy. Anyone may be appointed judge, and no less importantly, anyone, in theory, is eligible to participate in the process of appointing judges (Deut. 16:17). One could have thought of any number of bodies that could have been charged with appointing judges: the king, the prophets, the *kohanim*, or other judges. But the Torah insists: "Judges and officers you shall appoint for yourself" (16:18). The appointment of judges is mandated with the sole purpose of achieving the execution of justice, rather than the assignment of office to perpetuate the standing of a noble class. As Montesquieu noted in the eighteenth century, it is critical that the people appoint judges, so that they have faith in the justice that is meted out. The only source prior to Montesquieu to arrive at this insight was the Torah.

GOD THE ECONOMIST

The Torah understood that in order to create an egalitarian order, it would also need to re-envision the economic structure of society, for without equity, there is no equality. What the Torah proposes is the Western tradition's first prescription for an economic order that seeks to minimize the distinctions of class based on wealth, and instead to ensure the economic benefit of the common citizen.

A ubiquitous feature of the socioeconomic landscape of the ancient Near East was the threat faced by the common person of falling into irreversible insolvency. Social stratification would emerge as the common people would have to sell off their farm animals, their land, and even their own freedom. Famine, drought, or war could lead to precisely the kind of economic landscape we witness in the account of Egypt under Joseph, in Genesis 47. The Torah sought to remedy this through radical legislation on several fronts. Elsewhere, the norm was that land was owned by the palace and by the temple. The Torah, in contrast, knows of no landholding for either king or cult. Instead, nearly the entire land is given to the people themselves, in an association of free farmers and herdsmen, subsumed within a single social class. The idea that wide tracts of available land should be divided among the commoners was unprecedented. Perhaps the most famous example of such an initiative from modern times is the American Homestead Act of 1862. With the Great Plains open to mass settlement, nearly any person twenty-one years of age or older could acquire, at virtually no cost, a tract of 160 acres that would become his after five years of residence and farming. For millions of new arrivals and other landless Americans, the Homestead Act was an opportunity to acquire assets and to bring equality of economic standing in line with equality before the law.

The Torah also took specific aim at the institution of taxation. Elsewhere, taxes to the state and to the cult were deeply integrated. In the Torah, no taxes are specified for the state. Of course, no regime would be able to function without taxing its populace – but the Torah apparently envisioned that taxes would be levied without sacral sanction, as was so prevalent elsewhere. God would not be invoked as the taxman. Moreover, far less surplus is demanded from the people of Israel for the Temple than was customary in the imperial cults of the ancient Near East. The *kohanim* and *Leviim* who serve in the Temple are considered by the Torah to be a divine honor guard.

Whereas elsewhere, cultic personnel controlled vast tracts of land, the Torah balances the status that these groups maintain in the cult by denying them arable lands of their own. They are dependent upon the people they represent for their subsistence, and in some passages are even grouped together with other categories of the underprivileged. The Torah further legislates that one type of tax – the *maaser ani* – should not be paid to the Temple at all, but rather distributed to the needy – the first known program of taxation legislated for a social purpose (Deut. 14:28–29).

What is most remarkable about the Torah's economic reforms is the manner in which the new economy is incorporated into a new measure of time. Elsewhere in the ancient Near East, the calendar was based upon readily perceptible astronomical rhythms: the counting of days stems from observing the rising and setting of the sun; of months, from observations of the waxing and waning of the moon; of years, from observing the seasons and position of the sun. The ancient Near East, however, knows no calendar that incorporates the notion of a week. The week is the invention of the Torah, and is rooted, of course, in the Torah's account of Creation, in which God worked for six days and rested on the seventh. The result is that throughout the Torah the Shabbat principle determines the schedule of the laws of social welfare, and serves as a great equalizing force between haves and have-nots. Shabbat day is a day of rest for all. In the seventh year – the Sabbatical year – the field lies fallow and is available for all to enjoy, and debt release, as we saw earlier, is enacted. Time itself is marshaled in the establishment of the egalitarian agenda.

A REVOLUTIONARY DOCUMENT

What power interest could have been served by this program? We have already seen that it was a program that favored neither the king, nor the rich, nor the priesthood. Prophets are hardly mentioned in the Torah, and the criteria set out for validating an individual as a prophet are exacting in the extreme. Sages, or philosophers, are nowhere mentioned at all. No immediate candidate jumps out of the pages of the Torah as the interested party in the formulation of this new egalitarian order.

Throughout the ancient world, the truth was self-evident: all men were *not* created equal. They saw the world they had created and, behold, it was good. It was good, they deemed, *because* it was ordered around a rigid hierarchy, where everyone knew his station in life, each according to his class. For the first time in history, the Torah presented a vision to the masses in which the gods were something other than their own selves writ large, a vision with a radically different understanding of God and man. It introduced new understandings of the law, of political office, of military power, of taxation, of social welfare. It conceived in radically new ways the importance of national narrative, of technologies of communication, and of a culture's calibration of time. What we find in the Torah is a platform for social order marked with the imprint of divinity. Within the annals of political thought it is difficult to think of another document that revolutionized so much in such anonymity, and with so little precedent to inspire it.

Of course, these notions of equality are but early precursors of our more developed notions of equality today. Yet, as we saw in the last chapter, we are meant to apprehend God's instruction in the Torah as the first word, not the last word. The Torah instructs us with the implicit understanding that society changes, and with it, the form in which we fulfill God's will. The *peshat* level of the Torah speaks to the generation to which it was given. Already within the Torah itself, we can see how ideas and instruction given at an earlier stage were updated and reapplied later in different forms, and so it is here. We can marvel at how utterly removed the Torah's political thought was from the prevailing spirit about such things in ancient times. And, at the same time, we can appreciate that without believing that we are limited to the notion of equality as it had been expressed in those ancient times. Rather, the Torah serves as an inspiration for the further elaboration of those ideas as times change and events warrant so doing.

Throughout the book's first section, we explored some of the unacknowledged weaknesses in contemporary biblical criticism, noting that its reliance on modern conventions is a critical and recurring error. We saw that when the Torah is understood within its ancient context, many of the issues raised by the critical study of the Bible now appear in a new light. Moreover, we discovered that when we place the Torah in its historical context, we can more fully appreciate how truly revolutionary it is and was.

With that in mind, we embark on a new study, one in which we explore the history of our most treasured beliefs generally and our belief in the Torah's divine provenance in particular.

Part II

Appreciating Principles of Faith and the Principle of Torah from Heaven

Chapter 8

From the Mishna to the Rambam's Thirteen Principles of Faith

The question of the origins of the Torah goes to the very heart of Orthodox belief and practice. In light of the centrality of this issue, it is surprising that one cannot find anywhere in the classical sources of the rabbinic tradition a *systematic discussion* of what a Jew must believe about the origins of the Torah. By that, I mean that no figure of stature has ever set out to marshal the basic talmudic sources on the topic, followed by a review of the positions taken by *Rishonim* and *Aḥronim*, concluding with a ruling on the issue. Instead, the issue is subsumed within the tradition under a broader rubric: the acceptance and status of the Rambam's Thirteen Principles of Faith. Understanding what a Jew must believe about the origins of the Torah, therefore, is inextricably bound with the question of the status and acceptance of the Thirteen Principles of Faith. As with all matters of rabbinic tradition, these questions have a long history. And as with all matters of rabbinic tradition, what recent authorities have ruled and taught carries the greatest weight for contemporary thought and practice.

To appreciate the distinctive qualities and authority of the Thirteen Principles in general and how the sages of Israel have related to the question of the Torah's origins in particular, we must trace these issues from the beginning. This chapter explores how our earliest authorities related to these issues, from the Mishna until the composition of the Rambam's Thirteen Principles, using four sets of questions:

1. When and where did the very notion of "fundamental principles" of Judaism arise? Why did they arise at that time? Just what did it mean that a proposition was "a fundamental principle"? Were there different opinions of what this meant?

2. What implications did that have for one who affirmed or, alternatively, denied such a proposition?

3. What are the various opinions within talmudic sources concerning the origins of the Torah? Were these various opinions considered by their expositors to be "fundamental principles" of the Jewish faith? If not, why not?

4. The Rambam was not the first major rabbinic figure to compose a list of principles of faith. How did his set of principles differ from those proposed by his predecessors? And how did his opinions about the origins of the Torah differ from those of some of his contemporaries? What were the historical circumstances that led different authorities to different conclusions about these questions?

MISHNA SANHEDRIN 10:1 AND THE PRECEPT OF TORAH *MIN HASHAMAYIM*

The earliest and perhaps most cardinal source concerning what a Jew must believe about the origins of the Torah is the Mishna in Sanhedrin 10:1, which states that a person forfeits his place in the World to Come if he says "there is no *torah* from heaven," *ein torah min hashamayim*.

To properly understand this mishna and how it was understood by the Gemara, we need to probe the meaning of the term *torah* in the language of the Mishna, and in tannaitic literature more generally. Put differently, we must ask: What corpus is included in this *torah* that is from heaven? Most today would say that it refers to the text of the Torah.

This is but one position found in the *mesora* that in fact seems to arise only during the Middle Ages, but not earlier. Indeed, the Mishna does sometimes refer to the text of *the* Torah, but when it does it will almost always say *hatorah* or *batorah*, employing the definite article, or it will refer to a *sefer Torah*. In our mishna, however, the phrase *ein torah min hashamayim* appears without use of the definite article before the word *torah*. Consider the meaning of the term *torah* in arguably the most well-known mishna of all, the first mishna of Avot: "Moses received *torah* from Sinai and passed it on to Joshua." We would hardly say that *torah* here is limited to a Torah scroll, or to the text of the five books of the Torah. What Moses received and passed on was, to use our terms, the *mesora*, meaning the entirety of Torah, its written *and* oral parts. In fact, this is the sense in which we find the word *torah* used throughout the Mishna, in terms such as *divrei torah* or *talmud torah*. These phrases have never been understood as referring to the text of the five books of the Torah alone; *divrei torah* and *talmud torah* encompass the *mesora* as a whole, broadly conceived. In fact, in the entire Mishna and Tosefta, we never find the phrases *Torah Shebikhtav* and *Torah Shebe'al Peh*. There is, simply, *torah*, an unindividuated whole: the reading of the text through the eyes of the *mesora*. The word *torah* alone without the definite article never bears the narrow connotation of the text of the five books of the Torah.[1]

Even when the Mishna asks where something is found "in *the* Torah," it is far from clear that the reference is to the text of the Torah alone. Mishna Sanhedrin 10:1 offers a good case in point: "These are the individuals who do not have a place in the World to Come: he who says there is no resurrection of the dead from the Torah (*ein thiyat hametim min HaTorah*)." The biblical sources cited in Sanhedrin 91b–92a are all interpreted through the eyes of the *mesora*, and are not the literal, *peshat* meaning of those verses. True enough, the Gemara points to various verses as prooftexts, and that would seem to suggest that *torah* here refers to the text of the Torah. But in order to derive the concept of resurrection that the Mishna seeks, those verses are read through the prism of

---

1. On the polyvalent meaning of the term *torah* in early rabbinic literature, see Ephraim E. Urbach, *The Sages: Their Concepts and Beliefs* (Jerusalem: Magnes Press, 1975), 286–91.

derash; the text of Torah and the *derash* of Torah are meshed and fused. The idea of resurrection is not, in fact, found in the text of the Torah alone, unless it is accompanied by the prism of the *mesora*. In fact, one of the verses cited as proof of the basis for resurrection "in *the* Torah" is a verse from the book of Daniel (12:2)!

This now allows us to better comprehend our focus, the continuation of Mishna Sanhedrin 10:1. Among those who forfeit the World to Come is "he who says there is no *torah* from heaven (*ein torah min hashamayim*)." Note that the word *torah* here lacks the definite article; it does not say "one who says *ein HaTorah min hashamayim*." The mishna here does not address the denial of the divinity of the text of the Torah, but of the indivisible whole that is the text of the Torah and its received interpretation as passed down by the rabbis. As we shall see, the word *torah* in this phrase has been understood in various ways by various rabbinic authorities across the ages.

The mishna almost certainly stems from the socio-religious climate in which it was conceived. Those who forfeit their place in heaven include the *epikoros* and those who study "external books." These were real-life examples of Jews who were, in the eyes of the rabbis of the Mishna, straying from the true path. The mishna clearly has in mind challenges to the *mesora* that are rooted in the beliefs and practices of the age. There were indeed Greek anti-Jewish polemics that denied the Torah was a divine text.[2] But within the Jewish community, the debates were elsewhere. It was a given that the Torah was sacred; sectarian debates raged around the proper interpretation of the Torah. In such an environment, it would make sense for the mishna to stress that *torah* – the *mesora* as a whole – was divine.[3]

---

2. See Menahem Stern, *Greek and Latin Authors on Jews and Judaism*, vol. 3 (Jerusalem: Israel Academy of Sciences and Humanities, 1974–1984), 137. See also David Rokéah, *HaYahadut VeHaNatzrut BeRe'i HaPulmus HaPagani* (Jerusalem: Dinur Center, 1991), 18–21.

3. This view corresponds to the well-known dictum: "Mikra, Mishna, Talmud, and Aggada – even what a seasoned student would expound before his teacher – were all delivered to Moses on Sinai" (Y. Pe'ah 2:6 [16b]). For variations on this saying and the history of its interpretation see Aharon Schweka, "Luḥot HaEven, HaTorah, VeHaMitzva," *Tarbiz* 81 (2013): 343–66.

This understanding of the mishna may seem unfamiliar, or even radical, because many later expositors understood *torah* here as referring to the Five Books of Moses. But the more expansive definition of the term *torah* offered here was certainly the way that the Gemara understood it, and, indeed, as we shall see later, the way most of the great sages of Israel understood it as well in the twelfth and thirteenth centuries. When we translate the phrase *ha'omer ein torah min hashamayim* as "one who says *the Torah* is not from heaven," we inadvertently choose one side of this debate as the sole understanding of the phrase. Therefore, throughout this discussion, I shall translate the mishna's words *torah min hashamayim* as "*torah* from heaven" – leaving open the precise meaning of the term, so that we do not unwittingly read into the phrase a sole reference to the text of the Written Torah. Thus we can remain open to the different understandings of the sages of Israel that will be reviewed here.

I begin with the Gemara's understanding of "*torah* from heaven." To explicate this phrase, the Gemara (Sanhedrin 99a) brings three *baraitot*, all without comment, that expound upon the verse, "He has shamed the word of the Lord" (Num. 15:31):

Baraita 1

Our rabbis taught: "Because he has despised the word of the Lord, and has broken His commandment, that soul shall utterly be cut off" (Num. 15:31):

(1) This refers to one who says that *torah* is not from heaven.

(2) Another rendering: "Because he has despised the word of the Lord" refers to an *epikoros* (i.e., one who denigrates Torah sages).

(3) Another rendering: "Because he has despised the word of the Lord" refers to one who gives an interpretation of the Torah [not according to the halakha].

Baraita 2

Another [*baraita*] taught: "Because he has despised the word of the Lord" – this refers to one who says that *torah* is not from heaven. And even if he asserts that the whole Torah is from heaven, excepting a particular verse, which [he maintains] was not uttered by God but by Moses himself, he is included in "because he has despised the word of the Lord." And even if he admits that the whole Torah is from heaven, excepting a single point, a particular *kal vaḥomer* or a certain *gezera shava*, he is still included in "because he has despised the word of the Lord."

Baraita 3:

It has been taught:

(1) R. Meir used to say: He who studies the Torah but does not teach it is alluded to in "he has despised the word of the Lord."

(2) R. Natan said: [The verse, "he has despised the word of the Lord" refers to] whoever pays no heed to the Mishna.

(3) R. Nehorai said: [The verse refers to] whosoever can engage in the study of the Torah but fails to do so.

(4) R. Yishmael said: [The verse refers to] those who worship foreign gods.

The Gemara provides no comment to these three *baraitot*. What are we meant to derive from them? How do they elucidate the Mishna's term "*torah* from heaven"? We may safely come to two conclusions. The first conclusion concerns the lesson of the first *baraita*. This source reveals the prooftext for the Mishna's contention that one who says there is no *torah* from heaven forfeits his place in the World to Come. According to this *baraita*, that prooftext is Numbers 15:31, which states that he who has despised the word of the Lord shall be "cut off," i.e., will lose his place in the World to Come. The second conclusion we can safely determine is that the second *baraita* was brought because it defines the parameters of the *"torah"* that is from heaven. The answer this *baraita* gives is unequivocal: *torah* in this mishna includes the entirety of *torah*, its written and oral components. The discourse of the *baraita* is striking. Note the similar language that opens both halves of the *baraita*:

1. *Even if he asserts that the whole Torah is from heaven,* excepting a particular verse, which [he maintains] was not uttered by God but by Moses himself, he is included in "because he has despised the word of the Lord."

2. And *even if he asserts that the whole Torah is from heaven,* excepting a single point, a particular a *kal vaḥomer* or a certain *gezera shava* – he is still included in "because he has despised the word of the Lord."

The "Torah" is made up of *gezerot shavot* no less than it is made up of verses. All are part of the indivisible whole that is *"torah* from heaven."[4]

The talmudic source for the notion that God dictated every word of the Torah to Moses is found in a *baraita* in Bava Batra 14b–15a. This *baraita* states that Moses wrote the Torah, including the *parasha* of Balaam, and that Joshua wrote the book of Joshua and the last eight verses of the Torah, which narrate the passing of Moses. The Gemara later explores this contention concerning the last eight verses of the Torah:

---

4. This was also the understanding of *"torah* from heaven" adopted by the twelfth-century French Tosafist, Rabbi Yonatan of Lunel (c. 1135–c. 1210); Rabbi Meir HaLevi Abulafia (Spain, thirteenth century), *Yad Rama* Sanhedrin, ch. 11; Rabbi Isaiah di Trani the Younger (Italy, thirteenth century; *Piskei Riaz,* Sanhedrin ch. 11); and Rabbi Eleazar of Worms (thirteenth century) in *Sefer Roke'aḥ, Hilkhot Teshuva,* ch. 28. In time, however, classical commentators to the Mishna would define the phrase *"torah* from heaven" in our mishna only with reference to the first half of the *baraita* – that which refers to the text of the Five Books of Moses. See the commentaries on this mishna of Meiri (also thirteenth century) and *Tosefot Yom Tov.* It is also worthy of note that, taken together, these three *baraitot* offer eight different interpretations of what it means to "despise the word of the Lord." Strictly speaking, one might have thought that "the word of the Lord" refers to the words of the Torah. And yet, nowhere in the three *baraitot* is the "word of the Lord" equated with the text of the Torah alone.

"Joshua wrote the book which bears his name and the last eight verses of the Torah." This statement is in agreement with the authority who says that eight verses in the Torah were written by Joshua, as it has been taught: [It is written], "So Moses the servant of the Lord died there." Now is it possible that Moses being dead could have written the words, "Moses died there"? The truth is, however, that up to this point Moses wrote; from this point Joshua wrote. This is the opinion of R. Yehuda, or, according to others, of R. Nehemiah. Said R. Shimon to him: Can [we imagine the] scroll of the Law being short of one word, and is it not written, "Take this book of the Law"? No; what we must say is that up to this point the Holy One, blessed be He, dictated and Moses repeated and wrote, and from this point God dictated and Moses wrote with tears.

We may draw several conclusions from our review of talmudic literature. No opinion in the Talmud enunciates the opinion that there is a fundamental principle of Judaism that the entirety of the Torah was dictated by God to Moses. To be sure, R. Shimon in the *baraita* just cited maintains that this was the fashion in which Israel received the Torah. But neither R. Shimon in this *baraita* nor any other voice throughout the Talmud maintains that this position attains some ultimate status as a principle of faith. Mishna Sanhedrin 10:1, for its part, does not make this claim either. In fact, it says nothing about the role of Moses in the transmission of the Torah, nor does it offer a statement about the *text* of the Torah per se. Rather it seeks to buttress the notion that the entire *mesora* is of divine origin. The second *baraita* in Sanhedrin 99a cited before indeed insists that one must believe that the entire text of the Torah is divine, but makes no mention of the role of Moses in its transmission.

Furthermore, it would seem that Mishna Sanhedrin 10:1 is not to be taken as a comprehensive list of fundamental beliefs. Citing three different tannaitic opinions, it lists a total of six categories of individuals who lose their place in the World to Come. Four of these stem not from heretical beliefs but from prohibited activities. The only necessary beliefs listed are the belief in the resurrection of the dead and the belief in *torah* from heaven. By threatening the loss of the World to Come, the Mishna buttressed these beliefs against those who would challenge them. We see here a key strategy in rabbinic tradition addressing the issue of beliefs, one that we will revisit time and again in the coming pages: rabbinic tradition does not address theology in either systematic or comprehensive fashion. Rather, the sages highlight beliefs on the basis of the challenges and spiritual needs of the moment. When a particular issue is at the center of a challenge facing traditional Judaism, rabbinic leaders will respond by underscoring its importance.

THE BEGINNINGS OF PRINCIPLES OF FAITH IN THE RABBINIC TRADITION: RABBI SAADIA GAON

The first rabbinic figure to lay down a list of Judaism's fundamental beliefs was Rabbi Saadia Gaon (Baghdad, 882–942), who lived some two centuries prior to the Rambam. His list is not widely known, let alone studied. It appears in a work he composed on the Song of David (II Sam. 22), in his commentary on verses 2 and 3 of that chapter (which parallel word for word Ps. 18:2).[5] These verses contain ten terms of salvation and Rabbi Saadia Gaon (hereafter: Rasag) interprets each word to refer to a different fundamental tenet of Judaism. The specifics of the ten tenets need not detain us; they contain elements that are familiar to us from the Rambam's list: the eternity of God; that God is the first cause of the world; that His rule of the world is just; that the wicked are punished; that the righteous merit the World to Come.

But what is most remarkable about Rasag's list – beyond any of the particular tenets he mentions – is the very fact that he is the first major Jewish figure to ever compose such a list. Nowhere in the Tanakh or in talmudic literature do we find a list of the basic tenets of our faith. This is astonishing because articles of faith would seem to be critically important. And it is even more astonishing given the minute detail with which so many other aspects of the *mesora* are presented – think of the list of kosher animals listed in Leviticus 11, or the thirty-nine *avot melakha* listed in Mishna Shabbat. How could it be that something as central as fundamental beliefs had never been produced?

---

5. The full text can be found in Yosef Qafiḥ (Kapach), *Perushei Rabbenu Saadia Gaon al HaTorah* (Jerusalem: Mossad HaRav Kook, 1984), 175–76. See Haggai Ben-Shammai, "Aseret Ikkarei HaEmuna shel Rav Saadia Gaon," *Daat* 37 (1996): 11–26.

Framing the question in this way suggests that there is something deficient about biblical and talmudic thought for which we need to account. But this is hardly the case when we examine the issue in a wider perspective. Consider this: All of the cultures of the ancient Near East, from Egypt to Mesopotamia, were deeply religious ones and peoples there no doubt believed many things about many gods. Archaeologists have unearthed religious texts of various sorts left by these cultures – omen texts, prayers, formulae for temple rituals, epics about the gods, and more. But none of these cultures ever produced a list of basic religious beliefs. In fact – and this is truly revealing – none of these cultures even had a word for *belief*. Coming back to our own sources we see the same thing: it is not merely the fact – astonishing in itself – that neither the Tanakh nor Ḥazal ever produce a list of basic beliefs; neither in biblical nor in talmudic Hebrew do we even find a word that parallels our modern word *belief*, as a noun, as in "one of the Torah's basic *beliefs* is. …" The nouns employed to convey this idea – *emunot, de'ot, yesodot,* and *ikkarim* – are all post-talmudic.

If ancient religious cultures – whether sacred or pagan – indeed contained what we would call "beliefs," why did they produce no word for this seemingly critical concept? Why did they not compose concise lists enumerating these beliefs? Why was Rasag the first rabbinic figure to posit such a list?

To understand why ancient cultures never formulated lists of beliefs let us consider by way of analogy something closer to home: marriage. Imagine that you are tasked with coming up with a list of the ten most important ingredients for a healthy marriage. If you are married, you certainly know that there are many lessons one must learn in order to achieve and sustain a happy marriage. In the course of your married life you probably give thought to these on a regular basis. Yet, even if you have been happily married for decades, you would have difficulty penning such a list, and you certainly have not been rehearsing a little digest of such principles during all your years of marriage.

Successful marriage is indeed predicated on many noble ideas and attitudes, but these go unexpressed in systematic prose formulation. For husband and wife, the ideals of love, loyalty, sharing, compromise, partnership, empathy, sacrifice, and more are communicated, nurtured, and clarified not through abstract and concise articulation but through lived experience, in complex and changing ways. Without even thinking which ideal is more important, or how to define any of them precisely, a couple learns intuitively what is required of them and to what they aspire. An example: Every couple knows the importance of communication. But it is useless to state "communication is very important for a good marriage," unless a much larger context is included. After all, if I am feeling something strongly, does that mean that I should immediately share that with my spouse? Should I tell her everything I am feeling? Suddenly a host of other considerations and ideals colors and shapes exactly what it means to engage in constructive communication. Communication between partners is not a value that stands in isolation; it is best understood and learned in the complex web of a lived relationship.

It is the same with religious ideals and precepts. The Tanakh and the Talmud expect that Judaism's core ideals will be best communicated, nurtured, and clarified through a life lived fully within the context of a committed community. Our sources do indeed communicate ideas in writing, but always with only partial expression, framed and developed for the needs of the given situation. And what was true for Jews in the biblical and talmudic periods was true for inhabitants of the ancient Near East generally. Their thought systems also were part of the warp and woof of daily experience, lived and modeled by family members, neighbors, and fellow tribesmen and countrymen.

When and where, then, did the concept of a *catechism* – a list of beliefs – arise? The watershed moment comes with the rise of Christianity, for Christianity was unlike any religion that preceded it.[6] All peoples of the ancient world held beliefs in and about the gods. But they never saw themselves as charged by their gods to proselytize to others, to encourage them to take on a new faith commitment to a religious system they had not known previously. Christianity was the first religion that sought to recruit and indoctrinate others into a new faith. When a religion such as Judaism expresses itself through a complex web of ideas and practices, it can only be transmitted effectively through a life lived

---

6. Wilfred Cantwell Smith, *The Meaning and End of Religion* (Minneapolis: Fortress Press, 1963), 180.

within a community of faith and observance. There have always been individuals who converted to Judaism, and today, we see estranged Jews who return to faith. But these phenomena have always been peripheral in terms of their sheer numbers. There has never been a mass conversion to Judaism, nor has there ever been a mass return to Judaism. Our system does not easily lend itself to those types of movements. If you wish to proselytize to others, your religion needs to be relatively easy to grasp; otherwise it will be difficult to win over adherents in any number.[7] And this is where catechisms became necessary for Christianity as a proselytizing religion – to bring salvation to the many. The uninitiated needed only to affirm a basic list of beliefs in order to become members of the faith in good standing.

Just as Christianity had sought converts, so too did Islam, and like Christianity, Islam promulgated catechisms of basic beliefs that were easy to understand and disseminate.

Judaism's encounter with Islamic culture in the time of the *Geonim* was much more intimate than had been the encounter between Ḥazal and Christianity at any point in the tannaitic and amoraic periods. Rasag's move to enumerate Judaism's principles was part of a broader approach that he employed of observing what worked for Islam and incorporating those strategies within Jewish life as well.[8] For example, Muslims at this time were reading their Scripture – the Quran – according to its simple, plain meaning, and Rasag sensed the value for Judaism of encouraging Jews to read our holy Scripture in the same way. His commentary on the Torah ushered in a new emphasis on *peshuto shel mikra*, reading the Tanakh for its simple meaning and not only through the eyes of the Midrash. Just as Muslims wrote in a style of Arabic that would imitate the Quran as the paradigm of all good Arabic writing, so too Rasag championed writing in Hebrew in a style that imitated the Hebrew of the Tanakh. Another area of adaptive innovation spearheaded by Rasag was in the realm of religious philosophy, at which Muslim

---

7. See discussion in *Encyclopedia Britannica*, s.v. "Creed," accessed June 23, 2019, https://www.britannica.com/topic/creed.
8. For an overview of Rasag's openness to innovation, see Robert Brody, *Sa'adyah Gaon* (Oxford: Littman Library of Jewish Civilization, 2013).

theologians excelled. The midrashim of Ḥazal had long conveyed all manner of religious ideas. Rasag's *Emunot VeDeot*, a full-length systematic treatment of Judaism's philosophy, was the first rabbinic work of its kind. The succinct list of basic beliefs – the catechism, if you will – that he composes to the words of Psalms 18:2 is likewise influenced by the success of such practice within Muslim settings. Rasag understood that such a list could be well-received by Jews as well, set within a mnemonic device that could help the faithful to remember cherished beliefs.

Although Rasag lists these as fundamental beliefs, the implications of that designation are limited. Rasag nowhere suggests that these beliefs are necessary to merit salvation in the World to Come. Nor does he argue that one's membership within the Jewish people is contingent upon their acceptance. He does not suggest that they be recited or studied regularly. He does not showcase the list as a freestanding composition, but rather as a part of his commentary on II Samuel 22. Instead, Rasag's list serves simply as an educational and mnemonic device; by remembering the ten words of a well-known verse from the Psalms, a person could thereby access ten beliefs central to the faith.

A closer look at Rasag's catechism of ten beliefs reveals that there is no mention whatever of the Torah and its origins. The closest reference – a veiled one at that – is Rasag's sixth principle, that we are bound to perform God's commandments as related to us by His messengers, the prophets. There is nothing in Rasag's writing that suggests that anyone other than Moses had a hand in writing the Torah, but he does not make this issue a fundamental tenet. What is fundamental for Rasag in his Psalms commentary catechism is that God communicates His will to His messengers, the prophets, and that we are bound to follow their dictates because the source of what they instruct is divine. There is no differentiation between the status of Moses vis-à-vis the other prophets, and no claim made about the origins of the text of the Torah itself.

PRINCIPLES OF FAITH IN THE WRITINGS
OF RABBENU HANANEL OF KIROUAN

The next rabbinic figure to compose a list of principles of faith was Rabbenu Hananel ben Hushiel of Kirouan (965–1055), best known as the first figure to pen a commentary on the Babylonian Talmud, printed in the standard Vilna version of the Talmud. Rabbenu Hananel also wrote a brief commentary on the Torah, most of which was lost until the twentieth century.[9] In his comments on Exodus 14:31, which mentions Israel's "trust" in God (*vayaaminu baHashem*), Rabbenu Hananel lists what he calls the four primary dimensions of *emuna*. Like Rasag before him, Rabbenu Hananel makes no mention of the origins of the Torah nor any mention of Moses. And like Rasag, Rabbenu Hananel claims that one of the principles of belief is that we affirm that God appoints His messengers, the prophets, to deliver His word, and that we are duty bound to follow their dictates.

However, what is significant in Rabbenu Hananel's comments about fundamental principles is not which precepts make his list and which do not; largely, they are a condensed version of what Rasag had postulated. What is significant here is the *function* of the fundamental principles: "He who believes [in these precepts] merits great reward... and merits entering the Garden of Eden... and he who does not believe in these [precepts]...has exacted from him punishment, for they comport themselves in haughtiness, and do not merit life." For Rasag, the catechism was an *educational tool*; by recalling the well-known verse of II Samuel 2–3, the faithful would have access to one-line formulations of the foundational tenets of the Jewish faith. For Rabbenu Hananel, however, the catechism contains the ideas that are central to salvation and meriting the World to Come.

IBN HAZM THE ANDALUSIAN AND THE LIBEL
OF THE FALSIFICATION OF THE TORAH

Attention to the origins of the Torah within Jewish catechisms rises dramatically shortly thereafter, however, in the wake of the pernicious writings of a single man – the Muslim theologian Ibn Hazm the Andalusian.

Abu Muhammad Ali ibn Ahmad ibn Sa'id ibn Hazm al-Andalusi (c. 994–1064) was born to an aristocratic Cordoban family. In time, Ibn Hazm would achieve acclaim as one of medieval Islam's greatest

---

9. Rabbenu Hananel's commentary is found in the *Torat Ḥayim* edition of *Mikra'ot Gedolot* published by Mossad HaRav Kook.

theologians.[10] Of interest for our purposes is a tract he composed on Jewish and Christian Scripture, *Treatise on the Obvious Contradictions and Evident Lies in the Book Which the Jews Call the Torah and in the Rest of Their Books, and in the Four Gospels, All of Which Establish That These Have Been Distorted and Are Different from What God, Mighty and Exalted, Revealed.*[11] Islam had traditionally adopted a dual posture toward the Hebrew Bible generally and the Torah in particular. On the one hand, Mohammed was the greatest prophet, and the Quran the highest of God's revelations. But the Hebrew Bible and the Gospels had achieved acclaim over many centuries and were recognized as divine as well. Already the Quran had directed how the Torah should be regarded: The original Torah had been given to Moses. And when read properly, it told of the rise of the prophet Mohammed. But early Muslims also held the doctrine of *taḥrīf* – that the Jews had falsified their Scripture – and thus many other references to Mohammed were lost.

In short, two contradictory approaches to the Hebrew Bible and the Gospels emerged: On the one hand, they were divine in origin and could be marshaled for Islamic apologetics. On the other hand, they were deficient, as they had become falsified over time.[12] It is against the backdrop of this dual tradition that Ibn Hazm penned his treatise on the Hebrew Bible and the Gospels. Ibn Hazm's treatise was without precedent. He maintains that the Torah must have been written by an imbecilic simpleton, unlearned in arithmetic, astronomy, geography, and theology, and unreflective in his writing.[13] Ibn Hazm deemphasizes the use of Jewish and Christian Scripture as sources that portend Mohammed's ministry, and instead focuses on how these writings are rife with

---

10. On the life and background of Ibn Hazm, see Theodore Pulcini, *Exegesis as Polemical Discourse: Ibn Hazm on Jewish and Christian Scriptures* (Atlanta: Scholars Press, 1998), 1–11; Camilla Adang, *Muslim Writers on Judaism and the Hebrew Bible: From Ibn Rabban to Ibn Hazm* (Leiden: Brill, 1996), 59–69.

11. The treatise is today found printed as part of a larger compendium, *Kitāb al-fiṣal fī l-milal wa-l-ahwā' wa-l-niḥal* (*The Book of Opinions on Religions, Sects and Heresies*) extant only in the original Arabic.

12. Pulcini, *Exegesis as Polemical Discourse*, 13.

13. Ibn Hazm, *Book of Opinions*, 1:214–16.

falsehoods. He claims that the Torah is the product of many hands, as evidenced by what he takes to be its glaring contradictions.[14]

The tone Ibn Hazm adopts in the composition is far more antagonistic than that found in earlier works that assessed the Jewish and Christian Scriptures. For example, he says of the Jews that they are the

> foulest in their appearance, the ugliest in their faces, the most revolting in their general foulness, the most complete in their depravity, the most extreme in their dishonesty, the most cowardly in their souls, the lowest in their baseness, the most duplicitous in their language, the weakest in their ambition and the most unsteady in their character. [15]

Some scholars believe that Ibn Hazm composed the treatise out of intense jealousy of Samuel Ibn Naghrillah, also known as Shemuel HaNagid, who had received a plum post as vizier in the royal court of Granada that he himself coveted.[16] In an almost Haman-like spasm of jealousy, Ibn Hazm sought to undermine not only Shemuel HaNagid himself, but indeed the entire Jewish people, by defaming the Torah as falsified.[17]

It is difficult to overestimate the influence of this libel on the Muslim imagination, even to this very day. It is commonplace in Muslim thought that the Jews falsified their Scripture. In fact, there are numerous references within medieval rabbinic literature to this pernicious lie and its consequences. In his famous letter to the community of Yemen, the Rambam relates to the libel and pressure from the Muslim host culture on this issue. He states that even the Muslims themselves do not accept the so-called "proofs" that the Torah contains hidden references to the ministry of Mohammed. Left without proofs for their prophet, he says, they turn to libeling the Jewish people and their Torah: "They were

---

14. Pulcini, *Exegesis as Polemical Discourse*, 13.

15. Ibn Hazm, *Kitāb al-fiṣal fi l-milal wa-l-ahwā' wa-l-niḥal* (*The Book of Opinions on Religions, Sects and Heresies*) 1:201, quoted and translated in R. David Freedman, "The Father of Modern Biblical Scholarship," *Journal of the Ancient Near Eastern Society* 19 (1989): 35.

16. Adang, *Muslim Writers on Judaism*, 67–68.

17. Freedman, "Father of Modern Biblical Scholarship," 35.

compelled to accuse us saying, 'You have altered the text of the Torah, and expunged every trace of the name of Mohammed therefrom.'"[18]

In a similar vein we find in an essay attributed to the Rashba, Rabbi Solomon ben Adret (Barcelona, 1235–1310), with reference to Ibn Hazm:

> How could this crazy man come to corrupt the holy Bible of truth that our fathers pored over all their lives, discussing letters, counting the verses – and even the letters – of all the books, noting full and defective spellings and *ketiv-keri* variants, and words that are read but not written, and many other details? ... But that witless idiot, how did he come to impute into the venerated and so carefully and painstakingly examined Scripture that has no rival among any book in any language? This is just blindness and madness and mental illness that afflicts him.[19]

The libel of *taḥrīf* may have influenced rabbinic exegesis to the Bible as well. Consider the well-known comment by Ibn Ezra (1089–1167), who was an older contemporary of the Rambam. The Torah says (Deut. 1:1) that Moses spoke to Israel "on the other side of the Jordan." On this, Ibn Ezra writes, "And if you understand the secret of the twelve, then also 'And Moses wrote' (Deut. 31:22), 'The Canaanites were then in the land' (Gen. 12:6), 'And God's Mountain he shall be seen' (Gen. 22:14), 'Behold his bed is a bed of iron' (Deut. 3:11) – then you shall know the truth." What is most significant about this passage is that it is cryptic. Ibn Ezra refers here to "a secret," and to a "truth" about these passages that is not apparent at first blush. The foremost supercommentary to the Torah commentary of the Ibn Ezra is that of Rabbi Joseph ben Eliezer (Toledo, Spain, fourteenth century), the author of the *Tzafnat Paane'aḥ*. He explains that Ibn Ezra wanted to intimate here that there

---

18. Moses Maimonides, *Epistle to Yemen*, ed. Abraham Halkin, trans. Boaz Cohen, section viii (New York: American Academy for Jewish Research, 1952), available at https://en.wikisource.org/wiki/Epistle_to_Yemen/Complete.

19. For Hebrew text, see Joseph Perles, *R. Salomo b. Abraham b. Adereth: Sein Leben und seine Schriften* (Breslau, Poland: Schletter, 1863), Hebrew section, 2–3.

are passages in the Torah that were not written by Moses. One reason he offers for Ibn Ezra's cryptic language is that "there are peoples that accuse us, saying that our Torah had been true, but that we have falsified it, and introduced changes into it."[20]

Even as late as the early sixteenth century we can still hear the reverberations of the charges of *taḥrīf*, in the responsa of Rabbi David ben Solomon ibn Zimra, the Radbaz, who lived in Safed and Egypt, under Ottoman rule (1479–1573). The Radbaz writes that he took upon himself a personal crusade to amend all of the Torah scrolls in the city, so that there were not even the minutest differences between them. He writes,

> There are those among these peoples who claim that we have altered the Torah, supplemented it, deleted parts of it, and have done with it what we please, and especially now, should they see that our *sifrei Torah* contradict one another. I therefore personally went to the copyist's house and found three new and approved scrolls, and I corrected them and returned the crown to its former glory.[21]

All of this provides the backdrop for us to understand the import of the next catechism written by a Jewish author after Rabbenu Hananel, roughly a century after Ibn Hazm, a little-known work by Judah ben Eliyahu Hadassi, the Karaite of Constantinople. In 1149 he published a theological treatise in Hebrew called *Eshkol HaKofer*.[22] In it, he lists his catechism of ten principles of Jewish faith. Here we discover for the first time a catechism that relates specifically to the special role of Moses in the transmission of every word of the Torah:

> The fourth principle is: "To know clearly the awe of His Torah, that He sent a messenger by His command, Moses the son of Amram, of blessed memory, as well as all of the other prophets

---

20. *Tzafnat Paane'aḥ* to Gen. 12:5.

21. *Teshuvot HaRadbaz* 4:101.

22. On Hadassi generally, see Daniel Lasker, *From Judah Hadassi to Elijah Bashyatchi: Studies in Late Medieval Karaite Philosophy* (Leiden, Netherlands: Brill, 2008).

whom He sent." The fifth principle is: "To know by clear knowledge that what He sent was the Torah, which is truth, *and all of its words are truth* by His command."[23]

For Hadassi, it was insufficient to state that God had transmitted the Torah through Moses. To counter the libel of *taḥrīf*, Hadassi had to emphasize to the faithful that the Torah had been transmitted to Moses, down to its every word.

THE EIGHTH PRINCIPLE OF FAITH IN THE RAMBAM'S INTRODUCTION TO *PEREK ḤELEK*

Some twelve years after Hadassi published the *Eshkol HaKofer*, the Rambam embarked on his project to compose his commentary on the Mishna, a project that he completed in approximately 1168. In his introduction to the tenth chapter of Sanhedrin, *Perek Ḥelek*, the Rambam composed his Thirteen Principles. Here, too, we discover a principle of the Jewish faith not enumerated in the earlier Rabbinite catechisms of Rasag and Rabbenu Hananel, that every word of the Torah was transmitted by God to Moses. There is no reason to believe that the Rambam was familiar with Hadassi's *Eshkol HaKofer*.[24] A Karaite, Hadassi had determined that this was a principle of faith without recourse to the talmudic sources we surveyed earlier. The fact that both Hadassi – a Karaite – and the Rambam determine that it is a principle of faith to believe that every word of the Torah was given by God to Moses while no earlier figure had done so speaks volumes to the impact that the Muslim doctrine of *taḥrīf* had upon the Jewish community of the twelfth century.

Let us review the eighth principle with an eye toward understanding how the Rambam interpreted the talmudic sources we surveyed earlier:

The eighth fundamental principle is that the Torah came from heaven. We are to believe that the whole Torah was given us through Moses our teacher entirely from God. When we call

---

23. Translated in Lasker, *From Judah Hadassi*, 53.
24. Lasker, *From Judah Hadassi*, 169, n. 54.

the Torah "God's Word" we speak metaphorically. We do not know exactly how it reached us, but only that it came to us through Moses who acted like a secretary taking dictation. He wrote down the events of the time and the commandments, for which reason he is called "Lawgiver." There is no distinction between a verse of Scripture like "The sons of Ham were Cush and Mizraim" (Gen. 10:6), or "His wife's name was Mehetabel" (Gen. 36:39) "and his concubine was Timna" (Gen. 36:12), and one like "I am the Lord your God," and all are the Torah of God, perfect, pure, holy, and true. Anyone who says Moses wrote some passages on his own is regarded by our Sages as an atheist of the worst kind of heretic, because he tries to distinguish essence from accident in Torah. Such a heretic claims that some historical passages or stories are trivial inventions of Moses and not Divine Revelation. But the sage said that if one accepts as revelation the whole Torah with the exception of even one verse, which Moses himself and not God composed, he is referred to in the verse, "he has shamed the Word of the Lord" (Num. 15:31), and is heretical. Every word of Torah is full of wisdom and wonders for one who understands it. It is beyond human understanding. It is broader than the earth and wider than the sea. Each man must follow David, anointed of the God of Jacob, who prayed: "Open my eyes that I may behold wonders out of Your Torah" (Ps. 119:18). The authoritative commentary on the Torah is also the Word of God. The sukka we build today, or the lulav, shofar, tzitzit, phylacteries, etc. we use, replicate exactly those God showed Moses which Moses faithfully described for us. This fundamental principle is taught by the verse: "And Moses said, 'Thus shall you know that the Lord sent me to do all these things, and that they are not products of my own mind'" (Num. 16:28).[25]

---

25. Rambam's "Introduction to Chapter Ten of Mishna Sanhedrin," in Isadore Twersky's *A Maimonides Reader* (New York: Behrman House, 1972), 20–21, available at http://www.mhcny.org/qt/1005.pdf, with slight modification.

The Rambam's opening point, that every word of the Torah was dictated by God to Moses, represents the opinion of R. Shimon in the *baraita* in Bava Batra 15a, against the first opinion offered in the *baraita* (either R. Yehuda or R. Neḥemiah) that the last eight verses of the Torah were written by Joshua. His contention that the "authoritative commentary" on the Torah is also the word of God is an adaptation of the second *baraita* brought in Sanhedrin 99a, in definition of the mishna's phrase "*torah* from heaven." That *baraita* had stated that not only was every word of the Written Torah divine in origin but also that every point, every *kal vaḥomer*, and every *gezera shava* – everything found in the Oral Law – were also divine in origin. The Rambam scales this back. What is of divine origin is now restricted to "the authoritative commentary" on the Torah. In his introduction to the Mishna, the Rambam explains which aspects of the Oral Law are included in this authoritative commentary. The Rambam opens the eighth principle by giving it a heading: "*torah* from heaven," a reference to the phrase in Mishna Sanhedrin 10:1. It is clear from his formulation of the eighth principle that he understands "*torah* from heaven" as comprising not only the text of the Written Torah but a significant portion of the Oral Law as well.[26] The Rambam's formulation of the eighth principle seems to reflect a synthesis of positions found in the Talmud, suited to address the theological challenges of his day. "*Torah* from heaven" had been an imperative of Jewish belief since the time of the Mishna. What was innovative in the thought of the Rambam was the newfound emphasis on the singular nature of Mosaic prophecy and the transmission of the entire Torah through him. Haym Soloveitchik has speculated that the Rambam "would never have raised the notion of the 'primacy of Mosaic revelation' to the level of an *ikkar* (principle), were its opposite not a defining tenet of Islam"[27] – namely, the singular prophecy of Mohammed and the doctrine that every word of the Quran was dictated to him.

---

26. On the Rambam's definition of the Oral Law given at Sinai, see Gerald J. Blidstein, "Mesoret VeSamkhut Mosadit LeRaayon Torah SheBeAl Peh BeMishnat HaRambam," *Daat* 16 (1986): 11–27.

27. See Haym Soloveitchik, "Two Notes on the Commentary on the Torah of R. Yehudah he-Hasid," *Turin* 2 (2008): 243, n. 6.

POST-MOSAIC ADDENDA IN THE EARLY
MEDIEVAL RABBINIC TRADITION

Throughout the twelfth and thirteenth centuries we find a variety of rabbinic voices contending – contrary to the Rambam – that the Torah contains verses and passages that were composed after the passing of Moses. Some of these figures are members of the pantheon of Jewish biblical exegesis across the ages. Others are less-known figures, and still others are known to us only from manuscripts that have surfaced in recent times. My aim is not to argue for the authority of these positions today against the position of the Rambam, or to argue that their contentions about the growth of the biblical text are more historically accurate than the stance adopted by the Rambam. My aim is, simply, to survey the range of opinions that were circulating among learned, pious Jews at this time. We saw that the Rambam's position was informed by a study of the sources, but also by the spiritual currents prevailing in the world around him. At the close of this section, I will probe the same question with regard to these exegetes: What were the circumstances in which they lived and worked that allowed them to suggest that portions of the Torah postdate Moses? And how did they understand the talmudic sources surveyed above on the subject of the Torah's origins?

I assess the positions these exegetes maintain with regard to four basic questions: (1) Who is authorized to add passages to the Torah? (2) What are the limits on the size of these additions? (3) What limits are there on the content of these additions? (4) How are we to understand in these works the attribution of passages in the Torah to the *sadran/ sofer/baal hasefer* – terms that seem to mean "editor"?

1. Who is authorized to add passages to the Torah?

Tzafnat Paane'aḥ on Genesis 12:5 holds that addenda may be added by a prophet. In his words, "Since we are beholden to believe in the received tradition and the words of prophecy, what difference does it make whether Moses wrote the passage or whether it was another prophet, inasmuch as all of their words are true and prophetic?" Earlier, I cited the comments of Ibn Ezra on Deuteronomy 1:2 that suggest that some passages of the Torah were composed by agents other than Moses.

Although Ibn Ezra says no more on the issue, *Tzafnat Paane'aḥ* believes that Ibn Ezra held that these agents possessed prophecy.[28]

However, other exegetes also propose post-Mosaic addenda without underscoring that the source was prophetic. Rabbenu Yehuda HeHasid (Germany, 1150–1217) attributes addenda to either Joshua or to the Men of the Great Assembly.[29] It is unclear whether Rabbenu Yehuda HeHasid believed these figures possessed prophecy. The Torah provides a list of Edomite kings "who ruled in the land of Edom prior to the rise of a king in Israel" (Gen. 36:31–43). There is a medieval manuscript which attributes to Rabbi Samuel ben Meir, or Rashbam (Troyes, 1085–1158), the opinion that this passage was composed "during the period of the Judges," without detailing the nature of the figure who would, according to Rashbam, have had license to add this passage.[30] Numbers 22:1 reports that Israel "encamped in the steppes of Moab, *across the Jordan*, opposite Jericho.*" In one manuscript version of Rashbam's commentary, we find that he writes, "The phrase 'across the Jordan' is appropriately written after they [i.e., the Israelites] had crossed [to the west side of]

---

28. This is the way in which many rabbinic figures have understood these comments by Ibn Ezra. For references see Marc B. Shapiro, *The Limits of Orthodox Theology: Maimonides' Thirteen Principles Reappraised* (Oxford: Littman Library of Jewish Civilization, 2004), 108. See also Warren Zev Harvey, "Spinoza on Ibn Ezra's 'Secret of the Twelve,'" in *Spinoza's 'Theological-Political Treatise': A Critical Guide*, ed. Yitzhak Y. Melamed and Michael A. Rosenthal (New York: Cambridge University Press, 2010), 41–55.

29. Rabbenu Yehuda HeHasid, *Perushei HaTorah*, ed. Y. Lange, 1st ed. (Jerusalem: self-pub., 1975), on Genesis 48:20; Deuteronomy 2:8. Rabbi Moshe Feinstein was of the opinion that the manuscript that formed the basis of this publication was a forgery; see *Igrot Moshe* 3:114 and 115. As noted by Haym Soloveitchik, "That the composition is that of R. Yehudah he-Hasid there can be little question; there are too many citations from this commentary, specifically attributed to him, in medieval writings to leave room for doubt." See Soloveitchik, "Two Notes," 242. Rabbi Feinstein was unfamiliar with these other manuscripts and it is unclear what bearing these might have had on his opinion of the issue and upon his ruling. Some scholars have posited that some of the questionable interpretations may have originated with the son of Rabbenu Yehuda HeHasid, Rabbi Moshe Zaltman. See Eran Viezel, "R. Judah he-Hasid or R. Moshe Zaltman: Who Proposed that Torah Verses Were Written After the Time of Moses?" *Journal of Jewish Studies* 66, no. 1 (2015): 97–115.

30. The manuscript is ms Paris 260, which contains *Moshav Zekeinim*, a collection of Tosafist insights to the Torah.

the Jordan. From their point of view the plains of Moab [on the east side of the Jordan] are called 'across the Jordan.'"[31] Here, too, Rashbam does not relate to the question of the authority of the agent responsible for this addendum.

2. What are the limits on the size of these addenda?

Tzafnat Paane'aḥ claims that addenda are permitted only as explanatory glosses, notes that help make the text clearer: "If a prophet added a word or several words in order to clarify a passage in accordance with its accepted interpretation, *this is not considered an addendum*."[32] There is a nuance in his claim that should not be missed: it is not that a prophet is entitled to add to the text; rather, explanatory material is not considered an addition to the text. To understand what *Tzafnat Paane'aḥ* is stressing we need to appreciate that he lived in a textual culture very different than our own. We live in a world in which classic texts – Jewish or non-Jewish – are inviolate. To take a prosaic example: to our sensibilities, you cannot tamper with the text of Shakespeare to make his meaning clearer. That is considered unacceptable. If there is something unclear in the text of Shakespeare we

---

31. According to Rashbam scholar Martin Lockshin, this is the authentic version of the Rashbam's commentary. The standard printed edition of the Rashbam in most *Ḥumashim* today relies upon the work of the nineteenth-century scholar David Rosin. Lockshin provides extended arguments to demonstrate that Rosin emended the text of Rashbam's commentary in order to bring it into compliance with contemporary sensitivities. See his *Rashbam's Commentary on Leviticus and Numbers: An Annotated Translation* (Providence, RI: Brown Judaic Studies, 2001), 260–61. Note that both here and in the case of ms Paris 260 – cases in which Rashbam posits a post-Mosaic addendum – there are other manuscripts of his commentary that read differently. A priori two options exist to explain this pair of discrepancies. One is to say that Rashbam really holds like the majority of exegetes, and does not believe that any part of the Torah postdates Moses. The two variant attributions, by this view, are frauds; later copyists or scribes with heterodox opinions sought to advance their view by ascribing their views to an illustrious figure such as Rashbam. It should be noted that this phenomenon is not witnessed with regard to any other major medieval exegete. However, the existence of two such instances suggests the opposite – that these comments are authentically the Rashbam's but that later scribes sought to bring his commentary in line with accepted Orthodoxy, and thus censored the heterodox elements of his commentary.

32. *Tzafnat Paane'aḥ* on Genesis 12:5.

would say that an editor of an edition of the play should add a clarifying footnote at the bottom of the page. We would insist that there be a clear demarcation between the "classic" or "canonical" text of Shakespeare and the later editor's note of clarification. And if this is true of the classics of general literature, then it is truer still when we consider notes that "clarify" Scripture. But in the world before the printing press, classical texts – Jewish or otherwise – were never copied with commentaries at the bottom of the page, like we have today. Copyists in the pre-modern age were often faced with a dilemma: What to do when a classical, revered text contained material that was liable to be misunderstood or misconstrued? Often, rather than taking the risk that readers might misunderstand the import of the text, copyists would amend the text to make it clearer in light of the traditional understanding of the text.[33] This was considered an act of preservation, and not one of addition or tampering. This is how the *Tzafnat Paane'aḥ* can claim that an explanatory gloss does not consti-tute an "addition," even though in our climate and culture it surely would.

Other exegetes, however, allowed for a more expansive view of post-Mosaic addenda as more than just explanatory glosses. Genesis 48:20 reads, "So he blessed them that day saying, 'By you shall Israel invoke blessings, saying, "May God make you like Ephraim and Menashe."' And so he put Ephraim before Menashe." For Rabbenu Yehuda HeHasid, it is self-evident that Jacob had put Ephraim before Menashe. He therefore comments that the final clause of the verse – "and so *he* put Ephraim before Menashe" – refers to *Moses* putting Ephraim at the head of an encampment (Num. 2:18), and that the clause was written either by Joshua or the Men of the Great Assembly. This constitutes a significant addition to the narrative itself, albeit only a few words long. It may be that Rabbenu Yehuda HeHasid considered Moses's act a fulfillment of Jacob's blessing and thus worthy of insertion. As we saw, one medieval source attributes to Rashbam the view that an entire passage, the list of Edomite kings in Genesis 36:31–43, was composed by a later hand. Ibn

---

33. See Sigbjørn Olsen Sønnesyn, "Obedient Creativity and Idiosyncratic Copying: Tradition and Individuality in the Works of William of Malmesbury and John of Salisbury," in *Modes of Authorship in the Middle Ages*, ed. Slavica Rankovic (Toronto: PIMS, 2012), 121.

Ezra apparently felt that a later figure was responsible for at least part of the narrative frame of Deuteronomy, again more than just a gloss. Deuteronomy 1:1 says, "These are the words that Moses spoke to all of Israel on the other side of the Jordan." As noted earlier, Ibn Ezra's comment that this is one of a number of verses that inheres a "secret" is generally understood to mean that these are verses that were written after the time of Moses.[34] He understands this verse as reflecting the perspective of someone who resides west of the Jordan, and therefore dates to a time after Moses. Ibn Ezra does not clarify how much of the narrative frame is to be attributed to this writer – indeed, this may be the "secret" to which he alludes, but does not make explicit. Likewise, all of the verses that he identifies here provide information or perspective appropriate for a writer living after the time of Moses. *Tzafnat Paane'ah* pointed to these verses cited by Ibn Ezra as merely explanatory glosses. However, the example from the beginning of Deuteronomy reveals that the issue is far from clear. It may be that Ibn Ezra believed that a late hand introduced only the words "on the other side of the Jordan." But Ibn Ezra could also be understood as maintaining that the narrative frame of Deuteronomy in much larger part also postdates Moses, and that these are the words that prove it.

Perhaps the most expansive view of such post-Mosaic addenda is raised by Rabbi Elazar ben Rabbi Matitya Hasid (France/Byzantium/Israel, thirteenth century).[35] He writes the following:

> As is known, when Jeshurun was in the Babylonian Exile, the Torah was forgotten until the arrival of Ezra the *kohen, sofer mahir* in the Torah of the Lord. He returned the Torah to them, and

---

34. In his comments on Genesis 36:31–39, Ibn Ezra takes to task a Karaite scholar who dates that list of Edomite kings to the time of Jehoshaphat. However, it is unclear whether Ibn Ezra objects because a priori he rejects the possibility of post-Mosaic addenda of that scale on theological grounds, or whether he believes that the verses in question do not provide enough of a basis to date them to that late date.

35. Four manuscript copies of his supercommentary on Ibn Ezra's Torah commentary are known to us today. There are references to mystical works that he published and that were respected in his day and he was a signatory to ten *takanot*, or ordinances, of the city of Kandia (Greece) in the early thirteenth century, and recognized there as a halakhic authority.

did not change anything from all of the commandments which God commanded Moses. Regarding the narrative portions, however, in which there is no harm in expanding and embellishing in the spirit of the words already there, this prophet (i.e., Ezra) did not desist. And it may be that by the word of God he added what he added.[36]

3. What limits are there on the content of these addenda?

Tzafnat Paane'aḥ maintained that additions could only be made to the narrative portions of the Torah, and the passage cited above from Rabbi Elazar ben Rabbi Matitya Hasid maintains the same. However, we have two examples in which emendations are proposed for legal material in the Torah as well. Rabbi Moshe Zaltman, the son of Rabbenu Yehuda HeHasid, suggests that in the verse *velo tashbit melaḥ brit Elokekha me'al minḥatekha* ("You shall not omit from your meal offering the salt of your covenant with God," Lev. 2:13), the term *brit Elokekha* is a later addition.[37] Concerning the Yom Kippur sacrificial service, the Torah says that one of the lots drawn determines which goat goes to Azazel (Lev. 16:8). Rabbi Shlomo ben Shemuel HaTzarfati (Ashkenaz, 1160–1240), a student of Rabbi Shemuel HeHasid and of his son, Rabbenu Yehuda HeHasid, writes in his supercommentary on the commentary of Ibn Ezra:

> And do not be surprised that this word (Azazel) is written in Aramaic, for he (i.e., Moses) did not write this verse. And this is a secret that we share, that Moses did not compose this verse, but rather someone else wrote it. And do not be taken aback by what I write that someone else wrote it, for there are others like it in Scripture; that is, there are many that Moses our master did not state, for example, "And Moses went up" until the words "before the eyes of all of Israel" (Deut. 34:1–12).[38]

---

36. Hebrew text found in Naftali Ben-Menachem, *MiGinzei Yisrael BaVatican* (Jerusalem: Mossad HaRav Kook, 1954), 128ff.

37. Found in Rabbi Yehuda HeHasid, *Perushei HaTorah*, 138.

38. The passage is cited in Israel Ta-Shma, "Al Bikoret HaMikra BeAshkenaz BeYemei HaBeinayim," in *Knesset Meḥkarim: Iyunim BeSafrut HaRabbanit BeYemei HaBeinayim*, vol. 1, *Ashkenaz* (Jerusalem: Bialik, 2004) 276–77.

4. The *Sadran/Sofer/Baal HaSefer*

Several medieval sources refer to compositional and editorial activities within the text of the Torah by a figure that in rough terms we would call an "editor": *sadran, sofer,* and *baal hasefer.* Are these simply other epitaphs or titles for Moses? Or are these figures that postdate Moses?[39]

In one of these sources, it appears clear that the *sadran* is a figure who lives after the time of Moses. I Samuel 4 describes Israel's battle at a site called Even HaEzer, lit., "The Stone of Salvation." However, the book of Samuel reports that the site received this name only following the later battle that occurred there in I Samuel 7:12, when Israel received salvation from her Philistine foe. Rabbi David Kimhi, or Radak (Provence, 1160–1235), comments that when the first battle took place, the site was still called by its original name (commentary on I Sam. 4:1). Following the salvation of the second battle, the name of the site was changed. Because this is how the site was known when the book was written, the *sofer,* writes Radak, used that new name even to describe the location at the time of the first battle.[40] Radak then concludes, "And so it is with 'and he gave chase unto Dan'" (Gen. 14:14). The reference is to Abraham's pursuit of the five kings. Of course, at the time, there was no region in the land called "Dan," an appellation that only could have been given later. Radak therefore equates the two literary phenomena. Just as the *sofer* of the book of Samuel retroactively referred to the site of the battle of I Samuel 4 as Even HaEzer because that was the name of the site in his own day, so too, the *sofer* employs the name Dan to describe the events of Genesis 14 that occurred there, because that was how the site was known in his own time. One might suggest that Radak believed that God dictated the verse to Moses precisely as we have it. However, if this were the case, it is unclear why Radak would say that this is the activity of the *sofer* and not simply ascribe it to either God or Moses. His use here of the relatively obscure term *sofer* seems to imply that the

---

39. For an overview of the issue see Richard Steiner, "A Jewish Theory of Biblical Redaction from Byzantium: Its Rabbinic Roots, Its Diffusion and Its Encounter with the Muslim Doctrine of Falsification," *Jewish Studies Internet Journal* 2 (2003): 123–67.

40. If you will, it is similar to referring today to the siege of St. Petersburg during World War II; at the time, the city was named Leningrad.

ascription of the name Dan came only once the name would have made sense to Israel, which is to say, following entry into the land. In this case, then, it was the literary activity of a *sofer*. If this interpretation is correct, it is likely that for Radak, the *sofer* only introduces explanatory glosses such as these and nothing more.

The use of the term *sadran* is similarly found in a context that suggests editorial activity in a post-Mosaic context. Consider the following comment of Rabbi Menahem ben Shlomo (Italy, twelfth century), in his work, *Midrash Sekhel Tov*. Earlier we saw the comment attributed to the Rashbam that the list of Edomite kings in Genesis 36:31–43 was added during the period of the Judges. *Midrash Sekhel Tov* here writes that Scripture included this list in Genesis because it wanted to quickly dispose of what would be with Edom so that in the remainder of the Torah and on into the former prophets, it could sustain its focus upon Israel. In the words of *Midrash Sekhel Tov*: "The *sadran* listed them here to finish off discussion of the chaff [i.e., Edom] and to remove them from the kernel (i.e., Israel)." Note that the use of the term *sadran* here coincides with content that extends beyond the lifetime of Moses. To maintain that *sadran* here is an epithet for Moses – a possibility – we would need to assume that according to *Sekhel Tov*, Moses wrote this with prophecy and that the names were listed for Israel to see long before these kings even existed, and thus would have been unintelligible. We would also need to accept that for *Sekhel Tov*, precisely at the moment that Moses inscribes such detailed prophecy, his name is not used, and instead here – for unexplained reasons – he is called the *sadran*. By contrast, if this section was added by a later figure, we can easily understand why *Sekhel Tov* employs the term *sadran* here.[41]

We may reach the same conclusions regarding the comment of *Midrash Sekhel Tov* to Genesis 47:26. That verse reads, "And Joseph made it into a property edict in Egypt, *valid to this day*, that a fifth should be Pharaoh's; only the land of the priests did not become Pharaoh's." On this verse, *Midrash Sekhel Tov* writes, "*To this day* – these are the words

---

41. It should be noted that there are three points at which *Sekhel Tov* employs the term *sadran* to account for various textual phenomena, even when there is no issue of events that might have postdated Moses. See *Sekhel Tov* to Genesis 26:32, 41:4, and 42:34.

of the *sadran*." Had this merely been a gloss added by Moses, it would seem that *Sekhel Tov* would have written, "These are the words of Moses" as he does elsewhere where he believes that Moses added a retrospective gloss of his own.[42]

The term *baal hasefer* is similarly found in a context that could suggest post-Mosaic editorial activity. The Torah writes (Gen. 35:20), "And Jacob erected a pillar over her grave; it is the pillar at Rachel's grave to this day." Rabbi Joseph ben Isaac Bekhor Shor (Orleans, twelfth century), one of the Tosafists and a disciple of Rabbenu Tam and Rashbam, comments: "This is said by the *baal hasefer*: It is the pillar at Rachel's grave that has been standing all this time unto this day."[43]

BETWEEN JEWS UNDER CROSS AND JEWS UNDER CRESCENT

We may now take an overview of the rabbinic sources that entertain the possibility of post-Mosaic addenda to the Torah and arrive at a remarkable conclusion. The Ibn Ezra stands out in one regard. He engages a discourse of hedging; when he intimates that a passage is post-Mosaic, he never says so explicitly; rather it is "a secret" that only the discerning will understand. The other exegetes we surveyed seemingly offer their remarks with little or no attempt to carefully navigate the theological minefield in which they tread. Why is Ibn Ezra the only one to do so?

---

42. E.g., note *Sekhel Tov* on Genesis 32:32: *Al ken lo yokhlu Benei Yisrael. Zehu sipro shel Moshe Rabbenu, alav hashalom, shekatav issur gid hanasheh bemakom sippur hamaaseh;* "Therefore the children of Israel do not eat – this is narrated by our master, Moses, who referred to the prohibition of the sciatic nerve within the account of the origin of the prohibition itself."

43. Bekhor Shor also uses the term *baal hasefer* in his commentary on Genesis 32:20, in a context that does not stem from chronological concerns. The gloss to the verse is then quoted nearly verbatim, using the term *baal hasefer* in the thirteenth-century commentary of Hezekiah ben Manoah – or *Ḥizkuni* – on that verse. It should be noted, however, that Bekhor Shor states that Moses "arranged" the Torah for them (*sider lahem et HaTorah*) in his commentary on Deuteronomy 1:1, leaving open the possibility that the *baal hasefer* here in Genesis 35:20 is Moses as well. Bekhor Shor says explicitly that Moses wrote the Torah (commentary on Gen. 1:31; Deut. 1:1).

These other exegetes that we surveyed share a striking commonality: their place of residence. These exegetes hailed from Toledo, Provence, France, Ashkenaz, Italy, and Byzantium. That is, *they all lived under Christian rule.* These figures had no libel of *taḥrīf* with which to contend. Jews and Christians disagreed about many things. But on this there was unanimity: Scripture, including the Torah, was a sacred text, and without rival. Jews and Christians would disagree about the proper interpretation of Scripture, but not about the status of the text itself as revered and sacred. To be sure, most medieval authorities living in Christian Europe were staunch proponents of the position that the entire Torah was dictated by God to Moses.[44] But in these lands there was theological room for some exegetes to experiment with the notion that some parts of the Torah may have postdated Moses. Haym Soloveitchik's comments about the circle of *Ḥasidei Ashkenaz* speaks for all of those surveyed here:

> At that time and place ... [their comments] contained no concession to the surrounding culture; no Pandora's box of questions .... In their world these words did not abut any slippery slope of a "documentary hypothesis" or a "Jewish forgery."[45]

It is perhaps no coincidence that the terms for editor – *sadran, sofer,* and *baal hasefer* – are found with regard to post-Mosaic passages in the Torah only in the writings of these exegetes. These terms are not found in the commentaries of rabbinic exegetes residing in Muslim lands. Were these terms simply epithets for Moses, we might have expected commentators in Muslim lands as well to employ them with regard to Moses. That they do not suggests that these are terms appropriate for minor addenda to the Torah of Moses, and thus are only found in an environment in which the Bible's status as sacred Scripture was unchallenged.

Ibn Ezra is the only medieval exegete who hailed from a land under Muslim rule who was open to the notion that some parts of the

---

44. See, for example, the introduction of the Ramban to his Torah commentary and Abarbanel on Numbers 21.
45. Soloveitchik, "Two Notes," 246.

Torah were post-Mosaic in origin, and it is easy to understand why he was such an anomaly in this regard. To affirm the existence of post-Mosaic addenda to the Torah is essentially to claim a concession to the libel of *taḥrīf*, and a proof from within the camp of rabbinic Judaism itself that Ibn Hazm had been right all along – even the Jews write that later hands tampered with the text that Moses received. It is no surprise, then, that Ibn Ezra discusses the phenomenon of post-Mosaic addenda with caution and a discourse of hedging.

POST-MOSAIC ADDENDA AND THE TALMUDIC SOURCES

For many traditional readers, the opinions that I have surveyed above raise eyebrows, as they do not conform to the Rambam's eighth principle: "How could they say or write that? Did they not 'know' that such positions are heretical?" However, to ask such questions is to impose later theological presuppositions in an anachronistic manner. Some of these figures are recognized within the pantheon of the great sages of Israel and their names and works still have currency today. We must assume their piety no less than their learning. These exegetes do not share with us how they read the various talmudic sources concerning the origins of the Torah, but we may retrace how they did so.

As a general rule, it would seem that many of these exegetes agree with the opinion of R. Yehuda in Bava Batra 14b. R. Yehuda opined that Joshua had written the last eight verses of the Torah, because it was not possible for Moses to know the particulars of events that would occur following his death, in spite of the high level of his prophecy. Therefore when some of these exegetes ascribe the list of Edomite kings in Genesis 36:31–36 to a later writer, they are essentially employing the same logic as R. Yehuda.

Tzafnat Paane'aḥ held that some passages could come from a non-Mosaic source, as long as they were added by a prophet. It may be that *Tzafnat Paane'aḥ* accepts the position of R. Yehuda in Bava Batra 14b that Joshua composed the last eight verses and assumes that Joshua was a prophet. With an insistence on prophecy behind every word of the Torah, the position of *Tzafnat Paane'aḥ* satisfies the mishna in Sanhedrin that one who denies that *torah* is from heaven does not have a place in the World to Come. The Mishna does not mandate that one believe that the Torah was given to Moses, only that it and the accompanying *mesora* emanate from heaven. The position of *Tzafnat Paane'ah* also satisfies the second *baraita* in Sanhedrin 99a, which mandates that we believe that every word of the Torah is from heaven.

However, other exegetes that we surveyed do not explicitly state that every word must be from a prophetic source. It may well be that some – perhaps all of them – agree with this requirement. Rabbenu Yehuda HeHasid attributes all of the post-Mosaic addenda he proposes to either Joshua or the Men of the Great Assembly and may well agree with the Rambam[46] that the Men of the Great Assembly were endowed with prophecy.

Others, such as Ibn Ezra and Rashbam (and perhaps also Bekhor Shor and *Midrash Sekhel Tov*), do not explicitly write that prophetic agents were responsible for the addenda they propose and it may be that they did not share the opinion of *Tzafnat Paane'ah*. Due to the enormous sway of the Rambam's position on the *mesora*, there is a tendency to want to read his opinion as much as possible into other opinions. There is a natural proclivity to want to "limit the damage," as it were, and insist that surely they must have believed that these agents were at the very least prophets. However, that does not stem from a simple reading of their positions. Rabbenu Yehuda HeHasid is careful to always tell us the identity of the agent he believes responsible for the post-Mosaic addendum. When Rashbam notes that the list of Edomite kings "was written during the time of the Judges," or when other commentators ascribe a passage to the *sadran* or *baal hasefer*, we would expect them to underscore that these agents were prophetic. Put differently, the fact that they display no uneasiness whatsoever about ascribing verses to agents other than Moses, using prosaic terms such as *sadran*, suggests one of two conclusions: either (1) that these terms are nothing more than synonyms for Moses, a proposition that inheres problems of its own, as discussed earlier, or (2) that they may have believed that there are parts of the Torah that were not added by prophets.

---

46. *Guide for the Perplexed*, I:59.

Of course, all of these figures were pious, God-fearing sages, and all of them were learned and well familiar with the sources I have cited here. They may have reached such conclusions on the basis of their understanding of the mishna in Sanhedrin 10:1, and the phrase *ein torah min hashamayim*, and the three *baraitot* that the Gemara brings in Sanhedrin 99a. To be sure, classical commentators on the Mishna, such as Rabbi Menachem ben Solomon Meiri (1249–1306) and *Tiferet Yisrael* (Rabbi Israel Lifshitz, Germany, 1782–1860), all understood the mishna in light of the second *baraita* cited in that Gemara that *ein torah min hashamayim* means that every verse of the Torah was from God, and not a single verse from a human agent. But the fact that the major commentators on the Mishna explained it thus does not mean that all exegetes had the same understanding. As we noted earlier, the phrase *ein torah min hashamayim* lacks the definite article. These exegetes could be relying on the position of R. Yehuda in Bava Batra, who said that Joshua composed the last eight verses of the Torah, and also believe that Joshua was not a prophet. Of course, they affirm that "*torah* is from heaven," but take that to refer to a statement that the *mesora* generally is divine in nature, aimed against sectarian heterodoxies, and not a comment on every word of the text of the Torah. Moreover, the Talmud in Sanhedrin 99a does not suggest that any of the three *baraitot* that it brings is the preferred reference for the line in the mishna, "one who says there is no *torah* from heaven." The Rambam and *Tzafnat Paane'aḥ* clearly aligned with the second *baraita*, and thus insist that all words in the Torah must be ascribed to a divine source. However, other exegetes might have chosen to adopt either the first or the third *baraita*. In all, the three *baraitot* offer seven interpretations of the phrase, "he has despised the word of the Lord." Only one refers to the divinity of the entire text of the Torah.

To summarize, we have seen an important lesson about how our sages establish theological priorities. We saw that in Mishna Sanhedrin 10:1, the mishna raised two beliefs above all others – resurrection of the dead and the divinity of *torah*. The Mishna did so not because these are the two most paramount beliefs; rather, the Mishna denied a place in the World to Come to those adhering to six beliefs and practices, all of which were contested at the time. They did not meditate upon the identity of

Judaism's most important acts or most important beliefs. Rather, they identified challenges and sought to meet them head on, by stressing the great importance of the issues under attack. It would be the same in the early Middle Ages with regard to the question of the origins of the text of the Torah. The divide between sages living under Muslim rule and those residing in Christian lands is stark. Here, too, we are reminded that a sage's theological stance can be in large measure a derivative of earlier rabbinic sources, but is also a reflection of the world around him and his attempt to respond to the theological challenges of his own day.

Chapter 9

The Rambam's Principle of Torah from Heaven: From His Introduction to *Perek Ḥelek* to the *Mishneh Torah*

Beliefs matter and they matter halakhically. A person whose beliefs about the origins of the Torah render them a *kofer baTorah* is ineligible, for example, to perform kosher *sheḥita*. The key question is how to define exactly who is considered a *kofer baTorah*. As we shall see later in our survey, *posekim* since the *Shulḥan Arukh* have unanimously adopted the definition of heretics referred to in halakhic literature found in the Rambam's *Mishneh Torah*, in the third chapter of *Hilkhot Teshuva*, halakhot 6–8. At the same time, of course, it has long been accepted that the Thirteen Principles of Faith found in his Introduction to *Perek Ḥelek*[1]

---

1. *Beit Yosef, Yoreh De'ah* 158; *Baḥ, Yoreh De'ah* 158; *Knesset HaGedola, Yoreh De'ah* 2; *Levush, Yoreh De'ah* 158:2 and *Ḥoshen Mishpat* 425:5; *Sefer Me'irat Einayim, Ḥoshen Mishpat* 425. See also *Divrei Yatziv, Yoreh De'ah* 49. My thanks to Michael Broyde for these references.

represent the fundamental tenets of Judaism. What often escapes notice, however, is that these two sources – the Rambam's Introduction to *Perek Ḥelek* and the *Mishneh Torah* – are in disagreement about a range of issues pertaining to the questions of beliefs. Put differently, our *mesora* has sanctioned and hallowed two divergent sources in the writings of the Rambam concerning mandated beliefs. My purpose here is to delineate the ways in which these two sources differ on the question of beliefs. Here, we will focus on two questions:

1. Generally speaking, how does the Rambam's treatment of the Thirteen Principles in the *Mishneh Torah* vary from his treatment of the principles in the Introduction to *Perek Ḥelek*? How have the sages of Israel explained this difference?
2. More specifically, how does the Rambam's delineation of the principle of "*torah* from heaven" in the *Mishneh Torah* differ from his treatment of this issue in the eighth of his Thirteen Principles in the Introduction to *Perek Ḥelek*?

PRINCIPLES OF FAITH IN THE INTRODUCTION TO *PEREK ḤELEK* AND THE PRINCIPLES IN THE *MISHNEH TORAH*

Different Principles

In the Introduction to *Perek Ḥelek*, the Rambam concludes his composition of the Thirteen Principles of Faith by offering several remarks about their import:

> When a man believes in all these fundamental principles, and his faith is thus clarified, he is then part of that "Israel" whom we are to love, pity, and treat as God commanded, with love and fellowship. Even if a Jew should commit every possible sin, out of lust or mastery by his lower nature, he will be punished for his sins but will still have a share in the World to Come. He is one of the "sinners in Israel." But if a man gives up any one of these fundamental principles, he has removed himself from the Jewish community. He is an atheist, a heretic, an unbeliever who "cuts among the plantings." We are commanded to hate him and to destroy him. Of him it is said: "Shall I not hate those who hate

You, O Lord?" (Ps. 139:21). I have spent too much time on these matters, leaving the general subject of my book. But I have done so because I saw their fullness for faith. So I have collected a number of scattered but useful statements from our great books. You must know them well. Repeat them frequently. Meditate on them carefully. If your mind seduces you into thinking that you comprehend them after one reading – or ten readings – God knows you are deceived! Do not read them hurriedly, for I did not just happen to write them down. Only after careful research and introspection, when I came to see which opinions are clearly true and untrue, did I come to know what to accept; I have proved each point systematically. May God fulfill my wish and lead me on the way of goodness.[2]

Here we see the broadest definition of the *functions* of a catechism that would ever be expressed in rabbinic sources. For the Rambam:

1. The catechism is the sole test of whether a Jew has excluded himself from the Jewish collective – one's status as a member of the Jewish people is contingent upon acceptance of the Thirteen Principles. Even if one commits every sin yet still affirms these principles he is considered "Israel," a Jew. Belief is what determines membership, not actions.
2. Affirmation of the catechism alone is what entitles a Jew to communal support – we are bound to love, pity, and treat with fellowship only one who affirms the Thirteen Principles. Conversely, one who denies the principles is to be "hated" and "destroyed."
3. Only one who affirms the principles can merit a place in the World to Come.
4. The catechism is an organic whole – denial of even a single precept is enough to deny a person membership in the Jewish people.

---

2. Rambam's Introduction to chapter 10 of Mishna Sanhedrin, in Isadore Twersky's *A Maimonides Reader* (New York: Behrman House, 1972), 23, available at http://www.mhcny.org/qt/1005.pdf. I have made small modifications.

5. The catechism must be afforded deep study and contemplation, and should not be read quickly. We are mandated not merely to affirm the principles, but to strive to *understand* with ever-greater comprehension, as the Rambam strived to do himself.

Moving to the *Mishneh Torah*, however, we see the principles enumerated by the Rambam in the Introduction to *Perek Ḥelek* handled differently. Nowhere in the *Mishneh Torah* are the Thirteen Principles presented as a unit, and the Rambam's discussion of these principles is dispersed across several of the *Mishneh Torah's* fourteen books. In the *Mishneh Torah*, of course, we have an entire book, *Hilkhot Yesodei HaTorah*, where many of these precepts are addressed – many, but not all. Some of the thirteen are addressed at various junctures in *Hilkhot Teshuva* and in *Hilkhot Avoda Zara*.[3] In the *Mishneh Torah*, the Rambam does not identify the Thirteen Principles as a composition to which one must devote sustained study.

Moreover, we find in the *Mishneh Torah* that the various principles are given different degrees of weight. In the opening chapter of *Hilkhot Yesodei HaTorah*, the first four principles comprise parts of two separate *mitzvot aseh*, and as such receive an elevated status not afforded the other principles. The definitions of the different categories of heresy in *Hilkhot Teshuva* chapter 3 revolve around some of the ideas contained in the Thirteen Principles as laid down in the Introduction to *Perek Ḥelek*, but hardly all of them.[4]

Accounting for the Differences Between the Two Sources

There are two strategies proffered by our sages to account for the discrepancies between the Rambam's comments concerning principles of

---

3. The thirteen principles enumerated in the Introduction to *Perek Ḥelek* are reformulated in the *Mishneh Torah*; see the table on pp. 229–30. For more on how the formulation of the principles in the *Mishneh Torah* and then in the *Guide for the Perplexed* differ from the original handling of the principles in Introduction to *Perek Ḥelek*, see Charles M. Raffel, "Maimonides' Fundamental Principles *Redivivus*," in *From Ancient Israel to Modern Judaism – Intellect in Quest of Understanding: Essays in Honor of Marvin Fox*, ed. Jacob Neusner, Ernest S. Frerichs, and Nahum M. Sarna (Atlanta: Scholars Press, 1989), 77–88.

4. See discussion in Rabbi Shlomo Goren, *Torat HaShabbat VeHaMoed* (Jerusalem: HaHistadrut HaTzionit HaOlamit, 1982), 570.

faith in the Introduction to *Perek Ḥelek* and in the *Mishneh Torah*. The first strategy places the issue within the wider context of the discrepancies found between these two works. There are literally hundreds of similar instances in which the Rambam's position in the *Mishneh Torah* does not align with what he wrote in the Commentary on the Mishna. The sages of Israel have always been aware of this, and have universally adopted an interpretive strategy laid out already by the Rambam's own son, Rabbenu Avraham ben HaRambam. The assumption of this interpretive strategy is that the Rambam composed the Commentary on the Mishna at an early age, while his magnum opus, the *Mishneh Torah,* was composed in his later years, and represents his most developed thinking. Hence, the views expressed in the *Mishneh Torah* are given pride of place.[5] To be clear, this stance maintains that we do not attempt to harmonize between the Commentary on the Mishna and the *Mishneh Torah*; the positions espoused in the *Mishneh Torah* are to be taken as normative. In light of this, we well understand why *posekim* have always pointed to *Hilkhot Teshuva* chapter 3 as the text that determines the halakhic parameters of the various categories of heretic, and not to the Introduction to *Perek Ḥelek*; in doing so, they were simply following the standard practice regarding discrepancies between the Rambam's stance in the Commentary on the Mishna and in the *Mishneh Torah*. The *Mishneh Torah* is normative; the Commentary on the Mishna is not.

On this basis, the former chief rabbi of Israel, Rabbi Shlomo Goren, wrote that while each of these principles still played a vital role in the Rambam's thought and jurisprudence, it would appear nonetheless that the Rambam in the *Mishneh Torah* abandons the notion of an organic unit of thirteen principles.[6] Instead, he sought to address each one separately, each with its own implications, and with many of them redefined. However, even if Rabbi Goren is correct, later sages adopted the Thirteen Principles in a process we shall explore further in the next two chapters.

---

5. See the responsum of Rabbi Avraham ben HaRambam in *Sefer Maaseh Nissim* (Paris, 1866), responsum #7, p. 82; see also the responsum of Rabbi Menachem Azaria da Fano (Italy, 1548–1620), *Shut Rama MiFano* (Venice: BeVet Daniel Zaneti, 1600), #117 and the commentary of the Maharik (Rabbi Joseph Colon ben Solomon Trabotto, Italy, fifteenth century) on *Hilkhot Terumot* 11:1.

6. Goren, *Torat HaShabbat VeHaMoed*, 570.

A second strategy, more localized to the text of the Introduction to *Perek Ḥelek*, is found in the writings of Abarbanel. Commenting on the Rambam's intentions in Introduction to *Perek Ḥelek*, Abarbanel writes,

> [The Rambam]'s intention was, rather, correctly to guide those men who did not delve deeply in the Torah.... Since they could not comprehend or conceive of all the beliefs and sciences which are included in the divine Torah, the Rambam chose the thirteen most general beliefs... in such a way that all men, even the igno- rant, could become perfected through their acceptance. From this point of view, he called them principles and foundation, adopting [his language] to the thinking of the student, though it is not so according to the truth itself.... He postulated the principles for the masses and for beginners in the study of Mishnah, but not for those individuals who plumbed the knowledge of truth for whom he wrote the Guide.[7]

By this line of thinking, the differences between the Introduction to *Perek Ḥelek* and the *Guide* are not a product of evolution in the Ram- bam's thinking, but reflect the fact that the Rambam chose to explicate his theological stances in two separate genres, each aimed for a specific audience. Indeed, in the *Guide*, the Rambam writes of two types of beliefs: true beliefs and necessary beliefs.[8] The latter are popularly dis- seminated because they promote conformance with tradition. These include the notions that God gets "angry" at bad behavior and that God instantly responds to the prayer of someone wronged or deceived. While Abarbanel proposes this division with regard to the relationship between the Introduction to *Perek Ḥelek* and the *Guide*, it may be that the distinctions between the principles as laid out in the Introduction to *Perek Ḥelek* and as presented in the *Mishneh Torah* also reflect a dif- ference in genre and audience, and not an evolution in the Rambam's

---

7. Abarbanel, *Rosh Amanah*, ed. Menachem Kellner (Ramat Gan: Bar-Ilan University Press, 1993), 197–98.

8. *Guide for the Perplexed*, III:28.

thought.[9] To be clear, this view has no bearing on the question of the acceptance of the Thirteen Principles by later generations. Even if we accept the Abarbanel's contention that the presentation of the principles in the Introduction to *Perek Ḥelek* accords "to the thinking of the student, though it is not so according to the truth itself," in later times, the sages of Israel would still be within their right to accept these as the fundamental principles of the faith.

TORAH FROM HEAVEN: FROM THE INTRODUCTION TO *PEREK ḤELEK* TO THE *MISHNEH TORAH*

As noted, some of the principles laid out by the Rambam in Introduction to *Perek Ḥelek* are reformulated in the *Mishneh Torah*, at times with significant differences between them. The Rambam's eighth principle, concerning *torah* from heaven, is a prime example of this. Let us follow how the Rambam reworked this principle and recall the eighth principle in Introduction to *Perek Ḥelek* which we saw earlier:

> The eighth fundamental principle is that the Torah came from God. We are to believe that the whole Torah was given us through Moses our teacher entirely from God. When we call the Torah "God's Word" we speak metaphorically. We do not know exactly how it reached us, but only that it came to us through Moses who acted like a secretary taking dictation. He wrote down the events of the time and the commandments, for which reason he is called "Lawgiver." There is no distinction between a verse of Scripture like "The sons of Ham were Cush and Mizraim" (Gen. 10:6), or "His wife's name was Mehetabel" (Gen. 36:39) "and his concubine was Timna" (Gen. 36:12), and one like "I am the Lord your God," and all are the Torah of God, perfect, pure, holy, and true. Anyone who says Moses wrote some passages on his own is regarded by our Sages as an atheist of the worst kind of heretic, because he tries to distinguish essence from accident in Torah. Such a heretic claims

---

9. As suggested by Marc Shapiro, *Limits of Orthodox Theology* (Oxford: Littman Library of Jewish Civilization, 2004), 119–21.

that some historical passages or stories are trivial inventions of Moses and not Divine Revelation. But the sage said that if one accepts as revelation the whole Torah with the exception of even one verse, which Moses himself and not God composed, he is referred to in the verse, "he has shamed the Word of the Lord" (Num. 15:31), and is heretical. Every word of Torah is full of wisdom and wonders for one who understands it. It is beyond human understanding. It is broader than the earth and wider than the sea. Each man must follow David, anointed of the God of Jacob, who prayed: "Open my eyes that I may behold wonders out of Your Torah" (Ps. 119:18). The authoritative commentary on the Torah is also the Word of God. The sukka we build today, or the lulav, shofar, tzitzit, phylacteries, etc. we use, replicate exactly those God showed Moses which Moses faithfully described for us. This fundamental principle is taught by the verse: "And Moses said, 'Thus shall you know that the Lord sent me to do all these things, and that they are not products of my own mind'" (Num. 16:28).[10]

We may compare this with the Rambam's discussion of *torah* from heaven in the *Mishneh Torah, Hilkhot Teshuva* 3:8:

There are three kinds of deniers of Torah:

(1) those who say the Torah is not from God; and even those who only claim that a single verse or word of the Torah was written by Moses himself deny the whole Torah;

(2) those who deny the interpretations of the Torah, which is the Oral Torah, and those who repudiate its transmitters as Zadok and Boethius did;[11] and

---

10. See Twersky, *Maimonides Reader*, 20–21.

11. According to talmudic sources, these were the founders of heretical movements who interpreted the Torah improperly. See *Avot DeRabbi Natan* 5:2.

(3) those like the Muslims and Christians who say that God exchanged one mitzva for another, or that the Torah has been nullified, even though it was [originally] from God. Each one of these three is a denier of the Torah.

Elements (a) and (b) correspond to the eighth principle as expressed in the Introduction to *Perek Ḥelek*, although with significant modification. The definition of a *kofer baTorah* in *Hilkhot Teshuva* does not mention that the Torah was given via dictation from God to Moses, nor does it mention that every word in the Torah was revealed to Moses by God. The formulation here underscores the divine origin of the Torah, but does not attend to the identity of the prophetic agency through which it was communicated. How may we account for the varying presentations of the principle of *torah* from heaven in the Introduction to *Perek Ḥelek* and in the *Mishneh Torah*? The Rambam's writings present us with conflicting evidence and there are two ways to assess his opinion. Below I present each assessment, and follow with an analysis of the strengths and weaknesses of each approach.

HARMONIZING THE FORMULATION IN THE INTRODUCTION TO *PEREK ḤELEK* WITH THE FORMULATION IN THE *MISHNEH TORAH*

The classical commentaries on the *Mishneh Torah* do not explicate the Rambam's definition of *torah* from heaven in *Hilkhot Teshuva* 3:8. Certainly, for many today the intuitive reading of *Hilkhot Teshuva* 3:8 would be to read it in light of what the Rambam writes in the Introduction to *Perek Ḥelek* and to assume that what the Rambam writes in the Introduction to *Perek Ḥelek* is what he means in *Hilkhot Teshuva* 3:8: one who denies that every word of the Torah was dictated to Moses is a *kofer baTorah*. Such a reading is buttressed by the fact that within the *Mishneh Torah* itself the Rambam tells us that the whole of the Torah – even the last eight verses of it – were dictated by God to Moses (*Hilkhot Tefilla* 13:6). There is a harmonizing and thus satisfying effect to reading *Hilkhot Teshuva* 3:8 this way. Because in our time we have accepted the Thirteen Principles – which are based on the Introduction to *Perek Ḥelek* – as the foundational principles of Judaism, we desire to read these back into the Rambam's halakhic formulations concerning the definition of a *kofer baTorah* in *Hilkhot Teshuva* 3:8. By this interpretation, there is enough in common between the formulation in *Hilkhot Teshuva* 3:8 and the longer formulation of the eighth principle in the Introduction to *Perek Ḥelek* to say that the Rambam is merely presenting a shorthand version in the later source (i.e., *Hilkhot Teshuva* 3:8) of what he wrote explicitly at greater length in the earlier source, Introduction to *Perek Ḥelek*. Moreover, we have writings of the Rambam that postdate the *Mishneh Torah* in which the Rambam expresses the same opinion. In his epistle to one Joseph ibn Jabbar of Baghdad, the Rambam writes that the belief in *torah* from heaven requires us to affirm that every word of the Torah was transmitted by God to Moses.[12] Since this is his belief in an early writing – the Introduction to *Perek Ḥelek* – and in a late composition – the epistle to ibn Jabbar – this most certainly must have been his view in the intervening time, when he wrote the *Mishneh Torah*.

The Autonomy of *Hilkhot Teshuva* 3:8 Over Against the Formulation of the Introduction to *Perek Ḥelek*

There are good reasons, however, to reject the reading that harmonizes *Hilkhot Teshuva* 3:8 with the Introduction to *Perek Ḥelek* on the question of *torah* from heaven. The literary and theological autonomy of *Hilkhot Teshuva* 3:8 should be respected on the basis of five arguments. Before laying out these arguments I emphasize again that I do not claim that the "true" Rambam is that found in the *Mishneh Torah* nor that in the Introduction to *Perek Ḥelek*, or that today we should accept the formulation in the *Mishneh Torah* as opposed to the formulation in the Introduction to *Perek Ḥelek*. My claim is that we have accepted *both* formulations, but in different ways and for different purposes that I will chart in the next two chapters. My sole aim here is to argue that *Hilkhot Teshuva* 3:8 must be understood independently of the Introduction to *Perek Ḥelek*.

---

12. Yitzchak Shilat, *Igrot HaRambam* (Jerusalem: Shilat, 1987), 410–11.

The *Mishneh Torah* as Authoritative

The first argument stems from the traditional interpretive strategy noted earlier: the rabbinic tradition has consistently maintained that when we encounter discrepancies between the Commentary on the Mishna and the *Mishneh Torah*, we do not attempt to harmonize them, and read the *Mishneh Torah* in light of the Commentary on the Mishna. Rather, we view the formulation of the *Mishneh Torah* as independent and authoritative. By this reading, the definition of a *kofer baTorah* in *Hilkhot Teshuva* 3:8 is limited to one who denies the divinity of the Torah. To be sure, the Rambam still stated in the *Mishneh Torah* that the whole of the Torah was dictated by God to Moses (*Hilkhot Tefilla* 13:6). Were one to hold that a later prophetic figure had added to the Torah at God's command, the Rambam would consider this an erroneous position – erroneous, but not heretical; it would not be sufficient to brand one a *kofer baTorah*.[13]

The Absence of the Rambam's Eighth Principle in *Hilkhot Yesodei HaTorah*

The second argument that supports an independent reading of *Hilkhot Teshuva* 3:8 stems from an examination of this halakha within the wider scope of the Rambam's reformulation of the Thirteen Principles in the *Mishneh Torah*. As noted, many of the Thirteen Principles are discussed in the *Mishneh Torah* in *Hilkhot Yesodei HaTorah*. Consider the following schematic table that summarizes the Rambam's treatment of the principles in the Introduction to *Perek Ḥelek* and *Hilkhot Yesodei HaTorah*:

Precept	Introduction to *Perek Ḥelek*	*Hilkhot Yesodei HaTorah*
Existence of the Creator	Principle 1	1:1–6
Unity of God	Principle 2	1:6–7
Incorporeality of God	Principle 3	1:7–8
Eternal nature of God	Principle 4	1:1–5

---

13. There is, of course, the related issue of the seventh principle, the belief in the distinct prophetic stature of Moses, and the relationship between these two principles. See discussion below in this chapter.

Precept	Introduction to *Perek Ḥelek*	*Hilkhot Yesodei HaTorah*
Worship Only God	Principle 5	*Hilkhot Avoda Zara* 2:1
Existence of Prophecy	Principle 6	7:1
Prophecy of Moses	Principle 7	7:6; 8:3
Torah from Heaven	Principle 8	-----
Immutability of Torah	Principle 9	9:1
Divine Omniscience	Principle 10	2:9–10

The table shows that the Rambam relates to the first ten principles found in Introduction to *Perek Ḥelek*, with the exception of the fifth principle, in *Hilkhot Yesodei HaTorah*.[14] Principles 1–4 are largely covered in the first chapter of *Hilkhot Yesodei HaTorah*. Principles 6–9, those that discuss issues relating to prophecy, are covered in *Hilkhot Yesodei HaTorah* chapters 7–9. I would like to focus on these chapters with greater resolution to examine what elements are carried over from the Introduction to *Perek Ḥelek*. Here we see a striking pattern. Regarding principle 6 (Existence of Prophecy), principle 7 (the Prophecy of Moses), and principle 9 (Immutability of Torah), the discussions in *Hilkhot Yesodei HaTorah* are *expansions* of what we find concerning these elements in the Introduction to *Perek Ḥelek*. *Hilkhot Yesodei HaTorah* chapter 7 expands upon principles 6 and 7. *Hilkhot Yesodei HaTorah* chapter 9 expands upon principle 9.

The striking difference is seen with regard to principle 8 – *torah* from heaven. The eighth principle in the Introduction to *Perek Ḥelek* highlighted three points with regard to the Written Law – The Torah: (1) that the Torah was transmitted to Moses through something akin to dictation; (2) that *every word* of the Torah was revealed to Moses and written down by him; and (3) that one who claims that Moses made up even a single verse on his own is a heretic. None of these

---

14. Understandably, the Rambam elects to treat the fifth principle, worship to God alone, in *Hilkhot Avoda Zara*. The issues raised in the final three principles – reward and punishment, resurrection of the dead, and the coming of the Messiah – are addressed at other points in the *Mishneh Torah*.

points appears in *Hilkhot Yesodei HaTorah* even though the other aspects about prophecy contained in the Introduction to *Perek Ḥelek* – the existence of prophecy in precept 6, the nature of Mosaic prophecy in precept 7, and the immutability of the laws of the Torah in precept 9 – are not only included in *Hilkhot Yesodei HaTorah* chapters 7 and 9, but all appear in expanded formulations.[15] I bring these observation to buttress a single point: when we see in *Hilkhot Teshuva* 3:8 that the *kofer baTorah* is defined without the insistence that Moses received the entire Torah via dictation – a notion so central to the eighth principle in the Introduction to *Perek Ḥelek* – we can be sure that this is intentional as there is also no mention of this in *Hilkhot Yesodei HaTorah*, despite that composition's extended attention to the issue of prophecy in general and Mosaic prophecy in particular. The omission of this notion from *Hilkhot Yesodei HaTorah* lends credence to the reading of *Hilkhot Teshuva* 3:8 as standing in contrast to what the Rambam writes in the eighth principle of faith in the Introduction to *Perek Ḥelek*.

I am unaware of any classical rabbinic literature that attends to this striking lacuna in *Hilkhot Yesodei HaTorah*. Humbly, I offer a conjecture as to why the notion that the entire Torah was dictated to Moses is absent from both *Hilkhot Yesodei HaTorah* and from *Hilkhot Teshuva* 3:8. As we know from many of the Rambam's writings, the only laws that he considers to be from Sinai are those that are not subject to dispute.[16] For the Rambam it is axiomatic that the tradition is pristinely preserved. Dispute over a matter is prima facie evidence that the matter at hand is not part of the tradition given to Moses

---

15. It is true that the seventh principle of the Introduction to *Perek Ḥelek* and the seventh chapter of *Hilkhot Yesodei HaTorah* address the prophecy of Moses at length. But these are accounts of the *nature* of his prophetic experience and how it differs from the experience of other prophets. Neither the seventh principle of the Introduction to *Perek Ḥelek* nor the seventh chapter of *Hilkhot Yesodei HaTorah* mentions the Torah and Moses's role in its transmission. That was the subject of the eighth principle in the Introduction to *Perek Ḥelek* and is omitted in *Hilkhot Yesodei HaTorah*. Chapter 9 of *Hilkhot Yesodei HaTorah* does ascribe some parts of the Torah to Mosaic prophecy, but not the entirety of the Torah; see discussion below.

16. The Rambam's longest explication of this is in his introduction to the Commentary on the Mishna.

by God at Sinai.[17] Although the Rambam states this with regard to legal matters, perhaps the Rambam believed that the *mesora* also included the matters of faith. For a principle to attain the status of a foundational precept and to be included within his legal magnum opus, the *Mishneh Torah*, it had to be one that was accepted unanimously in the talmudic sources.[18] As we saw in the previous chapter, however, the subject of Moses's role in the transmission of the Torah is a disputed one. According to one opinion in the *baraita* cited in Bava Batra 14b–15a, Moses received the entire Torah. But according to another opinion in that *baraita*, there were verses that were not communicated to Moses but to Joshua. The Rambam himself would continue to maintain, even in the *Mishneh Torah*, that all of the Torah was dictated to Moses (as per *Hilkhot Tefilla* 13:6), but due to the disputed nature of this claim, he did not establish this belief as a "yesod haTorah," a fundamental belief, when writing the *Mishneh Torah*. The tenets concerning prophecy in chapters 6, 7, and 9 of *Hilkhot Yesodei HaTorah* are not the subject of dispute in the Talmud, and are thus granted a full airing in this book of the *Mishneh Torah*. Even if this hypothesis is found wanting, the fact remains that the notion that the entire Torah was dictated to Moses is absent from *Hilkhot Yesodei HaTorah*. The relative de-emphasis of this idea in the *Mishneh Torah* stands in contrast to the high emphasis placed on this idea in his more popular work, the Commentary on the Mishna (and with it, the Introduction to *Perek Ḥelek*), composed in Arabic for a wide audience.

---

17. See discussion in Moses Halbertal, *Maimonides: Life and Thought*, trans. Joel Linsider (Princeton: Princeton University Press, 2014), 99–107; within classical rabbinic sources, the issue is addressed in Maharatz Chajes, *Torat Neviim*, maamar *Torah SheBeAl Peh* (found in *Kol Sifrei Maharatz Chajes* [Israel, 1988], 1:115); Rabbi Yair Chaim Bacharach (Germany, 1638–1701), *Shut Chavot Yair*, sec. 192. My thanks to Gil Student for bringing these sources to my attention.

18. Although there is an opinion in Sanhedrin 99a, attributed to R. Hillel, that "Israel has no messiah," many commentators have maintained that R. Hillel did not mean to deny the coming of the Messiah. For an overview of these opinions, see Rabbi Akiva Kahana, "Emuna BeViat HaMashiaḥ: Kama Hi Ikkarit VeYesodit?" Portal HaDaf HaYomi, https://daf-yomi.com/DYItemDetails.aspx?itemId=40122.

The Source for the Omission of the Dictation of the Torah to Moses in *Hilkhot Teshuva* 3:8

The third argument for maintaining that *Hilkhot Teshuva* 3:8 should not be harmonized with the discussion of *torah* from heaven in the Introduction to *Perek Ḥelek* stems from the Rambam's handling of the talmudic sources in his formulation of this halakha. His source here is one we saw earlier, the second *baraita* concerning "*torah* from heaven" found in Sanhedrin 99a:

Hilkhot Teshuva 3:8	Sanhedrin 99a
שלשה הן הכופרים בתורה:	תניא אידך: כי דבר הי בזה –
האומר שאין התורה מעם הי	זה האומר אין תורה מן השמים.
אפילו פסוק אחד אפילו תיבה אחת אם אמר משה אמרו מפי עצמו	אפילו אמר: כל התורה כולה מן השמים, חוץ מפסוק זה שלא אמרו הקדוש ברוך הוא אלא משה מפי עצמו –
הרי זה כופר בתורה,	זהו כי דבר ה' בזה.
וכן הכופר בפרושה והוא תורה שבעל פה והמכחיש מגידיה כגון צדוק ובייתוס	ואפילו אמר: כל התורה כולה מן השמים, חוץ מדקדוק זה, מקל וחומר זה, מגזרה שוה זו.

Hilkhot Teshuva 3:8	Sanhedrin 99a
There are three who deemed *kofrim baTorah*:	Another [*baraita*] taught: "Because he has despised the word of the Lord" –
He who says that the Torah is not from God.	this refers to one who says that *torah* is not from heaven.
Even a single verse or even a single word – if he says Moses uttered it on his own accord,	And even if he asserts that the whole Torah is from heaven, excepting a particular verse, which [he maintains] was not uttered by God but by Moses himself,
He is deemed a *kofer baTorah*.	he is included in "because he has despised the word of the Lord."

Hilkhot Teshuva 3:8	Sanhedrin 99a
And so, too, one who denies its interpretation, that is, the Oral Law, and one who rejects those that promulgate the Oral Law, such as Zadok and Boethius.	And even if he admits that the whole Torah is from heaven, excepting a single point, a particular *kal vahomer* or a certain *gezera shava*.

In his introduction of the various categories of heresy in *Hilkhot Teshuva* 3:6, the Rambam states, "These are the individuals who have no place in the World to Come." When he comes to the category of those who have no place in the World to Come on account of their beliefs about the Torah, the Rambam formulates his definition by invoking talmudic sources that address the issue squarely. As we saw, the mishna in Sanhedrin 10:1 states, "These are the individuals that have no place in the World to Come: he who says ... there is no *torah* from heaven." The Gemara on Sanhedrin 99a then initiates a discussion about this category of heretic by invoking several *baraitot* that offer excurses on the verse, "he has despised the word of the Lord" (Num. 15:31). The formulation of *Hilkhot Teshuva* 3:8 is constructed entirely from one of these opinions. Put differently, when addressing which individuals forfeit their place in the World to Come by dint of their heresy, the Rambam hews closely to the sources he found on the subject in the Gemara, which focus on the divinity of the Torah, but not on the prophetic agency involved in its transmission. The Rambam's formulation in *Hilkhot Teshuva* 3:8 is not a shorthand version of a talmudic source that states that every word of the Torah was dictated to Moses. Nor is the formulation here a shorthand version of what appears in the eighth principle in the Introduction to *Perek Ḥelek*. To be sure, when the Rambam wrote in the Introduction to *Perek Ḥelek* that God revealed to Moses every word of the Torah as dictation, he could cite a talmudic source – the opinion of R. Shimon in Bava Batra 15a. However, that source never states that he who denies the role of Moses in the transmission of the Torah is deemed a *kofer baTorah* – the subject of *Hilkhot Teshuva* 3:8. The Rambam's formulation in *Hilkhot Teshuva* 3:8 is a tight paraphrase of a source that itself also omits the notion that God dictated every word of the Torah to Moses – the second *baraita* on Sanhedrin 99a. The formulation of the issue, then, in

Hilkhot Teshuva 3:8 is rightly read as standing in contrast to what the Rambam wrote on the matter in his Introduction to *Perek Ḥelek*.

The *Mishneh Torah* as a Stand-Alone Reference

A fourth argument for the independence of *Hilkhot Teshuva* 3:8 from the parallel formulation of the eighth principle in the Introduction to *Perek Ḥelek* is well understood in light of twelfth-century material limits and textual culture. The Rambam writes that he composed the *Mishneh Torah* so that communities throughout the Diaspora could have a single resource from which to receive halakhic guidance, without need for any other work. The Rambam lived and wrote three hundred years before the printing press. For a community to procure a copy of the entire *Mishneh Torah* was itself an enormous expense. If we assume that the Rambam formulated *Hilkhot Teshuva* 3:8 with the supposition that his readership had access to the Commentary on the Mishna, that would mean that his *Mishneh Torah* was not a freestanding resource, as he claims, but one that was dependent on procuring the accompanying text, the Commentary on the Mishna, a further hefty expenditure. Moreover, we know that the Rambam composed the *Mishneh Torah* in simple mishnaic Hebrew so that it could enjoy the widest circulation and access across the breadth of the Diaspora of his time. To make the understanding of the *Mishneh Torah* dependent on familiarity with the Commentary on the Mishna (let alone a private correspondence with ibn Jabbar) would have erected an enormous barrier blocking proper understanding of the Rambam's intent. Many in the Diaspora would have had no way of understanding the Commentary on the Mishna; it was written in Arabic. Clearly, then, the Rambam could not have been relying on his readership's familiarity with the Introduction to *Perek Ḥelek* when he composed *Hilkhot Teshuva* 3:8.

The Relationship Between the Heresy Categories in *Hilkhot Teshuva* and the Tenets of Faith in *Hilkhot Yesodei HaTorah*

The fifth argument in support of reading *Hilkhot Teshuva* 3:8 independently of the eighth principle as formulated in the Introduction to *Perek Ḥelek* stems from the relationship between the attention to the principles in *Hilkhot Yesodei HaTorah* and the presentation of the principles in *Hilkhot Teshuva*. In *Hilkhot Yesodei HaTorah*, the Rambam lays out detailed formulations of each of these *yesodot*, or fundamental precepts, which partially overlap with the Thirteen Principles in the Introduction to *Perek Ḥelek*. In the third chapter of *Hilkhot Teshuva*, the Rambam lists the different categories of heresy: the various denials that lead a person to forfeit their place in the World to Come. Since he had already offered detailed accounts of each *yesod* in *Hilkhot Yesodei HaTorah* (and, in the case of the fifth principle, in *Hilkhot Avoda Zara*), in *Hilkhot Teshuva* he refers to each with the briefest epitaph, of only a few words, without offering detailed definition. By referencing each principle with just a few words, the Rambam signals that he expects the reader to know that he has explicated these more fully in the earlier sections of the *Mishneh Torah*. However, in his composition of these epitaphs, we discover one anomaly, which is graphically evident in this schematic table:

Precept	Introduction to *Perek Ḥelek*	*Hilkhot Yesodei HaTorah*	*Hilkhot Teshuva*
Existence of the Creator	Principle 1	1:1–6	3:7a; 6 words
Unity of God	Principle 2	1:6–7	3:7b; 8 words
Incorporeality of God	Principle 3	1:7–8	3:7c; 9 words
Eternal nature of God	Principle 4	1:1–5	3:7d; 5 words
Worship Only to God	Principle 5	*Avoda Zara* 2:1	3:7e; 12 words
Existence of Prophecy	Principle 6	7:1	3:8a; 12 words
Prophecy of Moses	Principle 7	7:6, 8:3	3:8b; 5 words
Torah from Heaven	Principle 8	-----	3:8d; **32 words**
Immutability of Torah	Principle 9	9:1	3:8e; 17 words
Divine Omniscience	Principle 10	2:9–10	3:8c; 6 words

When the Rambam defines the individual who denies the principle of "*torah* from heaven," the description he offers is far and away the longest of any of the labels that he offers for the heretics who deny any of the other nine Principles of Faith. As we saw earlier, in *Hilkhot Yesodei HaTorah* the Rambam does not devote even a part of a single halakha – let alone an entire chapter – to the topic of the eighth principle, *torah* from heaven. For the Rambam to define in *Hilkhot Teshuva* what constitutes a *kofer baTorah*, he could not suffice with a one-line epitaph that refers the reader back to a previous section of the *Mishneh Torah*, because no such section exists. Were it his expectation that the readers of the *Mishneh Torah* return to the Thirteen Principles as laid out in the Introduction to *Perek Ḥelek*, there would be no need for the Rambam to elaborate concerning the principle of *torah* from heaven in *Hilkhot Teshuva* 3:8. He could have referred to the principle with a brief epitaph, as he does with the previous categories of heresy. The fact that this is the only category of heresy in *Hilkhot Teshuva* that is given detailed delineation is proof positive that the Rambam expected his readers to interpret this chapter of *Hilkhot Teshuva* by reference to the earlier chapters of the *Mishneh Torah* and not the Introduction to *Perek Ḥelek*.

THE PROPHECY OF MOSES AND THE TEXT OF THE TORAH: *HILKHOT YESODEI HATORAH* 9:1

As I noted earlier, although the Rambam expounds on the nature of Mosaic prophecy in both the seventh principle of his Introduction to *Perek Ḥelek* and the seventh chapter of *Hilkhot Yesodei HaTorah*, there is no indication in either of those sources as to the content of that prophecy. We do get a sense, however, of how this relates to a *part* of the Torah in the ninth chapter of *Hilkhot Yesodei HaTorah*, where the Rambam discusses the eternal and unchanging nature of the Torah's laws. *Hilkhot Yesodei HaTorah* 9:1 reads:

> It is clear and explicit in the Torah that it is [God's] *command-ment, remaining forever without change, addition, or diminishment,* as [Deut. 13:1] states: "All these matters *which I command to you, you shall be careful to perform.* You may not add to it or dimin-ish from it," and [Deut. 29:28] states: "What is revealed is for us

and our children forever, to carry out all the words of this Torah." This teaches that we are *commanded to fulfill all the Torah's directives forever*. It is also said: "It is an everlasting statute for all your generations," and [Deut. 30:12] states: "It is not in the heavens." This teaches that a prophet can no longer add a *new precept* [to the Torah]. Therefore, if a person will arise, whether Jew or gentile, and perform a sign or wonder and say that God sent him to: a) *add a mitzva*, b) *withdraw a mitzva*, c) *explain a mitzva in a manner which differs from the tradition received from Moses*, or d) if he says that *the mitzvot commanded to the Jews are not forever*, but rather were given for a limited time, he is a false prophet. He comes to deny the prophecy of Moses and should be executed by strangulation, because he dared to make statements in God's name which God never made. God, blessed be His name, commanded Moses that this *commandment* is for us and our children forever, and God is not man that He speaks falsely.[19]

We might have expected that the eternal nature of the Torah would mandate that one who tampers in any way with the text of the Torah – either its legal or narrative sections – abrogates its eternal nature, and thereby denies the prophecy of Moses. Indeed, the Rambam surely believed that tampering with any part of the text of the Torah was a very grave matter. But that is not his focus here in the ninth chapter of *Hilkhot Yesodei HaTorah*, and by extension is not the definition of one who changes the Torah in *Hilkhot Teshuva* 3:8. Note that throughout the halakha cited above, the sustained attention is to the *legal* passages of the Torah alone. The Rambam does not say here that one who adds a verse or deletes a verse from the Torah denies the prophecy of Moses. Rather only one who adds a mitzva, deletes a mitzva, or claims that a mitzva is not eternal is deemed to be one who "den[ies] the prophecy of Moses." We see that same limited scope in *Hilkhot Teshuva* 3:8. One must claim that there has been a change concerning a mitzva of the Torah in order for one

---

19. Translation taken from Eliyahu Touger, trans., "Yesodei haTorah – Chapter Nine," *Mishneh Torah*, http://www.chabad.org/library/article_cdo/aid/904993/jewish/Yesodei-haTorah-Chapter-Nine.htm. Slight modifications have been made.

to be labeled a *kofer baTorah*. As we saw, the Rambam himself believes that every word of the Torah was dictated to Moses. But according to the Rambam, if one believes that at God's command a prophet added to the narrative of the Torah, such an individual is not deemed to have denied the prophecy of Moses. Only if one believes that at God's command a prophet added something that were to "explain a mitzva in a manner which differs from the tradition received from Moses" would such a person be deemed to have denied the prophecy of Moses.

This understanding of *Hilkhot Yesodei HaTorah* 9:1 implies a hierarchy between the narrative and legal parts of the Torah that matches a distinction the Rambam himself makes at the beginning of the introduction to his Commentary on the Mishna. There, he writes that when God would issue the mitzvot, Moses would write down the dictation, and that these first texts would be studied with Aaron, Joshua, and the elders, together with the received oral interpretation concerning the correct understanding of these passages. Only at the end of the forty years in the desert, prior to his death, did Moses compose the whole of the Torah – its legal passages now embedded within a narrative frame – as dictated by God.

The logic for this distinction between the narrative and halakhic portions of the Torah stems from imperatives guiding the Rambam that we mentioned earlier. For the Rambam, issues disputed within the Talmud cannot be deemed to be part of the tradition given to Moses at Sinai. And surely, for the Rambam, the *yesodei haTorah* – the fundamental precepts of the Torah – must be part of that tradition. But in the *baraita* in Bava Batra 14b one *Tanna* was of the opinion that Joshua added eight verses to the Torah following the death of Moses. Put differently, this *baraita* demonstrates that there were opinions in the Talmud that believed that it was possible for some verses to be added to the Torah, even without the prophetic agency of Moses. The Rambam believes that the prophecy of Moses is unique and sacrosanct. But he cannot maintain that the denial of the prophecy of Moses extends to one who adds any verse to the Torah, and also maintain that such a belief constitutes one of the *yesodei haTorah*. The dispute in the *baraita* of Bava Batra disallows this. And so the Rambam seeks to limit the scope of the dispute found in that *baraita*. All eight verses in question are narrative. There is no source, however, that suggests that later figures added verses to the halakhic portions of the Torah. The Rambam therefore can state in *Hilkhot Yesodei HaTorah* 9:1 that one may not claim that a later prophet added to the halakhic portions of the Torah anything which would "explain a mitzva in a manner which differs from the tradition received from Moses." To accommodate both opinions in the *baraita* of Bava Batra 14b, however, he cannot make the same claim concerning the narrative portions of the Torah.

To conclude, I have offered here two assessments of the Rambam's intent in the formulation of his definition of a *kofer baTorah* in *Hilkhot Teshuva* 3:8. Each bears a burden of explanation. The view that I have advanced here claims that the Rambam's view in *Hilkhot Teshuva* is that one must believe that all of the Torah is from heaven. If one believes that at God's behest another prophet added to the narrative portions of the Torah, then for the Rambam, that person is erroneous in his belief, but not deemed a *kofer baTorah*. Yet, if this is so, why does the Rambam explicitly state otherwise in the Introduction to *Perek Ḥelek* and in his epistle to ibn Jabbar? For this explanation to stand, we must fall back on the Abarbanel's understanding of the Introduction to *Perek Ḥelek* cited at the outset of the chapter. The Rambam writes in different genres for different audiences. In the Introduction to *Perek Ḥelek*, his genre is hortatory and aimed for a popular audience. In the *Mishneh Torah*, his target is a learned audience, and he must abide by the restraints he adopts for precise halakhic formulation. When the Rambam claims that one is a *kofer baTorah* for believing that even a single word postdated Moses, it is surely no coincidence that we find these statements only in compositions he wrote in Arabic. In the epistle to ibn Jabbar, we learn that the interlocutor, by his own admission, could not understand a text in Hebrew. Given the theological realities discussed in the previous chapter – the libel of *taḥrīf* rife in the Muslim world – it is no surprise that the Rambam insists that the divine transmission of every word of the Torah to Moses was a principle of the highest order.

But the opinion that imposes harmony between the Rambam's formulation of *torah* from heaven in the Introduction to *Perek Ḥelek* and the formulation in *Hilkhot Teshuva* 3:8 bears a great burden of explanation as well. The Rambam is clear that the *Mishneh Torah* is meant to stand on its own, without recourse to any other work to elucidate it. This harmonizing approach is hard pressed to explain how the Rambam's intended audiences for the *Mishneh Torah* could have understood the intent of *Hilkhot Teshuva* 3:8 without recourse to the Introduction to *Perek Ḥelek*. Although we maintain that the Rambam is a master of precision in his formulations in the *Mishneh Torah*, this opinion is forced to concede that the Rambam's formulation of *Hilkhot Teshuva* 3:8 is imprecise. Standing on its own, *Hilkhot Teshuva* 3:8 does not clearly indicate that one is a *kofer baTorah* if one believes that the entire Torah is divine, but that some verses may have been delivered at God's behest through another prophet. Finally, and perhaps most crucially, the view that harmonizes *Hilkhot Teshuva* 3:8 with the eighth principle in the Introduction to *Perek Ḥelek* is hard pressed to explain why the notion that God transmitted every word of the Torah to Moses is entirely absent from *Hilkhot Yesodei HaTorah*, even though chapters 7–9 of that work expand every other aspect of prophecy that had been raised in the Introduction to *Perek Ḥelek*.

"HE WHO SAYS ...": TWO OPEN QUESTIONS

I conclude these remarks about the handling of the Principles of Faith in the *Mishneh Torah* by raising two questions in light of the Rambam's formulations concerning heretical positions in *Hilkhot Teshuva* chapter 3. In halakhot 6–8, the Rambam begins each case with the same formulation: "He who *says*, x, y, and z." The language hews to that of Sanhedrin 10:1, "He who says there is no resurrection of the dead," or "He who says there is no *torah* from heaven." When the Rambam writes, "He who *says*," does he mean that a person is deemed a heretic only if he or she makes a verbal statement, written or oral? Put differently, if a person harbors such thoughts, but never shares them, is he or she considered a heretic? Indeed, in nearly every case in which the Rambam writes *Ha'omer*, "He who says," the implication is that a verbal communication is made (e.g., *Hilkhot Avel* 1:11; *Hilkhot Ishut* 3:9). Nonetheless there are also instances where the phrase implies mental processes alone (*Hilkhot Teshuva* 4:4), and it may be that the Rambam employs this language here in *Hilkhot Teshuva* 3:6–8 because this was the language of the mishna in Sanhedrin 10:1. The issue is critical from a halakhic standpoint, because one who is a *kofer baTorah*, for example, cannot perfom *sheḥita*. But how shall we know if someone is indeed a *kofer baTorah*? If we take the Rambam's language here in its most literal fashion, then an individual is only rendered a *kofer baTorah* if he issues a statement of such heretical beliefs. So long as a *shoḥet* has made no heretical statements, there would be no need for us to probe him for his beliefs. But if the Rambam believes that it is sufficient to harbor heretical thoughts to render a person a *kofer baTorah*, how could we ever rely on a *shoḥet* without interrogating him concerning his beliefs at the moment of the *sheḥita*? It seems more reasonable to say that for the Rambam (and hence for all the *posekim* who rely on his ruling), one can become a halakhic *kofer baTorah* only by stating such beliefs. Put differently, halakhic heresy has a social as well as a theological component to it. I am unaware of any discussion of this issue within classical rabbinic sources, and simply raise here what seem to be two possible interpretations of the issue.

The Rambam's repeated formulation in *Hilkhot Teshuva* 3:6–8, "He who *says*," raises a second question, crucially important for our own day: What if a person harbors doubts about a particular issue, but is not fully convinced of the heretical position? Leaving aside the previous issue of whether heresy must be communicated, we ask here: Is someone who is unsure what to believe concerning one of the principles equivalent to someone who fully rejects? The language of "He who *says*" could imply that if a person harbors doubts or questions concerning the divinity of the Torah, for example, they are not categorized as a *kofer baTorah*; only one who fully affirms his opinion that the Torah is a human creation receives that designation. In this context, I would invoke *Hilkhot Yesodei HaTorah* 1:6. In the previous halakhot of that chapter, the Rambam laid out the mandate to believe in the Creator. In *Hilkhot Yesodei HaTorah* 1:6, the Rambam writes,

> Knowledge of this matter is a *mitzvat aseh*, as it is written, "I am the Lord your God" (Ex 20:2). *And anyone who considers* that there might be another divine figure other than Him is guilty of a transgression, as it says, "You shall have no gods other than Me" (Ex. 20:3) and he is a *kofer ba'ikkar*, for this is the principle upon which all else is predicated.

In this halakha the Rambam entertains and critiques the category of doubt in a way that is not expressed with regard to the various categories of heresy in *Hilkhot Teshuva* chapter 3.

The status of believers who struggle with doubts – even concerning the Principles of Faith – is an issue that, unsurprisingly, has garnered greater attention in recent generations, and I offer here only a brief survey of opinions. The Rambam himself states at the conclusion to the Introduction to *Perek Ḥelek* that one who even harbors doubts about the veracity of the Thirteen Principles is considered a heretic and must be hated. In the *Mishneh Torah*, however, this sentiment seems to be walked back, especially when the doubts are a function of the spiritual climate in which the doubter is raised (*Hilkhot Mamrim* 3:3). Rabbi Haym Soloveitchik of Brisk is cited as maintaining that according to the Rambam, one is rendered a heretic (*epikoros*) not only for *doubt*, but even for *ignorance*; if a person is ignorant of or unfamiliar with any one of the Thirteen Principles, he or she is thereby rendered an *epikoros*.[20] By contrast, more recent authorities – including Rabbi Avraham Yitzchak HaKohen Kook, Rabbi Yehuda Amital, and Rabbi Norman Lamm – have ruled that one who struggles with uncertainties even about principles of faith does not attain the status of a heretic.[21]

As we have seen, through the time of the Rambam, the very notion of fundamental principles of faith was only beginning to take hold and precise definitions of the tenet "*torah* from heaven" were varied. The path toward our acceptance of the principles of faith would be a long one, and we trace its early steps in the next chapter.

---

20. Cited in the *Ḥidushei HaGriz HaHadashim*, no. 88. Far be it for me to judge whether this is an accurate reading of the Rambam. Needless to say, however, on the operative level, such a ruling would render the vast majority of upstanding heaven-fearing Jews today *epikorsim*.

21. See Rabbi Avraham Yitzchak HaKohen Kook, *Iggerot HaRaaya*, vol. 1 (Jerusalem: Mossad HaRav Kook, 1984), letter 20, pp. 20–21; Rabbi Yehuda Amital, *Jewish Values in a Changing World* (Alon Shevut: Ktav, 2005), 178–79; Rabbi Norman Lamm, *Faith and Doubt: Studies in Traditional Jewish Thought* (New York: Ktav, 1971), 17. See also chapter 2 of *Sefer Ḥazon Ish al Inyanei Emuna, Bitaḥon, VeOd* of the Hazon Ish (Benei Berak: Sifriyati, 1997), which speaks of the status of those of "weak faith." My thanks to Gil Student for bringing these sources to my attention.

Chapter 10

The Thirteen Principles from the Rambam until the Dawn of Emancipation

oday we take it as axiomatic that the Rambam's Thirteen Principles are *the* fundamental principles of the faith. But that status was a long time in coming. In this chapter, I trace how this acceptance grew from the time of the Rambam in the twelfth century until the dawn of Emancipation at the end of the eighteenth century. As we will see in the next chapter, Emancipation brought with it tremendous challenges and changes for the *mesora*, and the Thirteen Principles would play a big part in meeting those challenges. But to understand that function, we need here, in this chapter, to understand the role and standing of the principles before that period. Here we will attend to two primary questions:

1. Many voices during these centuries would have agreed with the claim that the Thirteen Principles were now "accepted" as the Principles of Faith. But just what did "acceptance" of the principles mean at that time? Who decided that they had become

accepted and on what basis was that decided? How were the principles used? What were the consequences for disagreeing with one of the principles, or even all of them? As we shall see, the best answer that we can give is that the principles were only partially accepted at the time.

2. What version of the principles was it that gained acceptance? That question might seem like a tautology, akin to asking, "Who is buried in Grant's Tomb?" After all, it is obvious that the Thirteen Principles were composed by the Rambam in his Introduction to *Perek Ḥelek*. As we shall see, though, when Jews spoke of the "Rambam's Thirteen Principles" they could actually have had many different texts in mind. Why is this? What are the differences between each of these texts, and specifically as each pertains to what a Jew must believe about the origins of the Torah?

THE EARLIEST STAGES OF ACCEPTANCE: THE THIRTEENTH AND FOURTEENTH CENTURIES AND THE ROLE OF *PIYUT*

For more than two hundred years after the Rambam penned the Introduction to *Perek Ḥelek*, and with it the Thirteen Principles of Faith, we find no discussion of the Rambam's catechism in any major rabbinic work. There are no sources of enduring note that openly embrace it, or take issue with it, in whole or in part. In fact, there is no discussion of the general topic of principles of belief at all in any major rabbinic work until the fifteenth century.[1] Yet, noting this silence by the rabbinic elite overlooks an important development, one, arguably, that has shaped our attitude toward the Thirteen Principles more than any other: their employment by the composers of the *piyutim*, many of them anonymous. We have in manuscripts from this period some one hundred *piyutim* that are based on the Rambam's Thirteen Principles.[2] The most famous of

---

1. See Menachem Kellner, *Dogma in Medieval Jewish Thought: From Maimonides to Abravanel* (Oxford: Oxford University Press, 1986), 66.
2. These have not been published in any accessible compendium and remain largely in manuscript form. For a sample example of these, see Alexander Marx, "A List of Poems on the Articles of the Creed," *Jewish Quarterly Review*, New Series, 9, no. 3/4 (Jan.–Apr., 1919): 305–33.

these remain both familiar and popular today – *Yigdal* and *Ani Maamin*.[3] Only by understanding how these *piyutim* relate to the Rambam's formulations in his Introduction to *Perek Ḥelek* can we understand how the *mesora* came to accept the Thirteen Principles.

When a *paytan* composes a *piyut* based on the Rambam's principles, he does so, of course, out of great esteem; he does so out of a desire to further inculcate these ideas into the popular liturgical discourse of everyday Jews, who may not be learned, and who – given early medieval contexts – may not be literate. The challenges that faced the *paytan* in the Middle Ages were very much those that face moderns who wish to get their word out to as wide an audience as possible. By reflecting on modern modes of publicizing an idea, we can get a better grasp of the medieval genre of *piyut* and the role it played in popularizing the Rambam's Thirteen Principles.

You wish to publicize an idea, or an opinion. If you compose a long-form essay your writing can be comprehensive, systematic, and precise. But the longer the piece is, the more limited its readership will be. Only an elite audience of readers has the patience or interest to read a long essay. To reach a wider audience, you might boil down your long-form essay into a nine-hundred-word op-ed piece or a blog post on a highly read website. You bite the bullet of cutting down the size, losing nuance and depth, in the hopes that you will purchase a wider readership, and thus greater influence. You will also need to make the shorter essay free of specialized jargon, and relevant to the here and now, and you will need to employ good rhetoric – the competition out there for people's attention is fierce. Maybe if you hook some readers with a short, punchy op-ed piece, many of them will be drawn to actually invest the time to read your long-form essay. But even a blog post or an op-ed piece will reach a limited audience. To reach the widest possible audience will require even greater brevity, and even more attention to the rhetorical and aesthetic appeal of the message – think of a tweet, a one-frame comic, or

---

3. *Ani Maamin* lacks the meter and poetic style we generally associate with the genre of *piyut*. Nonetheless, *Ani Maamin* is properly categorized as *piyut* because, like *piyutim* generally, it is composed for a popular audience, to be committed to memory, and was penned by an author who was likely not a member of the rabbinic elite.

a bumper sticker. The upshot of all this is that there is an inversely proportional relationship between the breadth of audience you can reach and the length, nuance, and sophistication of what you write.

The Rambam was well aware of this dynamic. That is why he developed ideas to their fullest in the *Guide for the Perplexed,* whereas some of the same ideas are expressed more simply and in greater brevity in the Introduction to *Perek Ḥelek* and in the presentation of the Thirteen Principles. The Rambam hoped, as he writes at the end of the Introduction to *Perek Ḥelek,* that Jews would commit to intense study of the Thirteen Principles. This would prove an aspiration that would go unfulfilled. No community has ever undertaken the popular, sustained, in-depth study of the principles.

Enter the many *paytanim* who sought to communicate the Rambam's ideas in poetic form. They understood that the Rambam's catechism could have enormous popularity. Think of all the blog posts and articles you have seen that take the form of "Five keys to achieving such and such," or, "Seven things to do when x, y, or z." The Rambam's principles were the medieval version of "Thirteen key things to know about God." Here was a template that *paytanim* knew could inspire audiences toward greater piety, and one that was associated with that greatest of sages, the Rambam. But they realized that to succeed they would need to adapt the Rambam's Thirteen Principles in three ways. First, of course, they would need to express the catechism in poetic form so that it would be appealing and easier to commit to memory. Second, their compositions would put a premium on brevity. Thirteen principles would need to be expressed in about as many lines of verse. This, by necessity, forced difficult decisions. The Rambam himself had offered title sentences to each of the principles: "reward and punishment," "*torah* from heaven." Yet these titles gained clarity through the detail he provided thereafter. The *paytan,* therefore, would need to undertake the delicate task of either leaving the principle broad and vague, or of highlighting at most one salient aspect of it.

But these *paytanim* also needed to recast the principles in a third way which is far less appreciated today, but extremely important: they would need to *alter* ideas as well, to make them more palatable or appealing to their audience than what the Rambam had actually written.

We can see how *paytanim* went about their work of reconfiguring the principles by taking a look at the two *piyutim* from this period that have becomes classics of our liturgy: *Yigdal* and *Ani Maamin*.

Yigdal and *Ani Maamin*: Two Expressions of the Principles

Yigdal was written in the early fourteenth century by one Daniel ben Judah of Rome. For an example of how the *paytan* abbreviated the Rambam's formulations in his Introduction to *Perek Ḥelek*, we may look at the principle that concerns us, the eighth principle. Recall that for the Rambam, the eighth principle entails four propositions: (1) that every word of the Torah was given to Moses by God; (2) that this was transmitted by God through something akin to dictation; (3) that the Torah contains secrets, and that one must beseech God for inspiration to understand them; and (4) that "the traditional understanding of Scripture that is in our hands" was also spoken by God, such as the form of the shofar, sukka, tefillin, lulav, and tzitzit. In *Yigdal*, this is all abbreviated to a single line: *torat emet natan le'amo El al yad nevi'o ne'eman beito*, "A true Torah was given by the Lord to His people, by the agency of His prophet, the most faithful of His house." To be sure, the line is accurate, insofar as the idea it expresses is indeed found in the Rambam's eighth principle. Crucially, however, it omits any explicit reference to the Oral Law and its divine origin. Perhaps with the words "a true Torah" the *paytan* meant the entirety of Torah, its written and oral components. But the concise formulation may also be understood as a reference to the text of the Written Torah. Brevity is given pride of place in the *paytan*'s set of priorities, and he chooses to highlight what he considers the most salient aspect of the principle. A second example: the Rambam's eleventh principle is the belief in reward and punishment, specifically the belief that these are meted out not in this world but in the World to Come. The eleventh line of *Yigdal* omits the other-worldly nature of this recompense: *gomel le'ish ḥesed kemifalo, noten lerasha ra kerishato*, "He rewards a man according to his merits, and issues punishment to the wicked according to his wickedness." The abbreviated version in *Yigdal* fundamentally alters the Rambam's principle. At the same time, the line in *Yigdal* allows the simple of faith to believe that they will be able to see divine justice with their own two eyes here in this world – a more palatable proposition, even if it deviates from the Rambam's view.[4]

However, we also see in *Yigdal* a propensity to not only condense what the Rambam had formulated, but to deviate from it as well. In his fifth principle the Rambam posits that one cannot turn to angels or heavenly bodies as intermediaries to the Almighty; He alone is worthy of our appeal. The corresponding line in *Yigdal*, however, reads, *hino adon olam lekhol notzar, yoreh gedulato umalkhuto*, "for He is the Master of the Universe; and every creature shows His greatness and majesty." This may be a true sentiment, and one with which the Rambam would agree – but it hardly conveys the intent of the fifth principle.[5] It is likely that the author of *Yigdal* felt his audience would find the Rambam's fifth principle objectionable, as the appeal to angels as intermediaries of entreaty to the Almighty was widespread. To successfully disseminate his version of the Rambam's Thirteen Principles, the *paytan* needed to adapt his *piyut* to accommodate widely accepted practices – even when they directly contravened what the Rambam had written.

These dynamics of adaptation are also evident in the other *piyut* which has become a staple of our liturgy – the *Ani Maamin*. Here we can see a number of ways in which the author – whose identity is unknown to this day – reconfigures the original ideas of the Rambam to make them more palatable to his audience. At several junctures, the Rambam's principles call upon us to affirm that certain entities exist: God "exists" (first principle); prophecy "exists" (sixth principle). But the "existence" of something is somewhat of an abstract concept, and so the author of *Ani Maamin* reformulates these principles using terms that a popular audience can more readily grasp. In *Ani Maamin* the first principle is no longer that God exists, but that God is the Creator of the world that He guides.[6] The Rambam's sixth principle is reformulated

---

4. See Admiel Kosman, "Yud-Gimmel Ikkarim LaRambam BePerush HaMishna, BeYigdal UVeAni Maamin," in *Sefer HaYovel Minha LeI"sh*, ed. Itamar Warhaftig (Jerusalem: Beit Knesset Beit Yaakov, 1990), 346.

5. Ibid., 341.

6. Abraham Melamed, "Maimonides' Thirteen Principles: From Elite to Popular Culture," in *The Cultures of Maimonideanism: New Approaches to the History of Jewish Thought*, ed. James T. Robinson (Leiden, Netherlands: Brill, 2009), 186.

as an affirmation that the words of the prophets are *true* – a comforting notion for a despised nation in exile.[7] Perhaps to our minds these propositions are relatively interchangeable, but the Rambam clearly formulated the wording of each of his principles and the adjustment points to the license the author of *Ani Maamin* felt he could take. In his thirteenth principle – belief in resurrection – the Rambam writes that this is available for the righteous alone. *Ani Maamin* makes no mention of the righteous in this principle, and the oblique implication is that all of the dead shall one day rise.[8] Had the author of *Ani Maamin* remained vigilantly faithful to the Rambam's formulation, he would have needed to introduce a disturbing notion for some of those reciting his composition – that they themselves might not qualify as righteous, and might never rise from the dead.

Rambam's Eighth Principle in the *Piyutim*: A History

For our purposes we are concerned most specifically with the Rambam's eighth principle, and I trace now the dynamic of reconfiguration that takes place concerning this principle between the Rambam's original formulation in the Introduction to *Perek Ḥelek* and the *piyut* of *Ani Maamin*, or, more precisely, the *different versions* of *Ani Maamin* known to us today. We assume that the author of *Ani Maamin* wrote his work inspired by the original formulations of the Rambam in his Introduction to *Perek Ḥelek*. And while this might be true, we also know today something quite surprising about the *Ani Maamin* printed in our siddurim – that its author composed this as a condensed version of an earlier, longer composition, discovered only in recent decades in an archive in Parma, Italy. I shall refer to this earlier composition as Proto-Ani-Maamin, or simply, Proto-AM.[9] It is remarkable to see how the anonymous author of this manuscript reconfigured the eighth principle as presented in the Introduction to *Perek Ḥelek*, and then how the author of our *Ani Maamin* refashioned it further. Later still, this version of *Ani Maamin*,

7. Kosman, "Yud-Gimmel Ikkarim LaRambam," 343.

8. Melamed, "Maimonides' Thirteen Principles," 187.

9. For the text of ms Parma 1573, see Eli Gurfinkel, "Hashpaat Temurot Maḥshavtiot al Nusaḥei 'Ani Maamin,'" *Kenishta* 4 (2010): 51–112.

which has appeared in Ashkenazic siddurim for four hundred years, was condensed further in the version of the *piyut* appearing in Sephardic siddurim since the early nineteenth century. What is remarkable is that none of these three versions represents the Rambam's eighth principle fully or accurately.

Let us trace the progression between these versions of the *piyut* and identify the prerogatives that motivate each author. Recall that the Rambam stipulated four tenets in the eighth principle: (1) that every word of the Torah was given to Moses by God; (2) that this was transmitted by something akin to dictation; (3) that the Torah contains secrets, and that one must beseech God for inspiration to understand them; and (4) that "the traditional understanding of Scripture that is in our hands" was also spoken by God, such as the form of the shofar, sukka, tefillin, lulav, and tzitzit. The problem for any *paytan* wishing to rework this is especially challenging with regard to the fourth clause here. Just what did the Rambam mean by the enigmatic phrase, "the traditional understanding of Scripture that is in our hands"? Which aspects of the Oral Law are included in that definition and what is delimited here by referring to the sacral items he lists? The author of Proto-AM reformulates the eighth principle as follows:

> I believe with perfect faith that the entirety of the Torah, the Written Law and the Oral Law, now in our possession that we study, is the very Torah given to Moses our teacher, peace be to him, at Mount Sinai amid blasts, flames, and shofarot; that this Torah in its interpretation of the commandments was in its entirety given, as it states, "The Torah and the commandments, which I have written to instruct them" (Ex. 24:12). *Torah* – this is the Written Law; *the commandments* – this is the Oral Law (Berakhot 5a); all of it originates at Sinai, through the transmission of dictation.

His agenda is clear. He wishes to make the concepts simple: the entirety of the Written Torah and the Oral Torah were given to Moses at Sinai. By reworking the Rambam's formulation of the eighth principle in this way, he brings the Rambam in line with the *baraita* in Peah 1:1 (cited in Berakhot 5a) and the second *baraita* in Sanhedrin 99a that we referred to earlier, to wit, that the entirety of the Oral Law, no less than the Written Law, was given at Sinai.

However, there are two shortcomings in this strategy of adaptation. The first is that it misrepresents the Rambam. The Rambam was surely familiar with Mishna Peah 1:1, and had he wished to assert that the entirety of the Oral Law was also given to Moses at Sinai (and through dictation, no less), he could have said so. As we saw in the previous chapter, the Rambam deliberately rejected the notion that the entirety of the Oral Law was given at Sinai. For the Rambam, the Oral Tradition from Sinai can include only issues upon which there is unanimity in the Talmud. Dispute between Sages is a sign of a breakdown in the line of transmission, and for the Rambam, the line of transmission must be pristine. Thus only a part of what we term the Oral Law, for the Rambam, was given to Moses. The second shortcoming inherent in the work of Proto-AM is that the *paytan* opted for greater comprehensiveness over ease of recitation and memorization. The formulation here, like all the other principles in this work, is too lengthy to commit easily to memory.

We can easily see the prerogatives at work in the composition of what in time would be adopted as the Ashkenazic version of *Ani Maamin*. Its anonymous *paytan* worked from the copy of Proto-AM in front of him:

Ani Maamin	Proto-AM
אני מאמין באמונה שלמה שכל התורה המצויה עתה בידינו היא הנתונה למשה רבינו עליו השלום.	אני מאמין באמונה שלמה שכל התורה כלה שבכתב ושבעל פה המצויה עתה בידינו שאנו הוגים בה היא היא אשר ניתנה למשה רבינו עליו השלום בהר סיני בקולות ולפידים ובשופרות שהתורה הזאת בפירוש המצות כלה ניתנה דכתיב "התורה והמצוה אשר כתבתי להורותם" (שמ' כד:יב) תורה - זו תורה שבכתב, והמצוה זו תורה שבעל פה (בבלי ברכות ה'.); והיא כלה מסיני בהגעה הנקרא "דבור".

Ani Maamin	Proto-AM
I believe with perfect faith that the entirety of the Torah now in our possession is the very Torah given to Moses our teacher, peace be to him.	I believe with perfect faith that the **entirety of the Torah**, the Written Law and the Oral Law, **now in our possession** that we study, **is the very Torah given to Moses our teacher, peace be to him**, at Mount Sinai amid blasts, flames, and shofarot; that this Torah in its interpretation of the commandments was in its entirety given, as it states, "The Torah and the commandments, which I have written to instruct them" (Ex. 24:12). Torah – this is the Written Law; the commandments – this is the Oral Law (Berakhot 5a); all of it originates at Sinai, through the transmission of dictation.

The reformulation of the eighth principle in *Ani Maamin* reads: "I believe with perfect faith that the entirety of the Torah now in our possession is the Torah given to Moses our teacher, peace be to him." But what corpus is implied by the phrase "the entirety of the Torah"? It may be that the author intended the phrase to cover the entirety of the Written and Oral Law, the terms explicitly found in the version of Proto-AM. What clouds the issue is that in the Rambam's original formulations in the Introduction to *Perek Ḥelek*, the phrase "entirety of the Torah" refers solely to the text of the Written Torah. The Rambam does not employ the phrase "Oral Law" to refer to the *mesora*. Rather he uses the phrase "the received interpretation" (*peirushah hamekubal*). Therefore, when the author of *Ani Maamin* writes, "I believe with perfect faith that the entirety of the Torah that we possess today is the Torah given to Moses our teacher, peace be to him," wittingly or unwittingly, he is borrowing a phrase that the Rambam himself used only with regard to the text of the Written Law.

It is difficult to know which of these readings was intended by the author of *Ani Maamin*. What is clear is that over time – certainly in our own time – this formulation of the eighth principle has been taken as a principle about the text of the Torah, rather than about the *mesora* – the written text and its accepted interpretations. Consider the move here in historical terms. As we saw in a previous chapter, the Mishna, the Gemara, and a consensus of early *Rishonim*, including the Rambam himself, had all posited that the principle of *torah* from heaven referred to the divinity of the *mesora* as a whole. No voice in the tradition had ever decoupled the text of the Torah from the interpretive lens of the *mesora*.[10] No voice had ever given a greater place of pride to the Written Law over the Oral Law. Thus, the author of *Ani Maamin* sets the stage for a new path – again, wittingly or unwittingly – in the theology of how Israel would view the Torah.

Centuries later, another anonymous *paytan* would reduce the *Ani Maamin* further and create what has become the accepted version of the principles in Sephardic siddurim. His composition opens with a declarative statement that introduces all of the Thirteen Principles: *Harei ani maamin be'emuna sheleima bishlosha asar ikkarim shel haTorah hakedosha,* "I declare that I believe with perfect faith in the Thirteen Principles of the holy Torah." He then lists each of the principles, in bullet form, putting a premium on brevity and ease of memorization; each of the thirteen clauses averages just six words in length.

The eighth principle reads: *veshehaTorah netuna min haShamayim,* "and that the Torah was given from heaven." The formulation here represents a further process of truncating. It draws word for word from the opening sentence of the Rambam's eighth principle in his Introduction to *Perek Ḥelek*. It departs from the Ashkenazic *Ani Maamin* in that it highlights the Written Law's divine origin, but with no mention of the role of Moses in its transmission.[11]

---

10. It would appear that within commentators to the Talmud, the notion that the term "*torah* from heaven" in Mishna Sanhedrin 10:1 refers to the Written Law alone first appears in the commentary of the Meiri (late thirteenth century). This interpretation is picked up by later commentators on the Mishna, such as the nineteenth-century *Tiferet Yisrael*.

11. Note that the language here includes the definite article *haTorah*, unlike Mishna Sanhedrin 10:1. In the Rambam's eighth principle in the Introduction to *Perek Ḥelek*, the term *Torah* refers exclusively to the text of the *Ḥumash*; the Oral Law is referred to as its "accepted interpretation."

The fact that these *piyutim* depart in significant ways from the Rambam's original formulations of the principles does not suggest that they are defective or, worse, fraudulent. Indeed, no one has ever leveled such claims against these *piyutim* or their authors. These *paytanim* neither ascribed their works to the Rambam nor claimed that their poetic compositions were somehow perfect representations of what the Rambam had intended in his formulation of the principles in the Introduction to *Perek Ḥelek*. Indeed, it is folly to think that the Rambam's theology in his Introduction to *Perek Ḥelek* could be faithfully rendered in condensed lyric form, any more that it would be possible with the Rambam's halakhic writings. These *paytanim* sought to create compositions that were consciously and openly *adaptations* of the Thirteen Principles, with the hope of creating works that would be broadly accepted and lead the faithful to greater piety. As we shall see later, few figures ever insisted on understanding the Thirteen Principles exactly as expressed in the Introduction to *Perek Ḥelek*. In fact, as we will see, most authorities since the seventeenth century who embraced the Thirteen Principles as *the* principles of the faith have taken liberties with its tenets, sometimes at a great remove from the intentions of the Rambam in the Introduction to *Perek Ḥelek*.

We can learn much about the importance of these *piyutim* and how they shaped views of the Rambam's principles from a comment about them by the Maharil, Rabbi Yaakov Moelin (Mainz, 1360–1427):

> The rhymes and poems that people write in Yiddish on the unity of God and the Thirteen Principles – would that they were not written! For most of the ignorant believe that all of the commandments depend on this, and they despair of various positive and negative commandments, such as tzitzit and tefillin and the study of Torah, and the like. And they believe that they fulfill their obligation by saying those rhymes with pious intent. And yet those rhymes bear but a hint to what is fundamental in the faith of Israel, while mentioning not one of the 613 commandments that Jews are commanded.[12]

---

12. *Sefer Maharil*, Spitzer ed. (Jerusalem: Mekhon Yerushalayim, 1989), 626. See discussion in Marc Shapiro, *Limits of Orthodox Theology* (Oxford: Littman Library of Jewish Civilization, 2011), 19.

The comments of the Maharil attest to the immense sway that the Rambam's catechism had on the popular imagination. Common people were so taken by the notion of the fundamental principles of the faith that they mistakenly saw them as the key to proper service of the Almighty, perhaps reflecting the penetration of Christian ideas of salvation by correct faith. The Maharil's comment also attests to an important and ironic trend that would snowball with the passage of history: The celebrated stature of the Rambam's principles would stem not from a direct engagement with the Rambam's own writing in his Introduction to *Perek Ḥelek*. Rather, the masses adopted the "Rambam's" principles as they knew and understood them from the popular *piyutim* they recited. And in his time, it would seem, the masses to which the Maharil refers might not even have had the Hebrew literary skills to engage the Introduction to *Perek Ḥelek* in translation; the *piyutim* that achieved popularity were those composed in Yiddish. It is easy to understand why the principles became popularized through *piyut* and not through study of the text of the Introduction to *Perek Ḥelek* itself. Even for the more educated, it often would have been difficult to obtain a copy of the Introduction to *Perek Ḥelek* and actually read what the Rambam had written. In the textual culture of the Middle Ages, that meant that very few would ever actually even see a copy of the Introduction to *Perek Ḥelek* in their lifetime. By contrast, the dissemination of a *piyut* like *Yigdal* required no text at all. Recited aloud during collective prayer, it could spread easily, even among those who had no knowledge of reading or writing, let alone the means to procure hand-copied texts of lengthy works.

The Origins of the Torah According to Rabbinic Thought in the Later Middle Ages

Although there is no explicit discussion of the Rambam's principles among major rabbinical figures for the better part of the thirteenth and fourteenth centuries, we do see a shift in rabbinic attitudes toward the composition of the Torah. No longer can we find voices that maintain that various passages of the Torah postdate the time of Moses. Major biblical exegetes such as Radak, the Ramban, and Ralbag all adopt the position that the entire text of the Torah was given to Moses by dictation from God.[13] Does this attest to the great sway of the Rambam and his eighth principle? Perhaps, paradoxically, it attests to the great sway of Ibn Hazm and his libel. Perhaps exegetes – even those in Christian lands – became aware of the Muslim claim about the falsification of the Tanakh and refrained from any comment that could lend theological ammunition to the enemies of Israel, as we saw stated in explicit terms in the writings of the *Tzafnat Paane'ah*.[14] What is certain is that none of these exegetes mentions the Rambam's eighth principle as a source of inspiration for his position. Moreover, none of these exegetes takes to task any of their predecessors who suggested that certain passages were post-Mosaic. As an illustration of what I mean here, consider the Ramban. The Ramban tells us that he believes that the entire Torah was given to Moses. As we saw earlier, Ibn Ezra did not believe that the prophecy through which God communicated the Torah to Moses was verbal. Nor did he believe that Moses authored every word in the Torah. It is well known that the Ramban was highly critical of Ibn Ezra at many junctures across his commentary on the Torah. Yet he never critiques Ibn Ezra for his positions regarding the composition of the text of the Torah.[15] He surely disagreed with Ibn Ezra on these accounts. But his silence on these positions speaks volumes: there is no polemic surrounding Ibn Ezra or his works. Thus, we see that to the extent that the Rambam's eighth principle is accepted at this time, it is not in the fashion that the Rambam himself had laid out at the conclusion of the Introduction to *Perek Helek*. For the Rambam, one who denied even one of the principles was deemed a heretic and lost his standing within the people of Israel. For the Rambam, affirmation of the catechism of the Thirteen Principles delimited who was a Jew and who was not. There

---

13. See Radak, introduction to his commentary on Genesis (and commentary on Gen. 2:14, 5:29, 7:24); Ramban, introduction to his commentary on the Torah; Ralbag on Leviticus 25:1; Numbers 18:8, 25:9; Deuteronomy 1:1.

14. See above, p. 200.

15. It may be that the Ramban was not critical of Ibn Ezra because the latter was not explicit about the authorship question. However, in his commentary on Deuteronomy 34:31, Ibn Ezra writes explicitly that Joshua composed the final twelve verses of the Torah via prophecy. The Ramban on this chapter makes no reference to this opinion.

is no indication that within the world of the Middle Ages any rabbinic voice of stature shared that opinion.

THE HEYDAY OF CATECHISM IN
THE FIFTEENTH CENTURY

Until the late fourteenth century, the sages of Israel focused their intellectual energies on the Talmud and the halakha. There was no pressing need to clarify issues of Jewish philosophy and theology. Exegetes to the Tanakh, obviously, wove insights on these issues into their commentaries, but the explorations of these issues following the Rambam and prior to the fifteenth century was never systematic.[16] However, in the late fourteenth century and throughout the fifteenth century, the Iberian Jewish community faced an unprecedented assault, not only on Jews, but on Judaism itself, at the hands of the Christian authorities. This took the form of disputations, forced sermons, and incentives for Jews to convert. Christianity is a religion centered around creed and the crisis mandated that Jews and Judaism confront these challenges on the adversary's playing field by clarifying central concepts of Jewish theology.[17] Leading figures would need to delve into theological definitions and categories, even though these had never been the hallmark of rabbinic learning.[18] Among the notable figures that contributed to this debate were Rabbi Shimon ben Tzemah Duran (1361–1444, in his work *Magen Avot*), Rabbi Hasdai Crescas (1340–1411, in his work *Or Adonai*), Rabbi Joseph Albo (1380–1444, author of the *Sefer HaIkkarim*), Rabbi Isaac Arama (1420–1494, in his work *Ḥazut Kasha*), and Don Isaac Abarbanel (in his work *Rosh Amana*).

Of particular importance here is the position staked out by Abarbanel. Abarbanel believed that the very enterprise of articulating fundamental principles of the Torah is fundamentally foreign to Judaism. Commenting on the motivation of the Rambam and his followers to create a catechism of principles, Abarbanel writes:

---

16. Kellner, *Dogma in Medieval Jewish Thought*, 217.

17. Ibid., 81.

18. Ibid., 80.

[He] was brought to postulate principles in the divine Torah only because they were drawn after the custom of gentile scholars as described in their books. For they saw in every science, whether natural or mathematical, roots and principles which ought not to be denied or argued against…. Our scholars, having been dispersed among the nations and having studied their books and sciences, learned from their deeds and copied their ways with respect to the divine Torah. They said, *How do these gentiles pursue their sciences?*[19] By positing first principles and roots upon which a science is based. I will do so also and postulate principles and foundations for the divine Torah.[20]

What is most striking about this comment from Abarbanel is his willingness to critique the Rambam by placing his efforts within a certain historical and cultural context, thereby undercutting the validity of his enterprise. This is often viewed by many within the Orthodox world as itself a "foreign" or "academic" approach, and yet it appears here in full view – and not for the final time, as we shall see in the next chapter; Abarbanel was not the last major figure to critique the Rambam's enterprise of principles in this fashion.

Abarbanel goes on to stake out his own position on the issue:

Therefore, I said, "This I recall to my mind" (Lam. 3:21) that the divine Torah, with all its beliefs, is completely true. All of its commandments were divinely revealed. The validation and substantiation of all the beliefs and commandments, minor as well as major, is the same. The validation of one is like the validation of another. I, therefore, believe that it is not proper to postulate principles for the divine Torah, nor foundations in a matter of beliefs, for we are obliged to believe everything that is written in the Torah. We are not permitted to doubt even the smallest

---

19. The Hebrew here is a pejorative reference to seduction in Deuteronomy 12:30, "How do the gentiles serve their gods? Perhaps I shall do the same myself."
20. Abarbanel, *Rosh Amanah*, ed. Menachem Kellner (Ramat Gan: Bar-Ilan University Press, 1993), 194–95.

thing in it that it should be necessary to establish its truth with those principles and roots. For he who denies or doubts a belief or narrative of the Torah, be it small or great, is a sectarian and *epikoros*. For, since the Torah is true, no beliefs or narrative in it has any advantage over any other.[21]

The comments are important, because here Abarbanel essentially gives voice to the unstated position adopted by the great majority of sages who preceded him, in the Talmud and thereafter, who felt no need to engage in the formulation of the fundamental principles of Judaism.

Duran, Crescas, Albo, and Abarbanel represent the end of an era – the era of interest in Jewish dogmatics, the articulation of creed. All of these figures lived and responded to the events of fifteenth-century Spain. Their compositions were born out of the polemic with Christianity and the need to formulate just what Judaism took as its foundational principles.[22] The aim of these works was to sharpen what distinguished Judaism from Christianity, rather than what divided believing Jews from heretics.[23] At no point during this time do we see any of these writings used in order to determine the question of who is or is not considered a member of the Jewish faith. With the passing of the polemical challenge from Christianity, the interest in catechism would entirely fade into the background, and, indeed, no subsequent rabbinic thinker has taken to composing a catechism of his own. In fact, one is hard pressed to identify a major commentary on any of the medieval catechisms, even the Rambam's Thirteen Principles. Thoroughgoing, systematic explorations of principles of faith quite literally disappeared from the Jewish intellectual agenda.[24]

PRINCIPLES OF FAITH FROM THE SIXTEENTH CENTURY UNTIL THE DAWN OF THE EMANCIPATION

The fifteenth century, then, concluded with the question of principles of the faith very much an open issue. Does Judaism even possess such

---

21. Abarbanel, *Rosh Amanah*, 196–97.
22. Kellner, *Dogma in Medieval Jewish Thought*, 215.
23. Ibid., 69.
24. Ibid., 208.

a concept? Many sided with Abarbanel and concluded that the concept itself was foreign to the *mesora*. Others, like Albo, Crescas, and Duran, believed that Judaism did possess fundamental principles, but differed as to what they were or how to classify them. The notion that the Rambam's Thirteen Principles were *the* defining principles of the Jewish faith was far from an accepted conclusion. How have we come to the situation today where there is universal agreement among Orthodox authorities that the Thirteen Principles are indeed Judaism's fundamental principles of faith?

In this next section, I trace this development from the sixteenth century – the age that immediately followed the golden age of catechisms in Spain – until the dawn of the Emancipation in the late eighteenth and early nineteenth centuries. Our sources paint an uneven picture of how this process of acceptance unfolded. It is not that different *sources* say different things about the Rambam's Thirteen Principles; it is that different *genres* of rabbinic literature say different things about these principles. To get clarity about how the principles were accepted, and indeed what it meant to say that they were "accepted," I examine references to the principles in three different genres of rabbinic literature: (1) the responsa and halakhic literature; (2) homiletic literature (*derashot*); and (3) the literature of liturgical contexts – siddurim and *sifrei minhagim*. These references taken together will paint a fuller picture of what acceptance of the principles meant at this time.

The Standing of the Thirteen Principles in the Responsa and Halakhic Literature

Sages throughout this period do indeed address the various halakhic categories of heretic and apostate (*epikoros, min, kofer*). But the texts they cite in definition of these deviants are always halakhic texts – particularly the definitions established by the Rambam in the *Mishneh Torah*, in the third chapter of *Hilkhot Teshuva*.[25] This, in turn, refers largely to *Hilkhot Yesodei HaTorah*, where the Thirteen Principles are reconfigured, as we saw earlier. I have been unable to find any evidence that either

---

25. See *Baḥ, Yoreh De'ah* 158; *Knesset HaGedola* to *Yoreh De'ah* 2; *Levush, Yoreh De'ah* 158:2; *Ḥoshen Mishpat* 425:5; Sma, *Ḥoshen Mishpat* 425.

the text of the Introduction to *Perek Ḥelek* or even the very concept of "principles of faith" (*ikkarei emuna*) is ever invoked in halakhic writing through the end of the eighteenth century.

Elsewhere in the responsa literature we find *posekim* addressing the standing of the very concept of the principles of the Jewish faith. It would appear that no *posek* in a halakhic work at this time champions the Rambam's Thirteen Principles as the undisputed principles of the Jewish faith. In some of these sources, especially in the earlier centuries, the notion of principles of faith is rejected altogether, as we find in the responsa of Rabbi David ben Solomon ibn Abi Zimra, or Radbaz (Safed, 1479–1573). In one of his more than three thousand responsa, Radbaz is asked if he agrees with the position of the Rambam or of Rabbi Hasdai Crescas or of Rabbi Joseph Albo concerning the fundamental principles of the Torah.[26] The very question suggests that all three have some currency, and that at this time there is no clear consensus on the issue. Radbaz replies that he rejects all three, because he rejects the notion of fundamental principles in the Torah, and sides with Abarbanel that each and every facet and detail of Torah constitutes a fundamental aspect of Torah. A contemporary of the Radbaz, Rabbi Shlomo Luria (the Maharshal), was also quite pointed in his rejection of the Rambam's project of principles of the Torah:

> My teacher, our teacher Rabbi Shalom [Shahna] said that there is a trace of heresy in the fixed recital of the Thirteen Principles of Faith in the *Ani Maamin* which contains thirteen principles, for there are some who claim and who think in their heart that when they affirm the thirteen principles, even though they have perpetrated every abomination imaginable, they wish to believe that they can achieve salvation, but this is not so.... Indeed, the very composition of these thirteen principles was done only because this had been the practice of ancient philosophers to establish general principles, and this sort of enumeration had not been previously done; our rabbis came and likewise established general principles. And so it is in *Yidgal Elokim Ḥai*, where

---

26. *Shut Radbaz* 1:346.

the thirteen principles are likewise enumerated, and my teacher would recite neither *Yigdal* nor *Ani Maamin*.[27]

Like Abarbanel before him, the Maharshal does not merely disagree with the Rambam's program of establishing principles of faith. He sideswipes and undermines the effort by historicizing it and attributing it to outside influence. This he is prepared to do because of the deleterious effects he sees that the principles have in his day: the uneducated de-emphasize the proper performance of the mitzvot in the improper understanding that belief is the key to their salvation. Put differently, we see here a view of the principles that will become more prominent in later centuries: the validity and high standing of the principles is a direct function of their *utility*. What validates the principles is not their deep roots in talmudic sources, nor is it the consensus of rabbinic opinion that has surrounded them. The validation of the principles hinges on whether they achieve the one goal that is always paramount in the minds of great Torah authorities: bringing Israel to the pious observance of Torah and mitzvot. In his time and place, the Maharshal deemed that the principles were having quite the opposite effect.

Later figures during this period felt no compunction in rejecting individual tenets that the Rambam had included in his Thirteen Principles. In his ninth principle, the Rambam states that the Torah and its laws will never change. In that light, consider the following comment by Rabbi Jacob Emden (Altona, Hamburg, 1697–1776):

> We absolutely do not admit that which Maimonides laid down, that the entire Torah will not change, for there is no decisive proof for this – neither from reason and logic nor from the Bible. Verily, the Sages tell us that the Holy One will give a new Torah in the future. If our King should wish to change the Torah, or exchange it for another, whatever the King wishes, whether it be to descend on Mount Sinai or another of the mighty mountains,

27. *Hanhagat Maharshal*, ed. Yitzhak Rafael, in Y. L. Maimon, ed., *Sefer Yovel Mugash Likhvod HaRav Dr. Shimon Federbush* (Jerusalem, 1961), 326 (paragraph #42).

or even a valley, there to appear a second time before the eyes of all the living, we would be the first to do His will, whatever be His bidding.[28]

Even where *posekim* were prepared to acknowledge the category of principles of faith, we find that they were ready to offer at least as much credence to the principles enumerated by Rabbi Joseph Albo as they do to those enumerated by the Rambam. In a singular and remarkable passage, we find the Thirteen Principles of the Introduction to *Perek Ḥelek* accessed in a halakhic context, only to be subordinated to the primacy of the principles laid down by Rabbi Albo. This is found in a responsum of the *Yeshuot Yaakov* of Rabbi Meshulam Yaakov Oren-stein (Poland, 1775–1839). The *Shulḥan Arukh* (*Oraḥ Ḥayim* 126) rules that certain heresies listed in the Gemara render a person unfit to lead services. Later *posekim* had to determine what contemporary heresies would likewise render a person unfit to lead services in their own time. The *Yeshuot Yaakov* rules as follows:

> It seems to me that in truth a *min* is one who either does not believe in the existence of God, or does not believe in Torah from heaven, or does not believe in divine reward and punishment, the three primary principles of the religion. Concerning the other principles enumerated in the words of the Rambam, one who denies them is indeed evil, but nonetheless does not forfeit his standing as member of the religion, as written in [Rabbi Joseph Albo's] *Sefer HaIkkarim*, in the first treatise.[29]

At the very end of the period under question, we see again that Rambam's Thirteen Principles have yet to establish themselves as the unchallenged principles of the Jewish faith. Rabbi Moshe Sofer (Schreiber), the Ḥatam Sofer (1762–1839), was asked whether he believed that there are Thirteen

---

28. Rabbi Jacob Emden, *Migdal Oz* 26b, translated in Bezalel Naor, *Post-Sabbatian Sabbatianism* (Spring Valley, NY: Orot, 1999), 8–9. See discussion in Shapiro, *Limits of Orthodox Theology*, 125.

29. *Yeshuot Yaakov* on *Oraḥ Ḥayim* 126:1.

Principles of Faith, as posited by the Rambam, or whether there are only three principles, as articulated by Rabbi Joseph Albo. The very question is unimaginable today, and itself reflects the fact that the issue was far from clear in the early nineteenth century. The *Ḥatam Sofer* responded that he could discern no difference between them, except in name alone. He further noted that the sages of the Kabbala rejected the very project of identifying principles of faith, as they believed that all facets of Torah are an indivisible whole, and thus are all principles of the faith.[30]

However, to identify the place of the Thirteen Principles in the halakhic literature of this time, it is insufficient to attend to the overt references to them. We must attend to where the sources are silent as well, to the places where we would expect *posekim* to invoke them and yet they do not. These silences are no less a comment on the standing of the Thirteen Principles at this time. Recall that in the eighth principle as presented in the Introduction to *Perek Ḥelek*, the Rambam maintained that not only was the Written Torah given to Moses at Sinai, but that with it, Moses also received "the traditional understanding of Scripture that is in our hands." In his introduction to the Commentary on the Mishna, the Rambam writes that these are laws that have never been subject to argument or difference of opinion. Concerning these laws there has always been one and only one understanding of the issue. To illustrate what he has in mind, the Rambam in the eighth principle points to the shofar, sukka, tefillin, lulav, and tzitzit as articles whose form was divinely revealed to Moses and therefore must be accepted. Thus, when the Rambam rules (*Hilkhot Tzitzit* 1:2–3) that tzitzit with *tekhelet* should have one string of *tekhelet* and three strings that are white, this for the Rambam is something that was divinely revealed to Moses at Sinai. The number of strings and their color are basic to the form of the mitzva of tzitzit, and thus constitute an element of the eighth principle of the faith.[31]

---

30. *Shut Ḥatam Sofer, Yoreh De'ah* 356.
31. In more than a dozen places in his Commentary on the Mishna, the Rambam gives a verbal description of a physical entity and then writes, "and this is its form," where it is clear that the Rambam had originally included a line drawing. The "form" of an entity for the Rambam in the Commentary on the Mishna, therefore, is a rather detailed rendering that clarifies and adds resolution unavailable in verbal description alone. For the Rambam, then, to reveal the "form" of tzitzit to Moses was to give him

Nonetheless, we find that the Taz and the *Mishna Berura*, for example, rule like Rashi and *Tosafot*, that tzitzit with *tekhelet* should have two strings of *tekhelet* and two white strings.[32] Put differently, these *posekim* not only rule counter to the Rambam's ruling in the *Mishneh Torah*, but counter to his stated position that these halakhic issues are principles of faith, and adherence to them is mandated by our belief in *torah* from heaven. It is worth noting that no major halakhic work has ever challenged this ruling of the Taz, or the *posekim* who rule like him, under the contention that the ruling contravenes the Thirteen Principles of Faith.

Similarly, we may point to the way in which many *posekim* have disregarded the Rambam's ruling concerning the form of the shofar. The Rambam rules that the shofar must be curved and that it must be fashioned from the horn of a ram (*Hilkhot Shofar* 1:1). If the shofar is straight, or if it is made from the horn of any other animal, the shofar is not kosher for the performance of the mitzva, even ex post facto (*bedi'eved*). Nonetheless, here too, we find that the *Shulḥan Arukh* (*Oraḥ Ḥayim* 586:1) and many *posekim* in his wake – including the *Mishna Berura* (586:2–5) – rule that if one used a shofar that was straight or from another animal, ex post facto, the individual has fulfilled the mitzva. Here, too, we find that the *Shulḥan Arukh* felt no compunction ruling against the opinion of the Rambam even when the latter claimed that the issue was one of the Principles of Faith. And here, too, we find that no major halakhic work ever challenged this ruling of the *Shulḥan Arukh* on the basis of the fact that the ruling contravenes one of the Rambam's Principles of Faith.

The Thirteen Principles in the Homiletic Literature

In the homiletic literature of the period in question, we see that both the principles of Rabbi Joseph Albo and the principles of the Rambam share status as the principles of the Jewish faith. In fact, in this literature, the principles of Rabbi Albo are cited more frequently. Sometimes these are mentioned alone, but more often they are cast as the three

---

a more detailed understanding of the mitzva than one could derive from the verbal description found in the Torah. The same may be said about the mitzva of shofar, as per the discussion that follows immediately thereafter.

32. Taz, *Oraḥ Ḥayim* 9:3. See, likewise, *Mishna Berura* 9:7.

primary principles that encompass the others that the Rambam lists. Rabbi Moshe ben Yosef Mitrani – the Mabit (Safed, 1500–1580) – opens a homily with reference to Judaism's three fundamental principles, and lists those enumerated by Rabbi Joseph Albo, namely, the existence of God who created the world, Torah from heaven, and reward and punishment.[33] The Maharsha, Rabbi Shmuel HaLevi Eidels (Poland/ Ukraine, 1555–1631), writes that the three paragraphs of the recitation of the *Shema* correspond to the three fundamental principles laid out by Rabbi Joseph Albo – the existence of God, belief in Torah from heaven, and belief in heavenly reward and punishment.[34] He identifies these as "the three principles concerning which there is consensus among most commentators." A respected disciple of the Maharshal, Rabbi Moshe ben Avraham Matt of Przemyśl (Poland, 1551–1606), cites the *Sefer HaIkkarim* in his work *Mateh Moshe*, stating that the three sections of *Musaf* on Rosh Hashana – *Malkhuyot, Zikhronot,* and *Shofarot* – correspond to these three principles. He also includes an interesting note at the outset of his homily: "Although there are thirteen fundamental principles according to the Rambam, these are subordinate to three of them, the existence of God, reward and punishment, and Torah from heaven. These three are the chief fundamental principles; all the other are subordinate."[35] In like fashion, the Shela, Rabbi Yeshaya HaLevi Horowitz (Ashkenaz/Israel, 1558–1630), writes that the three tefillot of Shabbat correspond to these three fundamental principles, "which are the three principles that encompass all of the principles."[36] Moving to the eighteenth century, Rabbi David Hirschel Fränkel (Berlin, 1704–1762), the author of the commentary *Korban HaEda* on the Jerusalem Talmud, writes that Korah's three challenges to the authority of Moses revolved around these three fundamental principles.[37] Rabbi Tzvi Elimelekh Shapira (Poland, 1783–1841), the author of the *Benei Yissaskhar*, found

---

33. Mabit, *Beit Elokim, She'ar Yesodot,* ch. 1.
34. Maharsha, *Ḥidushei Aggadot,* Berakhot 13a.
35. *Mateh Moshe, Amud HaAvoda, Dinei Shofar,* sec. 807.
36. Shela, Tractate Shabbat, *Torah Or,* sec. 74. Likewise the Shela writes that the Exodus from Egypt demonstrated the three cardinal principles. See Tractate Pesaḥim, *Matza Ashira,* homily 3, sec. 385.
37. *Shayarei Korban,* Sanhedrin, ch. 10.

significance in the first word of the Torah relating to these three cardinal principles. The letters of בראשית, though not in order, could spell ראשית אמונת ישראל בורא, תורה, שכר ("the fundamentals of the faith of Israel: Creator, Torah, reward").[38]

Of note here is the single homily that we find during this period that uses as a referent the Rambam's longer list of principles. This is found in the work *Givat Shaul*, a collection of fifty sermons on the Torah by Rabbi Shaul Levi Morteira (Amsterdam, 1596–1660), one of the members of the community board of Amsterdam that excommunicated Benedict Spinoza. For this author, the breastplate of the *kohen gadol* contained the names of each of the twelve tribes, and in addition, the names of the patriarchs, thus creating thirteen "units," which the *Givat Shaul* sees as corresponding to the Thirteen Principles of the Rambam. However, the *Givat Shaul* feels the need to offer an "apology" as to why he ascribes such status to the Rambam's principles:

> For the Thirteen Principles are considered by all "principles," whether they are called principles, derivatives, or derivatives of derivatives, whereby if one denies them, they forfeit their place in the World to Come. And Rabbi Isaac Abarbanel in his book, *Rosh Amana,* restored the glory of [the Rambam] to his former splendor, and removed from him and from his enumeration of principles all of the difficulties that had been leveled against them.[39]

Even as the Thirteen Principles form the basis of his homily, Rabbi Morteira must gainsay the claim that the principles of Rabbi Albo are of greater stature, and hence the need to buttress the status of the Rambam's list of principles.

It is perhaps not surprising that Rabbi Albo's list of three principles gains the upper hand in most of this literature. After all, it is easier to weave a homily highlighting three cardinal principles than thirteen, and more textual and theological phenomena are likely to come in groups of three than in groups of thirteen. Nonetheless, several of these

---

38. *Igra DeKala, Bereshit, Tzerufei Bereshit,* sec. 79.

39. Saul Morteira, *Givat Shaul* (Brooklyn: Hayim Eliezer Reich, 1991), 76a.

sources went to pains to declare that the shorter list was the primary one, and nowhere during this period do we find a homiletic source that declares that the Rambam's Thirteen Principles have greater status than do Rabbi Albo's.

The Thirteen Principles in Liturgical Literature

However, the homiletic literature of the period does not tell the full story of the reception of the Thirteen Principles at this time. To round out the picture, we need to attend to liturgical developments as well. Consider the responsum of the Maharshal we saw earlier. In content, it is very similar to the responsum of the Maharil. Both *posekim* decry the deleterious spiritual effects they witness in the ignorant who place undue emphasis on the recital of *piyutim* that are affirmations of the Thirteen Principles. But the responsum of the Maharshal bears witness to an important development. The Maharil – written around the turn of the fifteenth century – notes the practice of "poems written in Yiddish." There were apparently several in circulation that he had in mind. The Maharshal, though, specifically labels the *piyutim Yigdal* and *Ani Maamin* as the sources of his consternation. Writing in the middle of the sixteenth century, the Maharshal lived in an age when the printed siddur was now widely available. Scholars have noted that siddurim from this period regularly included both *Yigdal* and the *Ani Maamin*.[40] The ubiquitous nature of the siddur in Jewish communal life meant that for all intents and purposes, the agent that contained the Thirteen Principles was now the *piyut*, specifically *Yigdal* and *Ani Maamin*, and not the text of the Introduction to *Perek Ḥelek*, which – though printed from as early as 1502 – was not nearly as accessible and known as were these *piyutim*. From the early eighteenth century we find siddurim that specifically instruct that the *Ani Maamin* be recited daily.[41] Rabbi Pinhas Shapiro

---

40. For sources concerning *Ani Maamin*, see Gurfinkel, "Hashpaat Temurot Maḥshavtiot," 52–57. For sources concerning *Yigdal*, see Yosef Ezra Zaleikha, "Amirat Yigdal," *Paamei Yaakov* 37–38 (2007): 47–56. The custom, however, has not been accepted universally. The *Ani Maamin* is printed neither in the Siddur HaGra nor the siddur of the Baal HaTanya. See Gurfinkel, "Hashpaat Temurot Maḥshavtiot," 57, n. 32.

41. See *Or Hayashar* (Amsterdam, 1709) and *Keter Yosef* (Berlin, 1700); Gurfinkel, "Hashpaat Temurot Maḥshavtiot," 52.

of Koretz (1726–1791), a disciple of the Baal Shem Tov, had declared that the recitation of the *Ani Maamin* daily was an amulet for earning a good living.[42] While both *Yigdal* and the *Ani Maamin* were popular in European Ashkenazic circles, in Sephardic culture, the *Ani Maamin* was unknown at this time. *Yigdal*, while widely known throughout Sephardic Jewry, was recited on Shabbat, festivals, and festive occasions, but was not recited daily.

"RAMBAM'S" THIRTEEN PRINCIPLES: IN WHAT SENSE ARE THEY "HIS"?

To conclude this review of the place of the Thirteen Principles until the end of the eighteenth century, I explore a question that has engendered a great deal of misunderstanding concerning the reception history of the Rambam's Thirteen Principles. What precisely do we mean when we use the phrase, "*Rambam's* Thirteen Principles"?

Consider two ways in which this term is often used. The phrase can suggest that these are the principles of the Rambam, because he *created* them. No prior thinker or source had ever spoken of Thirteen Principles. Had the Rambam not composed the Introduction to *Perek Ḥelek*, the very notion of a catechism of Thirteen Principles would not exist. Those within the tradition who rejected the very notion of principles of faith, such as Radbaz or the Ari, certainly would subscribe to this formulation. For these figures, the principles are "the Rambam's" and not ultimate truths inherent to the religion. The second use of the phrase "the Rambam's Thirteen Principles" is often found as a shorthand, referring to their textual form and content. To wit, when we refer to the Rambam's Thirteen Principles, we mean the full text of the principles as laid out in the Introduction to *Perek Ḥelek*. So, to illustrate the matter, when we speak of the Rambam's eighth principle, we mean all of the points that he raised in the Introduction to *Perek Ḥelek* concerning both the Written and Oral Torah. And when we speak about the Rambam's eleventh principle – reward and punishment – we mean the things he writes about how divine justice becomes manifest primarily in the World to Come.

---

42. Rabbi Pinhas Shapiro of Koretz, *Midrash Pinḥas* (Lemberg, 1872), 119; Shapiro, *Limits of Orthodox Theology*, 17.

These two uses of the term "Rambam's Thirteen Principles" – as a reference to the fact that the Rambam created them, and/or as a reference to the precise textual content found in the Introduction to *Perek Ḥelek* – might seem obvious, and unworthy of any note. But consider the ascription of the principles to the Rambam in the following homily by the Shela:

> The principles of the faith are thirteen in number. The Rambam enumerated them in [his Commentary] on the Mishna, *Perek Ḥelek*. And they are: (1) existence of God; (2) [divine] unity; (3) divine incorporeality; (4) creation ex nihilo; (5) God and God alone is to be worshipped; (6) prophecy; (7) the prophecy of Moses our teacher, peace be to him; (8) *Torah* from heaven; (9) the immutability of Torah; (10) divine knowledge; (11) reward and punishment; (12) Messiah; (13) resurrection of the dead. And it is on this basis that the great paean *Yigdal Elokim Ḥai* was composed. And now I shall explain each of them, and in the process explain the great paean *Yigdal*, and thereafter I shall delineate how each of the Thirteen Principles are alluded to through the thirteen attributes of mercy, and I shall explain the matter thoroughly through the truth contained in the secrets of the Kabbala.[43]

The Shela ascribes the principles to the Rambam, but rejects both of the implications of that ascription that I described before. The Shela untethers the Thirteen Principles from the Rambam. By the Shela's account, the Rambam did not *create* the principles. Nor are the principles precisely as laid out in the Introduction to *Perek Ḥelek*. The Thirteen Principles, for the Shela, are not the text of the Introduction to *Perek Ḥelek*. Rather, "Messiah," "reward and punishment," etc., are preexisting, higher-order abstractions that the Rambam identified. The Rambam fleshed them out one way in the Introduction to *Perek Ḥelek*, but the Shela feels no commitment to the Rambam's specific explications. They are the Rambam's Thirteen Principles only in the sense that he was the first to identify them, not because their authority or truth originates with him. The

---

43. *Shaar HaOtiot*, Letter Alef, sec. 13.

phrase "Rambam's Thirteen Principles" has the same implication as the phrase "Newton's law of gravity." The law of gravity is an immanent part of nature; Newton merely drew our attention to it. Because the principles exist in and of themselves and prior to the Rambam, the Shela is free to offer his own explication of their meaning, at times entirely independent of the Rambam's intent. During the sixteenth and seventeenth centuries, the philosophical approach of the Rambam was in deep eclipse behind the rising specter of the Kabbala. Ironically, in this passage from the Shela we see how a philosophical structure created by the Rambam – the Thirteen Principles – is now appropriated. It is not rejected, or done away with; the concept of thirteen principles was immensely popular. And so the external structure of thirteen principles is emptied of its philosophical content, and refilled with content from the ascendant Kabbala.

Let us look at an example of how the Shela expresses his independence from the Rambam's formulations in the Introduction to *Perek Ḥelek*. For the Rambam, the eleventh principle, that of reward and punishment, receives its greatest expression in the World to Come where the righteous will be rewarded and the wicked punished. In contrast, this is what we find in the Shela's homily:

> The eleventh principle is reward and punishment. And [in *Yigdal*] it says, "according to *his* deeds (*kemifalo*)," and "according to *his* wickedness (*kerishato*)." This teaches…that rewards and punishments are not assigned by [divine] fiat or decree; rather they are natural and immanent within the act itself. For the reward for a mitzva is the mitzva itself, and the recompense for a transgression is the transgression itself.[44]

The Shela understands reward and punishment in a way radically removed from the intent of the Rambam in the Introduction to *Perek Ḥelek*. Moreover, the text that bears the principles is no longer the text of the Introduction to *Perek Ḥelek*, but the text of *Yigdal*; after all, it is through the *piyut* that people know the principles in the first place. His

---

44. Ibid.

prooftext for his understanding of the principle is a close reading of that *piyut*'s eleventh line. Reward is given to a person "according to *his* deeds" or "according to *his* wickedness."

And so we see a figure that fully affirms the centrality of the Thirteen Principles, and yet takes the license of full autonomy from the definitions of those principles offered by the Rambam. Nor is the Shela an outlier in this regard; in fact, many voices in the tradition that affirm the standing of the Thirteen Principles of Faith likewise affirm that we are speaking of archetypes, identified by the Rambam, but not limited to his definition of them. The untethering of the Thirteen Principles from the Rambam is also witnessed in the *Daat Tevunot* by the Ramḥal, Rabbi Moshe Ḥayim Luzzatto (Italy, 1707–1746). The first section of this treatise on Jewish thought is set up as a dialogue between the Soul and Reason. The treatise opens with the Soul appealing to Reason to offer assistance in understanding some of the thirteen principles of the faith. No mention is made of the Rambam. The Ramḥal proceeds to explicate several of the principles by setting a veiled reference to kabbalistic literature regarding those concepts, at a far remove from the rationalistic explication given them by the Rambam.[45]

Perhaps the earliest evidence of interpretation of thirteen principles untethered from the Rambam's formulations in the Introduction to *Perek Ḥelek* is witnessed in the homiletic writings of Rabbi Moshe Alshikh (Safed, 1507–1600). In a homily about the Ten Commandments, he argues that allusion to all thirteen principles are found in the Ten Commandments, and he lists the thirteen. The principles are not listed in the same order in which they are found in the Introduction to *Perek Ḥelek*. Moreover, at least one of the thirteen seems to suggest a different content than what the Rambam had in mind. For the Rambam, the ninth principle concerns the immutability of the Torah. In the Introduction to *Perek Ḥelek*, the Rambam directs us to passages in his introduction to the Commentary on the Mishna, where he underscores that this principle teaches that no *laws* of the Torah may be abrogated in the future, even

---

45. See similar independence in explication of the principles in Rabbi Eliezer Rokeah (Poland/Amsterdam, 1665–1741), in his commentary on the *Mishneh Torah, Arbaah Turei Aven (Hilkhot Teshuva* 3:7).

by a bona fide prophet. For the Alshikh, however, the principle of the immutability of the Torah (for him, the thirteenth principle), refers to the immutability of the *text* of the Torah; nothing in the Written Torah may be altered.[46] It may be that the Alshikh here responds to the charges of *taḥrīf*, which, as we saw earlier, featured prominently in the writing of his Safed contemporary, the Radbaz.

Later, the nineteenth and twentieth centuries would witness the rise of the genre of commentaries on the Thirteen Principles. To a one, the authors of these commentaries believed the principles to be thirteen higher-order abstractions that could be fleshed out without conforming to the manner in which the Rambam had explained them.[47]

ANALYSIS: THE THIRTEEN PRINCIPLES OF FAITH AT THE DAWN OF EMANCIPATION

By the end of the eighteenth century, many Jews across the Diaspora would readily have agreed that the Rambam's Thirteen Principles were the fundamental tenets of the Jewish faith. But this acceptance of the principles was not in the form that the Rambam himself had intended when he composed the Introduction to *Perek Ḥelek* six centuries earlier. The Rambam had composed a nuanced and carefully crafted text. But this text had never been widely accessed by Jews the world over. Instead, what most common people knew about the principles was what they could glean from the *piyutim*, specifically *Yigdal* and *Ani Maamin*. When sages at this time wished to refer to one of the principles, it was not the text of the Introduction to *Perek Ḥelek* they cited, but rather the appropriate line from *Yigdal*. As we saw, these *piyutim* not only omitted much of what the Rambam had written, but in places altered the ideas as well. Yet, from the Rambam's introduction to his *Sefer HaMitzvot* we know that he believed the genre of *piyut* to be unsuitable for theological instruction. Theological truths, he believed, require the precision of systematic prose, which can only suffer when subject to the requirements of meter, rhyme, imagery, and so on. For the Rambam, the principles are not merely to

---

46. Alshikh, *Shemot, Parashat Yitro*, ch. 20.
47. For references, see Gurfinkel, "Hashpaat Temurot Maḥshavtiot," 58, n. 38.

be affirmed but are to be probed and understood ever more deeply. No community ever committed to the study of the principles in this way.

When we move from the genre of *piyut* to the homiletic writings of the sages of Israel, we find that the text of the Introduction to *Perek Ḥelek* fares no better. Many respected figures in the homiletical literature defer to the three principles of Rabbi Joseph Albo as the principles of the faith, or state that the Thirteen Principles of the Rambam are subsumed under the principles laid down in the *Sefer HaIkkarim*. And when authorities do affirm the Thirteen Principles as the principles of the faith, they do so with reference to the principles as higher-order abstractions which they are free to explicate in ways at variance with how the Rambam had understood them.

Moreover, the Rambam had cast the principles as the boundary markers of Jewish identity. One who affirmed all thirteen principles could be deemed *Yisrael* – a member of the Jewish people. Whoever denied even one of these principles was denied the status of *Yisrael*, and was therefore ineligible for communal support, or any of the reciprocal responsibilities that Jews are commanded one for the other. By the end of the eighteenth century, in the six centuries that had passed, no *posek* had adopted this position. Even during the mass defections of the conversos in fifteenth-century Spain, no authority ever adjudicated their status with reference to the Principles of Faith.[48]

Moreover, never during the sixteenth to eighteenth centuries do we find any sustained debate concerning the principles. There is no record of debate as to whether there are indeed three principles of the faith or thirteen. Among those offering differing explanations of the principles as higher-order abstractions or categories, there is no debate about who is correct in their interpretation, and on what basis these issues should be decided. Thus, with regard to the principle of *torah* from heaven, there are no calls during this long period to censure the Ibn Ezra or his writings on the origins of the Torah in any way. The fact that Rabbi Joseph Albo categorizes belief in Mosaic transmission of the Torah as an ancillary belief rather than a primary one never earns him censure of any kind.

---

48. My thanks to Prof. Eric Lawee for sharing this insight with me.

We see at this time a veritable fire wall between the world of halakha and the world of principles of faith. As we saw, sages throughout this period defined halakhic heresy entirely with reference to the sources in the *Mishneh Torah*. Neither the text of the Introduction to *Perek Ḥelek* nor the very concept of principles of faith was invoked in halakhic settings at this time.[49]

For all of the attention that we have seen in these sources regarding the Thirteen Principles, two caveats are in order. The first is that interest in the principles was overwhelmingly an affair limited to the Ashkenazic world. It is true that the Sephardic world knew of and recited the *piyut Yigdal*. But it did so on Shabbat, holidays, and festive occasions. It had no tradition at all at this time of a version of the *Ani Maamin*. By contrast, in Ashkenazic communities the custom was widespread to recite both *Yigdal* and *Ani Maamin* on a daily basis. Virtually all of the homiletic literature touching upon the principles was produced in Ashkenazic circles. The second caveat is that specifically with regard to the question of the eighth principle, *torah* from heaven, we sense that there was no urgency about the issue in particular; there was no more discussion about this principle than there was about any other principle. In short, from the sixteenth to eighteenth centuries, the Rambam's Thirteen Principles had been accepted as a widely popular didactic tool, one of many in the rabbinic homiletical toolbox.

All of this would change, and radically so, within a short amount of time, as Jews emerged from the ghetto, embracing emancipated lifestyles and abandoning tradition. As the authorities of the *mesora* sought to meet this challenge, they turned to the catechism of the Principles of Faith. It is to this period – our period – that we now turn.

---

49. With the notable exception of the *Yeshuot Yaakov* on *Oraḥ Ḥayim* 126, mentioned earlier.

Chapter 11

The Thirteen Principles as Boundary Marker: The Nineteenth and Twentieth Centuries

The beginning of the Emancipation movement at the end of the eighteenth century engendered far-reaching consequences for the socio-religious condition of Jews across Europe. For the first time, the prospect of legal and social equality caused large numbers of Jews to abandon the beliefs and practices of the tradition.[1] Rabbinic leaders faced unprecedented challenges in meeting these new realities. Within this new and threatening situation, the role and prominence of the Thirteen Principles took on new dimensions. As we saw in the last chapter, the Thirteen Principles had long served as a didactic tool. But now they would define Orthodoxy. This status, more than two centuries in the making,

---

1. For an overview, see Shmuel Feiner, *The Jewish Enlightenment*, trans. Chaya Naor (Philadelphia: University of Philadelphia Press, 2004), 139–82.

was well summed up in the founding meeting of the Orthodox Jewish Congregational Union of America in 1898, which laid out in its charter that "we affirm our adherence to the acknowledged codes of the Rabbis and the thirteen principles of Maimonides."[2] Denial of even one of these principles has usually been enough for one to be considered a heretic.[3]

There can be no question that contemporary Orthodoxy has accepted a commitment to both the halakha and the Thirteen Principles as binding. But they have been accepted in different ways, and the acceptance of each is governed by different rules. Understanding that difference is the subject of this chapter. The rules of halakha are largely expressed through precise legal formulation in works like the *Shulḥan Arukh* and the commentaries written over the centuries. The only exceptions they allow are generally those that already are incorporated into the code itself, such as leniencies to save a life. Any act is assessed in light of the codes of halakha and determined to be either permissible or prohibited. By contrast, as we have already seen, the Thirteen Principles are not even encapsulated in a single, uniformly accepted text. Most authorities prior to the nineteenth century – and, as we shall see, even since – have viewed them as an authoritative list of higher-order principles, whereas their details have been given wide interpretation. Indeed, the rules that govern the acceptance of the Thirteen Principles have never been articulated by any authoritative rabbinic figure.

THE CONCEPT OF A BOUNDARY MARKER: A PERSPECTIVE FROM SOCIOLOGY

We can best understand the new role played by the Thirteen Principles beginning in the nineteenth century by appreciating several insights from the field of sociology. When a community is faced with a threat, the threat itself fosters a sense of mutuality and a feeling of unity among the people of the community by supplying a focus for group feeling. Israelis band together in the face of war. In the United States, residents

---

2. Text in Paul R. Mendes-Flohr and Jehuda Reinharz, eds., *The Jew in the Modern World: A Documentary History* (New York: Oxford University Press, 1995), 470.

3. For sources see Marc B. Shapiro, *The Limits of Orthodox Theology: Maimonides' Thirteen Principles Reappraised* (Oxford: Littman Library of Jewish Civilization, 2004), 21.

of California or of Houston feel a bond in the face of natural disasters such as forest fires or flooding. The father of the modern field of sociology, Émile Durkheim, noted that this same sense of bonding is engendered and fostered when a community faces secession by members who engage in what the community considers deviant acts. The deviant actions function in the same way as the floods or fires do; they foster a sense of mutuality and group feeling among those who are committed to rejecting the deviant activity. The deviance makes the normative community members more alert to the interests they share in common and draws attention to the values that constitute the "collective conscience" of the community.[4] In an environment in which deviance becomes increasingly widespread, a community will defend itself by establishing boundary markers that clearly set off those who are deviant, and thus outside of the community.

This way of thinking permeates our daily lives as Orthodox Jews as a sub-community and minority within the larger collective of the Jewish people. Think of what we mean and what we are doing when we meet another Jew, perhaps in the workplace, and we ask ourselves, "I wonder if he is *frum*?" By that, we often mean to ask whether the person is *shomer Shabbat* and *shomer kashrut*. Of course, to be a fully observant Jew means to follow all of halakha, but we do form an initial impression and classify someone when we learn that they keep Shabbat and that they keep kosher. They are one of "us," and we appreciate in them the same commitments that we ourselves make.

One noted sociologist has observed that when a boundary crisis ensues, issues that had not previously been "hot-button" issues can suddenly rise to the fore as the focal point of boundary maintenance,[5] and we can see the relevance of that observation to our "Shabbat/kashrut" measure of Orthodoxy. Shabbat observance has always had a special place in classical rabbinic sources, but much less so "keeping kosher."

---

4. See Émile Durkheim, *The Division of Labor in Society* (New York: Free Press of Glencoe, 1960), 102; within an Orthodox context, see Adam S. Ferziger, *Exclusion and Hierarchy: Orthodoxy, Nonobservance, and the Emergence of Modern Jewish Identity* (Philadelphia: University of Pennsylvania Press, 2005), 7.
5. Kai Erikson, *Wayward Puritans: A Study in the Sociology of Deviance* (New York: Wiley, 1966), 69.

Our talmudic sources make no distinction between the importance of refraining from non-kosher food and, for example, refraining from wearing *shaatnez*. But in the new reality of the nineteenth century and certainly by the twentieth century, with so many Jews abandoning tradition, "keeping kosher" emerged as an effective boundary marker that divided those who were remaining loyal to the tradition and those who were not.

Yet, even as we routinely think of keeping Shabbat and keeping kosher as the signs of whether someone is in or out of the Orthodox community, we will routinely make exceptions in both directions. Someone might be scrupulously observant of both Shabbat and kashrut, but if they attend services at a Conservative synagogue we will not as quickly consider them part of the Orthodox community. Conversely, if someone keeps Shabbat and kosher but will order the fish option in a non-kosher restaurant, we will likely still consider such an individual a member of the community if they attend services in an Orthodox synagogue and send their kids to yeshiva day school, even if their observance of the laws of kashrut is deficient. A prominent twentieth-century sociologist, Kai Erikson, explained this phenomenon well: when passing judgment on one another, members of a community will take a number of factors into account that are not immediately related to the deviant act itself – in this last case, a lapse in the observance of kashrut. Erikson writes that whether or not the person will be considered deviant will have something to do with his social class, his overall record within the community, and many other similar concerns which take hold in the shifting mood of the community.[6] This approach to assessing the acceptability of an act is poles apart from the way in which codified halakha operates. Neither one's piety nor one's prior record have any bearing on the permissibility of an act. *Treif* is *treif*, whether consumed by a sinner or by a *tzaddik*; indeed, were a *tzaddik* to consume *treif* food, he would be rebranded a sinner. But as we shall see, when the sages of Israel considered deployment of the boundary marker of the Principles of Faith, they did so with the spiritual résumé of the person in full view, and this broader context played a key role in determining whether a breach of the Thirteen Principles constituted deviance.

---

6. Erikson, *Wayward Puritans*, 7.

THE THIRTEEN PRINCIPLES AS A BOUNDARY MARKER: EARLIEST STEPS

The earliest record in which the Thirteen Principles serve as a boundary marker is found in a brief few lines of a responsa by Rabbi Shemuel Leib Kauders of Prague (1768–1838) in his 1823 collection of responsa, *Olat Shemuel*. The *Olat Shemuel* was a highly regarded figure in Bohemian Jewry in his time, and was the de facto chief rabbi of Prague at the end of his life. We know that the assimilationist tides sweeping across European Jewry were challenges that he faced personally, because two of his responsa (nos. 11 and 16) address issues concerning individuals who had been observant but had now abandoned the tradition. We can see the new deployment of the Thirteen Principles as a boundary marker between Jews in responsum no. 88. Here, the *Olat Shemuel* relates to an issue that we have touched on earlier – that many Jews appeal to angels as intermediaries to the Almighty, in contravention of the Rambam's fifth principle, which expressly forbids such worship. The *Olat Shemuel* notes that such practice is inappropriate, and then writes:

> It is prohibited…and touches upon one of the thirteen fundamental principles of the religion, and there is much to be said on this issue (nonetheless we must not judge all of Israel as wayward, Heaven forfend, and especially since the great sages of the generation have witnessed this and have not offered protest, which suggests that they did not see the matter as illicit).

The *Olat Shemuel* collection of responsa was better known in its own day than it is today. However, in terms of the history of the status of the Thirteen Principles in rabbinic writings, the comment is supremely important in three respects. To begin with, to the best of my knowledge, it marks the first time in seven and a half centuries – since the Rambam published the Introduction to *Perek Ḥelek* together with his Commentary on the Mishna – that the Thirteen Principles as a corpus are invoked as a source in a halakhic ruling in the genre of halakhic literature. We saw in the previous chapter that the principles had heretofore been referenced in liturgical and in homiletic writings, but never as a source in a halakhic argument. Indeed, in earlier times, other *posekim* had written against this very practice of appealing to intermediaries.[7] However, they had never appealed to the Thirteen Principles as a source regarding that issue, or any other halakhic issue, for that matter. What is even more striking here is that the *Olat Shemuel* could have invoked the Rambam's halakhic writings to oppose the practice of prayer to intermediaries. The Rambam proscribes such worship in *Hilkhot Avoda Zara* 2:2 and again in *Hilkhot Teshuva* 3:7, where he categorizes one who makes such appeals a *min*. Instead the authoritative text the *Olat Shemuel* cites is the Thirteen Principles.

Second, this is the first time that we see the principles invoked in the context of a boundary marker, distinguishing groups of Jews. As we saw earlier, the Rambam himself had written in the Introduction to *Perek Ḥelek* that affirmation of the principles was the sine qua non for the acquisition of the status of a *Yisrael* – a Jew in good standing – and that one who even harbored doubts about any of the principles was to be denied that standing. But in the more than seven centuries since then, this dictate of the Rambam had never been adopted or enforced, neither in halakhic literature nor even in homiletic sermonizing. No figure had ever invoked the Thirteen Principles in order to distinguish in any fashion between "good" Jews who maintained fidelity to the principles and others who did not. Here, the *Olat Shemuel* fears that these Jews will be branded "wayward" (*to'im*), by dint of the fact that their practice inherently contravenes one of the foundational principles of the faith. Put differently, we see that at this time the principles have now assumed the function of a boundary marker between Jews faithful to the tradition and those who have abandoned the tradition. In these new circumstances of widespread abandonment of tradition, and with it the new role played by the principles, the *Olat Shemuel* does not cite the Rambam's halakhic works to take issue with the practice of appealing to intermediaries. It is true that such behavior contravenes express halakhot. But it also contravenes the Thirteen Principles that have now emerged for the *Olat Shemuel* and for his audience as a social boundary marker.

---

7. See *Shut Maharam Schick, Oraḥ Ḥayim* 293, with references to the opinions of Rabbi Hayim Paltiel of Falaise (thirteenth century) and Rabbi Yaakov ben Moshe Levi Moelin.

This takes us to the third significant aspect of the *Olat Shemuel's* comments here. For the *Olat Shemuel*, individuals who appeal to intermediaries are undeniably in violation of the Rambam's fifth principle. He does not condone the practice. And yet, he insists that we cannot brand such a large segment of the community as "wayward." What we see here is the *Olat Shemuel* exercising the prerogative that Erikson described about how and when communities will deploy a boundary marker and declare certain members of the community as deviant – which, remarkably, is the word that the *Olat Shemuel* himself uses here – *to'im*. Erikson, recall, noted that members of a community will take a number of factors into account when they pass judgment on one another, which are not immediately related to the deviant act itself. And that is precisely what the *Olat Shemuel* argues here. The people who appeal to intermediaries may indeed contravene one of the Thirteen Principles, but they are entirely unlike the vast majority of people who are excluded by the rabbinic deployment of that boundary marker. In his time, as in ours, nearly all of those who rejected the principles did so within the context of an overall abandonment of fidelity to the tradition, in practice as well as in belief. But these individuals who appeal to intermediaries were for all intents and purposes indistinguishable from precisely the types of Jews the boundary marker is designed to champion: those committed to a life of pious observance of the mitzvot. Those who engage in this practice overstepped the line of the principles, but they did not threaten the social order; they neither pushed a revolutionary agenda nor challenged rabbinic authority.

The significance of the *Olat Shemuel's* ruling may be appreciated in light of a similar ruling by the twelfth-century Provencal authority Rabbi Abraham ben David, known by the acronym, Raavad. The Rambam states that one who believes in divine corporeality is a heretic (*Hilkhot Teshuva* 3:7). In his glosses to that halakha, Raavad writes, "Why does he call him a heretic? After all, several figures greater and better than he harbored this opinion in accordance with what they found in Scripture, and even more so in the *aggadot* that taint the mind." Like the *Olat Shemuel*, Raavad seeks to protect from harsh judgment the pious who harbor erroneous beliefs. However, Raavad lived only a generation after the Rambam, long before the Principles of Faith would attain universal status, and thus Raavad could take liberties that the *Olat Shemuel* could not. For Raavad, the path to protecting the pious who err is to undercut the Rambam, and this he does through belittling rhetoric and by rejecting the ruling itself. Raavad seems unconcerned that the issue at hand – divine incorporeality – is one of the Rambam's Thirteen Principles. By contrast, when the *Olat Shemuel* wishes to protect the pious who have erred he seeks to uphold the Rambam and the catechism of the Thirteen Principles as a boundary marker. Unlike Raavad, he does not maintain that the Rambam was in error. Instead he exonerates these otherwise pious Jews on the basis of the fact that their actions have not traditionally been perceived as rebellious.

Put differently, we witness in the ruling of the *Olat Shemuel* something that we will see again and again in the nineteenth and twentieth centuries: On the one hand, acceptance of the Thirteen Principles rises in prominence as *the* boundary marker between Jews in good standing and those deemed "wayward." At the same time, the sages of Israel will reserve the right to deploy this boundary marker as they see fit. When they are faced by antagonistic agents whose actions threaten the order of rabbinic authority and pious observance of the mitzvot, they will herald the inviolate standing of the catechism as a boundary marker so as to exclude them from the community. But when they are confronted with situations and individuals who do not constitute such a threat, they will make an exception and not deploy the boundary marker. This is precisely what we see here in the comments of the *Olat Shemuel*. The appeal to intermediaries in no way implied a desire to challenge rabbinic authority, to establish a new religious order, or even to declare a new set of theological principles. To brand such Jews as standing beyond the boundary marker and akin to those who had abandoned the faith because they acted counter to one of the Thirteen Principles would be, to borrow a contemporary image, to ensnare dolphins in nets set to catch tuna.

THE THIRTEEN PRINCIPLES IN THE NINETEEN LETTERS OF RABBI SAMSON RAPHAEL HIRSCH

The next engagement of the Thirteen Principles by a major nineteenth-century figure illustrates just how flexible rabbinic leaders could be in their use and deployment of the Thirteen Principles as a boundary marker. This is found in one of the early works of Rabbi Samson Raphael Hirsch (1808–1888), in his *Nineteen Letters,* penned in 1836. In one letter, Hirsch critiques the Rambam's very notion of principles of faith (italics added):

> [By] merely reconciling Judaism with the ideas from without, rather than developing it creatively from within…he gave rise to all the good and followed, as well all the bad. His trend of thought was Arab-Greek, as was his concept of life. Approaching Judaism from without, he brought to it views that he had gained elsewhere, and these he reconciled with Judaism. Thus, to him, too, the highest aim was self-perfection through recognition of the truth; and the practical concrete deeds became subordinate to this end. Knowledge of God was considered an end in itself, not a means toward the end; so he delved into speculations about the essence of God and considered the results of these speculative investigations to be *fundamental axioms and principles of faith binding upon Judaism*…the [mitzvot] came to be viewed as empty of spiritual content, were inevitably neglected and even came to be despised…. People should have taken a stand within Judaism and asked: Inasmuch as Judaism makes these demands upon us, what must be its view of the purpose of human life?… Instead they took their stand outside of Judaism and sought to adapt it to their viewpoint…people who now presumed themselves to be the possessors of the idea represented by the mitzvah assumed that they no longer needed to fulfill it in practice, since it was meant to be only a stepping stone toward the idea involved…. As a result, other men, who had a more profound grasp of Judaism, came to oppose this philosophical attitude, and in due course, became opponents of intellectual inquiry in general and the pursuit of philosophy in particular… [270–71] one ought to have asked himself: Moshe ben Maimon, Moshe ben Mendel – are they in fact Moshe ben Amram?[8]

8. Joseph Elias, *The Nineteen Letters: The World of Rabbi S. R. Hirsch* (New York: Feldheim, 1995), 265–71.

Hirsch's attitude toward the notion of "principles of faith" is determined by their impact on the spiritual life of Israel, and for Rabbi Hirsch that impact is toxic. The principles focus on beliefs, the affirmation of truths. In the Protestant milieu of nineteenth-century Germany, this manifesto is taken by some Jews to support the notion that what counts is what the heart feels and the mind believes, not what a person does in ritual.[9] Thus, for Rabbi Hirsch, promoting the Thirteen Principles as catechism actually serves to impede the pious observance of the mitzvot. Hirsch ascribes the root of this wayward attitude within Judaism to the teachings of Moses Mendelssohn, and hence the rhetorical question at the close of the passage: Are "Moshe ben Maimon" and "Moshe ben Mendel" authentic bearers of the tradition of "Moshe ben Amram"?

Rabbi Hirsch takes substantial liberties in his critique. Because the standing of the Thirteen Principles is so high at this time, he cannot achieve his aim by merely disagreeing with the enterprise of identifying principles of faith. He must discredit both the enterprise and its founder. He thus employs the hermeneutics of suspicion – that is, speculating on what really motivated the Rambam, perhaps even subconsciously: the Rambam's formulation of principles of faith stemmed from attitudes and concepts he had too eagerly embraced from Arab and Greek sources antithetical to the spirit of Judaism. We saw in the last chapter that both Abarbanel and the Maharshal had offered similar critiques of the Rambam and his enterprise of identifying a limited number of principles of faith.[10] But looking now at Rabbi Hirsch's critique alongside theirs, we can see that across the ages, the critique of the Rambam in this regard is in proportion to the standing of the principles. In nineteenth-century Europe, the Thirteen Principles enjoy broad status as a boundary marker between the faithful and the faithless, a status they had not attained during the time of Abarbanel or the Maharshal. Thus, in order to counter their status, Rabbi Hirsch must subject them to withering critique. The

---

9. Although Hirsch rejected the notion of a catechism, he nonetheless agreed with the contents of the principles themselves. On Hirsch's rejection of Protestant categories of thought, see Michah Gottlieb, "Oral Letter and Written Trace: Samson Raphael Hirsch's Defense of the Bible and Talmud," *Jewish Quarterly Review* 106, no. 3 (2016): 316–51.

10. See above, p. 258 and p. 263.

boundary is meant to deliver results: to bulwark the pious observance of the mitzvot and the standing of those who observe them. When the boundary loses its utility, it loses its validity.

THE THIRTEEN PRINCIPLES AND THE
BATTLE AGAINST REFORM JUDAISM

By the middle of the nineteenth century, the Reform movement had begun to gain steam. During the mid-1840s, the nascent Reform movement sponsored three conventions and produced manifestos detailing its departure from traditional practice. It is now that we find the Thirteen Principles invoked not only against Jews that have abandoned the faith but against an organized movement. This is found in the writings of Rabbi Tzvi Hirsch Chajes (Galicia, 1805–1855), the Maharatz Chajes, who penned a polemical treatise against the nascent Reform movement, *Minḥat Kena'ot* (1849). There he writes:

> Concerning major laws, and long-established halakhot that are based in the Written or the Oral Law, and even precautionary edicts founded on the Talmud or the *posekim*, we cannot enact any change or alteration (*ein lanu shinui vetaḥlif*). In particular, there is no challenging the fundamental principles of the religion, for around these precious positions are all of Israel united as one, in conformity with the teachings of our teacher the Rambam, in his Mishna commentary on Sanhedrin, on the mishna, "All Israel have a place in the World to Come," that is, the Thirteen Principles, which have been incorporated as well into our prayers.[11]

In the last chapter we saw that through the end of the eighteenth century, rabbinic sources had held in esteem two catechisms: the three-principle list of Rabbi Joseph Albo and the Rambam's list of thirteen principles. In the nineteenth century, we find far fewer references to Rabbi Albo's list as "the Principles of Faith," especially in the homiletical literature. Although the Thirteen Principles were held in high regard already in

---

11. Tzvi Hirsch Chajes, *Kol Sifrei Maharatz Ḥayot*, vol. 2 (Jerusalem: Divrei Ḥakhamim, 1958), 979–80. Translation is my own.

earlier times, here we find an unprecedented exclamation: "for around these precious positions are all of Israel united as one." The elevation of the status of the Thirteen Principles over Rabbi Albo's shorter list is well understood. The manifestos that emerged from the Reform conferences of the 1840s did not include well-articulated positions on issues of theology. But they did emphasize sweeping changes to the practice of Judaism. To counter the challenge, traditionalists needed to choose their rhetorical weapons accordingly. Highlighting Rabbi Albo's three principles would not have provided a rhetorical response matched to the challenge. Nothing in the platforms promulgated in these conferences stated that these figures rejected the three Principles of Faith as articulated by Rabbi Albo. In fact, nothing that they proposed even rejected the notion that the Torah was from heaven, even though it was likely that some of these figures were familiar with and accepted the findings of German biblical criticism. In the early half of the nineteenth century, even critically minded German scholars mostly believed that the Hebrew Bible was in some form the word of God. Traditionalists seeking to charge that the reformers were violating Judaism's most sacred and fundamental principles needed to look beyond Rabbi Albo's three principles – and the Rambam's Thirteen Principles provided the theological wedge needed. Above all else, reformers sought to enact *reform* of practice, and this ran afoul of the Rambam's ninth principle, affirming the unchanging nature of the Torah's laws. In the passage cited above, the Maharatz Chajes highlights this very charge: "Concerning major laws, and long-established halakhot that are based in the Written or the Oral Law and even precautionary edicts founded on the Talmud or the *posekim*, we cannot enact any change or alteration (*ein lanu shinui vetaḥlif*)." The phrase echoes the language of the ninth principle as formulated in *Ani Maamin*: "I believe with perfect faith that this Torah will not be supplanted (*lo tehei muḥlefet*)."

Just as the Rambam's Thirteen Principles rise to ascendance over Rabbi Albo's three principles at this time, the status of *Ani Maamin* rises in relation to the status of *Yigdal*. There is a major distinction of genre between *Yigdal* and *Ani Maamin*. *Yigdal* is a *piyut* of praise and fits naturally into the siddur. The *Ani Maamin*, however, is a restatement of articles of faith. One recites it not to utter praise to the Almighty, as with

Yigdal, but to affirm theological propositions. Hence, the language of *Ani Maamin* is less poetic and simpler than the language of *Yigdal*.[12] We saw in the previous chapter that homiletical works frequently addressed the Thirteen Principles with reference to the lines of *Yigdal*. Because *Yigdal* is shorter than *Ani Maamin* and is lyrical in its composition, it has long been chanted as part of the prayers and thus is well known and committed to memory by most, to this day. I am unaware of any musical tradition that accompanies the entirety of the *Ani Maamin*. Nonetheless, in the nineteenth century the formulaic and propositional nature of *Ani Maamin* allowed it to attain new status as the Thirteen Principles rose as the bulwark and boundary marker separating the faithful from the faithless. This is seen in a steep rise in the literature of synagogue customs calling for its recitation, as well as in the new genre of commentary on the *Ani Maamin* as the base text through which the principles are known.[13] Orthodoxy had now established that membership in good standing would be contingent on the affirmation of these Thirteen Principles as the principles of the Jewish faith.

NINETEENTH-CENTURY EXCEPTIONS TO THE RAMBAM'S EIGHTH PRINCIPLE

Even as the Thirteen Principles grew in esteem and acceptance through the nineteenth century, we still do encounter voices that do not align with them. Here I look at two opinions that do not accord with the Rambam's eighth principle, that the notion of *torah* from heaven implies that every word of the Torah was dictated to Moses. The dynamics that allow these figures to veer from this principle differ from those that animated the previous two examples and are worthy of special consideration.

---

12. Admiel Kosman, "Yud-Gimmel Ikkarim LaRambam BePerush HaMishna, BeYigdal UVeAni Maamin," in *Sefer HaYovel Minḥa LeI"sh*, ed. Itamar Warhaftig (Jerusalem: Beit Knesset Beit Yaakov, 1990), 348.

13. For an overview of scholarly issues and sources pertaining to *Ani Maamin*, see Eli Gurfinkel, "Hashpaat Temurot Maḥshavtiot al Nusaḥei 'Ani Maamin,'" *Kenishta* 4 (2010): 51–58. For a list of nineteenth- and twentieth-century commentaries on the *Ani Maamin*, see Eli Gurfinkel, "HaIsuk BiIkkarim Aḥarei HaRambam: Bein Retzef LeTemura," *Alei Sefer* 22 (2012): 15, n. 78.

The first is the opinion of the Ḥatam Sofer in his commentary on the Torah, *Torat Moshe* (on Deut. 34:1). As we saw earlier, according to a *baraita* in Bava Batra 15a, R. Yehuda was of the opinion that the last eight verses of the Torah were written by Joshua – a position the Rambam rejects. These eight verses begin with Deuteronomy 34:5, "And Moses died." But the Ḥatam Sofer finds this explanation unsatisfactory; verse 1 of that chapter reports that Moses went up to Mount Nebo, which suggests that thereafter he would no longer be in a position to make further additions to the Torah. The Ḥatam Sofer asks: Did Moses bring a Torah with him? And did he inscribe the next four verses in which God addresses him prior to his death? And did then the children of Israel ascend the mountain and retrieve this *sefer Torah* after his demise? While he does not explicitly state that all twelve verses were written by someone other than Moses – presumably Joshua – he leaves the provenance of these verses unresolved (*tzarikh iyun*). Put differently, the Ḥatam Sofer entertains the possibility that there are verses that are post-Mosaic additions to the Torah, certainly beyond what the Rambam would have vouchsafed (which is to say, none at all), and even beyond those opinions attributed to R. Yehuda in the *baraita* in Bava Batra 15a.

A second voice that expresses openness to post-Mosaic additions to the Torah is found in the work of one Rabbi Shneur Zalman Dov Anushinski, who published a composition in Vilna in 1887 entitled *Matzav HaYosher*. At one point in the work, the author maintains that Ezra added words to the Torah.[14] The composition garnered hearty endorsements from leading Eastern European authorities, including Rabbi Joseph Saul Nathanson, the author of *Shut Shoel UMeishiv*; Rabbi Meir Leibush Wiser (or Malbim, 1809–1879); Rabbi Naftali Tzvi Yehuda Berlin (the Netziv); and Rabbi Isaac Elhanan Spektor (Russia, 1817–1896). Now, it may be that not all of these figures read the entire work. Nonetheless, none of these major figures seem to have expressed reservations that

---

14. Shneur Zalman Dov Anushinski, *Matzav HaYosher*, vol. 2 (Vilna, 1887), 28b. Anushinki offers support for this position from the statement in the Talmud that had Moses not preceded him, Ezra would have been worthy of having the Torah presented to Israel through him (Sanhedrin 21b). See discussion in Shapiro, *Limits of Orthodox Theology*, 112.

the author claims that Ezra added words to the Torah. The significance of the work rests not in the identity of its author, a minor figure at best, even in his own day. Rather, what is noteworthy here is that the work seems to have engendered no outcry with its release, where it surely would have been read by a wider audience.

Two factors can help explain how these sources could deviate from the Rambam's eighth principle, and do so, more importantly, without a ripple of opposition from within the rabbinic community. Recall that we noted that as early as the seventeenth century, in the writings of the Shela, Rabbi Yeshaya HaLevi Horowitz, major rabbinic figures could affirm that the Thirteen Principles are the fundamental principles of the faith, and yet take liberties in the explication of those principles.[15] Indeed, no authority had ever argued that the only legitimate understanding of the Thirteen Principles was that laid down by the Rambam in the Introduction to *Perek Ḥelek*. Rather, they viewed the Thirteen Principles as higher-order abstractions, the particulars of which have no set form; thus each figure explicated them in accordance with his own theology. It is telling that the *Ḥatam Sofer* reports in a responsum that he was asked whether the principles of the faith are those of Rabbi Joseph Albo or those of the Rambam.[16] He replies that so far as he can tell, they differ in name alone. Both the question posed to the *Ḥatam Sofer* and the somewhat dismissive answer he provides attest to a fluidity at the time concerning the content of the principles that the faithful were bound to affirm. It may well be that the *Ḥatam Sofer* subscribed to the Thirteen Principles. He certainly affirmed the principle of *torah* from heaven, as had all figures throughout rabbinic history. Yet, as we have seen, the sages of Israel across the ages understood the particulars of that doctrine in various ways. It would appear that the *Ḥatam Sofer* did not feel bound to the particular understanding of that principle as found in the Rambam's eighth principle in the Introduction to *Perek Ḥelek*.

The second factor that may have allowed these figures to experiment with the notion of post-Mosaic additions to the Torah is that it posed no concrete theological threat for these authorities. We find that

---

15. See above, p. 272.

16. *Shut Ḥatam Sofer, Yoreh De'ah* 356.

German authorities such as Rabbi Samson Raphael Hirsch and Rabbi David Zvi Hoffmann (1843–1921) were insistent that every word of the Torah was transmitted to Moses.[17] But these were figures who sought to engage and combat the theological challenges of German biblical criticism. In the East, however, where *Matzav HaYosher* was written and published, German was not widely spoken or read. Here the late nineteenth-century theories of the documentary hypothesis for the composition of the Torah associated with Karl Heinrich Graf and Julius Wellhausen swayed few Jewish minds or hearts. Anushinski's *Matzav HaYosher* was composed squarely within the world of the *beit midrash* and constituted no threat, and thus the sages of the time – those who gave their imprimatur to the book, and those who read it while it was in circulation – felt no impetus to act against it. The Ḥatam Sofer wrote his commentary on the Ḥumash in the early nineteenth century, before biblical criticism had emerged as a cultural challenge. Here, too, we can see how the deployment of the boundary marker of the Thirteen Principles is a function of its spiritual utility; in lands or in times in which biblical criticism is less known, we find greater openness to the idea that the notion of *torah* from heaven may not imply that Moses was the agent through which every word of the Torah was prophetically transmitted.

THE THIRTEEN PRINCIPLES IN THE NINETEENTH CENTURY: THE SEPHARDIC CONTEXT

The notion that the deployment of the Thirteen Principles as a boundary marker is a function of the spiritual needs of the time is well seen when we examine the place of the principles for Sephardic Jewry in the nineteenth century. As noted in the previous chapter, Sephardic communities, particularly in Morocco, had written and adopted into the liturgy several *piyutim* devoted to the principles. Yet, nowhere was there a custom of daily recitation of these *piyutim*; they were reserved for festive occasions. Moreover, as we also saw in the last chapter, homilies

---

17. See Hirsch's essay "Religion Allied to Progress" in Samson Raphael Hirsch, *The Collected Writings*, vol. 6 (New York: Feldheim, 1984), 112–113; David Zvi Hoffmann, *Sefer Vayikra*, trans. Zvi Har-Sheffer and Aharon Lieberman (Jerusalem: Mossad HaRav Kook, 1976), 1.

worked around principles of faith – whether those of Rabbi Albo or those of the Rambam – were far more prevalent in Europe than in the communities of Arabic-speaking lands. Early in the nineteenth century we encounter, for the first time, publication in a Sephardic siddur of a version of *Ani Maamin* and the beginnings of a daily custom of recitation. The Sephardic *Ani Maamin* is an adaptation of the one found in Ashkenazic siddurim, and it is no coincidence that the first Sephardic siddurim to contain this adapted *Ani Maamin* are printed in Europe.[18]

The Sephardic *Ani Maamin* departs from the Ashkenazic version in several regards. There is a difference in the order of some of the principles. God's intervention in the world is cast as part of the first principle, the existence of God, rather than in the tenth principle, divine omniscience. The issue of the distinct prophecy of Moses comprises not one but two principles. In terms of content, it departs from what the Rambam writes in the Introduction to *Perek Ḥelek*. The Rambam writes in the thirteenth principle that only the righteous will rise from the dead. But the Sephardic version of *Ani Maamin* states *shehameitim atidim lehaḥayot*, suggesting that all of the dead will one day rise. As we noted in the previous chapter, the notion of the Thirteen Principles is a fluid one; different authorities in different periods took license to parse them and explain them in ways that were often at great variance from the Rambam's account of the principles in the Introduction to *Perek Ḥelek*.

But the greatest difference between the Sephardic version and the Ashkenazic version is that the Sephardic one significantly reduces the length of each of the principles to statements of five words only, on average. I take here as an example the eighth principle. The Ashkenazic version reads, *Ani maamin be'emuna shlema shekol haTorah hazot hametzuya ata beyadenu hi hanetuna leMoshe Rabbenu alav hashalom* ("I believe with perfect faith that the entirety of the Torah now in our possession is the very Torah given to Moses our teacher, peace be to him"). As we noted in the previous chapter, the Ashkenazic version of the *Ani Maamin* is itself a curtailed version of a longer literary predecessor and

---

18. See Shlomo Elkayam, "Piyutei 'Ani Maamin' UMekomam BaTefilla," *Ḥemdaat* 5 (2006–7): 13.

does not encompass all that the Rambam had to say about the concept of *torah* from heaven, as it entirely omits any explicit mention of the Oral Law and its transmission by God to Moses. In the Sephardic version, this principle (now the ninth principle) reads simply: *ShehaTorah netuna min haShamayim* ("That the Torah was given from heaven"). As we have noted, it is clear the author of this version of the *Ani Maamin* did not feel bound by the order of the principles as laid down by the Rambam in the Introduction to *Perek Ḥelek,* and felt at liberty to explain at least some of the principles in a way that differed from the Rambam's own accounting. For the author of the Ashkenazic version of *Ani Maamin,* the principle of *torah* from heaven implied the transmission of the entire Torah to Moses, but made no explicit statement about the Oral Law, and indeed many today understand the formulation to refer to the Written Torah alone. Here it may be that the anonymous author of the Sephardic *Ani Maamin* affirmed everything the Rambam had said in the eighth principle of the Introduction to *Perek Ḥelek,* and intended no departure from those ideas in his curtailed formulation of the principle. Conversely, however, he may have believed that the principle of "*torah* from heaven" – as stated in Mishna Sanhedrin 10:1 – refers solely to the *divinity* of the Torah, but does not speak of the nature of its *transmission,* an opinion we saw implied in the work of several early medieval exegetes. Or alternatively, he may have believed that we are duty bound to affirm, simply, the general concept that God revealed His will to us in His Torah. In nineteenth-century central and western Europe, traditional Ashkenazic Jews were faced both with a host culture that increasingly questioned the origins of the Torah and with the rising threat of Reform Judaism. Here, traditional Jews scrupulously affirmed the language of their *Ani Maamin,* exactly as printed in the siddur: every word of the Torah was dictated to Moses. But Sephardic Jewry largely faced no Emancipation, no secular culture, no movement of Reform Judaism. Here, these Jews adopted a version of the *Ani Maamin* that made a simple statement about the divinity of the Torah.

The tides of history had now changed. In the twelfth and thirteenth centuries, under the pressure of the libel of *taḥrīf,* Jews in Muslim lands would affirm nothing less than the fact that every word of the Torah was transmitted by God to Moses through dictation. Meanwhile, the Jews

of Ashkenaz and elsewhere in Europe could experiment with the idea
that portions of the Torah were post-Mosaic in origin without feeling
threatened by their host culture, which universally accepted the sacred
and divine nature of the biblical text. By the nineteenth century we see
that the tables have turned. It is now European Ashkenazic Jewry that
holds fast to the idea that every word of the Torah was dictated by God
to Moses, while no such struggle exists for Sephardic Jews, who adopt
a version of the *Ani Maamin* that simply affirms the divinity of the text.

THE FLUIDITY OF THE THIRTEEN PRINCIPLES
IN THE WRITINGS OF THE ḤAFETZ ḤAYIM

As we move toward the end of the nineteenth century and into the twentieth, we see a new and nuanced approach to the principles: a *posek* will
relate to the Thirteen Principles as a boundary marker but in varying
ways, depending on the particulars of the situation. The prime example
of this fluid and situational deployment of the principles as a boundary
marker is found in the writings of Rabbi Yisrael Meir Kagan of Radin
(Poland, 1839–1933), the Ḥafetz Ḥayim.

The Ḥafetz Ḥayim was the first *posek* to invoke the Rambam's Thirteen Principles as laid out in the Introduction to *Perek Ḥelek* as the basis
for a halakhic ruling. In his work *Ahavat Ḥesed* (published in 1888), the
Ḥafetz Ḥayim addresses the halakhic parameters of the commandment
of charitable acts for the poor (*gemilut ḥasadim*), noting that the commandment is to assist individuals who qualify as a *Yisrael* – a Jew. One
who does not believe in the Thirteen Principles, he writes, forfeits his
status as a *Yisrael*, while one who transgresses a prohibition on a regular
basis, but nonetheless affirms the Thirteen Principles, retains this status.[19]
He cites the Introduction to *Perek Ḥelek* as his source for this ruling. No
prior *posek* since the Rambam had conditioned the conferral of the status of *Yisrael* upon an individual's affirmation of the Thirteen Principles.

However, we find a very different view of the Thirteen Principles
as a halakhic boundary marker in the *Mishna Berura* on *Oraḥ Ḥayim*
126:1. The issue here concerns an individual's eligibility to serve as the

---

19. This statement concerning the forfeiture of the status of *Yisrael* is echoed in his
writings in *Torat HaBayit*, ch. 13.

leader of a prayer service when he harbors heterodox views. Following the Yerushalmi (Berakhot, ch. 5) and the Tur (*Oraḥ Ḥayim* 126), the *Ḥaftez Ḥayim* rules that one is disqualified from leading services if he skips both the blessing of *teḥiyat hametim* and *boneh Yerushalayim* during the repetition of the *Amida*.[20] His omissions arouse suspicion that he does not believe in resurrection of the dead or in the coming of the Messiah. The *Ḥafetz Ḥayim* continues,

> It is clear, however, that if we know for certain that the individual denies the notion of the resurrection of the dead, or does not believe in the coming redemption, and all the more so if he does not believe in *torah* from heaven, or in reward and punishment, according to all he is a total heretic (*epikoros*) and cannot be asked to lead the service.

Based on the Yerushalmi and the Tur cited above, we can understand the basis for the *Ḥafetz Ḥayim's* ruling that denial of the resurrection of the dead or the coming of the Messiah are grounds for disqualification as a leader of the prayer service. What is curious here, however, is his further expansion of the list of heresies that would likewise serve to disqualify someone. Based on what the *Ḥafetz Ḥayim* had ruled earlier in *Ahavat Ḥesed*, we would have expected that in the *Mishna Berura* he would rule that one who denies any one of the Thirteen Principles ipso facto loses his status as a *Yisrael*, rendering him invalid to lead prayer services. Here, however, he lists only denial of the principles of *torah* from heaven and reward and punishment. The *Ḥafetz Ḥayim* cites as a source for this ruling the opinion of Rabbi Meshulam Yaakov Orenstein, in his commentary on the *Shulḥan Arukh*, titled *Yeshuot Yaakov*, which we encountered in the previous chapter. Recall that for the *Yeshuot Yaakov*, the Thirteen Principles are important, and one who denies even one of them is wicked. However, one is declared a heretic (*min*) only for denial of one of the three cardinal tenets laid down by Rabbi Joseph Albo in the *Sefer HaIkkarim*: the existence of the Creator, *torah* from heaven, and divine reward and punishment. In his own ruling on *Oraḥ Ḥayim* 126, the *Ḥafetz*

---

20. See *Ḥafetz Ḥayim, Oraḥ Ḥayim* 126, n. 2.

Ḥayim adopts the position of the *Yeshuot Yaakov* and rules that in addition to the categories of heretic disqualified by the Tur – those that deny resurrection of the dead and the coming of the Messiah – we must add those that deny *torah* from heaven and divine reward and punishment. The *Ḥafetz Ḥayim* does not include here one who denies the existence of the Creator, but the reason for that is obvious: one who elects to lead services implicitly demonstrates his belief in the Creator.

Strictly speaking, we find here a contradiction in the rulings of the *Ḥafetz Ḥayim*. In *Ahavat Ḥesed*, the *Ḥafetz Ḥayim* ruled that denial of any of the Thirteen Principles rendered an individual not only unfit to lead prayer services – it rendered him a non-Jew. And yet in *Oraḥ Ḥayim* 126, the *Ḥafetz Ḥayim* draws as his inspiration a source which explicitly downgrades the status of the Thirteen Principles and establishes as probative here only the three cardinal principles of Rabbi Joseph Albo. However, when the Thirteen Principles are understood as a boundary marker that is deployed in a fluid, situational fashion, we can well understand the two rulings. In *Ahavat Ḥesed*, the *Ḥafetz Ḥayim* addresses the distribution of funds for the poor, living and writing in the realities of late nineteenth-century Poland. Certainly relative to our own age, in that time and place funds were meager and needs were great. By insisting that only those who affirmed the Thirteen Principles were eligible for community support, the *Ḥafetz Ḥayim* enacted a form of spiritual triage. Those who were most spiritually worthy would be eligible to receive support, for only they were considered *Yisrael*. Across the *Ḥafetz Ḥayim*'s works we consistently see his inclination to establish boundaries demarking the faithful from those that have abandoned the faith; often these boundaries extend beyond what is demanded from talmudic sources alone. In fact, the *Ḥafetz Ḥayim* consistently rules those that have knowingly abandoned observance to be non-Jews.[21]

---

21. See Benjamin Brown, "The Hafetz Hayim on the Halakhic Status of the Non-Observant," in *Religion and Politics in Jewish Thought: Essays in Honor of Aviezer Ravitzky*, ed. Benjamin Brown, Menachem Lorberbaum, Avinoam Rosenak, and Yedidia Z. Stern (Jerusalem: Zalman Shazar Institute, 2012), 803–10. For an overview of literature on rabbinic views of the non-observant Jew in the nineteenth and twentieth centuries, see p. 789, n. 6.

By contrast, in his comments in the *Mishna Berura* to *Oraḥ Ḥayim* 126, the *Ḥafetz Ḥayim* faces no quandary such as how and to whom to distribute limited funds. Rather, the case addresses individuals who have come to shul to pray – already a sign of their commitment to the Almighty. These are individuals who might harbor erroneous beliefs on certain issues, but essentially see themselves as members of the faithful of Israel. Here, therefore, the *Ḥafetz Ḥayim* adopts the lenient position of the *Yeshuot Yaakov*, that a person is disqualified from leading the service only if he denies one of the three cardinal tenets of Rabbi Joseph Albo.[22]

The dynamic here is similar to what we witnessed in the responsum of Rabbi Shemuel Leib Kauders, the *Olat Shemuel*. Essentially pious individuals were acting in contravention to one of the principles. Rigid deployment of the principles as a boundary marker would have, idiomatically speaking, ensnared dolphins in the tuna nets. The same dynamic exists here in the ruling of the *Mishna Berura*. The *Ḥafetz Ḥayim* could easily have ruled as he did in *Ahavat Ḥesed*, and disqualified individuals who denied any one of the Thirteen Principles. The *Yeshuot Yaakov* is the only *posek* prior to the nineteenth century to invoke the Thirteen Principles of the Introduction to *Perek Ḥelek* in a halakhic discussion and it is remarkable that he rules against the Rambam's principles and states that the standard for rendering one a heretic (*min*) is delimited by the three-principle catechism of Rabbi Joseph Albo. The fact that the *Ḥafetz Ḥayim* cites that opinion demonstrates that he is prepared to reject the Rambam's catechism as the boundary marker between acceptable and unacceptable Jews when he feels that leniency will serve the spiritual needs of the moment: an inclusive stance toward those who wish to lead the prayers but may be erroneous in some of their beliefs. Once again, we see that the label of deviance is not determined on the basis of the deviant act, or belief,

---

22. Alternatively, we may say that the tension between the *Ḥafetz Ḥayim*'s ruling in *Ahavat Ḥesed* and his ruling in *Mishna Berura Oraḥ Ḥayim* 126:2 stems from methodological inconsistency, or that he cites the *Yeshuot Yaakov* without intending to bring to bear the implications of the latter's comment. I believe that the *Ḥafetz Ḥayim*'s decision to invoke the ruling of the *Yeshuot Yaakov* begs explanation, and thus I interpret these passages on the assumption that the *Ḥafetz Ḥayim* has chosen his words and his sources with care.

alone, but in consideration of the situational context and spiritual résumé of the person in question as well.

Conversely, however, we also find that the spiritual needs of the moment can bring the *Ḥafetz Ḥayim* to define the heretic in ways that deviate from what the Rambam prescribed, by adopting an even more stringent definition than that proposed by the Rambam himself. In his treatise on the laws of slander, the *Ḥafetz Ḥayim* notes that the prohibition does not apply when the subject of the slander is an *epikoros*, which he defines as follows:

> An *epikoros* is one who denies the notion of Torah and prophecy in Israel, which is inclusive of both the Written Law and the Oral Law. And even if one says, "All of the Torah is from heaven, with the exception of a single verse, a single *a fortiori* (*kal vaḥomer*), a single *gezera shava*, or a single talmudic inference" – this too is included [in the definition of the *epikoros*].[23]

Once again, we see how the *Ḥafetz Ḥayim* establishes a strong bulwark for the *mesora*. The Rambam had stated in the eighth principle of the Introduction to *Perek Ḥelek* that the *torah* which was from heaven included the text of the Torah as well as the relatively limited category of "its accepted interpretation," which refers to issues and opinions in the Talmud over which there is no dispute. The Rambam chose that language in contradistinction to the language contained in the *baraita* in Sanhedrin 99a, which includes virtually all of the elements of the Oral Law, claiming that these, too, are "from heaven." Writing in an age when the heavenly origins of the tradition were questioned in many quarters, the *Ḥafetz Ḥayim* breaks from the Rambam's definition of "*torah* from heaven" in the Introduction to *Perek Ḥelek* and seeks to safeguard the entirety of the Oral Law by reverting to the language of the *baraita* in Sanhedrin 99a and giving all content of the Oral Law the same high status – "from heaven." Just as the *Ḥafetz Ḥayim* could offer a more expansive definition of *torah* from heaven than did the Rambam, the *Ḥafetz Ḥayim* could elsewhere offer a more limited one. As we noted in the previous

---

23. *Ḥafetz Ḥayim, Hilkhot Leshon Hara*, 8:5.

chapter, the *Mishna Berura* rules against the Rambam concerning the requirements of the form of the shofar and the form of the strings of the tzitzit, even though the Rambam had said in the Introduction to *Perek Ḥelek* that the form of these objects constituted *torah* from heaven.[24]

In short, we see that the *Ḥafetz Ḥayim* invokes the Thirteen Principles in various ways. Sometimes he hews precisely to the Rambam's formulation, as we saw in *Ahavat Ḥesed*. Sometimes he will adopt a more stringent definition of a principle than that offered by the Rambam, and sometimes he will take a path less stringent than that prescribed by the Rambam. In all instances, however, what guides the *Ḥafetz Ḥayim* is a single constant: given the particulars of the situation at hand, what deployment of the Principles will contribute to the pious observance of the mitzvot.

THE FLUIDITY OF THE PRINCIPLES AS A BOUNDARY MARKER IN THE *IGROT MOSHE*

The practice of relating to the Thirteen Principles in a fluid and situational manner is witnessed as well in the writings of Rabbi Moshe Feinstein in his *Igrot Moshe*. Here, too, we see an approach to the Thirteen Principles that deploys the principles as a boundary marker only in consultation with the broader context of the persons and activity at hand. As we saw in the writings of the *Ḥafetz Ḥayim*, we shall see here, too, that these shifting priorities led Rabbi Feinstein at times to adopt a more stringent position concerning the principles than did the Rambam, and at other times a more lenient one.

In the postwar period in which Rabbi Feinstein served as American Orthodoxy's leading *posek*, Reform and Conservative Judaism experienced enormous growth, especially in the newly expanding suburbs. As they moved from Jewish inner-city neighborhoods to these new suburban communities, many Jews who were raised Orthodox chose to affiliate with other movements. Entire congregations that had been founded as Orthodox voted to reaffiliate as Conservative.[25] In this climate, Rabbi

---

24. See above, p. 267.
25. Jonathan D. Sarna, *American Judaism: A History* (New Haven, CT: Yale University Press, 2004), 282–93; Wolfe Kelman, "Moshe Feinstein and Postwar American Orthodoxy," *Survey of Jewish Affairs 1987* (1988): 175.

Feinstein sought to establish clear boundaries that would distinguish Jews who were Orthodox from those who were actively identifying as Reform and Conservative. In dozens of *teshuvot*, the *Igrot Moshe* refers to Reform and Conservative Jews generally, and their clergy in particular, as heretics (*kofrim*) who deny in statement or in deed "fundamental principles of the faith" (*ikkarei ha'emuna*).[26] Across the history of *pesak*, no authority refers as often and as forcefully to the notion and halakhic import of "principles of faith" as does the *Igrot Moshe*. Earlier *posekim*, especially the *Ḥatam Sofer*, had focused upon halakhic deviance in their condemnations of the followers of liberal Judaism.[27] More than any authority who preceded him, the *Igrot Moshe* looked to theology to discredit these movements, frequently invoking the notion of "principles of the faith" (*ikkarei ha'emuna*) and heresy (*kefira*). More fully than ever before, the Thirteen Principles emerged as *the* boundary marker separating Orthodox from non-Orthodox Jews.

At the same time, though, Rabbi Feinstein still felt a responsibility to include liberal Jews within the Jewish fold and thereby keep the door open in the hopes that efforts could be made to bring them back toward greater traditional observance. In turn-of-the-century Poland, the *Ḥafetz Ḥayim* had no direct encounter with liberal Judaism. Nonetheless, it is clear from his comments in *Ahavat Ḥesed* cited earlier that he would consider such Jews out of the bounds of *Yisrael*, as they denied the Thirteen Principles as an act of conscious rejection. This ruling, we noted, was predicated on the Rambam's position in the Introduction to *Perek Ḥelek* that only one who affirmed the principles was included within the people of Israel. The *Igrot Moshe* rejects this approach; on repeated occasions he states that even heretics (*kofrim*) who reject "the principles of the Torah" still retain their *kedushat Yisrael* – their status as members of the Jewish people.[28] For the *Ḥafetz Ḥayim*, the Thirteen Principles serve

---

26. For analyses of Rabbi Feinstein's approach to Reform and Conservative Jews, see Donniel Hartman, *The Boundaries of Judaism* (London: Continuum, 2007), 133–67; Harel Gordin, *HaRav Moshe Feinstein: Hanhaga Hilkhatit BeOlam Mishtaneh* (Alon Shevut: Tevunot, 2017), 177–93.

27. Hartman, *Boundaries of Judaism*, 104–32.

28. *Igrot Moshe, Oraḥ Ḥayim* 1:23, 2:19; *Yoreh De'ah* 3:39, 3:146; cf. *Igrot Moshe Even HaEzer* 4:83. See discussion in Hartman, *Boundaries of Judaism*, 145.

as a boundary marker that distinguishes between those who are Jewish and those who are not. For the *Igrot Moshe*, the Thirteen Principles distinguish between Jews who are Orthodox and those who are not.

Conversely, we also see how the *Igrot Moshe* retains license to lay aside the demands of a specific principle of faith where the deviant belief – indeed, the deviant *act* – poses no threat to the rabbinic order. In *Igrot Moshe* (*Oraḥ Ḥayim* 5:43:6), Rabbi Feinstein addresses the legitimacy of appeals to the dead to intercede before the Almighty. This is similar to the issue that we saw addressed early in the nineteenth century, in the responsum of the *Olat Shemuel*. There we saw that the boundary marker of the principles was deployed only within the larger context of the situation at hand, and that the *Olat Shemuel* was eager not to brand pious Jews with the blanket tag of deviance. No *posek*, however, ever placed such a premium on the principles of the faith as the boundary marker between Orthodox and non-Orthodox Jews as Rabbi Feinstein. Thus, we might have expected that he would be unbending, upholding the principles as an unconditional boundary, declaring those who appeal to the dead as intermediaries to be heretics. Yet, the *Igrot Moshe*, like the *Olat Shemuel*, seeks a way to avoid deploying the tag of deviance, although the mechanism through which he navigates the conundrum is different. Even as the *Igrot Moshe* lines up the arguments for and against such appeals, one senses Rabbi Feinstein's own discomfort with the practice throughout the responsum. Indeed, he even makes reference to the Rambam's fifth principle, stating that there is a rationale for prohibiting the practice, "by the very fact that this constitutes an appeal to one other than the Almighty" (*mitzad etzem habakasha zulat Hashem yitbarakh*), thereby invoking the language of the fifth principle as enunciated in *Ani Maamin: ShehaBoreh yitbarakh shemo lo levado ra'uy ve'ein ra'uy lehitpalel lezulato* ("That it is worthy to pray exclusively to the Almighty, may His name be blessed, to the exclusion of any other entity"). He brings no opinion that maintains that the Rambam could agree with the practice and that it may not, in fact, contravene the tenets of the fifth principle. Normally, when a question comes before a *posek* concerning a questionable practice, he rules that it is either permitted or prohibited. Alternatively, he may rule that it is permissible de facto (*bedi'eved*), but that it is preferable (*lekhathila*) to behave otherwise.

Here, the *Igrot Moshe* adopts a fourth path. He rules that each local *posek* can rule as he sees fit; some will choose to permit such appeals, while others will prohibit them. One senses that if asked for his own personal ruling, Rabbi Feinstein would dissuade someone from the practice. But at the same time, he is well aware that the custom has spread far and wide within the Sephardic and hasidic communities where Lurianic Kabbala holds sway. Put differently, the *Igrot Moshe* is not prepared to deploy the boundary marker and to tag as deviant otherwise pious Jews, and effectively trigger a theological battle with a wide swath of Orthodox Jewry. We see here, once again, that the seemingly deviant act – here, appealing to the dead as intermediaries – cannot be detached from its wider context. The "deviants" here are otherwise pious, committed Jews, continuing a rite that equally pious Jews had practiced for centuries. Thus, their deviant act that runs afoul of the boundary of the Thirteen Principles inheres neither challenge to rabbinic authority nor challenge to the halakhic order generally.

THE OPINIONS OF THE SAGES OF ISRAEL CONTRARY TO THE THIRTEEN PRINCIPLES: TO CENSOR OR NOT TO CENSOR?

To appreciate the dynamic nature in which the sages have deployed the Thirteen Principles as a boundary marker, we must go beyond what is expressly written and attend as well to a conspicuous and pervasive silence that arises from our sources. Although the Rambam's Thirteen Principles grew in stature over time, there are many examples in the last millennium of rabbinic writings of prominent voices within the tradition that take exception in one form or another to the Thirteen Principles as the principles of the Jewish faith.[29] I noted earlier that through the end of the eighteenth century, none of these voices had ever been challenged as heretical. As we have seen, though, the Thirteen Principles rise in prominence as a boundary marker beginning in the nineteenth century. How, then, do the rabbis relate to a long and varied heritage which contains views by prominent figures that are now considered beyond the pale? We can mention here Ibn Ezra's statements about the origins

---

29. See generally, Shapiro, *Limits of Orthodox Theology*.

of various Torah passages; his statements suggesting that the Torah was not dictated word for word;[30] and the opinion of Rabbi Jacob Emden that were a bona fide prophet to appear today we would follow his dictates, even if he told us to amend our halakhic practice.[31]

One can envision a range of moves Orthodox rabbinic authorities might have taken to ensure doctrinal purity and thereby fortify boundary maintenance. Most radically, one might have expected a movement to brand Ibn Ezra, for example, a heretic. A less radical step might have been to censor the commentary of Ibn Ezra by removing the now offensive passages from publication. At the very least, we would have expected a call to ensure that those passages be taught only with the disclaimer that the views expressed are no longer deemed acceptable. And so we might have expected to find with regard to the aforementioned position of Rabbi Jacob Emden concerning the mutability of the laws of the Torah, and many other statements issued before the time of the Rambam, and long after as well, that ran counter to the Thirteen Principles.[32]

Strikingly, the *mesora* bears not the slightest hint of a move in any of these directions. The commentary of Ibn Ezra continued – and continues – to be published and studied, and the same is true for the works of Rabbi Jacob Emden. In short, all of the works and authors that have taken issue with one principle of faith or another have maintained the same high status over the last two centuries that they enjoyed in earlier times before affirmation of the Thirteen Principles became the boundary marker denoting deviance.[33] Yet, how could rabbinic leadership declare the Thirteen Principles to be *the* Principles of Faith and a boundary marker between those considered Orthodox and those not, while tolerating the proliferation of books and ideas that undermine these very principles?

One might counter that the issue here is no different than a similar issue that we find across the entire breadth of halakhic literature. Over time, many halakhic opinions – from the *Tannaim* through modern-day

---

30. Abraham Ibn Ezra, *Yesod Mora VeSod HaTorah*, gate 1.
31. See discussion above, pp. 264–65.
32. The most thorough discussion of such opinions is Shapiro, *Limits of Orthodox Theology*, 107–8, 125.
33. See Shapiro, *Limits of Orthodox Theology*, 28.

posekim – have been expressed that today are not accepted as normative. And yet these were never erased from the books, or even declared
to be flawed and in error. And so what is good for halakha should be
good for beliefs: many opinions have been offered on the subject over
the ages, and, as in the world of halakha, some have gained acceptance
and others not.

The issues, however, are not the same. For the Rambam, the Thirteen Principles are fundamental truths that are eternal and unchanging.
The fact that the most authoritative Orthodox authorities have accepted
the Thirteen Principles as the principles of the faith yet continue to
proliferate the contrary opinions of earlier sages speaks volumes to the
dynamics of the deployment of the Thirteen Principles as a boundary
marker. When rabbinic leaders perceive a threat to rabbinic authority or
to the halakhic social order, they will deploy the principles as a boundary marker to exclude the threatening agents. But revered figures such as
Ibn Ezra and Rabbi Jacob Emden have been hallowed as part of the warp
and woof of the *mesora* for centuries, and as such constitute no threat.
Neither they nor their works challenged rabbinic authority or called for
the establishment of alternative religious movements. Recall here the
teaching of the sociologist Kai Erikson cited at the outset of this chapter: when a community is faced with a deviant act – in this case, beliefs
that run counter to the Thirteen Principles – it will not look at the act
alone in isolation, but will consider a broad range of factors surrounding the individual and the circumstances in question. This principle has
implicitly guided the sages as they have deployed the boundary marker
of the Thirteen Principles of Faith. The logic here is the same as we saw
with regard to the question of individuals who appeal to the departed
as intermediaries. Such individuals clearly contravene the Rambam's
fifth principle. But they will not be called out as heretics because they
are clearly acting within the fold of the faithful.

An intriguing comment about the Thirteen Principles penned by
the Ḥafetz Ḥayim sheds light on the status of the principles in his time
and within Orthodoxy more generally. In a missive to him in 1929, a cor-
respondent bemoans the harshness of the exile as experienced at that
time. In response, the Ḥafetz Ḥayim recommends that "in these days
when faith is waning due to our manifold sins, it is a meritorious deed

for each and every person to strengthen himself in this, and to recite [the Principles of Faith] after services, as was the custom of our fathers of yore."[34] The *Hafetz Hayim*'s call suggests that in his time the custom of daily recitation of the principles was no longer widely practiced. Over the course of the nineteenth century the Thirteen Principles assumed the status as the undisputed principles of the Jewish faith and as the boundary marker between the faithful and the faithless. Given that, one might have assumed that the catechism of the Thirteen Principles would be at the core of our schools' educational curriculum, and the frequent subject of sermons and *shiurim*, widely known, recited and studied regularly. Yet, the *Hafetz Hayim*'s call to "restore the custom of yore" to recite the principles points to a great irony: even as rabbinic authorities were relying on the standing of the principles with ever-greater weight to distinguish between acceptable and deviant Jews,[35] Orthodox Jews themselves were – and continue to be – mostly ignorant of their contents. Think of what we see and experience in our own communities. How widespread is knowledge of the Principles of Faith? Learned individuals often have difficulty identifying the Thirteen Principles even in general terms, let alone reciting their formulation as expressed in *Ani Maamin*. It is rare anywhere within Orthodox circles to hear public discourses on their content. Individuals who are familiar with the text of the Introduction to *Perek Helek* and what the Rambam writes about each of the principles are few and far between. No movement has ever been established to enshrine the study of the principles in a regular cycle of study. The Thirteen Principles of the Jewish faith are important and have been accepted not because Orthodox authorities insist that they need to be deeply understood, nor even because they need to be known by all in even a rudimentary manner. Rather they are important because they assist with the necessary work of boundary maintenance.

The rules that govern the deployment of this boundary marker, however, are far removed from the rules that govern our practice of halakha. Our halakha resides, largely, in set forms – the various codes,

---

34. Aryeh Leib Kagan, ed., *Mikhtavei HaRav Hafetz Hayim* (New York, 1953), letter no. 18 (Iyar 5689), 49.
35. See sources cited in Shapiro, *Limits of Orthodox Theology*, 16–17, 21–22.

such as the *Shuchan Arukh*, the *Mishna Berura*, and so on. These are carefully formulated, and we read and parse these with great precision to learn our halakhic obligations. But the Thirteen Principles have no set formulation. Instead, the sages have tended to refer to the principles as higher-order abstractions – such as "resurrection of the dead" or "reward and punishment" – that can comprise a range of meanings, some closer to what the Rambam wrote in the Introduction to *Perek Ḥelek*, some more distant. But this lack of one, precise formulation of the principles is itself deliberate and part of the system. As we have seen, it provides rabbinic authorities the flexibility they need to deploy the principles in a sensitive and effective manner.

Within the sources reviewed here, a clear dichotomy emerges: when a proposition that runs counter to the principles is enunciated by an agent who is squarely within the camp of tradition, and whose utterance trucks no challenge to the rabbinic order, the view is tolerated. Indeed, as we saw in the case of Rabbi Hirsch, when the principles are themselves deemed a threat, they are devalued. It is when the principles are denied within a context that authorities perceive as a challenge to rabbinic authority or to the stability of the halakhic order that they are deemed as heretical. As we have seen throughout these chapters, different authorities deployed the principles – as a whole and individually – in varying ways. And yet at no point do we find authorities challenging one another on the question of how and when to deploy this boundary, and how and when flexibility is in order. Unstated but implicit is the understanding that each *posek* faces circumstances that are complex and distinct to his own situation. Moreover, implicit is the understanding that an authority might rule in a fluid fashion, adjusting as the circumstances and the audience warrant. Thus, each authority is granted autonomy to deploy the boundary marker of the Thirteen Principles as he sees fit in order to achieve the broad goal shared by all of the sages of Israel across the ages: to bring *Klal Yisrael* to the pious observance of Torah and mitzvot.

Afterword

When We Are Left
with Questions

In this volume I have tried to relate to some of the most vexing challenges posed by critical study of the Tanakh for the Orthodox Jew: Are the accounts of the Tanakh historically accurate? Was there really an Exodus? Why are there discrepancies in the narrative and laws of the Torah? Is the Torah a divine text, and if so, how can we see that? The questions asked by critics are good ones. But oftentimes they belie a disposition that they – and indeed, we, too – possess as citizens of the modern era. For all of these questions, I claimed that proper understanding could come only through an exploration of the Torah's ancient context. And it is my hope that this context has proven as enriching for you as it has been for me through a lifetime of learning and studying.

In the second part of this book, I entertained the question: What are we bound to believe as Orthodox Jews committed to the principle of *torah* from heaven? I hope that our exploration of the richness of the tradition on this point and understanding of its development will serve readers to become more committed to their Maker and to His commandments.

Nonetheless, as I pointed out in the introduction, there are more points of contention between academic biblical studies and our *mesora* than can be considered in a single volume. As this book draws to a close, I offer *tzeida laderekh*, "provisions for the journey," a way of thinking about troubling questions. Consider this troubling question: What if we had incontrovertible proof that our transmission of the text of the Torah was defective? The question is hardly theoretical, and is, in fact, one that our sages faced. How they approached that challenge can teach us much about how to face troubling questions about the Torah's accuracy and authenticity.

As early as the period of the *Baalei HaTosafot* in the twelfth century, our sages realized that an error had fallen into the transmission of the texts of the Tanakh, including the texts of the Torah. They noticed instances in the Talmud and the Midrash in which a *derasha* rested on a reading of a verse that was at odds with the reading of the Masoretic Text – the text of the Torah found in our *sifrei Torah*.[1] In fact, Rabbi Akiva Eger lists dozens of discrepancies between the Masoretic Text and the readings of various verses according to midrashei Ḥazal.[2] Nearly all of these cases are instances of variant spellings. Most are variations of defective and plene (*maleh veḥaser*) spellings of the words. Some of these discrepancies concern verses in the Torah.[3] And in some cases, Sages of the Talmud derived halakhot on the basis of these variant readings. Here are two examples: The Talmud (Sanhedrin 4b) states that the word *totafot* appears three times in the Torah – twice spelled defectively, without a *vav* in the suffix (טטפת), and once with a *vav*

---

1. See *Tosafot*, Shabbat 55b, s.v. *Maaviram*. On this topic generally see Sid Z. Leiman, "Masorah and Halakhah: A Study in Conflict," in *Tehillah le-Moshe: Biblical and Judaic Studies in Honor of Moshe Greenberg*, ed. Mordechai Cogan, Barry L. Eichler, and Jeffrey H. Tigay (Winona Lake, IN: Eisenbrauns, 1997), 291–306, available online at http://leimanlibrary.com/texts_of_publications/74.%20Masorah%20and%20 Halakhah%20A%20Study%20in%20Conflict.pdf.
2. See Rabbi Akiva Eger, *Gilyon HaShas*, Shabbat 55b.
3. There are some instances, however, in which the Midrash seems to have been based on variant spellings that alter the meaning of the word. See Menachem Kahane, "Nusaḥ HaMikra HaMishtakef BiKhtav-Yad Romi 32 LeSifrei Bemidbar VeDevarim," in *Meḥkerei Talmud*, ed. Yaacov Sussmann and David Rosenthal, vol. 1 (Jerusalem: Magnes Press, 1990), 1–10.

(טטפות). From this R. Yishmael determines the number of *parshiyot* (sections) to be contained in our tefillin. He reasons that the occurrences spelled without the *vav* could be read consonantally as singular forms, and thus count for one *parshiya* apiece. The occurrence spelled with a *vav* can only be read as a plural form, and thus counts for two *parshiyot*, bringing the total to four *parshiyot*. However, according to the Masoretic Text found in our *sifrei Torah*, all three occurrences of the word *totafot* are spelled defectively (Ex. 13:16; Deut. 6:8; Deut. 11:18); none contain a *vav* in the suffix. Another example: In Mishna Zevaḥim 4:1, Beit Shammai and Beit Hillel debate the minimum number of times blood must be sprinkled on the corners of the altar when bringing a sin offering. The Talmud states (Zevaḥim 37b) that the calculation of Beit Hillel rests on the spelling of the word "corners" in three different verses, where twice the word is spelled defectively, קרנת, and once with the *vav* in the suffix, קרנות. However, in our *sifrei Torah*, we find that all three occurrences of the word (Lev. 4:25, 4:30, and 4:34) are written defectively, with no *vav* in the suffix.

Logically, these observations are nothing short of damning. It cannot be that the talmudic tradition of the midrashei halakha and the Masoretic tradition of our *sifrei Torah* both preserve accurate traditions of these verses. If the variants preserved in the midrashei halakha are correct, then our *sifrei Torah* do not contain an accurate record of God's word, and are not true to the original. Conversely, if the Masoretic Text is accurate, then the sages of Israel have derived halakhot from texts of the Torah that, in fact, do not exist. This could have the startling implication, at least according to the opinion of R. Yishmael, that our practice of inscribing four *parshiyot* for our tefillin is founded in error.

Furthermore, these observations cast a long shadow over the question of the general accuracy of our received texts. After all, only some five or six centuries had passed between the redaction of the Talmud and the first observations of this issue by the *Baalei HaTosafot*. Presumably, the discrepancies arose only after the redaction of the Talmud. But what then of the previous centuries, or even millennia? How many mistakes had crept into Israel's various traditions since the texts of Scripture were first written? How can we be sure that any of our texts are true to the original wording? How can we know that the divine word has not been corrupted by human error?

As we shall see, the rabbis attended to these potentially damning sets of data with no angst at all. But to understand why that is, we need to probe how our sages related to a fundamental question. We must ask: How can we know that our sages' determination of the halakha accords with God's desire? What if they simply got it wrong? For this, we turn to a well-known talmudic passage, the argument over the halakhic status of the oven of Akhnai, in Bava Metzia 59b. The Torah says that clay vessels can be rendered impure (Lev. 11:33). Shards of pottery cannot contract impurity; shards are not vessels. The oven of Akhnai is one in which shards of pottery were held together by sand. Does this construction constitute a vessel? R. Eliezer was of the opinion that this could not be considered a vessel, and thus could not be rendered impure. The rabbis believed that the oven of Akhnai constituted a vessel and therefore could contract impurity. The Talmud relates the following tale of dispute that unfolds in four rounds, each composed of four elements:[4]

Round 1

It was taught: On that day R. Eliezer responded with all the responses in the world, but they did not accept it from him.

a. He said to them: If the law is as I say, let the carob prove it.
b. The carob uprooted itself from its place and went one hundred cubits, and some say four cubits.
c. They said to him: One does not bring proof from the carob.
d. *The carob returned to its place.*

---

4. The following translation was rendered in consultation with that of Jeffrey Rubenstein, *Talmudic Stories. Narrative Art, Composition, and Culture* (Baltimore: Johns Hopkins University Press, 2003), 36–37. This version of the tale is preserved in ms Munich 95. I have placed in italics phrases that appear in this manuscript and are not found in the standard printed versions of the Babylonian Talmud; these are taken from the version of the tale in Y. Moed Katan 10 2:1. The text of this version in the Jerusalem Talmud is available at https://www.sefaria.org.il/Jerusalem_Talmud_Moed_Kattan.10b.1?lang=he.

Round 2

a. He said to them: If the law is as I say, let the aqueduct prove it.

b. The water turned backward.

c. They said to him: One does not bring proof from water.

d. The water returned to its place.

Round 3

a. He said to them: If it is as I say, let the walls of the *beit midrash* prove it.

b. The walls of the *beit midrash* began to teeter.

c. R. Yehoshua rebuked the [walls]. He said to them: When Sages contend with each other in halakha, what is the nature of your involvement in the dispute?

d. It was taught: The walls did not fall because of the honor of R. Yehoshua, and they did not return upright on account of the honor of R. Eliezer, and they remained inclined.

Round 4

a. He said to them: If it is as I say, let it be proved from heaven.

b. A heavenly voice went forth and said: What is it for you with R. Eliezer, since the law is like him in every place?

c. R. Yehoshua stood up on his feet and said: "It is not in heaven" (Deut. 30:12). What is "It is not in heaven"? R. Yirmeya said: We do not listen to a heavenly voice, since the Torah was already given to us on Mount Sinai and it is written there, "Incline after the majority" (Ex. 23:2).

d. R. Natan came upon Elijah. He said to him: What was the Holy One doing at that time? He said to him: He laughed and smiled and said, "My sons have prevailed over Me; My sons have prevailed over Me."

The tale reveals that while there is a divinely true law, that law bows before the law as determined by the rabbis. Specifically, the tale champions the rules and conventions the rabbis employ to arrive at their determination of the halakha. We see this through four rounds of argumentation, each of which contains a common structure of four elements:

In the *a* element of each round, R. Eliezer invokes Heaven to support his ruling. In each round, the *b* element demonstrates that there is, indeed, a divinely true form of the law: the divine sign signifies that God approves of R. Eliezer's ruling. In the *c* element of each round, the rabbis reject the divine sign as procedurally invalid evidence when determining the halakha. The fourth and final element, *d*, demonstrates that, in fact, God Himself concedes the position of the rabbis.

Let us explore the subtle differences between the four sections. Rounds 1 and 2 unfold in parallel fashion. For R. Eliezer, the task of the Sages is to arrive at the ideal law – the law as the Almighty envisions it. Hence in element *a* he invokes God to take sides in the debate, and a divine sign follows in *b*, first via the carob tree and then via the aqueduct. In element *c*, the rabbis do not deny that God has expressed His support for R. Eliezer's ruling. Rather they reject the sign on *procedural* grounds: "One does not bring proof from the carob tree/water." The statement "one does not bring proof from" suggests that determining the halakha is exclusively a process of invoking accepted legal processes and conventions, even when the ruling counters the divine ideal. The *d* element seals the rabbis' victory. Each round opens with God delivering a sign, but only when R. Eliezer calls for a sign to be delivered. By contrast, God acts on His own, even without the rabbis calling upon Him to do so when the rabbis proclaim the inviolate nature of the halakhic legal process. With no further prompting from them, the carob returns to its place, and the waters of the aqueduct return to their natural flow. Put differently, God Himself rejects the ideal divine law and accepts the limits and dictates of rabbinic legal processes.

In the third round, R. Eliezer ups the ante. The two previous signs came via agents external to the *beit midrash* and its deliberations – the carob tree and the aqueduct. Here, R. Eliezer invokes the walls of the *beit midrash* to signal that divine authority does indeed trump the conventions of halakhic jurisprudence. Moreover, the teetering walls not only signify divine approval of R. Eliezer's ruling, but threaten disapproval of the rabbis' position. Speaking on behalf of the rabbis, R. Yehoshua likewise ratchets up his rhetoric a notch, chiding the walls and excoriating them for overstepping their bounds and intruding upon the sacrosanct deliberations of the halakhic legal process. Here, too, the divine sign favoring R. Eliezer is aborted. This time, however, the walls do not return to their upright position. They remain at an incline – neither erect nor collapsing – signifying the tension between the ideal divine law championed by R. Eliezer and the law as determined by the rabbinic legal process championed by R. Yehoshua.

In round 4, R. Eliezer ups the ante even further, and elicits verbal divine approval for R. Eliezer's ruling. However, the divine voice does not merely declare that the halakha under debate – the oven of Akhnai – concurs with R. Eliezer. Rather, the divine voice employs the strategy of the rabbis against themselves. For three rounds the rabbis maintained that divine signs were invalid because they did not accord with the legal processes of the halakha. In this fourth and final round, the divine voice employs one of the rabbis' own legal conventions: "What is it for you with R. Eliezer, *since the law is like him in every place?*"[5] R. Yehoshua, in turn, responds in kind. He deflects the divine voice by citing a verse, that is, by citing the Almighty's own words to refute Him. The *peshat* meaning of the phrase, "It is not in heaven" (Deut. 30:12) has nothing to do with halakhic legal processes or divine revelation. It is simply a rhetorical flourish which underscores that following God's commands is within the grasp of ordinary members of the people of Israel, and requires no herculean effort. When R. Yehoshua invokes the phrase to reject the heavenly voice, he co-opts the simple meaning of God's words, and subjects them to rabbinic midrashic interpretation: the Torah is not in heaven, but rather has been given over to the Sages for interpretation.

R. Yirmeya's "proof," too, appropriates the simple meaning of the Torah, and reinterprets the text in question according to rabbinic midrash. Exodus 23:2 reads: *Lo tehiyeh aharei rabim velo taaneh al rav lintot aharei rabim lehatot*. The simple, or *peshat*, translation of the verse would be, "Do not follow the many to do wrong, and do not give false testimony in a dispute by following the multitudes." Within this *peshat* reading, the second half of the verse is an integral whole; grammatically, the words *aharei rabim lehatot* cannot stand alone. However, according to rabbinic *derash*, that is precisely what they do, and what emerges is a mandate to the judges of Israel to follow majority decision. Implicitly,

---

5. Cf. Eiruvin 62b; Yevamot 60a; Bekhorot 23b.

R. Yirmeya concedes that the voice heard is indeed a divine voice. And
its declaration that the law is like R. Eliezer in every place is itself one of
the conventions of the rabbinic legal process. Yet, argues R. Yirmeya, it
flies in the face of majority decision; only the rabbis can determine how
to balance the competing conventions, and they rule in favor of majority
decision. R. Yirmeya does not merely cite Scripture in his favor. Rather,
R. Yirmeya underscores his rejection of the heavenly voice because "the
Torah was already given to us on Mount Sinai." With the transmission
of the Torah to Israel, so too was transmitted the authority over its interpretation. This fourth round, like the three that preceded it, concludes
with the Almighty admitting the existence of the ideal law, yet bowing to
the authority of the rabbis to determine the law in accordance with their
legal process: "He laughed and smiled and said, 'My sons have prevailed
over Me, My sons have prevailed over Me.'" The Ran, Rabbenu Nissim
of Gerondi (Spain, fourteenth century) has well expressed the ethos:
"The [power of] decision was given over to the sages of each generation,
and what they agree to – that is what God commanded."[6]

When our sages confronted evidence that error had crept into
the transmission of the text of the Torah, they responded with calm and
confidence. Even when they saw that midrashei halakha were predicated
on readings of the Torah at variance with the Masoretic Text, at no juncture do we sense that this was a cause for angst. At no point do they raise
the fear that the halakha might be founded in error. Nowhere do they
wring their hands at the prospect that all of our *sifrei Torah* are invalid.
The dozens of discrepancies listed by Rabbi Akiva Eger never resulted
in concerns about the general accuracy of the received text of the Torah.
Our sages make no effort to review the discrepancies on a case-by-case
basis to determine as best they can which variant is accurate. The reason for all this is simple: Our sages do not have their eye on the "ideal"
or original Torah. It may be that our Masoretic Text does not match
the Almighty's Torah, the original version of the text. But for the rabbis,
this is of no consequence. "It is not in heaven." The Torah that we possess is the Torah that is sanctioned. Even though it may appear strong,
the evidence that some other hypothesized reading or version is more

6. *Derashot HaRan, derasha* 7.

accurate or more original is of no import for the spiritual world of the observant Jew. "The [power of] decision was given over to the sages of each generation, and what they agree to – that is what God commanded." So how did the rabbis address these discrepancies? True to the spirit of the talmudic tale of the oven of Akhnai, the rabbis arrive at the "right" solution by employing a series of legal conventions. With near unanimity, they declared that Israel should follow three rules:[7]

1. When several *sifrei Torah* contain variant readings of the same text, we amend the minority to conform to the majority.
2. When we find midrashei aggada that are predicated upon readings of the Torah that are at variance with our *sifrei Torah*, we neither amend our *sifrei Torah* nor declare the midrashim invalid.
3. Conversely, when we find midrashei halakha predicated on readings of the Torah at variance with our *sifrei Torah*, we are to amend our *sifrei Torah* to conform to the readings found in the midrashei halakha.

These rulings place a premium on pragmatism over dogmatism. The sages do not declare that the text in the midrashei halakha was at all times superior to the transmission of the Masoretic Text. Likewise, our rabbis never state that the midrashei aggada founded on readings at variance with those found in the Masoretic Text are mistaken and should be disregarded. In fact, they recognize that they do not have the resources to be able to ascertain which versions are the ideally correct ones.[8] Their sole aim is to provide instruction for Israel in pragmatic fashion: What shall be the text of our *sifrei Torah* moving forward? How may we safeguard the continuity of halakha, even when questions arise about the sources from which some of the halakhot are derived? Ultimately, these

---

7. See Meiri, Kiddushin 30a. Cf. also *Shut HaRashba* (attributed to Ramban), sec. 232; *Shut HaRadbaz* 4:101. It is remarkable that none of these sources attempts to mitigate the problem by insisting that the *derashot* might merely be *asmakhtaot*, and that the Torah laws putatively derived from them really had existed already.
8. Meiri, Kiddushin 30a.

issues – like all halakhic issues – are given over to them to decide. And what they decide "is what God commanded." Remarkably, although great sages for several centuries called for the amendment of our *sifrei Torah* to accord with the textual variants found in the midrashei halakha, their call was never heeded.[9] In fact, to this day our talmudic sources retain a handful of halakhic opinions based on readings of the Torah that are variants of what we find in our *sifrei Torah*. Over time, later voices in the tradition hallowed the Masoretic Text and declared it inalterable.[10] Logically, we should be aghast that we preserve inconsistency – two traditions of a given verse, at least one of which cannot conform to the original. Theologically, however, we embrace both. We follow, separately, the dictates of the halakha with regard to the midrashei halakha and with regard to the now inalterable nature of the Masoretic Text. Both courses of action have been sanctioned by our sages, and thus both are what God commanded.

The number of such textual discrepancies is small, and the degree of variance between the readings of the text is likewise minor. Nonetheless, probing how our sages approached these questions can offer us guidance for a range of challenges to the *mesora* that arise from the field of biblical studies. These challenges are only rarely rooted in hard-and-fast evidence that is incontrovertible. Rather, these challenges are hypotheses drawn from supporting evidence, sometimes stronger, sometimes more speculative. As we saw, however, even when the strongest evidence – a divine voice – rules against the rabbis, it is the rabbis' ruling that is operative for Israel. This is not because the rabbis' ruling must be the original, ideally true ruling. Their ruling is operative because "the Torah was already given to us on Mount Sinai."

To some, this theology will smack of self-serving rabbinic apologetics. Yet, consider this: No text of any genre, composed anywhere in the period of late antiquity, rivals the Talmud in length. No legal system

---

9. See sources above, n. 7, and discussion in Leiman, "Masorah and Halakhah," 304–6.

10. See the letter of approbation of the Ḥatam Sofer for the first edition of the work of Rabbi Solomon Ganzfried, *Keset HaSofer* (Ofen, 1835), whose author maintains that we do not amend the Masoretic Text in favor of the variants found in any midrashic source. See discussion in Leiman, "Masorah and Halakhah," 305–6.

produced during this time rivals it for its legal complexity. No people has experienced displacement and upheaval in the last two thousand years as have the Jewish people. And no people so dispersed has ever sustained a tradition of adherence to a legal system so vast. When I speak before non-Jewish audiences, one question inevitably rises: "Who is your pope? What body is Orthodoxy's governing council?" The questions are understandable. Humans are inherently fractious. And yet the rabbinic tradition has had no overarching authoritative body since the demise of the Sanhedrin during early talmudic times. The fact that Jews have observed talmudic law in uninterrupted fashion over all that time and into our own in spite of every upheaval imaginable is nothing short of miraculous, and a sign of the divine imprint on it. With calm we embrace the Torah as we have it today, confident that it is this text and no other that the Almighty wishes us to revere.

Index

The fonts used in this book are from the Arno family